Between the Tides

Between the Tides

A FASCINATING JOURNEY AMONG THE KAMORO OF NEW GUINEA

by **DAVID PICKELL**
Photos by **KAL MULLER**

PERIPLUS

Originally published as *Kamoro: Between the Tides in Irian Jaya*
in a limited edition by Aopao Productions, 2001

This updated and revised edition published by Periplus Editions (HK) Ltd

ISBN 0-7946-0072-7

Text editing by Leigh Anne Jones
Photography editing, cartography, and book design by David Pickell
Supervision of color separation by Mary Chia
Scanning, separation, and film casting by Unique Color Separation Pte Ltd, Singapore

Distributed by
INDONESIA PT Java Books Indonesia, Jl. Kelapa Gading Kirana, Blok A-14/17, Jakarta 14240

ASIA-PACIFIC Berkeley Books Pte Ltd, 130 Joo Seng Road, #06-01/03, Singapore 368357

JAPAN AND KOREA Tuttle Publishing, Yaekari Bldg., 3F, 5-4-12 Osaki, Shinagawa-ku, Tokyo 141-0032

NORTH AMERICA, LATIN AMERICA, AND EUROPE Tuttle Publishing, Airport Industrial Park,
364 Innovation Drive, North Clarendon, VT 05759-9436

Printed in Singapore

Set in the Dutch Type Library's Fleischman, a faithful digital adaptation of the Rococo types
cut in Amsterdam in 1738–39 by the German-born Johann Michael Fleischman. The decorative capitals that
begin each chapter are interpretations of motifs on Kamoro *kamar-apoka* from the early 20th century.

First photo spread ADAM IRAHEWA, HEADING HOME TO OTAKWA.

Second photo spread CONCLUSION OF THE KU-KAWARE, NEAR PARIPI.
Galus Mauria is wearing the *mbi-kao* mask costume.

Frontispiece MBITORO, TIMIKA PANTAI.
Represented on the carving is the late Saturnius Perayau,
a respected former chief of traditions.

Contents

Figures

For Engelbertus, Celestina, Wensislaus,
Berlinda, Franky, Ernestina, Augustinus,
Maria, Franco, and Nana Reyana.

Mbitoro, Paripi.

Preface

An Adventure in New Guinea

 EW GUINEA IS actually two places, one real, and one imaginary. But which is the shadow of the other? The real New Guinea is the world's second-largest island, yet few people could describe its location with confidence. Somehow it is always lurking on the far side of the globe. But the imaginary New Guinea is vivid. It is a dense, wet jungle, a wall of green with no apparent opening. The vines and trees have thick leaves, like human hands, and cast a deep shade even sound can't escape. Suddenly visible, though perhaps it was there all the time, is a human face, bright streaks of ocher and white hanging disembodied among the leaves. Then, with no movement at all, it is gone.

In the early 1960s, historian Gavin Souter wrote a book called *New Guinea, the Last Unknown,* still the best history in English of the island. In this volume—sadly, now out of print—he recounts the story of a French sailor who, in 1888, published an utterly fraudulent account of an expedition to New Guinea. In his *Adventures in New Guinea,* Louis Trégance reported the wonders of K'ootar, where King Hotar Wokoo ruled over gleaming cities of three thousand buildings and kept pet tigers on leashes of pure gold. Trégance had very likely never set foot on New Guinea, and his K'ootar was a typical and particularly French fantasy—a kind of orientalized Levant in blackface.

In the late 19th century, taxonomy and description ruled the biological sciences, and interest in the world's fauna and flora and—in a peculiarly clinical and racist way—in the world's people, was at its height in Britain and Europe. These were hard-nosed times for science, during which bones were counted and human heads and faces were measured with precision. Facts reigned supreme. But Trégance, Souter notes, was not immediately dismissed as a fantasist. The reason was very simple: he set his tale in New Guinea.

More than a century has passed since *Adventures in New Guinea,* yet I don't think things are fundamentally different today. If I wrote that, in New Guinea, there is a mammal with no recognizable face at all, just a lump of fur and spines and a fleshy probe of a nose, and that this unlikely creature wanders the forests and high meadows, fossicking with that probe for earthworms, which it sucks up with relish, I don't think my reader would abandon me. If I added, offhandedly, that the male of this curious species has a penis that ends in four knobs, and the female lays eggs, I still think nobody would toss the book aside as a work of fiction.

Fig. P.1 ZAGLOSSUS BRUIJNII. A long-beaked echidna, from the first published description of this unusual species, by Paul Gervais in 1877.

I could also write that in New Guinea there is a community of people for whom tradition dictates that the women, after a period of two or three days, exhume their buried relatives, carefully strip the flesh from the bones, and cook and eat it steamed in tubes of bamboo. I could further add that this practice provides the means of transmission for a strange disease that causes the women to die in a fit of frenzied twitching that appears like they are dying of laughter. Again, I think I would lose none of my readers.

The long-beaked echidna is now rare (alas, it tastes too good), and it has been more than twenty years since the American virologist and pediatrician Carleton Gajdusek won the Nobel Prize for solving the puzzle of the transmissible spongiform encephalopathy *kuru* in the Foré people, but these things are true.

There are languages in New Guinea that are so rare that they are spoken by only a few hundred people. There are bright green katydids the size of small lobsters that require two hands to pull from a branch. There are mountains almost five kilometers high

---

AGUS YAUNIYUTA, TIMIKA PANTAI. Assistants daub Agus's face with lime to prepare the boy for his role in the *karapao* initiation ceremony, after which he will be considered a man. He is, understandably, a bit nervous.

MAMBRUK. The beautiful *Goura scheepmakeri* lives only in New Guinea, and like the birds of paradise, has become an emblem of the island. This specimen is variety *sclateri,* found only in the lowland forest of southern Irian Jaya, from Etna Bay to the Fly River. The crown pigeon is as large as a chicken and considered by some to be even finer as a roasting bird. Although the genus has enjoyed legal protection since 1931, this *mambruk* was headed for the black market in Timika, where its captor intended to sell it as a cage bird. He estimated it would fetch the equivalent of $10.

capped by permanent snowfields. There are entire forests of moss. There are people, though now just a few, who have never used a fish hook. There are so many very curious things that one can truthfully say about New Guinea that if, like Trégance, I threw in some cities of gold or a cavalry of "Orangwoks," well, in context I don't think much additional benefit of the doubt would be needed.

The difficulty in writing about this wonderful place is not to allow one's text to be overrun by astonishment. There seems always to be justification for an exclamation point. For the reader, the difficulty is to resist the powerful image of a dripping green jungle and imagine a real place, where the leaves are indeed as fat as hands, and where men do paint their faces, but also where jet airplanes land, and telephones ring, and children get up in the morning and go to school.

I HAD BEEN PLANNING to write a book about Irian Jaya,* the western half of New Guinea island and a province of the Republic of Indonesia, since my first visit in 1991. Four notebooks from this trip remain on my shelf in their plastic bag (in Irian Jaya, you quickly learn to keep your notebooks in a plastic bag). But I was living in New York at the time, and my Upper West Side rent and the cost of keeping a full refrigerator in that city encouraged me to continue working as an editor, an occupation that promised to be more remunerative than writing a book about a place only a hundred people in the United States have heard of. But I always meant to return to my New Guinea project.

This book began in 1997, just after New Year's. I was in a hotel room in Jakarta, the energetic capital of Indonesia, sharing a bottle of duty-free Scotch with photographer Kal Muller. Kal and I had just spent the last forty-five minutes in the back seat of a Bluebird taxicab. It used to be that the Bluebird franchise cabs were the only ones in Jakarta that ran meters, but now Silverbird and a whole flock of others compete with them. Our trip had covered a distance of seven or eight kilometers, and frankly, we hadn't done too badly for a weekday late afternoon in this city of almost thirteen million. Still, we felt we deserved our Scotch.

I hadn't seen him in a few months, and Kal was anxious to show me some slides. These were of a traditional initiation ceremony in a place called Timika Pantai, a village on the south coast of Irian Jaya in the Kamoro area. The images were striking: young boys, smeared with pigments and dressed in bright cloths and comic sunglasses; a great carved pole standing in front of the ritual house; a ritual leader slashing open a coffin-like container of sago starch; drummers beating the lizard-skin heads of their drums.

The slides were wonderful. For the last year or so, Kal had held a regular job photographing for the

Freeport company, which runs a copper mine in southern Irian Jaya. This job, though interesting and lucrative, had not produced the most exciting photographic work he has done. While in the area working for Freeport, he caught wind of the Timika Pantai ceremony and organized a boat to take him and his cameras there. Sitting in Jakarta, Scotch in hand and with his slides spread out in front of us, he was more enthusiastic than I had seen him in several years.

"This," he said, "is the real thing. This"—tapping the plastic slide sheet—"is why I do what I do."

Kal Muller is Hungarian by extraction, but the extraction took place half a century ago. We have been friends for a decade, and have worked together on six or seven book projects. He spent most of his childhood and was educated in the United States, but since then his resumé would have to list Africa, France, the South Pacific, Mexico, and especially in the last two decades, Indonesia. His preferred photographic subjects are traditional people: the Huichol of Mexico, the Afar of Ethiopia, the Nambas of Vanuatu, and the many traditional groups in Indonesia.

Kal is sixty-two years old, disciplined, and at least while the sun is shining, tireless. He makes a "things to do today" list every morning, and ticks items off as the day wears on. He exercises regularly, in the hopes of postponing for a few more years the time when he won't be able to carry his own camera bag. If you saw the muscles on his chest and arms, you'd think that time must be at least thirty years away. In the last few years he has favored a short salt-and-pepper beard, because it's less bother, and so that when he comes back into town after two weeks in the field, people are less shocked by his appearance. By his own standards, the strangest thing he ever did was get a Ph.D. in French literature from the University of Arizona.

One of Kal's proudest moments came in the early sixties. He and some other young adventurers had decided to sail a small boat across the Pacific. They were going to look for Michael Rockefeller, who had disappeared in the Asmat area of what was then Dutch New Guinea. Also, given that these were healthy young men, I have to imagine that the more traditional charms of the South Seas islands played a role in their decision. One afternoon, after twenty-six days of blue, featureless ocean, Kal looked at his charts and predicted that they would reach their first island landfall the next morning. He had never used a sextant before that trip, and his boatmates—they had been friends when they left—were very far from believing him. In the morning the green hump of an island appeared. It was Nuku Hiva in the Marquesas of French Polynesia.

Like most people who spend a lot of time by themselves, Kal can be a bit set in his ways, many of which seem to have been shaped forty years ago. He sometimes uses language that would prompt enraged stares at a Berkeley cafe. He goes to bed before evening

---

* On January 7, 2002, too late to be incorporated into this manuscript, the province was officially renamed "Papua."

BOY INITIATES, TIMIKA PANTAI.
Yohanis, Fictor, and Robertus Maopeyauta are led by their chaperones to the initiation ceremony.

properly becomes night, and gets up before the sun. During one period while he was staying with me in New York, it happened regularly that I would be having the night's last cigarette when Kal came into the kitchen for his morning cup of coffee.

Kal and his boatmates never did land in New Guinea, having had the bad luck of arriving during the politically tense period of the transfer of the territory from Holland to Indonesia, when permits were impossible for young explorers to obtain. But he reached the New Hebrides, now Vanuatu, where he decided to learn about and photograph the Bunlap villagers of Pentecost Island. This group had stubbornly refused any "help" from the missionaries and colonial government, and it took Kal more than a year to earn their trust. His time in Bunlap village culminated in his participation in a ritual land-diving ceremony, in the course of which he jumped, tethered by vines, from a rickety tower in the jungle. One vine broke. These experiences were documented in a 1970 article he wrote and photographed for *National Geographic,* an article so well remembered that it is considered to have inspired the sport of bungee jumping.

Kal's passion is documenting the world's few remaining truly traditional people. There is a generation between Kal and myself, and I cannot say I fully understand his relationship to this subject. I do not believe it is something as rudimentary as the visual drama of a painted face with a bone in its nose. I think what he really sees when he photographs "the real thing" is a kindred spirit. Among traditional people, he finds a culture where basic human needs and instincts are not repressed or made embarrassing, but instead respected, even celebrated. What fascinates him, I think, is not the nakedness itself, but rather the pride and confidence that make clothing unnecessary.

ONE OF THE most surprising things about Kal's slides was that, as far as either of us knew, an event like the one he photographed was simply not supposed to happen any more. Maybe among the Asmat, the famous former head-hunters to the east, or among one or another of Irian Jaya's more remote groups. But not the Kamoro. Accounts suggested that all the good Kamoro woodcarvings were collected long ago, and that ceremonial life among this group had long since come to a full stop.

In fact these accounts paint a very sorry picture, and after reading one particularly unflattering text, Kal, with the inimitable humor that gets him in trouble in college towns, joked that the Kamoro must simply have been a hapless "prey species" for the Asmat.

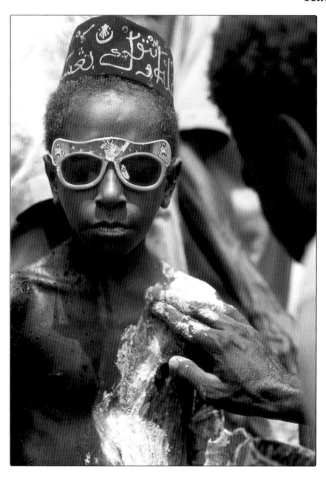

BENEDIKTUS MAMOPO, TIMIKA PANTAI.

NATALIS ONAMARIYUTA, TIMIKA PANTAI.

In a short treatise on the Kamoro (then still called Mimika), Father F. Trenkenschuh, O.S.C. writes:

> It is not a pleasant sight—a people totally indifferent to your presence; people educated but without a place in their own society. Mimika strikes a person as a dead area filled with zombies. There is no work and no interest in work. Religion of the past is no longer celebrated and the Christian religion means nothing to the people. The past is gone forever. The future holds no hope.

I don't think Father Trenkenschuh, who wrote this passage in 1970, meant to insult the Kamoro people. Like the American Crosiers and other missionaries who have been working with the Asmat since the 1960s, Father Trenk is a progressive, Vatican II–influenced cleric. I have seen these brothers and fathers come back from Catholic services, their faces painted with red mud and lime, breathless with excitement about a new element of Asmat tradition that had just been spontaneously incorporated into the Mass by their flock. They are not religiously conservative men.

Still, to these missionaries the Kamoro were a beaten down and lost people, somehow ruined by the intolerant and judgmental Dutch missionaries and Kei Islander catechists and teachers who converted them in the 1920s and 1930s. It is as victims of this great tragedy that the Kamoro are perhaps best known. Stripped of their culture, they stand, pathetic in their rags, as a kind of living rebuke to early forms of messianic Christianity and unenlightened Dutch colonialism. In Trenkenschuh's text and others like it, they become unwitting actors in a cautionary tale, an example for a new generation of Catholic missionaries of what not to do to the more recently proselytized Asmat. But for the Kamoro—and here one can see the heads shaking sadly back and forth—it is simply too late.

The contradiction between the cultural vitality of what Kal had just photographed and the "zombies" in the literature made us both intensely curious. So we decided, sitting in that hotel room sipping whisky, to spend some time in the area and write and photograph our own book on the Kamoro.

Most plans hatched at moments like this evaporate even before the bottle of Scotch, and by rights this one should have as well. As a rule, publishers do not look forward to being offered expensive, full-color book projects on subjects that almost nobody in the world has heard of. When it comes to evaluating the commercial possibilities of a title, Eric Oey of the Periplus Publishing Group is no less shrewd than his peers, but Eric differs from other publishers in that he knows about, and cares about, Indonesia and Indonesian subjects. He and his Asian Studies editor

Noor Azlina Yunus read the manuscript, liked it, and instantly agreed to bring out the title. I would also add that they both have a very good bedside manner. In discussions of potential sales figures, never once did I hear the word "dismal." Instead, Azlina gently reminded me that the market for serious titles on Southeast Asia is still, shall we say, underdeveloped.

There would have been no book for Eric to bring out had it not been for the good offices of Paul Murphy. At the time, Paul was the public affairs vice-president of P.T. Freeport Indonesia, the Indonesian subsidiary of Freeport-McMoRan Copper & Gold which is running the Grasberg mine in the highlands of Irian Jaya. When Kal and I approached him with our proposal, Paul—who has a great personal interest in the people and cultures of Irian Jaya, particularly south coast art—was able to find the funding for us.

Freeport's logistical and financial support made our travel and research possible. Outside of a few designated tourist areas, Irian Jaya is not a place a foreigner can move freely without a sponsor. From 1969 until 1998, the entire province was designated a Military Operations Area (Daerah Operasi Militar, or DOM).* Travel required a government-issued letter, and then registration with the authorities in each village visited. Such letters were not always forthcoming, particularly for writers and photographers, and even if they were, the local police sometimes had their own idea of their legitimacy. Transportation in most of the province remains very expensive, or simply unavailable.

The company's support also allowed the release of an Indonesian language edition, entitled *Kamoro: Diantara Pasang Surut Irian Jaya,* which Kal and I had planned for from the beginning. Although I have no way of judging the success of the translation, the fact that it exists—that the Kamoro and other Indonesians can read what I have written—is immensely satisfying to me as a writer. At first we even toyed with the idea of translating it into Kamoro, which would have made it the only non-liturgical book to appear in that language, but the expense and time required would have served only our vanity. Ninety percent of the Kamoro are literate in Indonesian, while fewer than half of these can read Kamoro, which is not traditionally a written language.

Although corporate and foundation support is a well-established tradition in serious non-fiction publishing, it may raise a few eyebrows that we have accepted money not just from a mining company, but from *this* mining company—Freeport is big enough, and controversial enough, to have spawned a very lively group of critics. This is not a book about Freeport, nor is it the place to discuss these criticisms. The company's presence in Irian Jaya is unavoidable, however, and where relevant, I discuss it in this text.

* In October 1998, five months after President Suharto's fall, the province's status was lowered one degree to "Critical Control Area" (*Pengawalan Daerah Rawan,* or PDR). Travel remains difficult.

In these cases, I have reported my impressions honestly. Freeport played no role in shaping the content of this book, nor did anyone at the company ever even suggest such a thing.

THIS IS A book about a group of people living at the far edge of what most of us would call the known world, at a very interesting time. Jet airplanes land daily in what, just thirty years ago, was a forested coastal plain unmarked by a single road or concrete building for hundreds of kilometers.

The Kamoro are not naked innocents, unaware of the modern world. Almost all have been converted by the Catholic Church and now speak the national language of Indonesia. As a culture, they are wrestling with the conflicting opportunities and demands presented by western religion, wage labor, and civil society. At the same time, they are trying to understand the identity "Kamoro," which only now, after decades of influences from Holland, Jakarta, and the United States, has begun to seem necessary—and possible.

Fig. P.2
KAMAR-APOKA.
Collected by H.A.
Lorentz,
c. 1907–1910. From
Nova Guinea, Vol.
VII, 1913.

This book is not a eulogy. I can detect no signs of prelapsarian grace in the few extant 19th- and early 20th-century photographs of the Kamoro, then still untouched and pure, standing naked except for their bamboo codpieces. I do not see wistfulness in those strange, distant eyes, only the blur of a long exposure, a common artifact of pictures taken with the slow film emulsions available in those days. An old *kamar-apoka* penis case is an interesting enough thing, but hardly the most important signifier of a living culture.

Anyway, this is an outsider's problem. A Kamoro man who speaks three languages and dresses for work in a shirt and slacks does not find it contradictory or otherwise troubling to paint his chest and don a headdress of feathers for a *karapao,* should the occasion arise.

This is an account of two visits to the Kamoro area, one of three weeks' length in January 1997 and another from early July through early September of the same year. I have tried to be accurate in my observations, but I have made no special effort to interpret them. I have neither the training nor the inclination to be an anthropologist, and this work does not belong to the literature of that field. It is, I suppose, nothing more or less than a kind of journalism.

I have tried to produce a book that will interest a Western audience as well as, because of the translation, western Indonesian and Kamoro audiences. At times, this may tug the text in strange directions, and what I have deemed of interest to one group might come across as dull or pedantic to another. I hope, should this occur, that it does not too grievously test the forbearance of any of my readers.

CHAPTER ONE

Two Brothers

The Story of Aweyau and Miminareyau

HE ONE STORY begins in the village of Uria, in the wet forest far to the east, hard up against the terrifying land of the Asmat, the We Manowe or Men-who-eat-men. The names of Uria are Tapapima, Monomonowe, Itirae, Imamukawe, Pimamowe, Kapauwe, Naegeripi, Amayeripi, I'ita, Matuta, Muawe, Matuawe, Tarowe'e, Mifae, and Woanaripi.

In the gray silence, after the night insects finished and before the birds began, the people with these names packed their nets and spears and slipped their narrow canoes into the brown river. A mist hung over the water, and in the sky, just perceptibly, rose the barest blush of dawn. The tide was running seaward, and with paddle strokes as sure as the beating of a bird's wings, the men and women of Uria followed.

The broad river wound first past open forest, then the crooked, stilt-rooted pandanus appeared, like huge spiders spilling over the banks. The river steadily narrowed, and finally disappeared altogether in the gnarled choke of the mangrove. Delicately, as if passing through the very bones of the earth, the men and women poled their canoes through dark, secret creeks to where the river once again spread wide and glinting, and the water tasted of salt.

Here, under a bright morning sun, the wispy branches of the casuarina trees yielded only the hint of shade. Drifting between crescents of gray-brown sand, they snared the mullet *tipoko,* with its sweet flesh and scales like pounded coins, and *ewako,* a fat-bellied catfish as thick as a man's leg. They stalked the huge sawfish *tawake,* an apparition of such ancient and unlikely form that it appears to be a composite of both fish and reptile. Their harpoons also found the bull shark *boako,* blunt-nosed and purposeful in the murky water, and *buru,* the river tortoise, its head rising from the surface like a clenched fist.

MBITORO ON PARADE, KEAKWA. After it is awakened, and before it is planted in the ground in front of the *karapao* building, the *mbitoro* goes on a wild, bucking tour of the village grounds. Few can stay astride it for long.

AGUSTINUS OMOANE, KEAKWA. Working by the light of a pressure lamp, Agustinus puts the final touches on a *mbitoro.* The ancestor pole will be raised during the upcoming *karapao* ceremony.

By the time the bellies of their canoes were full, the tide had again begun to rise, and one by one and in small groups, the people of Uria turned inland. Afternoon became evening, and finally, night, and still the canoes had not made it home. There was no moon. The air thickened, and the forest became strangely quiet. Then the night sky opened up, and rain fell in black sheets. Thunder exploded overhead, and bursts of lightning lit their way.

As the storm raged, a woman named Miminareya stopped her canoe at the place called Ayaretoko. She had gone into labor during the day, and though she paddled as hard as she could in an effort to reach the village, she knew now she must stop. There on the river bank she gave birth to a son, who lay sticky and wrinkled on the red sand. Miminareya collapsed. Staring up into the black night, unable to move, she felt the last of her human strength dissolve in the cold rain.

In her haste Miminareya's canoe was the first, but soon the others, also despairing of reaching Uria in the rain and cold, sought the familiar red sand of Ayaretoko. The night forest is not benign, and the men lit branches from the embers they kept sheltered under bark in their canoes. Each man took one of these torches in his left hand, freeing his right to carry his paddle, reversed to display its flame-hardened point which, when hurled in anger, can penetrate the hull of a canoe. Thus armed, the men climbed the bank to search the strand of trees for a dry campsite.

Halfway up the bank they heard a sound. At first it was so faint that each, individually, thought he had imagined it. They stopped moving. The sound persisted, and grew louder. A voice? It wavered eerily, in a pitch that has never been produced by a human being. The group exploded in panic, and dropping their torches, rushed blindly for the canoes. They forgot the cruel tips of their paddles. In the melee,

Fig. 1.1 SAWFISH.

the men tripped and fell, and by the time they reached the canoes, several were bleeding from their arms and legs. Others, pierced through in the stomach and neck, lay dead on the sand. No one stopped or even looked back until they were all well upriver.

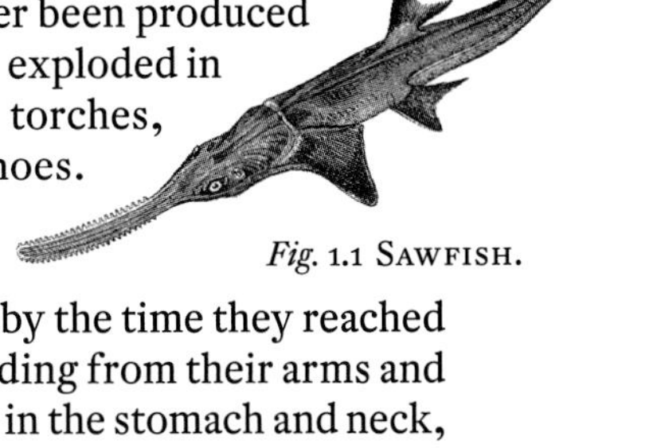

Nataiku Alowisius Wania, Timika.

One canoe, lagging behind the others, reached Ayaretoko after the men had fled. In it was a woman named Aweya. As she neared the fateful red sand she heard a voice, strangely familiar, and inexplicably found herself paddling toward the bank. When she reached it she saw her sister, Miminareya, carrying a child. But there was something odd and translucent about Miminareya, and Aweya fought back a shiver.

"I must give my son to you, sister," said the ghost. "But I will follow you wherever you go, and together we will raise him."

She took the boy, and leaving her sister's ghost on the bank, paddled toward home. She soon caught up to the others, who had stopped their canoes to tend their wounds. Aweya said nothing of her encounter, but when the others saw the strange child, they protested. "That is the child of the devil," they said, "Throw it in the river at once!" But the ghost of Miminareya was as good as her word, and had been following the progress of Aweya's canoe from the forest.

"Do not kill my son!" she boomed from the riverbank. "If you do, I will turn every tree in the forest upside down, and the trees, and you, and everything else in the world will die."

The people trembled at Miminareya's warning and did not molest the child. In silence, they continued paddling toward home and reached Uria late at night. Aweya's husband started a fire in the hearth and he and Aweya gently laid Miminareya's child and their own son, both now sleeping, on a mat by the fire. Cold and exhausted, Aweya and her husband laid down to sleep on either side of the boys.

Aweya was asleep for only a few hours before she stirred, feeling something strange in the bed. The fire was low, and she couldn't see. Instinctively, she reached over to touch her children. Rubbing them, she became alarmed. She jumped up and added wood to the fire. When it was bright enough to see, she slumped to the ground in amazement. By some unknown magic, both of the children had, within hours, become fully grown men.

THE STORY DOES not end here. The boys—now physically men—learn to make bows and arrows, to hunt, and to fish. They travel. They impart supernatural knowledge to the village, teaching the men of Uria how to make a *karapao* ceremonial house and how to pierce their noses. They become famous, and all too soon, infamous. They begin to steal food. As a warning, the men of a neighboring village kill their two uncles. Their thieving continues. Even their own village takes up arms against them. But the boys are resourceful. They invent spirit costumes, the *mbi-kao,* and donning these horrible masks spring from the forest and attack Uria. This, finally, is too much. The people of Uria pack their canoes and paddle as far away as they can. Eventually, and much later, a group of men from Imiyu village catch up with the boys near the Tipuka River and kill them.

The story was told to me by a man from Tipuka village, and this particular ending is specific to his recollection. In fact, the story has many endings or, more accurately, has none. Any sentence, any word, can itself unwind into another story, one as rich and endless as the one it came from. Like a child who outgrows and outlives her parents, and whose own child outlives her. Or like a tree that, when examined closely, appears more intricate and beautiful than the forest it grows in, and yet, when examined even more closely, each leaf of that tree shows itself to be more intricate and beautiful still.

The story of the human child and the spirit child, Aweyau and Miminareyau (Aweya is to Aweyau as John is to Johnson), contains the sum of all of Kamoro culture. The important *kaware* ritual cycle is there, the *mbitoro* ancestor poles are there, and the *karapao* initiation houses are there. Nose piercing is there. The *mbi-kao* spirit costumes are there. The *taparu* groups, the basic organization of Kamoro society, are there. Simple things, fishing and sago, are there, and the sea and the sky and the mangroves are there.

The history of the Kamoro is there, too, a history that begins in the East. Today, the people of the *taparu* named in the story live in an area that stretches from

Atuka village.

Kaugapu village to the Sempan area, in other words, from the Tipuka River eastward to old Uria. The narrative event that takes place when the men of Uria flee from the spirit masks recapitulates the historical event when the Kamoro people first moved onto this coast from a point of origin somewhere to the east.

The Aweyau (approximately "*Ah*-way-yow") and Miminareyau ("*Mim*-nah-ray-yow") story also reflects the resolutely matriarchal character of traditional Kamoro society. Aweya's husband is not named. He is with Aweya in the boat when she accepts the child from Miminareya, but the listener could be forgiven for not realizing this, because the storyteller never mentions it. The only acts he performs are to build a fire and fall asleep. (In some versions of the story Aweya doesn't have a husband.) Miminareya's husband is so irrelevant as not even to warrant passing mention. He is more of a ghost than Miminareya.

The Aweyau and Miminareyau story is always called the story of "the two brothers." Most Americans would call them cousins, but the Kamoro, who follow what anthropologists label the Hawaiian kinship system, call the sons of two sisters "brothers," or their daughters, "sisters." The combination of this lateral emphasis and matrilineal primacy in relationships means that, in many ways, a boy's relationship to his uncle—specifically his mother's brother—is more important than his relationship to his father. When Aweyau and Miminareyau persisted in stealing food, it was their uncles who were punished, not their fathers.

I HEARD THIS story from Nataiku Wania, who introduced himself to me by his Church name, Alowisius. Alowisius was an old man, shrunken and wiry, with the bright eyes of a naughty child. He reminded me of a bird. He was from the village of Tipuka, and he shared his last name with that of an important river. He wore a felt hat, and those bright eyes peered out from behind an ancient pair of glasses with lenses that had been rubbed so often they were more smooth than transparent, like bits of quartz found in a riverbed. He was one of the best storytellers I have ever had the pleasure of sitting across a table from, and I couldn't understand a word he said.

Alowisius told me his story in a dusty little cafe just across from the main market in Timika, a bustling settlement of about fifty thousand people and the only real town in the Kamoro area. We were joined by Didaktus Maoromako and Cansius Amareyau, two leaders of the local Kamoro development foundation Lemasko, and Apollo Takati. Apollo, a schoolteacher from Paripi who now lives in Timika, is a friend, and

25

one of our partners on this project.

The maitre d' and waiter of the cafe was a handsome young man from South Sulawesi. He wore a clean white shirt and pressed trousers, and affected complete disinterest in us and our story. He would usually bring another round of sodas after we asked three or four times. He spent the entire afternoon slouched on a stool near the register, his chin on his hand, staring out through the chicken wire windows. I don't think he saw the dusty street, the taxis and minibuses in the gravel lot, or the drab stalls hung with vinyl luggage or pots and pans of spun aluminum. I think he saw Makassar, the capital of South Sulawesi and the most cosmopolitan city in all of eastern Indonesia, with the sun glinting off the harbor and pretty Bugis girls walking along the dock.

Apollo translated Alowisius's story for me, and it was not an easy job. By late afternoon I had bothered our waiter at least four times for coffee and sodas, and not counting a short break for fried chicken and rice, the storyteller had been talking for about four hours. The process, because of the translation and my efforts to write it down, was almost excruciating.

It went like this. Alowisius, with wonderful choreography of gestures, pauses, and changes of pitch, would narrate a section of his story. His eyes were fixed on me. After a bit he would stop, and look expectantly at Apollo, who would then try to tell me what Alowisius had just said.

This wasn't always easy. The Tipuka dialect is different from that of Paripi, something on the order of a strong accent. Apollo, like a Southerner trying to understand a New Yorker (the Tipuka dialect sounds clipped and energetic compared to Apollo's western region dialect) was having a rough time.

Didaktus is a *kepala suku*—literally "tribal head"—of Nawaripi, and his dialect is closer to that of Tipuka than Apollo's. He saw the trouble Apollo was having and tried to help by offering some translation into Indonesian. At this point, however, Alowisius, who also speaks Indonesian, would step in himself with some point of disagreement over Didaktus's translation of his story. Cansius, for the most part, kept out of things. He is a great orator in his own right, but seeing that the pot already had three cooks attending it, he wisely decided just to listen.

At first I wanted to record every line, but after about an hour struggling with this, Apollo began summarizing. By late afternoon, fifteen minutes of Alowisius's dramatic monologue would, after sufficient discussion, be reduced to something like: "The boys went to their uncles' village, saw the uncles were dead, and returned home."

It became clear early on that Alowisius cared little whether his narrative were linear or coherent. Initially I would interrupt him and ask him to clarify points that seemed to be missing, or that I did not understand. For example: "Pardon, but Apollo, can you ask Alowisius where exactly on the map is Uria?" Alowisius became rather impatient with me over this. "Near Pece and Sumapero," he said. But his eyes said: "Does it matter?" Or: "Now wait, so her husband was in the boat all the time?" "Of course," he said, "she wouldn't be going so far away without her husband, would she?" And the eyes: "Can I get back to the story now?"

Although he found my questions distracting, Alowisius had his own strong opinions about which parts of the story were most important. When he reached these, he would wave his arms, widen his eyes, or otherwise offer some physical sign of emphasis. He listened carefully to Apollo's translation as well, and if at one of these key points I didn't seem to be writing much in my notebook, he would stop and tell Apollo to insist I write it down. However, since he did not understand English he sometimes got ahead of himself, and Apollo was constantly reassuring him: "Don't worry, I'll tell him, I'll tell him. I'm not there yet."

I could never predict which details Alowisius would find important. My first lesson came right away, when I tried to abridge the list of *taparu* names. He spotted my sloppiness immediately, and repeated the names slowly—and in exactly the same order—until I had written every one down. Some items he insisted I take down were that the sand at Ayaretoko was red, that the people carried their sharpened paddles in their right hands, and that Miminareya threatened not simply to kill the trees, but to turn them upside down.*

The cafe was hot and stuffy, and by late afternoon our faces were slick with oil and sweat. I could hardly concentrate any longer, and neither the coffee nor the Cokes were helping. Seeing my condition and the late hour, Apollo gallantly rescued me.

"I am afraid," he said diplomatically, "it is a very long story. We will listen to the rest, and I'll write down the basic points for you."

I did not put up much of a fight. I am sure Apollo and the other men were also quite happy to relax, sit back, and listen to the story without the constant interruption of translation. Alowisius was a very famous storyteller, and it was not every day that one got to hear him.† I treated the table to another round of sodas, said my goodbyes, and left.

The next day Apollo handed me his summary, neatly written on a single sheet of paper. It is the Cliffs Notes to Aweyau and Miminareyau. He did a very good job of reducing an evening's worth of Alowisius' performance to the basic skeleton of a western story: who did what to whom and where. He even included a line or two of dialogue. But the story on that sheet of

---

* When I later showed him this account, anthropologist Todd Harple speculated that turning the trees upside down might also be a way of bringing the underworld to the surface, which would unleash great torment on the people. It is actually a wonderful image, straight out of the worst kind of nightmare. Imagine a dead forest of black roots, populated by evil, clacking ghouls.

† Nataiku Alowisius Wania, sadly, passed away in 1998.

PAULINA IMIRIYU, KEAKWA.

YOHANES WAUKATEYAU, KEAKWA.

paper is as frail and colorless as a dried flower.

Trying to record Alowisius Wania's story was my one and only experiment with a method that is traditional to the anthropologist or folklorist, and I failed miserably. Although I mean no insult to Apollo, who did his job as well as anyone could, seeing the dry husk of his summary made me realize that if I were to try to do justice to a people and culture as rich as the Kamoro, I would have to learn from the old man of Tipuka. I cannot in any way offer a "translation" of Kamoro culture for my readers. Nor can I tell a story that will in any tidy or objective way "explain" the Kamoro. What I can do, I hope, is describe the color of the beach, let you know in which hand the men are carrying their paddles and, of course, warn you when somebody threatens to turn the trees upside down.

S INCE THE TIME that a relatively accurate map of New Guinea could be drawn, which was only in the past two hundred years, the shape of the island has always been compared to a bird. A bird perched, perhaps, on Australia's Cape York Peninsula. Modern maps label the large peninsula making up the northwestern limit of New Guinea "Kepala Burung," Indonesian for Bird's Head, and older ones label it "Vogelkop," which means the same thing in Dutch. In this metaphor, the bird's tail is the easternmost peninsula that ends at Milne Bay in Papua New Guinea.

This huge island covers 792,540 square kilometers and is 2,400 kilometers long. If the "beak" were on Seattle, the tailfeathers would touch Kansas City. Or, if the beak were on London, the tailfeathers would touch Ankara, Turkey. After Greenland, it is the largest island in the world. The Indonesian province of Irian Jaya covers 421,981 square kilometers of this island, which makes it slightly bigger than California, and has a population of 2,098,310. Slightly more than half of these people are indigenous Papuans, and the rest are relatively recent migrants from elsewhere in Indonesia. Eighty percent of the province's population is rural, and only a handful of towns can claim more than ten thousand people.

The only large city here is the provincial capital of Jayapura, on the north coast near the border with Papua New Guinea. Jayapura was called Hollandia during the colonial period and is still remembered by this name as the base from which General Douglas MacArthur began his island-hopping campaign to retake the South Pacific during World War II. The capital has a cosmopolitan population of 153,400.

Today's border, which approximately follows the 141st meridian, separates Indonesia from Papua New

ELISABET NATIPIA, GINEPERA AMAREYAO, AND WILHELMINA AMAREYAO, KEAKWA.

Guinea, an independent nation of 4.7 million people. Colonial Papua New Guinea had been divided into distinct German and British territories, Kaiser Wilhelmsland in the north and British New Guinea in the south. The British territory was renamed Papua in 1906 and transferred to Australian control. The German territory was conferred on Australia by a League of Nations mandate as "New Guinea" in 1920. The two territories, Papua and New Guinea, joined as independent Papua New Guinea in 1975.

New Guinea is only superficially an island. The Arafura Sea separating it from Australia is so shallow that only here and there does one encounter a sounding greater than about fifty meters. During the last Ice Age, which began retreating 15,000 years ago, enough of the earth's water was tied up in polar ice that the Arafura Sea was a broad sweep of open forest and woodland. Until just 7,000 years ago, New Guinea and Australia formed a single continent.

Scientists call the continent Meganesia, a still unfamiliar term that refers to those parts of the Australian tectonic plate that reach above the sea, including both New Guinea and Australia. New Guinea's bedrock, its unique community of plants and animals, and its aboriginal people are Meganesian.

The island's most distinctive topographical feature is the welt of mountains rising near the island's neck in the west and running in a great, curved, two thousand-kilometer-long spine to its tail in the east. Most of the limestone in these mountains first formed 170 million years ago in the Jurassic Period, when Meganesia was still part of the great agglomerated continent of Pangaea. When Pangaea broke up, Meganesia drifted north. When the edge of the Australian Plate, carrying Meganesia, met the Pacific Plate, the Australian Plate was subducted—that is, it was forced under the Pacific Plate. Like two hands placed flat on a table and forced together, one eventually buckled into a fist. New Guinea is this fist, and the high cordillera of mountains, the knuckles.

Although people popularly associate high, bleak mountains with age beyond measure, a geologist will note that such mountains are in fact the youngest. In geological time, New Guinea's barren peaks arose just yesterday, a mere tens of millions of years ago. Puncak Jaya, which at 4,884 meters is the highest point on the island, is so unweathered that you could literally cut your hand on its tip. Because there has been little time for erosion, extensive foothills have not formed, and the mountains near Puncak Jaya, in particular, rise so abruptly, and to such an unlikely height, that it is easy to mistake their distance. Standing on the shore of the

MANGROVE, INLAND FROM PARIPI.
Growing in regularly inundated soil, the *Bruguiera* tree produces 'knees'
so that its roots will have access to atmospheric oxygen.

Arafura Sea, the mist-shrouded mountain wall can appear to be just fifteen kilometers away, while the true distance is closer to one hundred kilometers.

New Guinea, more than anywhere else in the world of equivalent area, offers a taste of almost every terrain possible aside from true desert. Though it lies just a few degrees south of the equator, permanent snowfields, or firns, rest on the high mountains around Puncak Jaya. Mangrove forests ring the shore for hundreds of kilometers. In between are strange alpine swamps of lichens and tree ferns, lowland rainforest with a dense, thirty-meter canopy, plains of dry grassland, sluggish, meandering rivers and rushing waterfalls, shrubby karst pocked with sinkholes and caves, and clear, blue lakes.

The variety of habitats, and the abrupt changes between them, make the biology of the island extremely rich. In just a few square kilometers of the best lowland forest, a botanist could find more different species of plants than have been identified in all of North America. Many of these are still unnamed. For the entire island, I have seen an estimate of twenty thousand species of plants called "conservative."

Ornithologists have identified 712 species of birds here, and more than one-third of them live nowhere else. Herpetologists have so far counted 250 species of frogs, and before they are done they expect this total to exceed 500. The number of species of insects and other smaller animals living in New Guinea is almost limitless. An entomologist offered an estimate of 100,000 for the insects, but nobody really knows. Even the beetles, given the Creator's oft-stated fondness for them, would probably take more than one lifetime to catalog.

The wildlife of New Guinea, in addition to being very rich, is also exceptionally strange. All of the mammals, except for the bats and a few introduced species, are marsupial or, in the case of the two echidnas, egg-laying monotremes. The largest carnivorous mammal, the bronze quoll, is smaller than a housecat. The largest carnivore of any kind on New Guinea is not a mammal but a reptile – *Crocodylus porosus,* the saltwater crocodile. The largest bird, the cassowary, cannot fly, although it can outrun a man (but not a good hunting dog). Even the introduced animals seem strange. The dogs in New Guinea can't bark. They whine and howl like coyotes.

NEW GUINEA IS one of the oldest inhabited places on earth, and yet much of the prehistory of this island–and of Australia, to which for most of the period of human habitation it has been connected–is still poorly understood. Until recently, dates given by scientists for the first occupation of Australia and New Guinea hovered around 35,000 years ago. Today, with the development of genetic analysis and new physical dating techniques, the most promising being one called optically stimulated

thermoluminescence, the date of the arrival of the first New Guineans and Australians has been moved back to 50,000–60,000 years ago.

To put this in perspective, most archaeologists believe the first human footprint appeared in the soil of North America about 15,000 years ago, although recent genetic work suggests a date of perhaps 30,000 years ago. The new dates for the habitation of Meganesia mean that human beings reached New Guinea at about the same time they reached central Asia–and perhaps 20,000 years before they reached Europe–a puzzling fact for an area that is so far from Africa, where anatomically modern human beings first arose approximately 150,000 years ago.

The material culture and history of the people who

Fig. 1.2 NEW GUINEA AS A BIRD.
George Collingridge de Tourcey drew this whimsical map for his *The First Discovery of Australia and New Guinea,* published in 1906. His political boundaries reflect the colonial division of the island at that time.

first walked and paddled from East Africa to New Guinea, in the process first populating Southeast Asia and the islands that now make up Indonesia, are now matters chiefly of speculation, as these people have almost entirely been replaced by a more recent, and very successful wave of immigrants whom prehistorians call the Austronesians.

The Austronesians, who are the ancestors of most contemporary Southeast Asians, are thought to have left southern China 5,000–7,000 years ago and, via Taiwan, made their way across what is now the Philippines, Indonesia, Malaysia, Melanesia, and Polynesia. The Austronesians brought with them a number of innovations that allowed their culture to displace that of the earlier inhabitants of these islands: canoes affixed with stabilizing outriggers and sails; the domesticated chicken, pig, and dog; pottery; and, perhaps most importantly, irrigated rice agriculture.

The success of these Austronesian innovations is evident in the fact that today, except for a few tiny groups in the Philippines, Indonesia's Maluku islands, peninsular Malaysia, and the Andaman Islands, there are currently no indigenous dark-skinned, curly-haired people living in the ten thousand kilometers separating Africa and New Guinea.

CARVED PIGS, TIMIKA PANTAI.
Placed in front of a ceremonial house, these symbolic carvings are intended to bring the men luck in their hunt. In this case they did.

But what has been called the "Austronesian dispersal"—and it may have seemed more like an invasion in its day—stopped dead at New Guinea. Crops were domesticated on the island independently at least nine thousand years ago, and irrigated rice agriculture, with which the Austronesians supported the large, dominant populations that drove out existing people in the western islands, was not suited to very many places on New Guinea. The few groups of Austronesians who did become established on the island soon switched to locally gathered and domesticated crops: sago, taro, and bananas. Even the most famous Austronesian technical innovation—the outriggered canoe—would have been nothing more than a hindrance on New Guinea's twisting coastal rivers.

Evidence exists of trade contacts between the Papuans of New Guinea and the Austronesians—the pig and the dog reached the island a couple of thousand years ago and, at least one source suggests, the cuscus went the other way—but other than in a few coastal areas, the Austronesians never displaced the native New Guineans.

It is New Guinea's long, undisturbed human history, combined with the island's rich and diverse environments, that has made it so culturally and linguistically varied. Estimates of the number of distinct languages spoken in New Guinea exceed one thousand—256 for Irian Jaya, and 817 for Papua New Guinea. This single island thus holds one-fifth of the languages spoken in the entire world. Approximately one-quarter of the indigenous Irianese (230,000) speak one of the Dani or Lani dialects, and another 100,000 speak the Me (usually still called Ekagi or Ekari) language. A full 140 languages here are so rare that they are spoken by fewer than 1,000 people.

Whether the Kamoro have lived much as they do now, and in the same place, for the past 30,000 years, or only the past 300 years, will probably never be known. A culture that until very recently has found no use for a calendar or even a written language, no use for modifying the land for agricultural purposes, and a culture in which art, houses, and equipment like weapons, containers, and boats, are all made of wood and other rapidly perishable substances leaves very little evidence for an archaeologist to ponder. The Kamoro language is quite similar to the language of the Asmat, as are Kamoro art styles and material culture, and Kamoro narratives suggest an origin in the east, near the Asmat territories. But exactly when the Kamoro left Uria, pointed their canoes downstream, and settled the Kamoro coast, will probably always remain a mystery.

WHEN I TELL people in the United States where I have been working they usually mistake the name as "Iran Jaya" or, even more strangely, "Iran Gyra." The geographical knowledge of the average American presents an easy target for ridicule, but in this case, they can perhaps be forgiven. Irian Jaya is probably the most remote and least known place in the world. This territory is the easternmost frontier of the island nation of Indonesia, which despite its status as the world's fourth most populous nation, is itself little known aside from the famously exotic islands of Bali and Java.

The Indonesian archipelago stretches for nearly 5,000 kilometers from peninsular Southeast Asia to New Guinea. Fully 17,508 islands have been counted, of which approximately 6,000 are significant enough to have names and 1,000 are inhabited. The nation's 80,791 kilometers of coastline, if stretched out, would circle the globe twice. Most of Indonesia falls between the equator and about ten degrees south latitude, and it is for the most part a land of tropical rainforest, bright sand beaches, and coral reefs.

The Republic of Indonesia is part of the developing world and its population is still chiefly made up of rural rice farmers. Indonesia's standard of living, compared to the west and to Asia's "Tigers," is still relatively low, but economic growth over the last three decades has averaged a credible six percent, and at the time of my research in mid-1997, per capita gross domestic product stood at $1,300 (now less than $900). One-fifth of the economy is based on manufacturing, and another fifth on farming. The nation is also quite rich in minerals and petroleum, particularly natural gas, and in recent years tourism has grown to become a significant source of foreign exchange.

The population of Indonesia is 228,400,000 (2002 est.) and almost ninety percent of its citizens are Muslim, making it the largest Islamic nation in the world. Most Indonesians live in the western part of the archipelago, particularly on the island of Java, which is home to sixty percent of the nation's people and is one of the most densely populated places in the world. The sprawling capital city of Jakarta, in west Java, is the nation's largest city with a population of almost 13 million.

The archipelago's strategic position between the Indian and Pacific Oceans led to the growth of maritime empires based on the trade in spices, cloth, and aromatic woods. These goods both came and went north to China, west to India and the Middle East, and east to the far-flung islands of Maluku.

Indonesia's first great empire was the Buddhist Sriwijaya (c. A.D. 683–1025) centered at present-day Karanganyar, about eight kilometers west of Palembang in Sumatra. The empire fell when Sriwijaya's allies the Sailendras of Central Java, the rice bowl of the empire, were conquered by an East Java kingdom based along the Brantas River. Pre-colonial Indonesia reached its golden age with the rise of the Hindu-Buddhist Majapahit (1292–1528), an empire based in the twin cities of Bubat and Majapahit, about forty kilometers up the Brantas River from what is now the large city of Surabaya in East Java. At its height, in the late 14th century, Majapahit claimed more land than is currently part of Indonesia, although this was certainly a relationship of trading and tribute rather than direct rule.

By the time of Majapahit the Arabs had established a monopoly on the trade in the so-called fine spices—nutmeg, mace, and cloves—to the Middle East and Europe, and many Muslim traders lived in the coastal entrepôt cities of Sumatra and Java. In 1402, taking advantage of a civil war in the heart of Majapahit, the Sumatran prince Paramesvara established the port of Melaka (Malacca) on the straits of the same name between Peninsular Malaysia and Sumatra. Paramesvara converted to Islam sometime late in his reign (c. 1390 to 1413 or 1414), taking the name Iskandar Syah. For traders coming from the west, Melaka is fifteen hundred kilometers closer than East Java, and by the end of the 15th century this Muslim port dominated the spice trade.

Europe's Age of Exploration began with the search for a direct sea route to the valuable spices of the East, to circumvent the Arab monopoly and put the profits in European hands. In 1488, Bartolomeu Dias reached the Cape of Good Hope (King John came up with this name later, Dias called it "Cabo Tormentoso"), and subsequent Portuguese navigators soon reached India, and in 1511, Melaka. There they finally discovered the source of the fine spices: the Malukan islands of Banda, Ternate, and Tidore. The Portuguese and Spanish fought for control of the spice trade for a hundred years, but by the early 17th century, Protestant Holland owned a monopoly in the trade. First through the Dutch East Indies company and later through direct colonial rule, the Dutch controlled the "East Indies" for the next 350 years.

The Dutch East Indies fell quickly to the Japanese in 1942, and this effectively ended colonial rule of Indonesia. When the Allies won World War II, Holland attempted to retake her former colony, but two nationalist leaders—Soekarno and Mohammad Hatta—had declared Indonesia's independence in a small ceremony in Jakarta on August 17, 1945. It took a four-year colonial war and threats from the United States to cut off Holland's Marshall Plan money before the Dutch formally relinquished their colony on December 27, 1949.

Soekarno was Indonesia's first president, and Hatta the new nation's first vice-president. From 1950 through 1957, Indonesia was governed by a parliamentary democracy, with multiparty participation and a level of political freedom that has only recently re-emerged. As expected in a newly decolonized state, political and economic crises were numerous, but

Indonesia basically succeeded during this period in defining itself as a democratic nation, and made an important mark on the international stage by hosting the 1955 Bandung Conference of non-aligned nations.

The next year, serious divisions broke out within the military, and with covert support from the Dwight D. Eisenhower administration, a military rebellion began in Sumatra and North Sulawesi.* In response, Soekarno declared martial law and dissolved the parliament, giving increased authority to army chief of staff A.H. Nasution, who soon quashed the rebellion.

"Guided Democracy" is what Soekarno called the period that followed, but most commentators would say it was neither. With parliament gone, what remained was a more authoritarian president and an increasingly powerful military, both jostling for political control as the nation faced a series of crises. Soekarno aligned himself ever more closely with the Indonesian Communist Party, the PKI, which by this time was the most popular of the nation's political parties, and the only one untainted by recent scandal.

Soekarno was a skilled politician, deftly balancing the interests of the country's varied constituencies while presenting himself as a forceful leader and source of national pride. But Guided Democracy was an economic failure, and from 1961 to 1964, inflation in Indonesia averaged one hundred percent a year. By mid-1965 the price of rice was rising at a yearly rate of nine hundred percent.

Soekarno cooled towards the United States, and warmed to China and the Soviet Union, nations that were in any case more generous with their foreign aid. This, and his association with the PKI, increasingly alienated right-wing elements of Indonesia's military.

Late at night on September 30, 1965, a group of army officers attempted a coup in Jakarta, assassinating six generals and one lieutenant. Called GESTAPU (an acronymic abbreviation of the date), the coup attempt was quickly put down by Major-General Suharto, who happened to be on hand the next morning and whose name was not on the coup planners' list. An uncontroversial explanation for GESTAPU has not yet been found—some observers see CIA involvement, and most see it as a well-planned putsch by Suharto—but the PKI received the blame, and during the remainder of 1965 and into the next year, hundreds of thousands of people were killed as suspected communists.

GESTAPU effectively ended Soekarno's reign, and by March 1966, he had been forced to award extensive powers to Suharto. One year later, the Indonesian

assembly made Suharto acting president, and Soekarno spent the final three years of his life under house arrest. President Suharto began the "New Order," which emphasized economic development and ties with the West. By 1969 inflation was down to ten percent and the 1970s began a period of steady economic growth that lasted almost thirty years.

This situation changed suddenly in 1997, just as I left Irian Jaya. A pan-Asian currency crisis and years of questionable banking practices stripped the Indonesian rupiah of eighty percent of its value, while a popular reform movement leveled charges of corruption and cronyism against the president and his family. On May 21, 1998, Suharto stepped down after serving just two months of his seventh five-year term as president, leaving the country, facing its worst economic crisis in thirty years, to be led by the unpopular Vice-President Bacharuddin Jusuf Habibie.

Following the first free election in more than three decades, in October 1999 Indonesia's governing body chose Abdurrahman Wahid (Gus Dur) as president, and Megawati Soekarnoputri, Soekarno's daughter, as vice president. Wahid's term was short and rocky, and in May 2001 Megawati became president.

DUTCH NEW GUINEA was not among the territories Holland surrendered to the fledgling nation of Indonesia in 1949. Indonesia annexed the territory in 1963, when it became known as Irian Barat (West Irian). "Irian" is a traditional Biak Island word for the mainland of New Guinea, and the name was first put on record by Frans Kaisiepo at the Malino conference in 1946. Irian Barat was renamed Irian Jaya, approximately "Glorious Irian," in 1973.

Indonesia's annexation of Irian Jaya remains controversial to this day. Critics have called it "Jakarta Imperialism" and even "genocide." The Indonesian army maintains a heavy presence in the province, which can make Irian Jaya feel like an occupied zone. Jakarta considers the troops necessary because of the activities of a separatist movement called the OPM, the Organisasi Papua Merdeka or "Free Papua Organization," which seeks an independent, self-governed West Papua. Over the years, OPM activities have included—in addition to organizing, and lobbying foreign governments through overseas offices—sabotage, kidnapping, and armed resistance.

From the beginning, Soekarno intended for Netherlands New Guinea to be part of independent Indonesia. But as a condition of their vote on the 1949 Round Table Agreement, which transferred sovereignty from Holland to Indonesia, conservatives in the Dutch parliament forced a one-year delay in the transfer of West New Guinea. When this was not forthcoming, Soekarno conducted a ten-year campaign through the United Nations and other diplomatic channels to get Holland to relinquish its New Guinea colony.

By 1960, the Irian Jaya campaign had assumed a

---

* Until the Bay of Pigs, the CIA's support of the Permesta rebels was the agency's most spectacularly bungled operation. When pilot Allen L. Pope was captured on May 18, 1958, after his B-26 was shot down over Ambon, the CIA's cover was blown—Pope's papers clearly showed that his services were on loan to the CIA from the U.S. Army's Camp Bruckner in the Ryukyu Islands. Pope's capture effectively ended CIA participation in the rebellion. This fascinating and little known Cold War parable is told in Audrey R. Kahin and George McT. Kahin's *Subversion as Foreign Policy* (1995).

Frans Pakawa, Hiripau.

pitch of high nationalism that was almost as strong as the original anti-colonial struggle for Indonesia. Soekarno severed diplomatic relations with Holland in August 1960, and on a visit to the United States in 1961, he called the Dutch presence on New Guinea "a cancer in Asia." By the end of 1961 Soekarno was ready to force the Dutch out at gunpoint.

The military campaign for Irian Barat, called Mandala Jaya, was run by Major-General Suharto. The Dutch, with 7,500 troops on the island, were generally able to fend off Indonesian assaults. In the first naval battle, which took place thirty kilometers offshore from the Kamoro village of Yapakopa on January 15, 1962, Indonesia lost deputy naval commander Yos Sudarso and some fifty others aboard the patrol boat *Matjan Tutul*—the Leopard—when it was sunk by the Dutch frigate *Evertsen.* But once the military conflict started, Holland realized that the price of retaining New Guinea would be a protracted jungle war and criticism and sanctions from the United States.

The Cold War was at its height in the early sixties, and the United States was growing increasingly nervous over the influence of communism in Indonesia. Soekarno relied on the Soviet Union for armaments—although the United States, anxious to retain influence, also sold Indonesia arms—and the Kennedy administration, fearing that a long war in New Guinea would only push Indonesia closer to the Soviets, pressed Holland to settle with Soekarno.

In 1962, President John F. Kennedy sent his brother, Attorney General Robert F. Kennedy, to Jakarta to negotiate a solution to the conflict. The first round of talks broke down, but on August 15, 1962, in an agreement brokered by former U.S. ambassador to India Ellsworth Bunker, the Dutch finally agreed to relinquish their New Guinea colony. According to the terms of the Bunker Plan—it is also called the New York Agreement, from the city where it was signed—on October 1, 1962, Irian Barat was turned over to the United Nations, and on May 1, 1963, to Indonesia.*

The first few years of Indonesian rule were difficult ones in Irian Barat. The historical and cultural divide between western Indonesians and the Irianese is considerable even today, and was even more marked in 1963. Considering the "undeveloped" condition of the former Dutch colony, and the fact that Indonesia had just won what it considered an anti-colonial struggle on behalf of the Irianese, the Jakarta government expected to be welcomed to the province.

"The Indonesians pictured themselves as liberators," writes Australian journalist John Ryan in his 1970 *The Hot Land.* "Like the Dutch, German and British colonialists in 1884, the Indonesians in 1963 had entered New Guinea with the assumption that *anything* being offered from the civilized world outside would be greeted by the tribes as salvation from village anarchy and slaughter."

This was not the case. In the late fifties, as they saw their position in New Guinea eroding, the Dutch began an accelerated program of "Papuanization," rapidly increasing the number of West New Guineans in government and education. By 1961 more than three-quarters of the lower and middle positions in the civil administration were held by Papuans, as were twenty-three of the twenty-eight seats on a policy board called the New Guinea Council established in April 1961. The leading members of this council—Marcus Kaisiepo, Nicolaas Jouwé, Herman Womsiwor, Frits Indey, Frits Kirihio and Elizier Bonay—were all committed Papuan nationalists.

In October 1961, the Council formed a National Committee, which chose the name "Papua Barat" for their future independent nation and designed a flag. The flag shows a single star—representing the planet Venus—against a red field in the left, and nine white bands against a blue field on the right, and is informally called the Morning Star. It first flew next to the Dutch Tricolor on December 1, 1961. It came down for the last time—officially, at least—less than a year later when the territory was turned over to the United Nations. At this same time, many of the nationalist leaders went into exile in Holland and Senegal.

As a condition of the New York Agreement, Jakarta had agreed that by 1969 it would hold an "Act of Free Choice," a plebiscite of the Irianese to determine their willingness to become Indonesian citizens. When Soekarno withdrew from the United Nations the plebiscite was temporarily forgotten, but soon after he came to power Suharto rejoined the United Nations, and in August 1969 a group of 1,025 Irianese leaders voted unanimously to join Indonesia.

This "Act of Free Choice" was by no means a plebiscite, as specified by the New York Agreement, and there is considerable evidence that the members of the council organized by the Indonesian government were coerced into voting to join Indonesia. In its defense, Jakarta maintains that a true plebiscite of Irian Barat would have been too difficult to adminis-

---

*Soekarno considered John and Bobby Kennedy to be friends, and the feeling seems to have been mutual. This personal warmth had a lot to do with the success of the New York Agreement. So did Soekarno's pardon and release of the pilot Allen Pope, after a visit by Bobby and Pope's wife and daughters in February 1962. The pilot had been sentenced to death (although he was being held comfortably under house arrest). President Kennedy understood Soekarno's political predicament, and in 1961, referring to the Eisenhower administration's involvement in Permesta, said "No wonder Soekarno doesn't like us very much. He has to sit down with people who tried to overthrow him." Kennedy had planned a state visit to Indonesia for January 1964, and Soekarno built a special house for him on the palace grounds. After the assasination in November 1963, and Lyndon Johnson's ascension to the presidency, U.S. policy toward Indonesia became strongly anti-Soekarno. Johnson even revoked Kennedy's modest Indonesian aid package, which was one of the last pieces of legislation he signed before being assasinated. Overt and covert U.S. policy during this period seems to have exacerbated Indonesia's economic problems, and even contributed to GESTAPU and Soekarno's downfall. For a more complete discussion of this, see Peter Dale Scott's 1985 "The United States and the Overthrow of Sukarno, 1965–1967" in *Public Affairs* 58.

EDI MOYAU, HIRIPAU.

ter, and says that *musyawarah*, "reaching consensus," is a traditional and legitimate way to gauge opinion.

The early years of Indonesian rule were marked by economic chaos and widespread mistreatment of the Papuans, and scattered anti-government incidents began soon after the Indonesians arrived. The first counter-insurgency campaign launched by the Indonesian military, in 1964, was called Operasi Tumpas ("Crush"), followed by the more sensitively named Operasi Sadar ("Awareness"). By 1969, the military had switched to Operasi Wibawa ("Authority"). The province was brought under military control by the early seventies, although sporadic uprisings continued—and continued to be harshly quelled. According to a 1984 UNESCO report, a total of 109,278 Irianese were killed or disappeared in the first twenty years of Indonesian rule.

In the years before my visit, in 1997, conflicts between the military and the local people had been growing increasingly rare, and the quality and discipline of the soldiers has been improving. Still, there is widespread discontent among the Irianese over Indonesian rule, largely because of past abuses by soldiers and, more generally, the greater wealth of western Indonesian migrants to the province.

With the fall of Suharto in 1998, and the successful independence vote of the East Timorese, sentiment in favor of an independent West Papua has been on the rise. At the time this goes to press, in early 2002, the name change to "Papua" has been approved, and a package offering considerable economic autonomy has been planned for the province. Also, a prominent independence figure—Theys Eluay—has been murdered, apparently by rogue elements in the military. Stability in the province has still not arrived.

EIGHTEEN THOUSAND Kamoro live in a great stretch of swampforest along the wet belly of Irian Jaya. The Kamoro language is spoken in Etna Bay, a narrow hook of seawater on the south side of New Guinea's western neck, and the closely related Sempan language can still be heard along the watershed of the Sumapero River, almost four hundred kilometers to the east. The Kamoro are scattered in some three dozen villages, most with two to four hundred people, and a single town, Timika, a booming frontier settlement of fifty thousand Amungme, Kamoro, Dani, Ekagi (Me), Moni, and Biak Islanders from within the province, and Bugis, Javanese, Kei Islanders, Sumatrans, Manadonese, and Madurese from elsewhere in Indonesia.

The name "Kamoro" is a recent invention. Like

37

PURIRI ISLAND.
Fishermen and their families live seasonally on this tiny island, smoking and drying their catch.

most ethnic and linguistic groups that have long lived in relative isolation, the Kamoro never saw the need to coin a name for themselves. They identified themselves by clan group or *taparu* — Itirae, Naegeripi — or by a kind of village group — Paripia-we, literally the "People of Paripi." They had names for various outsiders, however, and for example the early Chinese traders were called Tena-we. Most of the other ethnic groups in New Guinea were the same. They had no names for themselves, but they had names for outsiders, or at least for their immediate neighbors.

Since many groups in New Guinea were less than fond of their neighbors, this led at first to the use of some very unflattering names by outsiders. For example, the Dutch first called the Asmat by a Kamoro name, We Manowe, which simply means "The Cannibals." While this may have been a meaningful appellation from the point of view of the Kamoro, who suffered at the hands of Asmat raiding parties, it is not particularly generous to the Asmat. Nor is it particularly descriptive, as the Asmat are far from being the only people in New Guinea who could accurately be called *we manowe.*

Some of the more benign of these imported names have now been accepted by the people to whom they refer. For example, the Yali living in the Irian Jaya highlands will identify themselves as such to an outsider, even though this name — which comes from the Dani word *ngalik,* meaning "over the mountain range" — was originally an import. By looking at the history of these names, one can often piece together the history of European expansion on the island. For example, the Ekagi living around the Paniai Lakes just inland of the Kamoro were first called Kapauku by the Dutch. "Kapauku" is a Kamoro word, meaning "people of the mountains," and since the Dutch reached the lakes from their outpost at Uta, in the Kamoro area, that is where they got the name. In turn, these "Kapauku" were asked to name the people living in the highlands just to their east, and they said: "Migani." This name persisted until the Moni — the name by which the Migani are now known — were contacted by the Dutch and had some say in choosing the term by which the outside world would know them.

The Mimika River, which reaches the sea near present-day Kokonao in about the middle of the Kamoro territory, was charted in 1902, making it one of the first rivers in the area to be properly explored by the Dutch. Because of this, the area became known as the Mimika district, a name that appears in accounts as early as 1912. In 1926, the Dutch located their first government station in the Kamoro area at the mouth of the Mimika River, and by this time the name "Mimika" came to be applied both to the district and to the people of the district. Most of the extant literature on the Kamoro people still calls them the Mimika.

The name "Kamoro" was first popularized by Dutch linguist and missionary Father Petrus Drabbe, who suggested in a 1947 issue of the journal *Oceania* that it was a more suitable term than "Mimika." "Mimika" was never more than a Dutch colonial construct, and even the original people of Mimika village, now combined with three other villages in the small town of greater Kokonao, call themselves Wakotu-me, not Mimikans. Not everyone has taken to Drabbe's suggestion. Dutch anthropologist Jan Pouwer, who wrote a long monograph on the Kamoro in the 1950s, continues to use the term "Mimika" in texts written as recently as 1991.

The Kamoro themselves have no such problems, however, and I never once heard anyone speak of Mimika except in two very narrow senses: that of the Indonesian political district and sub-districts which, following Dutch practice, are called Mimika, or that of the village of Mimika in Kokonao town. When not elevated to the status of a proper noun, *kamoro* means something like "life," or "living people," and connotes the difference between a human being and a ghost.

FLYING FROM JAKARTA to Timika takes about as long as flying from San Francisco to New York. Both are eastward flights, but their directions are not really the same. An Indonesian's cultural and historical sense of "east" is the same as an American's sense of "west." Flying east in Indonesia is flying toward the frontier, the newest and strangest part of the country. Irian Jaya is Indonesia's "Wild East." Kal has been working in Indonesia for so long that his internal map has adjusted to this. He can, when he is speaking to an American, say "east" when he means "west." Although we jokingly call this "directional dyslexia," he is only in error by the compass.

Because of the Freeport mining operations, Timika has one of the longest and best-surfaced airports in the province, and one of the few that can accommodate jet aircraft. But the small concrete-block terminal building feels more like a minor Eastern European border crossing station than a public airport. There is no piped music, nor are there restaurants or magazine stands or information booths. The building is so small that no one whose name is not on the flight manifest is allowed through the doors.

Kal and I arrived in Timika to begin work on this book in January of 1997. Our plane stopped far away from the small terminal, near the pads and hangers for the military helicopters and planes. Parked nearby, their huge diesel engines rattling in the heat, were two primer-colored buses, each a school bus shell grafted onto the chassis and drivetrain from a super heavy-duty Mack dump truck. The mine workers climbed directly from the plane into one of these, and were hauled immediately up the tortuous, hundred kilometer road to the mine. Kal and I and the other Timika-bound passengers climbed into the second bus, for the short trip to the terminal.

From the airport, we caught a bus to the Sheraton Inn Timika, a very unlikely oasis of four-star luxury that, without luggage, would be walking distance from the airport. Like the airport, the remarkable road to the highlands, the power grid, and the cellular phone transmitters, the hotel exists because of the needs of the mining company. It is almost impossible to exaggerate how strange this place, with its tennis courts, sculpted swimming pool, and painstakingly tended grounds appears in Irian Jaya's rainforest frontier.

The next day we went to see Tony Rahawarin. Tony worked for Freeport's community affairs department out of a small office in downtown Timika. At the time we went to see him, Tony was helping the Nawaripi Kamoro living along the East Levee of the company's tailings impoundment area. Tony's development projects seem modest, such as making sure that there is a regular bus so the Nawaripi people could bring their sago and other products to market in Timika. These small things, he said, can generate big headaches.

Tony is a Kei Islander, but he was born in Uta in the western Kamoro area. The Kei Islands are in Indonesia's Maluku Tenggara province, about four hundred kilometers from Timika. Kei Islanders enjoy a special relationship with the Kamoro, which began more than a half-century ago, when the Catholic Church recruited people from the Keis to serve as teachers and pastors in Kamoro communities. Tony's father was a schoolteacher and administrator in Uta during the Dutch colonial period.

Tony, who is fifty-one years old, has the build of someone well acquainted with a glass of beer. He is very soft-spoken, so much so that he seems tired, or resigned. It's hard to tell which. His command of English is excellent, and few Americans—and even fewer Californians—speak with such grammatical precision.

I hoped that Tony could recommend somebody to help me with this project. I speak no Kamoro and very little Indonesian, so I needed a translator at least. But what I really wanted was a kind of intellectual partner, somebody who would be as interested as I was in constructing a portrait of Kamoro life today.

Tony sat back on his chair for a minute. Using just two criteria, a functional knowlege of English and at least some education past grade school, he began listing the names of candidates, raising a finger for each. When he was done he still had three fingers left.

"Imagine," he said wearily. "In a hundred years, only these."

Two names stood out: Aloysius Akiniyau, with whom Kal had already worked several times on earlier photographic and fact-finding jaunts in the area, and Apollo Takati.

39

KASPARINA MAYARAIKU, VERONIKA MANEYAU, AND BERNARDA MANEYAU, YARAYA.

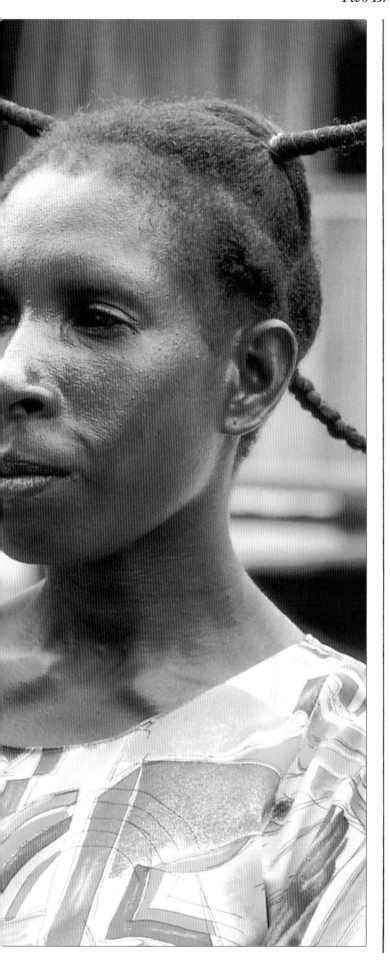

I MET APOLLO TAKATI for the first time the next evening, when I invited Tony and him to the hotel for a beer. I soon discovered that the two are good friends and, in fact, brothers in law. Apollo's wife is Tony's sister. No sooner had we poured our beers than Apollo began joking with Tony about a glass of beer, a cuscus, and a lizard. The joke, which collapses in translation, hinges on the similarity of these words in Kamoro, all of which are pronounced approximately "*wah*-kay." I liked Apollo immediately.

Apollo teaches at a junior high school in Timika, and is a leading member of LEMASKO, the largest local Kamoro development agency. In 2002 he became a member of the Mimika DPRD, a kind of district level legislature. He is an intellectual, of a careful and slightly conventional stripe. He has a very active sense of humor, and it is rarely long before he erupts in a burst of laughter.

Apollo is fifty-nine years old, and he and his wife Secilia Florentina live in a comfortable house in a residential neighborhood of Timika called Timika Indah. He has gained a bit of weight over the years, perhaps befitting his station in life. He and Secilia have seven children, ranging in age from twenty-seven-year-old Engelbertus (named after the singer Engelbert Humperdinck) to fourteen-year-old Maria.

"I don't follow the Kah-Bay," Apollo joked, referring to the initials of the Indonesian department of family planning. "Irian Jaya is a big place and we must have many people."

Apollo was born in the village of Paripi. His father Abraham had considerable status in the village, and served the Dutch colonial government as *mandur,* a kind of village foreman. Apollo took to school at an early age, which did not make his father or mother, Katarina Moukiyu, particularly happy.

"My brother was already a teacher, and they needed my help at home," he said. "Sometimes they did not allow me to go to school."

Education was still a bit of a novelty in Paripi fifty years ago, and his parents couldn't see losing a second son to the Dutch school system. Finally, Apollo said, he succeeded in convincing them that the hardship involved in his being away at school during his education would be outweighed by the money this would allow him to provide to the family later on.

When Apollo was a child, the ritual life of Paripi was still quite strong. His parents had not been formally schooled or brought up in the Catholic Church. "Apollo" is his church name; his parents called him by his *nama tanah,* or traditional name, Mautipuru. I had known Apollo for months before I got this piece of information out of him, and it required an additional several minutes of pleading to get the meaning: "Short Feet." The Dutch missionaries discouraged the use of *nama tanah,* dismissing them as "Hindu names." Since the nearest Hindus were more than two thousand kilometers away in Bali, nobody except the missionaries

MBITORO, TIMIKA PANTAI.
Raised during the first stage of the *karapao,* the carved poles stand for six
months or more until the second, initiation stage.

understood the intended slander. Still, their attitude made itself felt to the younger generation like Apollo, and he recalls getting angry with his parents, telling them: "I'm *educated,* stop using my Hindu name."

Although we laughed at "Short Feet," it must be understood that "short" is a relative term. Leather dress shoes are like hen's teeth in Timika, and on my second trip I brought Apollo a pair from the United States. They were size 10 $\frac{1}{2}$, and fit perfectly.

Apollo studied first in Kokonao, then the largest village in the Kamoro area and the center of the colonial government, and later attended teacher training school in Fakfak, a small city on the Bomberai Peninsula to the west.

"At that time, Fakfak was a good place," Apollo said. "We were treated well and lived well. We never really knew at the time who was taking care of us"–he laughed–"but of course it was the Catholic Church. We didn't continue our education after this training, but had to go right out to the villages to begin teaching."

He first taught primary school in Timika Pantai, and then was transferred to Paniai, in the highlands outside of the Kamoro area. Thanks to his three years there–and his gift for languages–Apollo can still speak the Ekagi language quite passably.

In the late 1960s, he continued his training in Jayapura, the largest city in Irian Jaya and the capital of the province. In 1970–in the period after the Act of Free Choice and before the first Indonesian election–he took advantage of a United Nations program and spent a year in Australia, studying at Macquary University. He lived with a British family on Epping Street in North Sydney, and remembers the Australians as being very friendly, and particularly tolerant of his then minimal command of English.

It was on a brief holiday in Kokonao after returning from Australia that he met his future wife, Secilia. She was just returning from Langgur, in the Kei Islands, where she had finished school. Actually, this wasn't the first time they met. He saw her years earlier when she was still a girl. Apollo had inherited a school principal's job from Secilia's father, who was returning to the Kei Islands. "I'm going to marry that pretty daughter of yours when she grows up," he joked. Five years later, in 1972, he did.

Apollo was enthusiastic about our project from the beginning. We planned to take a boat to the far western edge of the Kamoro area, stopping at as many villages as we could find time to. It had been years, and in the case of some villages, decades, since Apollo had found an opportunity to do this. I teased him that his years in Timika, and before that Kokonao and Jayapura, had turned him into a city boy, but he needed no encouragement. He was as curious as we were to see what was happening in the villages. Apollo's students were about to take their exams, so all we had to do was convince his principal to find a proctor and Apollo was free. A letter from the *bupati* took care of that.

ALOYSIUS AKINIYAU HAS had a more checkered past than Apollo. Whereas Apollo found a nice, middle-class career for himself within the Dutch Catholic, and later Indonesian, education system, Alo's luck has been, at best, seasonal, a fact that is etched on his personality. His humor tends toward irony, and he can be very philosophical. He always speaks frankly, which is refreshing in Indonesia, where indirection is strongly associated with politeness. He also has a real gift for language, and was continually impressing me with his turn of phrase.

"It takes a while for something bad to come out," he once said, on a subject I'd rather not elaborate. "Like a gecko that falls dead from the ceiling, and lands in a crack between the floorboards. It's only after a couple of days that it begins to stink."

Alo was born in Uta, but his family is from Atuka, which he considers his home village. He is fifty-one years old, and as tall and lanky as a Texas cowboy. A coffee cup disappears in his hand. Alo's parents would have been very unwise to give him Apollo's traditional name. I brought him back size 12 E shoes, and they are a little tight. (His parents called him Maratipiya, "The Hatchet.") Alo is very fine company in the quiet part of the evening, when the after-dinner coffee grows cold and the discussion tends to wander freely.

Alo's father, from Atuka, was a policeman for the Dutch colonial administration. He was stationed in Uta when Alo was born, but soon transferred to Merauke, in the southeastern corner of the province, near the Papua New Guinea border. Alo remembers life being very good in those days, particularly when he could join his father on hunting expeditions. As a policeman, his father enjoyed the rare privilege of owning a firearm. The land around Merauke, uniquely for Irian Jaya, is a dry savannah that seems more like Australia than New Guinea. Particularly in the dry monsoon, when the animals are desperate for a drink, a blind set up at a water hole quickly rewards the hunter. The family always had fresh venison, tree kangaroo, and fowl–wild goose was Alo's favorite.

In 1959, Alo's father moved the family to the capital, then called Hollandia. Alo had been attending the Catholic school in Merauke, and continued in his studies in Hollandia. The year of the transfer to Indonesia, 1963, was a troubled one in the capital, which was renamed Kota Baru, "New Town." Children of the educated elite spoke Dutch and their native language, and not a word of Indonesian. Some of them, particularly those who had studied abroad, held pro-Dutch or pro-independence political opinions, and the tensions between the Indonesian army and the students were high. At the time, Alo was getting into the usual trouble that thirteen-year-old boys do, but in this charged atmosphere he, together with the older Dutch educated students, was being branded anti-Indonesian.

To keep him out of trouble, Alo was sent to Kokonao and enrolled in school with the Catholic father there. Things cooled down after a few years, and in 1968 he returned to the capital to finish senior high school. It was at this time that he first met Apollo.

Alo and Apollo have been close friends for a very long time, although their personalities are so different that each can still be quite puzzled by the other. While he was going to high school, Alo was living with Apollo's brother in Abepura, just outside of Kota Baru—the capital was eventually renamed Jayapura—which is how Apollo came to meet him.

"At first, there was a bit of a problem," Apollo said. "He didn't talk much to me. There was too much difference in age and experience—he was a student, and I was a teacher."

This, in any case, is the way Apollo remembers it. Alo, for his part, countered that Apollo may have thought of himself as a bit too much of a big shot to pay attention to his brother's young lodger. "Also," Alo said, "If my memory serves I think you were spending all your free time chasing girls."

When Alo finished school in 1971, he tried to get a scholarship to the university in Bandung, but there was no money at the time. He was told to enroll at the University of Cenderawasih (UNCEN), in Jayapura, and that the scholarship to the better school in Java might be available later. He studied at UNCEN for one semester, but the promised scholarship never appeared. He didn't have the money even to continue at UNCEN, and headed south to the Timika area to find work.

In 1967, while he was still in Kokonao, Alo had heard about the activity in the Aikwa watershed, as Freeport began the initial viability studies on the Ertsberg mine. By the time the twenty-one-year-old Alo returned to the south coast, Bechtel-Pomeroy was already building the mine road. He was hired as a mechanic and trained to service heavy equipment.

At the time, the workers lived in Port-O-Camp temporary buildings at Amamapare, the company's portsite. Relatively high-paying jobs such as Alo's were scarce in the area, and some western Indonesians were not particularly happy to see an Irianese man get one. At one point, an Ambonese foreman demoted Alo to millright/mechanic level, where he was stuck until the foreman was transferred. The new foreman was an expatriate American, and he saw what had happened and reinstated Alo's position and salary.

Separatist activity heated up in 1976 and 1977, particularly in the highlands, and relations between the Irianese and western Indonesians deteriorated. In the Timika area, Alo had the bad fortune to be the first person rounded up by the military. The soldiers had commandeered a metal shipping container from the Freeport dock and used it as a makeshift cell. At first Alo was alone, but by the end of a fortnight, thirty people were sleeping in this hot, airless "jail."

The problem, as Alo describes it, was that the foremen and other workers, all of whom were Indonesians from outside Irian, pushed the Kamoro and other Iri-

anese workers around. Alo didn't like this very much. Even at age fifty-one, Alo has the height and build of someone you would not want to encounter on the other side of an argument. My impression is that the then twenty-seven-year-old Alo wasn't particularly reserved in expressing his anger at the way he and his peers were being treated. The fact that the Americans and Australians on the project liked and respected him just made things worse with the Indonesians.

Alo was released after two weeks, but he didn't go back to his old job. The same Ambonese man was back in the foreman position, and he made work impossible for Alo. At this stage in his life, Alo was so dejected that he decided to stow away on a ship to Australia. He had to get drunk to work up enough nerve to go through with his plan, however, and this unfortunately impaired his sense of time and motion. Thinking that he was safely out to sea, he came out of hiding only to find the ship still in port, whereupon he was politely—but firmly—escorted ashore.

In the late seventies, the Timika area was starting to expand dramatically. Alo got work with a survey crew, laying out roads and plots for transmigrant farmers who were moving to Irian from western Indonesia in increasing numbers.

Alo married Modesta Omaniyau, a former nurse, in 1983. Alo's father, who has since died, never approved of the match, but his mother always liked Modesta, and still lives in the Timika area. Alo and Modesta have three children: eight-year-old Nana Reyana, named for Nana Mouskouri, a singer I should have heard of but haven't; eleven-year-old Franco, named for Franco Nero, an actor I should have heard of but haven't; and twenty-two-year-old Franky, named for Frankie Avalon, a former teen idol I should have heard of and have. Alo was stunned that I hadn't heard of Mouskouri and Nero, and made me feel like a philistine. In my defense, I tried to emphasize the eleven-year difference in our ages, admittedly a weak ploy.

In the mid-eighties, Alo found a survey crew again, this time working around Akimuga in the Lorentz National Park. This park, covering a huge area from the coast to the highlands just east of Timika, is one of the most impressive natural reserves in the world, and has been declared a World Heritage Site. It is also one of Alo's favorite places.

"It is so beautiful, I cannot forget it," he said. "It's not like here"—pointing at the dusty roads of Timika— "there are no cut trees, no roads, no houses. They picked a very good spot."

In 1987, Alo was chosen for a five-year term on the Fakfak DPRD, but the experience was marred by the the corruption and dealing on the board at that time.

A few years ago, tiring of the stress and noise of Timika, Alo moved his family further south to Paumako, where they still live. In Paumako, he said, the sounds of the night insects are not drowned out by traffic noise, and the air still smells clean.

YUFENSIUS EWAKIPIYAUTA, TIMIKA PANTAI.
The large, decorated casket in the foreground is filled with sago for the *karapao* ceremony.

CHAPTER TWO

Karapao!

When the Mbitoro Awakes

WHEN KAL AND I first arrived in Timika, we found a letter waiting for us. It was an invitation from the people of Keakwa village to attend their upcoming *karapao* festival. When Kal stumbled upon the initiation festival in Timika Pantai several months earlier, he let it be known that he would like to photograph any other such events that might come up. Keakwa is the next village west of Timika Pantai. Through the somewhat mysterious pathways that substitute for the post in this area, which in this case included hand delivery to the *bupati*'s office and to Tony's office, the invitation found its way to the front desk of our hotel.

Actually, the letter was addressed to Kal, and since nobody yet knew about our plans for a book, I was going to have to go along as a gate-crasher. Another would be Kal's fifteen-year-old son Andres, who was taking a break from high school in Mexico and came to Indonesia to see just what it was that his father did for a living. Andres, who can be almost distractingly charming, is something of a prodigy in the sport of rock climbing, and most Mexican national-level free climbers dread the day he turns sixteen and begins to be formally ranked.

As a father, Kal provides a somewhat unusual mix of free-thinker and disciplinarian. He didn't mind Andres rolling himself an occasional smoke from our supply of shag tobacco, he was more or less indifferent to the shoulder-length dreadlocks, and he actually enjoyed the continuous soundtrack of Bob Marley and Jimmy Cliff that emanated from Andres's portable CD player. On the other hand, for the two weeks he joined our little expedition, Kal made sure Andres worked through his daily correspondence course lessons and, when it came time to haul our gear around, saw to it that his son's healthy fifteen-year-old

back performed its fair share of the lifting.

The scheduled date for the culmination of the Keakwa *karapao* was January 30, less than two weeks from the day we arrived in Timika. We decided to stop first in Timika Pantai, to see what we could learn about the ceremony Kal had photographed earlier, and then to continue on to Keakwa. Within days we had organized a boat, and on the appointed morning Kal, Andres, Alo, Apollo, and I met at the Freeport company dock at Amamapare, forty kilometers south of Timika.

The hour-and-a-quarter ride from Amamapare to Timika Pantai was beautiful. The sun fought constantly with dramatic rain clouds, and a rainbow stood in front of us most of the way. Our vessel was a strange, square workboat, about five meters long and two in beam, which was typically used to run errands and tend the larger ships around the docks. The boat, constructed of heavy gauge steel, had the apparent hydrodynamics of a brick, but when the twin engines opened up it climbed up on the water nicely, and we made good time along the crooked brown rivers.

The water was calm, and we followed the inland route all the way to Timika Pantai. Because we were a little late getting off, the outgoing tide briefly grounded us on one tight loop. After pushing and rocking the heavy boat, and restarting the engines half a dozen times, we squeezed through.

The Prasarana Marga company holds the logging concession here, and in many areas along the Mawka River the mangrove forest was being cut quite heavily. We passed countless stacks of cut trees, each the size of a small house and neatly labeled. Behind them lay a plot of stripped forest. The logs were short, and mostly only a few centimeters in diameter, and they seemed good for nothing except paper or chipboard. I have heard that mangrove logs make very good paper, but this environment is so ecologically important that I am skeptical of the wisdom of allowing any lumbering at all here.* Between the logging and the bottom-dragging shrimp trawlers that operate just offshore,

---

LIBERATUS IMUARO, TIMIKA PANTAI. While the chief of traditions for the village, Yufensius Nokoreyau, instructs the boys on their role in the upcoming initiation, Liberatus cannot resist a quick peek back at the photographer.

HERMAN AMORMAYARO, TIMIKA PANTAI. Lime from burned clamshells, charcoal, and ocher provide the color palette for the initiates. The patterns are specific to the boys' *taparu*.

* Even before I completed this manuscript, Prasarana Marga went bankrupt. The stacks of wood I saw are still there, now gray and dry-rotted, and not even usable as firewood.

YULIANUS AMATIMUKA, TIMIKA PANTAI.
This dance brings good weather for the ceremony, and a bright future for the young initiates.

this important estuary environment is getting it from both ends.

When we arrived Timika Pantai looked deserted, except for a small group of children who immediately ran over to meet our boat. We remembered then that it was Sunday morning. One of the older boys ran off to the church, where the entire village was gathered for Mass, and brought back the village schoolteacher. He led us to to the clinic, the best accommodation in town.

The clinic at Timika Pantai is a comfortable masonry block building with a concrete floor and jalousied-glass windows. One window even had curtains, which were neatly held open by passing the calico through two empty cigarette packs from which the top and bottom had been removed. The Indonesian brand Gudang Garam comes in a bright red and gold pack. Since the village was enjoying good health at the time, we were offered two beds with mattresses. The clinic's entire supply of bandages and medicines fit on one small shelf of a locked cabinet.

We took coffee in the kitchen, on a factory-made wooden table. One corner was taken up by a gross of garden spades, wrapped in burlap in neat bundles of twelve. Although the kitchen had a sink and space for a stove, nobody cooked there, and in traditional Kamoro style a cooking area with an open fire had

been added under a lean-to out back. The afternoon was quiet, and a dreaming puppy vibrated on the cool floor under the table.

The official government name for Timika Pantai is Tiwaka, a holdover from a time when the people of Wapuka and Aika villages were living together with the people of Timika. The acronymic name "Tiwaka" combines a syllable each from the three villages. The village should simply be called "Timika," but with that name now being used for the big city nearby, the specific *pantai* has been added to avoid confusion. In English Timika Pantai means something like "Timika-by-the-Sea." To further complicate matters, older maps still label the village "Timuka" or, using the Dutch spelling, "Timoeka." This misspelling comes from the Dutch having asked the wrong person for the name: the romanization "Timuka" is simply "Timika" as rendered in a dialect from further west.

Toward the end of our visit I heard rumors that Timika Pantai, which has been losing population to the greater Timika area, might join Keakwa village at a new, inland site. If this happens, of course, the "Pantai" will have to go. The joint village could end up with a hyphenated name, Timika-Keakwa, but I vote for the neologism "Keamika." In any case, one certainly must sympathize with the cartographer trying to make a map of this area.

THE KARAPAO IS enjoying a comeback throughout the Kamoro area. Between mid-1996 and mid-1997, *karapao*s were held in Timika Pantai, Keakwa, Hiripau, and Atuka, and perhaps a few villages further west. During the national election campaign in the spring of 1997, almost every village erected at least a small *karapao* building, although these were just a way for the village leadership to generate interest in the election, and no initiations took place.

The *karapao,* which is the name of both a ceremony and a structure, is a temporary building framed with lashed poles, with leaf mat walls and a thatched roof arranged, like a lean-to, with a single pitch. The width of a *karapao* is always about three meters; the length depends on the number of "doors," and these, in turn, depend on the number of boys being initiated. The largest ones I've seen are maybe thirty meters long.

In Timika Pantai, we sat with some of the older men in the village, showed them prints of Kal's slides, and asked about the *karapao* that had been held there the previous spring.

What Kal had witnessed was the second and final stage of a male initiation ceremony, they said. This is actually a modern interpretation of the initiation ceremony, and is all that is left of a more elaborate past cycle of three separate initiations. Traditionally, a Kamoro boy underwent his first initiation at age seven or eight, and his second at age fifteen or sixteen. This second ceremony, during which he traded his *tapena,* a kind of clothing for children, for the symbolic *tauri,* a

SERFASIUS WAUKATEYAU, KEAKWA.
A few days before the event, Serfasius carves the last details on the *mbitoro*'s banner or *tokae*.

palm frond covering for the penis, marked the passage to adulthood. The cycle included an additional stage, which took place only after the boy was fully adult and married. In this ceremony, which marked his initiation into the leadership of the community, his nose was pierced. This piercing, by the way, does not mean that the man puts a dainty gold ring in one nostril. It means that a hole big enough to pass a boar's tusk is punched through his septum. It is a bloody, painful procedure, and in the past infection and other complications were not uncommon.

Today there is only one ceremony, and although the boys vary in age, the average at Timika Pantai was probably around ten. Even in the old days there was never really a fixed age for initiation, and the men had to exercise some judgment in the matter. To determine whether a boy was ready for the second part of the traditional cycle, the real beginning of adulthood, the village men employed a simple test, Apollo said.

"A man would take a big piece of banana stem, walk up to the boy, and smack him as hard as he could. If the boy cried out, he wasn't ready yet. If he kept quiet, he was."

I was quickly assured that this test has gone the way of nose-piercing, which nobody can remember having taken place since at least the fifties. But Apollo

seemed a little too anxious to tell me this. The men of Timika Pantai offered no comment.

For the climax of the ceremony, as it is conducted today, the boys are tended by older brothers and other male relatives, who dress them in eye-popping finery. Their bodies are completely painted in soot and lime, stippled with rosettes produced by the conveniently shaped seed cap of the *Bruguiera* tree, and accented by bright orange ocher or red bixin from annatto seeds. The patterns are not random, but serve rather like a coat of arms to represent the boy's *taparu*. The final touches are wildly patterned pieces of cloth, crazy hats—anything from the Muslim's *peci* to baseball caps with rabbit ears—and novelty sunglasses.

Fig. 2.1
BRUGUIERA
SEED.

The villagers gather sago in great quantities, the women fish, and the men, taking their best dogs, hunt for wild boar. There is drumming and dancing and plenty of tobacco. This final stage of the *karapao* lasts several days, and during this period spirits are high and bellies are full. It is in no way a solemn event. It is much more like a carnival.

The ceremony that would take place at Keakwa in

INTERIOR OF KARAPAO BUILDING, TIMIKA PANTAI.

the next few days is the first stage of the *karapao*. The boys will not be initiated yet. First the huge *mbitoro* poles must be carved, painted, awakened, and, in the culminating gesture, raised and lashed to the front of the *karapao*. These stages are separated by about six months, sometimes even longer. The exact time is set by the village elders, according to their own traditional means of reckoning together with some consideration for today's modern exigencies, such as the school calendar and Indonesian national holidays.

WHEN OUR BOAT landed in Keakwa the next day, a cheering crowd greeted us like heroes. We were literally swept along to, again, an empty clinic building and marched up onto the porch. Obviously, someone had brought news from Timika Pantai, and the clinic had already been cleared out and set aside for us. The atmosphere was electric, and by the time we reached the building what seemed like the entire village, at least two hundred people, gathered in front of us and cheered. I have never in my life experienced such a hearty welcome.

As we stood before the crowd, not really knowing what to do or say, a woman leaped up onto the porch and smeared each of our foreheads with white sago paste. Then, quite mischievously, she stuck her hand in my pants pocket and began slowly going through its contents. I had no idea what she was doing, and I looked down the line at Alo and Apollo, but they seemed just as confused as I was. Finally, when she reached the second pocket, she came up with my cigarettes, and held them out. "It's traditional," she said, with what I swear was a wink, and the crowd roared. She moved down the line, relieving each of us in turn of our tobacco and a couple of coins or small bills.

Kal quit smoking two years ago, so he wasn't a good prospect for cigarettes. He did, however, have a roll of money in his pocket, which she pulled out. Unfortunately, it was about two hundred thousand rupiah, our fuel and supplies money for the next couple weeks, and I don't think the woman had ever seen cash in this quantity. She didn't even peel off a Rp1,000 note, she just slipped the wad back into his pocket like it was on fire and moved on to Alo and Apollo, where she had better luck.

When we arrived, the culminating day of the festival was still three days away, but already celebration was in the air. As we walked to the center of the village to see the work progressing on the *karapao* building, a woman ran up and hugged me with great enthusiasm, giggled, and ran off. Everyone in the village was laughing and carrying on, and they all wore dabs of sago paste on their foreheads.

Keakwa immediately presents itself as a tidy, attractive village, an impression helped by the clean sand and coconut trees. One house has a pineapple plant growing in front of it, another an orchid on a short post. All of the simple fencing along the main paths was in the process of being renewed, the better to show off the village during the upcoming ceremony.

Very quickly we were led down a small path away from the village to a shaded copse near the beach, where the carvers were finishing up work on two *mbitoro* poles. By tradition, women are not allowed to see the *mbitoro* until they are finished, and a makeshift blind had been placed around the site. This was hardly a real safeguard, and anyone walking back from the beach could have easily seen inside. But while I was there, at least, it seemed to me that the passing women politely averted their eyes.

In the past, the carving of the *mbitoro* would have been conducted far away from the village in a secret place, and for a woman or uninitiated child to have seen it would have violated a very serious taboo. Such an event has even been known to cause a war. I heard about the most famous one from Todd Harple.

Todd is a young American anthropologist who had been hired by Freeport to work with the Kamoro living in the area of the company's work contract, especially the Nawaripi and Tipuka people living in the area of the Iwinia, Tipukamiuka, and Muamiua rivers. Todd is an enthusiastic, sandy-haired Pennsylvanian who studied at the University of Pittsburgh and the University of Kansas. He reads Dutch and is learning Kamoro. It was from Dutch sources that Todd read an account of what has become known as the Tipuka War.

Just when this event took place is unclear, but since it was already fading into memory at the time of the earliest Dutch observers, a good guess would be about a century ago. Basically, Todd told me, the whole thing started with a *kaware* ceremony in Tipuka, to which people from nearby villages such as Mioko and Woanaripi were invited. Whether it actually happened or not is unclear, but these visitors became convinced that the men of Tipuka leaked secrets of the *kaware* to the women of the village. They kept quiet about it during the ceremony, but as soon as they returned to their villages, they met and organized a reprisal. The attack on Tipuka was swift and unexpected. Many of the men were killed, and the women taken as spoils of war.

It is this last point that continues to cause Todd headaches today. Because kinship in traditional Kamoro society emphasizes matrilineal descent, the Tipuka women's *taparu* lineages are now spread in a great web throughout the Tipuka and Wania watersheds and even across to the Nawaripi living along the Uamiua River. Todd keeps a big area map on his office wall on which he has tried to highlight these *taparu* connections, and it seemed to me he was running out of different colored pens.

It is impossible to imagine a similar breach causing such problems today. Kal later photographed a *karapao* in Atuka, and there he noticed that during the taboo parts of the ceremony several of the village leaders interrupted the proceedings and brought the women and children over to show them what was taking place. These leaders were attempting in this way to demystify the ritual, to make it more secular and less spiritually charged. In other words, to make it less of a ritual, and more of an entertainment.

These men have been influenced by a powerful local schoolteacher named J. Sukadi. Sukadi is Javanese by birth, although his wife of twenty years is Kamoro. He firmly believes that the *karapao* and other traditional ceremonies are recidivist nonsense, a step backward for the Kamoro. His prestige and political power in the village are considerable, and for almost two decades he was able to insure that Atuka did not hold a *karapao* at all.

Not everyone in Atuka is happy about Sukadi's meddling, and the reputation he has—at least out of earshot—is not exactly enviable. But his drive to "modernize" Atuka has brought benefits as well, including what are probably the most productive vegetable gardens on this coast east of Ararao. It was in Atuka, Kal claims, that he sampled the best-tasting pineapple of his life.

T HE CHIEF DECORATION of the *karapao* is the *mbitoro.* This is a kind of ancestor pole, serving to bring back the spiritual power and wisdom of a dead member of the community, always someone who had been strong and respected during his life. It is also, of course, a sign of respect, and in the context of an initiation, the men on the *mbitoro* are almost literally being held up as examples to be emulated by the boys.

The men who received this sign of respect at Keakwa were Esebius Waukateyau (traditional name: Iyakopateyau) of *taparu* Kanare-Kimara, a famous woodcarver who had died just two years before, and Amandus Weyau (traditional name: Potowae) of *taparu* Imiriaripiti, another famous woodcarver who has been dead for many years.

The two *mbitoro*—pronounced "*bee*-toe-roe," with just the hint of the em—being carved at Keakwa were somewhat unusual, because each bore the likeness of just one man. Most *mbitoro* I have seen show two faces, although I have also seen them with three, and once, four. The Keakwa *mbitoro* were the only ones I have seen with a single face.

The *mbitoro* were about five meters long, and carved from a local softwood called *kiyako.* This tree has plank-like buttress roots to prop it up in the soft mud of the mangrove where it grows. For a *mbitoro,* the entire trunk and the largest buttress root are used, and once the tree is inverted the root serves as the *tokae,* a kind of pennant or banner, at the top of the carving.

The carving work was being supervised by a master carver, a *maramowe,* named Serfasius Waukateyau. Serfasius learned his trade from his father Esebius, who is represented on one of the *mbitoro.* Under him were three apprentices. Serfasius tended to the more difficult designs and the finish work, while the others

roughed out motifs. Kamoro art is quite abstract, and appears very modern to a western viewer. The motifs have names that translate as "bird's egg hatching," "uku shell," and "sawfish bill," but they are stylized almost beyond recognition. Some, such as the *ma'ako,* which looks like a German iron cross, are strictly geometrical.

When we arrived, the men were putting the final touches on these two carvings, and they were not quite ready to begin painting them. While I was asking Apollo the names of some of the motifs, he stalled when I pointed to a small knob the size of a thumb along the edge of one of the *mbitoro.* One of the carvers, who saw where I was pointing, laughed. That is the penis, he said. In the past, this item would have been represented at a much grander scale, but it has gradually wilted under the disapproving influence of the Catholic Church and the Dutch colonial government. At least each carving included two, which might be of some solace to Esebius and Amandus.

The men finishing the *mbitoro* were not the only carvers at work, and out on the beach in front of the village we met Marselus Weyau. Marselus is Amandus's son, and woodcarving is as much in his genes as it is in those of Esebius's son Serfasius. Marselus was making a drum. A baseball cap proclaiming "New Town Project"—a reference to the town north of Timika that has since been named Kuala Kencana—would have kept the sun out of his eyes if he hadn't been wearing it backward.

Sitting next to a fire, Marselus was gradually hollowing out the interior of a piece of wood the size and shape of a fireplace log. Using wooden tongs, he placed a coal from the fire into the interior of the drum, and directed and intensified the burning by blowing through a length of bamboo. When the coal exhausted itself, he returned it to the fire, then scraped the charred surface of the drum with a rasp he had made by punching an old can a hundred times with a nail. He also kept a pile of wet mud nearby, with which he protected the finished parts of the drum from further combustion.

A Kamoro drum is shaped like an hourglass and is not quite a meter long, with a skin on one end and a handle along the side. There is rarely much decoration except on the handle, but a good one has walls of a very even thickness. What struck me as strange about Marselus's method was that, essentially, he was shaping the drum from the inside out. I would have guessed that one first carves the drum and its handle, and only then hollows it. Marselus's technique is something like building a doughnut around the hole; first he shapes the emptiness, and then carves the log to produce a thin, even layer of wood over it. Since it is the hollow that produces a drum's sound, Marselus's instincts in this matter are much better than mine.

I also would have guessed that such a job would take a very long time, but even though he wasn't very

DANCERS, ATUKA.
Dominika Emeyau, Margareta Kemeyau, and Marselina Mapareyau.

far along when I saw him, Marselus said he'd be finished in another couple hours. And he wasn't working at a particularly strained pace. In fact, later that evening I saw him in front of his house, carving the handle and attending to the other final detail work. The next morning the new drum was finished, and some men had already gone out to set lizard traps. The drum head requires a belly skin from a species of monitor lizard.

L ATE AFTERNOON WAS a quiet time in the village. While the women prepared dinner, the men carved drums or canoe paddles. Stacked behind each house was that family's allotment of thatch for roofing the *karapao,* and both men and women folded and pinned it into sections. Wives swept out their porches and under the house. Younger women returned in groups of three or four with bundles of firewood, in net bags or simply stacked on their heads. I occasionally saw men splitting logs, although more often it was women, but I never saw men carry firewood.

Tiny puppies fell asleep wherever they got tired, and sometimes I had to shuffle my feet to avoid stepping on them. Their mothers, heavy with their distended dugs, were smart enough to seek shade under the houses. The older dogs perfunctorily harassed the few village pigs, on principle I suppose.

Walking along the beach, we passed a group of teenage women lying in a circle and chatting. They stopped talking as soon as they saw us, and then, in unintended unison, burst out laughing. They were talking about their boyfriends, Alo said, but he was just guessing.

Some of the teenaged girls had worked their hair into spiky braids, and others affected abrupt ponytails. Many tattooed patterns of black dots on their cheeks, an effect against brown skin that is subtle and, like a beauty mark, attractive in an inexplicable way. The younger ones, I was told, prefer abstract designs, or arrange the dots to represent their initials, while the older ones, in a show of modest rebellion, form their boyfriends' initials. Both girls and boys sometimes render similar patterns on their forearms. The means of tattooing is a sharp, sappy twig from a tree something like a citrus. The sap of this tree is caustic, and permanently "burns" the design into the skin.

Kamoro women aren't shy. In midsummer I stopped in Timika Pantai with a group of prints from Kal's slides. I wanted to sit down with some of the villagers to make sure I had people's names spelled correctly, and to identify people I didn't know. Normally the men of the village would take the most active role in fraternizing with visiting writers, but they happened to be gone, scouting a possible new inland location for the village. So Apollo and I sat down with a group of about twelve women. Of course they knew the names of the people in the photographs right away, but my ability to write them down accurately did not impress them at all, and they weren't the least bit bashful about expressing their opinions on this matter. Apollo asked them to slow down so I could keep up, which they did, and we laughed together at my clumsiness. But they were a tough bunch, and I know they walked away thinking: he seems nice enough, but he sure isn't a genius.

The situation between men and women here struck me as dramatically different from that among the Asmat, an ethnic group living further to the east who are closely related to the Kamoro in language and history. Kal and I spent two weeks in the Asmat area in 1991, and there, each time we arrived in a village, the women pretty much disappeared. Asmat women crop their hair very short, and these austere haircuts, and the distance they kept, gave the impression of a caste of delicate nuns. This is not really true, of course, and in a big village like Agats or Atsj this shyness was not present to such an extent. Still, the Kamoro women are a lot bolder, and it is tempting to suggest that this is because of the inherent matrilineality of Kamoro kinship, which is very different from the patrilineal kinship structure of the Asmat.

Outsiders have also been in the Kamoro area for a lot longer than they have in the Asmat area, and Kamoro women long ago adopted the European fashion of wearing a shirt or blouse to cover their breasts. When they are out crabbing or fishing in the mangroves the older women are as blasé about going topless as French women on the beach, but even they will throw on at least a T-shirt when they approach the village.

In the Asmat area, at least in 1991, this introduced modesty was still new, and obviously had not yet been completely internalized. On several occasions while Kal and I walked through a village, a woman would have to remind one of her friends to run home and get something to cover her breasts. That this rule was followed in letter, rather than in spirit, was made obvious when the woman returned wearing a brassiere.

The brassieres that reach Irian Jaya apparently come in just one color, which in the United States would be called "nude." Of course this term is only sometimes accurate, as at least a quarter of Americans find out when they put on a Band-Aid. And take my word for it: a frilly pink bra on an Asmat woman results in exactly the opposite of modesty.

M Y FIRST NIGHT in Keakwa was one of the most uncomfortable I have ever experienced. Late January is still the dry monsoon, and a green coil of incense doped with pyrethrin kept away the occasional mosquito. Also, I was more

RAISING THE MBITORO, HIRIPAO.

or less used to Kal's snoring, and Andres was quick to poke him in the ribs when it became unbearable. It was the hard floor of the clinic, a piedmont of hand-hewn ironwood planks, that provided the greatest trial. From the outside, the clinic looked about like any of the other houses, except for the galvanized steel roof and some small louvered-glass windows. But the floors of traditional Kamoro houses are made of springy bark, making a mattress redundant. The clinic, with its "modern" construction, was insufferable.

The building wasn't much used. The nurse practitioner stationed here, we were told, was away on marriage leave. The leave was supposed to be for three months, but it had already been much longer (and

Fig. 2.2 SEA PIGS.

when I returned six months later and again stopped briefly at Keakwa, he still hadn't returned). People who fall ill in Keakwa go to Timika Pantai, which is just a few kilometers away, or simply recover on their own. The strangest feature of the clinic was its rainwater collection cistern, a blue-and-white fiberglass tank decorated with a large graffito representing a skull and crossbones. I never found out if this meant that the water it collected was not potable, and in any case since it was the dry season the cistern was empty. But it did seem a very odd symbol to display on a health services facility.

The village school is just behind the clinic, although a small tidal creek separates it from the village proper. This creek provides the back road to the village, and the women use it to fish and gather crabs in the mangrove. A walkway had been built for the children to cross, but all that was left of this was a rough frame of poles. So, at eight o'clock in the morning when school was ready to start, the children climbed in an old canoe, stationed there for this purpose, and pulled their way across by the remains of the old walkway. When school let out in the afternoon low tide reduced the creek to mud, and the children relied on several strategically placed planks and the grounded canoe to keep their uniforms clean.

In the late morning, a policeman appeared in the village to supervise the removal of the palm wine taps on the village coconut trees. This was to make sure that everyone would stop drinking, thus lessening the possibility of fighting or other unseemly behavior during the upcoming *karapao* celebration. I was told, sotto voce, that of course the men knew he would be coming and had hidden stashes of palm wine. I also noticed that, after collecting the last of the plastic jugs

from the trees, a group of men and the policeman himself disappeared down the beach for a couple of hours.

In the afternoon, Kal and I went out to the beach for a swim. The Arafura Sea is not the glistening turquoise of the postcard South Pacific, but it is shallow, and in the lee of the sandbars jutting out east of Keakwa, calm. On the coast the heat is not stifling, but the sun is strong enough that a newcomer who is not wearing sandals begins to run about halfway between the coconut trees and the water. The water, which is not really even cool, was still refreshing.

At the time of our swim the tide was slack low, and the height of the waves could best be measured in centimeters. The sea is shallow enough here that an adult could walk out a hundred meters before his or her chin would get wet. Kal and I weren't the only people in the water. A man and his wife had taken their small child out for a dip, and a group of young boys were splashing around noisily about a hundred yards away. Two men took advantage of the low tide to set posts for gill nets.

We also shared the water with the *babi laut.* In most of Indonesia, dolphins are called *lumba-lumba,* but in Irian Jaya people say "babi laut," which means "sea pig." This is not a very flattering name, and I wonder if, with it, the dolphin would ever have achieved the status it enjoys in the United States today, where it is revered as a creature of almost mystical intelligence, and serves as the totem of the marine environmental movement. I can't see people rushing off to Caribbean resorts so their children can swim with the sea pigs, or buying crystal sea pigs to set on their mantles.

I never liked the name *babi laut,* not because it was so unglamorous, but because it seemed like such a misnomer. The dolphins I had seen were playing in the wakes of boats, or chasing schools of fish along the surface. A comparison with a bird might make sense, but a pig? At Keakwa, I finally understood. Here, in the shallows, I saw dolphins rooting in the sand, and the comparison to pigs became obvious. They were chasing stingrays, and in their enthusiasm, often ended up in water shallow enough that their shiny backs were more out of the water than in. Once they were able to get a good grip on the stingray—not an easy proposition, considering its flat build and the poison barb on its tail—the dolphins had to twist and wiggle to get back to where it was deep enough to swim again. This display, which Apollo told me takes place only during times of calm seas, was very entertaining. I also made a mental note of the stingrays, and tried to remember to shuffle my feet when walking in the water.

Activities related to the *karapao* began again in the evening, after supper, in a small roofed shelter in front of the still uncompleted *karapao* building. There the *make ipikare* began singing. To an outsider, Kamoro music seems melancholy, and if written down would have to be rendered in a minor key. At the end of each phrase, the pitch of the note drops, the way the doppler effect alters the pitch of a passing car horn. The *make*

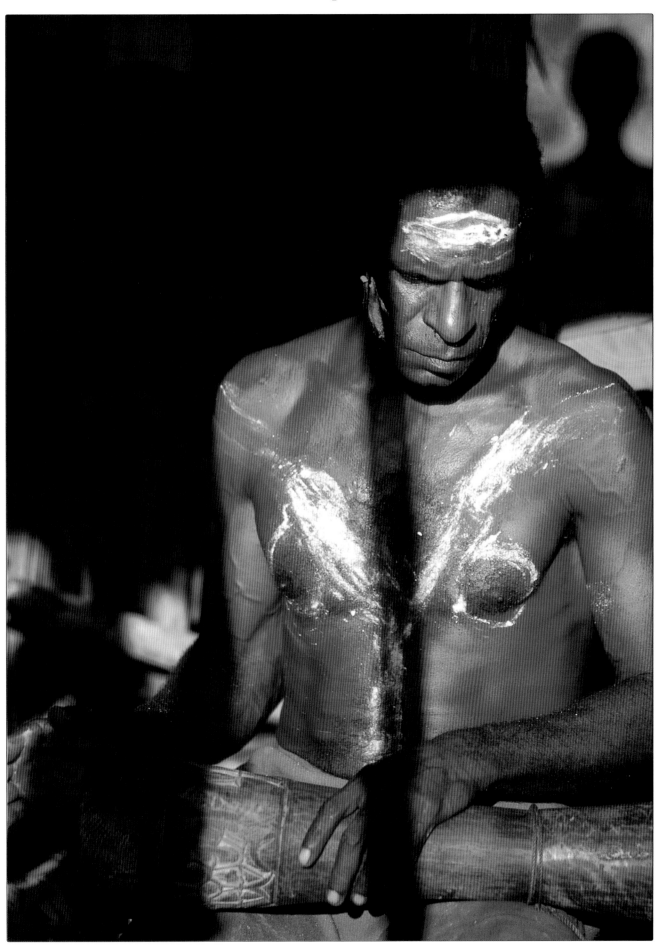

YOHAKIM MIKAMANIYU, TIMIKA PANTAI.

DRUMMERS, TIMIKA PANTAI.
Yoakim Mikamaniyu, Demianus Tiriyu, Samuel Tiriyu, Pontianus Yauniyuta, and Leo Ewakipiyuta.

ipikare, whose position is hereditary, is a man of great status and influence. He knows the old stories, and when he begins to sing, people quickly gather around. The language he sings in is a very refined form. In an oral culture like the Kamoro, his songs are the equivalent of high literature. The most famous *make we,* such as Liberatus Mutiyu, are the Shakespeares and Faulkners of the Kamoro language.

Keakwa's *make ipikare* began singing, accompanied by a single drummer, around eight o'clock, and continued, sporadically, for several hours. According to Apollo, his narrative mixed exhortations to the village to get into the spirit of the ceremony, segments of the old stories, news from other villages, and even social announcements, such as who was planning a marriage or had just had a child. The men in particular were very happy to lean against a post in the warm glow of the fire and listen to him all night long. I watched one man, who had found a particularly comfortable position, give his young son a cigarette and send him over to the fire to light it for him.

The *make ipikare* took regular breaks, and between sessions, the men played cassette tapes on a portable boom box. There was quite a bit of variety, but The Rolling Stones and Creedence Clearwater Revival seemed to be clear favorites.

I F YOU WALK along the beach from Keakwa, heading southeast, in about three kilometers you reach the broad mouth of the Timika River. Just across this estuary, about a kilometer away, is the village of Timika Pantai, and you can see signs of the village from the Keakwa side. If, at this point, you turn around and head into the forest just thirty meters, you will find yourself in a strange clearing, not very wide, but maybe one thousand meters long. This is an old, overgrown airstrip.

This site was the easternmost outpost of the Japanese Imperial Navy along the south coast of New Guinea. On April 1, 1942, naval units of the Japanese force sweeping through the Dutch Indies reached Fakfak, and by November, they were in the Kamoro area. At the time, the local Dutch administrative headquarters was in Uta, and the Japanese landed there first. In early December, two destroyers with four hundred and fifty Japanese marines landed at Keakwa, and within two weeks they began building the airstrip.

The economic depression of the thirties had greatly reduced Dutch colonial activities in the area, and the Japanese took the Kamoro area without firing a single shot. The Imperial Navy considered its fight to be against the Dutch, not the people of New Guinea, and at first relations with the Kamoro were cordial. But

DANCERS, TIMIKA PANTAI.
Front row: Luisa Kupakoreyau, Martha Wamenareyau, and Magdalena Matameka.

this did not last long. The soldiers needed food, and took what they needed from the Kamoro at gunpoint. When that still wasn't enough, they forced them to plant larger gardens. If they felt the men of the village weren't working hard enough, the soldiers flogged them publicly or, according to some accounts, staked them out on the sand flats during low tide, to be slowly drowned as the tide came in. When the soldiers wanted sex, they took whomever they wished.

When the Japanese captured the Dutch Indies, control of Kalimantan and all of the eastern part of the archipelago was assigned to the navy. Unlike Java and Sumatra—both army-controlled—the navy holdings were considered strictly strategic, and the Japanese did not even create the illusion of local political participation here, as they did in the western islands.

The airstrip at Keakwa was never to have any real strategic importance. According to a Dutch account, the Japanese landed only a single airplane there. After the war, it was used sporadically, and Apollo remembers landing there in a mission Cessna in 1962. But by 1967, when Freeport Sulphur's advance team reached the area to begin developing the mine, the strip was deemed too overgrown and low-lying to be useful (instead, they shipped in two helicopters and assembled them across the inlet at Timika Pantai). Today,

you couldn't drive a car down the airstrip, much less land a plane there.

Although the airstrip never proved important, the large anti-aircraft guns located closer to present-day Keakwa seem to have successfully downed at least several Allied planes. Australian troops were moving west along the south coast from Merauke and eventually reached, albeit briefly, the old Dutch post of Yapero at the mouth of the Otakwa River. From Keakwa, the Japanese sent scouting parties as far east as the Asmat territory, and to create a buffer between their outpost and the Australians at Yapero, they attempted to depopulate the intervening coastal villages. Some of the men of these villages were rounded up and taken to the main Japanese forward base at Kaimana to serve as laborers.

There are people in Keakwa who still recall World War II. One old man—he didn't know his age, but it must be considerable, since he was already married at the time—remembered a time when the guns reached an Allied plane.

"We were scared of the Japanese, and the noise of the guns, and watched from back in the trees," he said. "Many men floated down from the sky. Their parachutes stuck in the trees, and the soldiers found them. They were captured, and the Japanese cut off their heads with swords. The bodies were taken to a special place, and burned."

One of the villagers, who helped the Japanese by organizing work details, was said to have been given a samurai sword as a reward. I was assured that somebody in the village still has it, but nobody was anxious to tell me who, or to show it to me.

Any hints of collaboration between the Kamoro and the few remaining Dutch missionaries and colonial officers in the area enraged the Japanese. Father H. Tillemans, M.S.C., one of the pioneering Catholic missionaries in the area, kept a residence and ran the mission center in Uta. When the Japanese reached Uta, Tillemans was in Yapero, making his rounds. A Kei Islander teacher named Alowisius Farneubun wrote a note to Tillemans, telling him not to return, and sent it with two of his Asmat assistants to deliver to Yapero, which is on the way to the Asmat area. The Japanese caught the men near what is now the Freeport portsite, found the note, and forced them to reveal the name of its author. When they captured poor Farneubun, they boiled him alive—in front of the whole village—in a fuel drum of water.

The Japanese never caught Father Tillemans, nor did they catch his good friend Jean Victor de Bruijn, who was the district officer of Enarotali in the Paniai Lakes area of the highlands. De Bruijn enjoyed a very good relationship with the Ekagi, and he and his friends decided to stay behind and go underground during the Japanese occupation. His work with the famous Oaktree group, providing critical intelligence by radio to Australia on Japanese troop movements, earned him the Netherlands Bronze Cross and Cross of Merit. De Bruijn's biographer, Lloyd Rhys, dubbed him the "Jungle Pimpernel" in a 1947 biography of the same name.

With some of the men of the village as our guides, we stumbled through the brush near the old airstrip, and were led to some of the relics of the Japanese occupation: a small, tidy graveyard with wooden crosses; bits of landing gear from an Allied bomber; a cache of rifle shells, now reduced to rotten casings and long, thin slugs jacketed in brass.

The strangest item we were shown was a tiny tracked vehicle, a kind of miniature tank. The remains of a swivel mount were still visible, presumably for a small automatic gun, and the engine block sprouted weeds. What was remarkable was how small it was, the whole being no bigger than a kitchen table. Either the vehicle had no roof or it had been removed, and what remained was a box of rusting six-millimeter steel. We climbed in to pose for a picture, and standing, packed like sardines, it could just accommodate six people. I couldn't see how even two soldiers could fit sitting down.

This tank, I realized, must have been what the old man was talking about the previous night when he mentioned a "robot"—Apollo was precise about this translation—the Japanese used to scare the people of Keakwa. The soldiers kept this robot near their graveyard, and the villagers assumed that it was the supernatural source of their power.

We were told that the Japanese stationed their airforce near the airstrip, their navy in the deep channel of the Keakwa estuary, and their army near the antiaircraft guns. The soldiers' combination bar and "comfort woman" facility stood next to where the school is today, on a site that is now a watermelon patch, neatly surrounded by a tight twig fence to keep out the pigs. An old bomb casing still serves as the schoolbell.

One old woman in the village is said to be the illegitimate daughter of a Kamoro woman who had an affair with a local Chinese man who was working for the Japanese as a spy. (My informant seemed clear that it was an affair, not rape.) In her fifties now, the woman is shy, and keeps to herself. At the end of the war, the few Japanese who were unfortunate enough not to have been evacuated were hunted down by the Kamoro and, with the tacit encouragement of the returning Dutch administrators, killed. This woman, although dark-skinned like her mother, inherited her father's straight hair, and to this day she keeps her head shaved.

ON THE FINAL day of preparation for the *karapao*, I found Apollo sitting on the porch of the clinic in just his shorts and a towel. He had his toothbrush in a cup and looked worried. I asked what was wrong.

"I'm frightened," he said.

I looked around, but didn't see any obvious signs of danger. It was broad daylight, and there didn't appear to be anyone else around.

"Of what?"

"That woman," he said, pointing toward the shadow of the house just across from the clinic. There stood a woman, who was staring right at us and wore an expression of absolute delight. She carried one arm behind her, obscuring something. I couldn't tell what.

"You're frightened of *her*?"

"She's trying to hit me."

"Apollo? What's going on here?"

It turned out that this day, like the day we arrived, was one on which required some *adat*. "Adat," an Indonesian word, means customs or traditions, customary law, or more losely, manners. The women were once again out smearing foreheads with sago paste and rifling pockets for cigarettes. But a new twist had been added. On this day the women enjoyed a kind of license to practice mischief on the men, such as sneaking up behind them and smacking them with a rattan rod, or dousing them with a bucket of water. Retaliation was not allowed. The mischief this grinning woman was perpetrating, Apollo said, involved a long ironwood stick, and he didn't like the look of it.

It seems that Apollo had been innocently walking to

CLIMAX OF THE KARAPAO, TIMIKA PANTAI.
Initiates Irianto Minayau and Serenius Kirupi. Serenius's chaperone,
looking at the camera, is Dominikus Maopokia.

MARSELENA MAPAREYAU, ATUKA.

our bathing area, which was behind a house not a hundred meters away, when he was beset by his tormentor. In his nearly naked state, he must have been an irresistible victim. The woman hadn't landed a blow with her stick, but she had succeeded in confining him to the porch of the clinic. And I think he lost his soap and toothpaste in the chase.

Eventually she got bored and went searching for other victims, but Apollo kept looking over his shoulder for the rest of the day. I received a smear of sago and lost another pack of cigarettes, but as an outsider I seemed to be immune to serious attacks. When I began telling him the story, Alo found Apollo's plight very humorous—that is, until we were interrupted by an assault on a man sitting on the ground nearby.

Alo watched, horrified, as a woman crept up silently behind this man, who was peacefully rolling a cigarette, and dropped a meter-and-a-half-long python onto his lap. The man literally erupted from the ground, and the snake ended up six meters away, where its sudden presence caused a second eruption. The python was dead, but people flung it away so quickly that they never had a chance to find this out.

Alo does not like snakes. Once, when he was working on a survey crew in the Sempan area of the Lorentz National Park, he was talking to a man who had stopped in his canoe. They were just exchanging pleasantries and passing the time of day when Alo happened to look down. The bottom of the canoe was piled high with a mixture of fish and snakes of all kinds. This, he said, is the most horrible image he can recall, and he still can't describe it without shivering. The Sempan eat snakes. The rest of the Kamoro most emphatically do not, and seeing them in such numbers mixed with fish is about like an American seeing a sirloin steak crawling with maggots. In Keakwa, once he saw that there was a snake involved, he became as restless as Apollo.

In the afternoon, a small argument broke out. The village head was still away, and one man, deciding that people weren't doing enough to get ready, decided to take charge of affairs. He began by lecturing a group of young men playing volleyball on the sand out near the *karapao* building, basically telling them to quit goofing around and get to work. Nobody paid any attention to him. In fact, the village already looked quite tidy. The sand had been swept clean, and all the fenceposts and rails were brand new. The man's lecture was delivered in Indonesian, and although most Kamoro are bilingual, public arguments and exhortations like this often seem to be delivered in the imported tongue.

Big events like the *karapao* always involve some

negotiation of people's status and privilege, which can lead to friction in the village. At the time of the initiation, there will be eighteen "doors" on Keakwa's *karapao*. Each door can accommodate several initiates, although they must all be from the same family group. Perhaps not every door is equal, however, as we witnessed a heated argument between a man who wanted his son to be initiated in the center door, and the man in charge of the door, who did not seem to want to allow this.

In the late afternoon, the two *mbitoro* were moved from their hiding place and laid out in front of the *karapao* building. The carving was finished and the *mbitoro* had been powdered white with a paste of lime, but no additional color had yet been added. A pile of orange dye roots and green leaves had been placed nearby. The men brought the *mbitoro* out into the open with as little fanfare as possible, and the dramatic carvings just quietly appeared. Ordinarily this would be a very lively stage of the ceremony, but a son of one of the men represented on the *mbitoro* was not yet back from Kokonao. It would have been an insult if the ceremony proceeded loudly in his absence.

One small part of each carving had not yet been completed. Esebius and Amandus, the two men represented on the *mbitoro*, still had closed eyes. At sunset, it was time to open them. This minor bit of surgery required the skill of Serfasius, the head carver, but he was nowhere to be found. I asked Apollo to find out where he was.

"They say he is out fishing, but that is not true," Apollo said.

"Where is he then?"

"He's at home."

Serfasius was sitting peacefully in his living room not a hundred meters from the *mbitoro*. A group of men had gone to his house to plead with him to come open the eyes. This ritual cajoling, which involves some cigarettes and several rounds of compliments, is a kind of traditional good manners, a way of showing respect for both the carver and for the event itself. Apollo assured me that Serfasius wasn't being a prima donna. Both sides were simply acting out a traditional role. After an hour the carver appeared, squatted down with a small chisel, and quickly performed the operation. It was now getting dark, and kerosene pressure lamps were brought out to illuminate the *mbitoro* so they could be decorated.

While the artists worked on the *mbitoro*, drummers assembled inside the *karapao* building nearby. They continued, with occasional breaks, all night long. Between songs, one man began wailing. His tears looked real, and he had to be comforted by two of his companions. Apollo said he was mourning the loss of the two men on the *mbitoro*, specifically, "He is sad that they can not be here for the ceremony." The drummers' work is to remedy this, to bring the spirits of Esebius and Amandus to life in the *mbitoro*.

The drummers keep a fire going in the middle of their group, and each maintains a smoldering joint of wood to heat the head of his drum between songs. The lizard skin loses its tautness rapidly in the humidity, and must be dried out frequently to keep the drum in tune. The men also tune the drums by rolling a mixture of beeswax and sap into small lumps, and pressing these onto the skin. This is said to give the drum a richer tone.

The men of the village gradually drifted in, sometimes with their young children, and took up comfortable positions to listen to the drumming. Everyone who sat down first pitched a pack of cigarettes or a pouch of tobacco into a plastic bowl, and these offerings were distributed by the lead drummer. In addition to the drumming, there was plenty of storytelling and just plain gossip. One of the sessions was recorded on a portable cassette recorder. The ceremony requires the drumming to continue all night, and this tape was played whenever the drummers took a break.

The *mbitoro* are decorated in shades of white, red, black, and green. These first three colors are traditional, but the green is a recent innovation. The pigments are mixed into a paste with a bit of water, and painted on with fingers, a crumpled leaf, or a twig with one end pounded into fibers. The white color comes from clam shells, which are ricked in a fire and burned—calcined—to yield white lime. The preferred species for this purpose is the granular ark clam (*Andara granosa*) which the Kamoro call *poro*. This thick-shelled animal is found in the muddy estuaries and rivers rather than the sea. The red comes from mangrove bark (deep red) or ocherous clay (more a brownish orange) or plant roots (various shades of red to yellow), and the green from crushed leaves that have been mixed with shell lime.

In the past, the black pigment was simply charcoal, perhaps mixed with a bit of animal grease to make it stick better. But today there is a readily available supply of a better substance—the black paste electrolyte inside old flashlight batteries. Anyone who has traveled in Indonesia will be familiar with the little cylinders of frustration produced by the ABC battery company. These are not the high-capacity alkaline cells of Duracell and Energizer fame. Using ABC batteries, I don't think the famous bunny would have enough power even to tap out S.O.S. on his little drum. But alkaline cells are filled with a plastic membrane containing a bluish, very caustic substance. ABC's carbon-zinc cells are filled with nice black paste. And they wear out so fast there's always plenty of it around.

V ERY EARLY IN the morning, before sunrise, the process of awakening the *mbitoro* began. By then the *mbitoro* were fully painted, decorated with cloths, and lying supine on the sand in front of the *karapao*. The drummers picked up the beat, and men

MARSELUS WEYAU, KEAKWA.
The first stage of making a drum requires burning out a log with coals.

straddled the *mbitoro,* hopping and dancing along their length. Men with painted faces lined both sides of the carvings, and one stood between the two figures, beating a bronze gong. Life was being brought into the *mbitoro* in a gradually building crescendo of drumming and movement. A dozen women, their faces painted with ocher and wearing long grass skirts, shook their backsides back and forth in time with the drums.

At last Theo Amareyauta, the head of traditions or *kepala suku,* leapt astride the *mbitoro.* He worked each figure in turn. Theo bent dramatically to the *mbitoro*'s face and then pointed to his own eyes. Turning to the side, he grabbed his eyes and forced them wide open with his fingers. Then he leaped and danced, and with a line of men holding each side of the carving, the *mbitoro* itself began slowly to wobble. The carving's head shot up a foot into the air, then fell back down again. Then the foot. Finally, without warning, the whole *mbitoro* was two meters in the air, bucking like a horse, and Theo was riding it.

Normally at this point the *mbitoro,* with their riders hanging on for dear life, would go on a bucking-and-prancing tour of the village. This time, however, the celebrants quieted down and, it seemed, took a break. The men were stopping, Apollo learned, to pay respects to a family who had lost a child the night

before. Once we heard this, we did the same.

The child was just three years old, and had died in the night from an infected boil, or abscess, on his stomach. His parents were clearly deep in grief; the father could barely bring himself to speak, and his wife was powdered head to toe in sand, with great streaks under her eyes from tears. We offered our condolences, and gave the family some money for the funeral. Alo was unusually quiet during this affair, and even seemed sullen. He didn't say a word until we got back to the clinic house.

"That is a perfect example of the basic problem with the character of the Kamoro people," Alo said. "That child had been sick for a month. A *month!* The clinic in Timika Pantai is not even thirty minutes away by canoe. Until parents will take their child to a neighboring village when they're sick, it is hard to get anywhere."

Both Alo and Apollo were disgusted. They could see no excuse for the child's death other than plain laziness on the part of his parents.

"When we look at the people in their kitchens, they seem happy," Apollo said. "But when you look closer, you realize that they aren't really happy. When they have food on their plates, fine. But they aren't willing to work for anything more. If the basis of develop-

NATALIS MOPORTEYAU, KEAKWA.
Awakening the newly carved *mbitoro.*

ment is mindset, sometimes I think we are starting from null."

"The Kamoro way," Alo said bitterly, "is *cari gampang*—'look for the easy way.'"

He said parents take their children out of school because they don't want to work to raise a few dollars for uniforms, or they'd rather spend the money on cigarettes. Some people, Alo said, actually leave their village and move to the outskirts of Timika just to avoid the modest amount of communal work—gardening, fence repair and the like—that village life requires. In Paumako, where Alo lives, there are people from Keakwa who could easily get work as stevedores unloading goods from the many small boats stopping at the port there. But they don't even try, he said. They do the minimum necessary to get by.

"Maybe the Church didn't lay down the necessary foundation," Alo said. "Maybe the missionaries were interested in the coast only as a stepping stone on the way to the interior. Maybe they just wanted Christians in name, not in reality."

There wasn't anything I could say to cheer them up. The conversation ended, and we sat silent over our morning coffee. The festivities had ended temporarily not only because of the unfortunate child, but also because the village was waiting for the arrival of some of the more important guests, including the *bupati,* the head of the local administrative district, who was on his way from his home in Timika.

BY MID-MORNING THE village again buzzed with activity. The *mbitoro* were up and leaping into the air, their riders hanging on as best they could. A shouting throng of men led them down the main thoroughfares of the village, stopping occasionally to hurl them into the air. The *mbitoro* leapt to a meter above the men's outstretched hands; the riders another meter above this. A company of dancing women and shouting spectators followed the *mbitoro* in a wild crowd, and by the time they headed back to the *karapao* building, the mob was running at full speed.

Two deep pits in front of the *karapao* had already been prepared in which to root the *mbitoro.* A group of men acted out a kind of ritual death and awakening in these receptacles, sanctifying them for the *mbitoro.* The poles were thrust in the ground, and dozens of arms forced them skyward. Within seconds they were vertical, lashed to the *karapao* frame, and the sand at their bases firmly tamped. A deafening roar erupted from the crowd, and the drums and dancing grew wild.

The dancing women fanned out in two groups on

67

either side of a little shelter in front of the *karapao*. The shelter, where the *mbitoro* had been painted the night before, now provided ringside seats for visiting dignitaries and the village leaders. Kal climbed one end of the *karapao* frame to capture a panorama of the scene, and I decided to take a few portraits of the dancing women.

The women dance with their waists bent slightly and with their backsides thrust out and rocking rhythmically back and forth with the drums. The dance is quite sexually charged. The dancers were pleased with the attention of my camera, and I was rewarded by each of my subjects with an affectionate cheek-rub. First one cheek, slick with sweat and paint, was rubbed against mine, then the other. Then, slowly, each side of the nose. One woman even surprised me with a bold little peck on the lips at the end, which her dance partners found very amusing. By the time I got my photographs I had as much ocher on my cheeks as the women did.

The ceremony culminated in a series of speeches by the village leaders and important visitors delivered from the front of the *karapao*. Each orator climbed up the frame of the building, between the *mbitoro,* and while perched there, offered his speech to the crowd. The speakers were free to gesticulate and otherwise move their arms—a freedom they exercised constantly—because they were being held in place by a crowd of assistants. A dozen strong arms pinned them to the *karapao* frame by the shoulders, legs and chest. In fact, these dignitaries never even touched the wood with their own flesh. Assistants would quickly place their feet under the speaker's feet, and their arms behind his shoulders, to make sure he is comfortably perched.

One of these dignitaries was Frater John Djonga, a popular Catholic lay pastor stationed in Kokonao. "Frater John," as he is universally called, is a lively, teasing character who is impossible to dislike. He showed up in a bright red shirt with a pattern made up of little black bull's heads, a rather bold expression of political sympathies for 1997 Irian. (He traded this outfit for something a bit more sober before his speech.) Frater John, originally from the island of Flores, is the kind of cleric who is more concerned with the economic and social welfare of his flock—and the survival of Kamoro tradition—than mere church attendance.

Titus O. Potereyauw was born in Keakwa, and his arrival at the *karapao* was a very special occasion. He is the *bupati* of the Kabupaten Mimika, which includes Keakwa and all but the westernmost part of the Kamoro area. The *bupati* is sometimes called a "regent," and the *kabupaten* a "regency"; if one can imagine such a thing in the United States as a governor of a county, the *bupati* would be it, although it is actually a much more important position than this suggests. Titus Potereyauw is the highest-ranking Kamoro man in the Indonesian government, and he

was returning to Keakwa this day as a native son who has done very, very well. The *kabupaten* of Mimika was a brand new political division, and the *bupati*'s term of office had just begun. The *karapao* was the occasion for perhaps his first important public speech.

Both the *bupati* and Father John delivered speeches full of hard medicine: "You must educate yourselves to bring your community up!"–Titus Potereyauw; and "If you forget your traditions the Kamoro people are as good as dead!"–Frater John. Since both men are very popular, and good and lively speakers, the people listened attentively.

Frater John and the *bupati* spoke in Indonesian, a language that is understood by probably ninety percent of the Kamoro population. Kepala suku Theo Amareyauta, and Cansius Amareyau, from the Kamoro development agency LEMASKO in Timika, both spoke in Kamoro.

A small but significant number of Kamoro are not fluent in any Kamoro dialect. These are, unfortunately, usually the best-educated members of the community, particularly those who have moved away from the Kamoro area. Alo, for example, who left Atuka when still young to follow his father's career in the police department, speaks Indonesian like a diplomat, and speaks an impressive amount of English as well. But he knows very little Kamoro. Apollo, whose parents were more traditional than Alo's and whose career kept him in the villages of the Kamoro coast, speaks fluent Kamoro in addition to his professor's Indonesian, as well as Ekagi and good English.

The speeches of Father John and the *bupati* drew enthusiastic applause. But Theo and Cansius inspired wild cheers, and in the latter case, even a few tears. It is very easy to see why these men have the positions they do. If I were somehow facing ten years of jail in Keakwa, I would want Cansius to deliver the final arguments in my defense.

The ceremony concluded by the end of the afternoon, but there was still plenty of excitement left in the village. Ceremonies mean good food, and fresh sago and fish were cooking over every fire. Nightly dancing and drumming would continue for several days before the first stage of the *karapao* would truly end. Then the building would stand mute for six months or even a year, until the time was right to put up the walls and paint the boys for initiation. Only then would the initiation cycle be finished.

Before a year passes the *mbitoro* will look like they are a hundred years old. The driving rain quickly washes off their colors, leaving the glare of the equatorial sun to bleach the wood to a cracked, dry gray. The spirits of Esebius Waukateyau and Amandus Weyau will by then have finished their job, and the *mbitoro* become mere wood again. At the right time the carvings will be respectfully burned, and the ashes scattered so as not to waste even the residual spirits of these great, departed men.

CANSIUS AMAREYAU, KEAKWA.
Addressing the crowd from the wall of the *karapao* building.

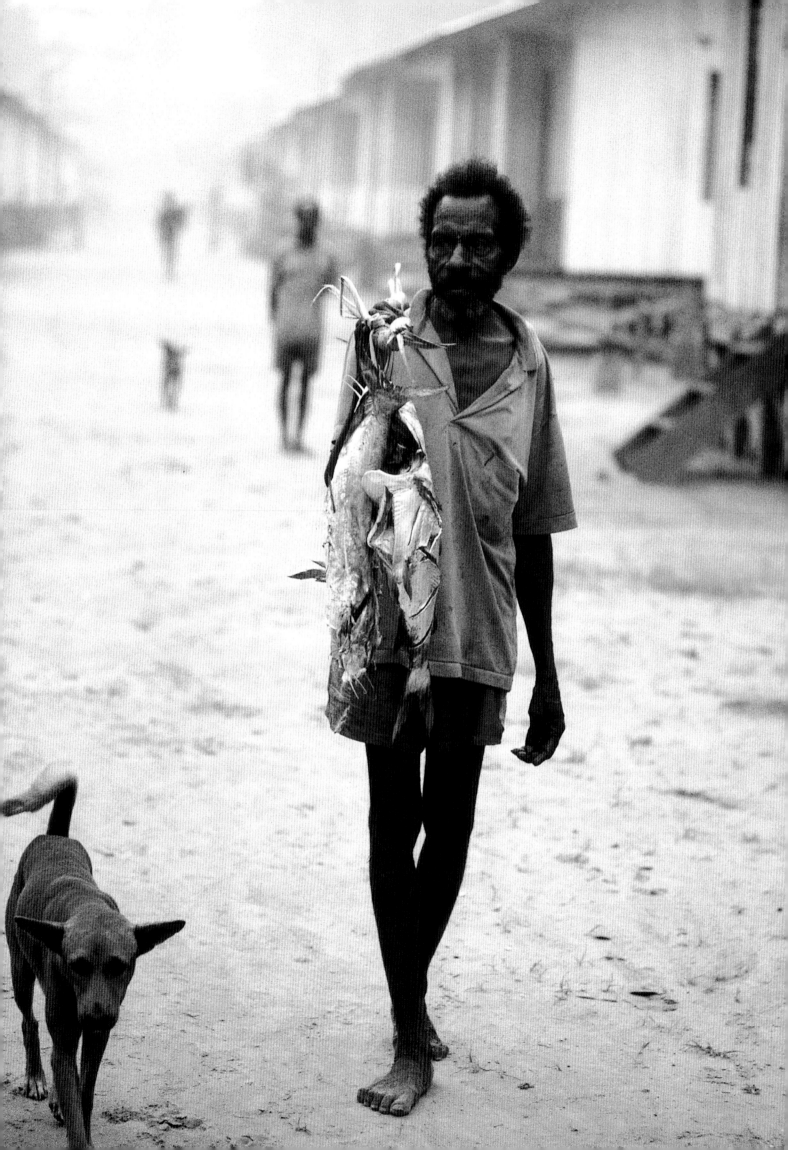

CHAPTER THREE

The Wild, Wild East

Where the Streets are Paved with Copper

 IMIKA, IT IS now said, is the fastest growing town not just in Irian Jaya, but in all of Indonesia. I don't know if this is true, and neither—if they are being honest—does anyone else. But it feels like it could be. It is, for example, a good place to make a living as a taxi driver.

Late one morning Kal and I found ourselves in the familiar position of needing a cab for an afternoon's worth of errands and unable to raise one by telephone. Kal has been a guest at the Sheraton Inn Timika often enough that the bellhops don't say "How are you today, sir?" but rather, "Hello Mr. Muller, and how is your son Andres doing in Guadalajara?" so when Kal asked the assistant manager if he would drive us the short distance to the airport parking lot, where we could find a taxi, he was happy to oblige, and disappeared to get one of the hotel's cars. While we waited we met a woman who needed to get to the airport, but had missed the Sheraton's bus. Kal, always charitable, offered her a ride with us.

Our passenger was young, maybe twenty-five, and was blessed with the kind of looks and figure that men feel compelled to comment upon. She said she was from Palu, a medium-sized city in Central Sulawesi, and was talked into buying a ticket here by an acquaintance who insisted that Timika was booming, and that a talented, fast-talking woman like herself could make her fortune here.

Her conversation, and "monologue" would probably be the better word, was conducted entirely in Indonesian and addressed to Kal. From the snippets I could follow—she was not given to long pauses—and a few strategic asides from Kal I was able to glean the kernal of her complaint which, approximately, was:

"Why I listened to that fool I don't know. But you can keep this cowboy town. I'm going back to civilization."

TERESIA YAWA, KAOGAPU. The 100cc Honda is the beast of burden in urban Indonesia. This bridge leads across the Wania River to a new transmigration settlement.

YOSEP IRAHEWA, OTAKWA. This village houses a fishing operation that transports the catch to the Timika market.

She didn't appear to have been crushed by the experience, however. As soon as we stopped she opened her door, thanked us, and bounced across the lot to the terminal building. In the short time it took us to find a taxi willing to take us on our errands, we noticed that she was already standing in the shade, talking to two well-dressed men. As we pulled away Kal said, smiling, "I guess I'm not too worried about her."

Timika is a busy, hot, charmless town with a population of more than fifty thousand—closer to eighty thousand if the Freeport mine developments and the surrounding communities of transmigrant farmers from western Indonesia are taken into the total. Its ethnic diversity is considerable, mixing Amungme, Dani, Ekagi, Moni, Nduga, and Damal from Irian's highlands, Kamoro and a few Asmat from the south coast, immigrant Indonesians from Sulawesi, Java, and Maluku, and a few hundred expatriate Americans, Australians, and Europeans. It cannot really be called a melting pot, however. The different people living in greater Timika are for the most part balkanized into ethnically defined neighborhoods: Amungme in Kwamki Baru, Kamoro in Koperapoka and Sempan Barat, and Bugis in the downtown areas. The expatriate and Indonesian mining company employees live in the model company town of Kuala Kencana, just north of Timika.

Timika is a brand-new town, what Alo once called "murni" or pure, meaning that it has no roots that go back to the Dutch colonial period. Until Freeport built the airport and associated facilities in 1971, there was nothing here, and it wasn't until the late seventies that a small community of highland Amungme had moved into an area near the airport called Kwamki, an Amungme word for the bird of paradise. Construction south of the airport began in earnest in the early eighties, and only by the middle of the 1980s could Timika be called a small town. Since then its growth has been exponential. A stack of red lumber and a pile of sand now claim every empty lot along the main roads.

When we arrived in midsummer of 1997, ENSO— the southern oscillation of El Niño—had stolen the monsoon rains, and Timika was dry and suffering. People unlucky enough to have houses facing the main

73

streets tossed out buckets of water in a vain effort to keep the dust out of their homes. Some of Timika's streets are paved and some aren't, and the tiny yellow minivans that serve as buses negotiate the worst stretches in wide, careful esses, to avoid the kind of potholes that can snap off a suspension arm.

Although it will never be recommended in a tourist guide, this energetic town is not without a certain kind of motley charm. Saccharine love ballads blare from the tinkling speakers of the passing minibuses. Groups of schoolgirls, hand-in-hand in their clean uniforms, skip happily along the sidewalks. A small knot of Amungme men, each with a bow over his shoulder and a quiver of arrows, stand on a streetcorner laughing and chatting quietly. Behind the big, new market, a Javanese man squats shirtless on the gravel, riveting aluminum mesh and bar stock together to make satellite dishes. Out front, young Bugis men, draped over their 125cc mounts, stare through mirrored sunglasses and langorously smoke Marlboros, their cowboy image spoiled only by the Walt Disney characters on their T-shirts. Highland women, bent horizontal against their tumplines, haul string bags bursting with sweet potatoes to the tiny old market, which now specializes in mountain staples: sweet potatoes, taro, *singkong*.

Timika is by far the largest settlement between Fakfak and Merauke, and the only town in the Kamoro area with high schools, banks, movie theaters, a post office, hotels, and well-stocked pharmacies. It is, for example, the only place within at least three hundred kilometers where one could buy a television. Or a chainsaw. Or an outboard motor. Or just about any other imported item, useful or otherwise.

But a sense of frustration and even anger underlies the current of activity here. The spoils of economic growth are never distributed evenly, and the shiny motorbikes and cassette tapes are almost all bought by immigrant Indonesians, not Irianese. I never once saw a black face behind the wheel of a car in Timika.* The town is less than thirty years old, and only for twenty of these has it been anything more than a logistics station for the Freeport mine. This is simply not long enough for members of such disparate groups to have developed a shared history. People will tell you they live in Timika, but nobody calls himself a "Timikan."

Timika is a major post for the Indonesian armed forces in the province, and the number of soldiers here—by some estimates, almost three thousand—contributes to the uneasy feeling. The army is here to protect the mine, which is the government's most valuable asset in the province, and to keep a lid on the ethnic and economic tensions in Timika. These had last surfaced on March 12, 1996, when the town erupted in two days of rioting that left several people dead. Police are also stationed here in larger than usual numbers, and at times they can seem slightly menacing. Timika is the only place in Indonesia where I have seen a policeman wear his sidearm while not in full uniform.

Nobody lives here because of the weather (it is relentlessly hot, with no breeze), because of the view (there is none, both the mountains and the sea are fifty kilometers away), because they have lived here for generations (before the late sixties, the Kamoro hunted here, but there was no village), because the soil is good (it's fine, but not better than elsewhere), because the fishing is good (it's better downriver), or because of the sago trees (the sago belt is closer to the coast). This diverse group of people has been drawn into a peculiar and sometimes tense community by a powerfully attractive force—money, from the jobs and market created by the Freeport mine.

O N DECEMBER 5, 1936, at about seven o'clock in the morning, three young Dutch alpinists stood on the highest point in New Guinea, and in fact, the highest point between the Andes and the Himalayas: the glaciated summit of Ngga Pulu, one hundred and thirty kilometers inland from the coast near Timika. Succeeding where two much larger British expeditions had failed, they became the first outsiders to reach the top of the snow-capped mountains Dutch navigator Jan Carstenszoon had seen from the sea in 1623, more than three centuries earlier.

Theirs were very likely the first human footprints on Ngga Pulu, which at the time stood at 4,906 meters, or more than 16,000 feet.† The local Amungme were familiar with the glaciers, of course, but not with boots and crampons and wool jackets. More importantly, they lacked the European drive to "conquer" the world's mountains. I cannot imagine an Amungme of sound mind struggling up a barren ice face to an elevation where it is bitter cold and hard even to breathe, just to be the first man to have done it.

The three men on this history-making expedition were Dr. Anton H. Colijn, the son of Holland's prime minister and the manager of a Dutch oil exploration team at Babo in Bintuni Bay; Frits J. Wissel, a pilot for the oil company and the first European to see the Paniai Lakes (for a while they were called the Wissel Lakes); and Jean Jacques Dozy, an exploration geologist for the oil company and one of the world's first photo-geologists.

The men were such avid mountaineers that this grueling expedition was organized during one of the infrequent, two-month vacations—informally called "Java leave," after the island where most workers spent theirs—allowed by the oil company. But Dozy was a geologist twenty-four hours a day, and during the expedition he noted rock formations and faults, and took as many samples as he was able to carry. In late November, when the team had reached an alpine meadow they called the Carstenszweide, Dozy sketched it in his notebook. At the southern end of the

---

* This has changed noticeably in the last five years.

† Ngga Pulu's ice has been gradually melting, and today Puncak Jaya, at 4,884 meters, is the highest of the Carstensz mountains.

CARSTENSZ SNOWFIELDS FROM THE COAST.
This sight inspired the first expeditions to the highlands.

weide was a large, dark outcrop of rock. Dozy wasn't able to explore this interesting feature until the next day, but when he did, he discovered that the greasy black rock was copper ore. In his book, he penciled in: "Ertsberg," Dutch for Ore Mountain.

The story, as it is usually told, jumps from here to the Freeport mine we know today, with one Jean Jacques Dozy as the heroic discoverer of the huge ore deposit. But even Dozy, who is still alive, would be quick to point out that this is a misreading. Colijn was the leader of the expedition—which was called the Colijn Expedition—and he wrote the popular account of their ascent, which remains in print in Holland to this day. Dozy was not famous; Colijn was the son of Holland's prime minister. The three men entered the history books for having scaled the Carstensz, not for finding an unusual ore outcrop exposed by the scouring of glaciers. None of them, Dozy included, thought Ertsberg was a discovery with any economic value, and it is only in retrospect, with the evidence of today's multi-billion-dollar Freeport mine, that this seems strange. At the time, "It was like a mountain of gold on the moon," Dozy has said. Ertsberg was interesting, but only in a geological sense, and its description found an appropriate place in a relatively obscure technical journal published in Leiden.

MORE THAN TWENTY years passed before Jan van Gruisen, working for a Dutch mining concern called the East Borneo Company, encountered Dozy's description during a routine literature search. In 1959, Van Gruisen was looking for nickel prospects in Dutch New Guinea because his company, called Oost Borneo Maatschappij or OBM in Dutch, had recently lost their mines in Borneo and Sulawesi to Indonesian President Soekarno's nationalization program. Van Gruisen was intrigued by what he read, and showed it to his friend Forbes Wilson, the head of exploration for an American company called Freeport Sulphur.

Wilson was looking for nickel prospects for the same reason as Van Gruisen. Freeport, which had formed in 1912 to extract sulfur from the salt domes along the Gulf Coast of the United States, had diversified into nickel in 1940, and through the war years the metal had proved profitable enough that the company had built a smelter near New Orleans. The company had been mining nickel in Cuba, but in 1959, just when operations at Moa Bay had produced their first shipment of ore, Fidel Castro nationalized Freeport's mine. Wilson was trying to find ore to feed his new smelter when Van Gruisen showed him Dozy's report.

75

A painted bench at Mwapi, just south of Timika.

"My reaction was immediate," Wilson writes in *The Conquest of Copper Mountain,* a lively account of what was to become the Freeport–OBM expedition to Ertsberg. "I was so excited I could feel the hairs rise on the back of my neck."

Wilson wasted little time organizing an expedition to New Guinea, and in the spring of 1960 a joint American and Dutch team followed the Omawka watershed to the highlands. They brought back 300 kilograms of ore samples from Ertsberg, which when assayed yielded a remarkably rich 3.5 percent copper. At this stage, the political turbulence of the early sixties in Irian Barat interfered with the company's plans. No foreign company would attempt a venture as risky as Ertsberg under the left-leaning Soekarno administration, but the situation changed dramatically when Suharto took over—and Freeport's connections with the Johnson administration gave the company early notice of the change in power. Suharto welcomed foreign investment, and on April 5, 1967, Freeport signed a contract of work to develop Ertsberg.

Freeport and its contractors took just over five years to build a working mine. By December of 1972, when the first Ertsberg ore poured down a slurry line to the coast, they had built a one hundred-kilometer-long road that began near the coast and ended in a wet valley 2,624 meters up in the highlands, as well as an airport, a mill, a powerplant, a tramline to carry ore, and a compact little company town nestled between two streams at an elevation of 1,800 meters. The road alone presented such a challenge to its builders that the huge engineering firm Bechtel, which built it in partnership with Pomeroy, has called it the most difficult project the company has ever completed.

The strangest thing about this mine is that no businessman with a cool head would ever have built it. As soon as a drilling team reached Ertsberg in 1967 to take an accurate measure of the deposit, they found that Wilson's estimate of 50 million metric tons of ore at 3.5 percent copper was very optimistic; the reality was more on the order of 33 million metric tons at 2.5 percent copper. Since the project was projected to cost $100 million in good, hard 1960s currency (it finally cost twice this), and would only be processing 6,500 metric tons a day, the return seemed pretty poor even if it hadn't been, as Dozy said, on the moon.

"To me a project this expensive, this small, and in this location appeared to be sheer madness," writes George Mealey in the preface to *Grasberg,* a comprehensive recent history of the mine. During the years that Ertsberg was being developed, Mealey was working at the huge El Teniente copper mine in Chile, and he watched the development of the tiny Freeport mine with a kind of morbid fascination. He was sure it would fail. It didn't, however, thanks to President Richard Nixon's controversial wage and price controls of the early seventies, which artifically propped up the price of copper, and thanks to a very supportive

Indonesian government, which offered the fledgling mine a tax holiday during its difficult early period. Mealey's opinion changed, and when he wrote his 1996 book he was the outgoing President of Freeport-McMoRan Copper & Gold, the parent company of P.T. Freeport Indonesia.

Freeport's mine early on captured the imagination of the Suharto government. Freeport was the first foreign company willing to sign an agreement with his administration, and the mine was the most important economic development in Indonesia's new, and at the time still politically unstable, province. In May 1973, when Suharto arrived to formally open the mine, he christened both the company town—Tembagapura, "Copper City"—and, in a move that surprised everybody, the province itself. With a single speech Irian Barat had become Irian Jaya, literally "Glorious Irian." The company had to re-engrave all of the plaques it had prepared for the ceremony.

The Ertsberg mine ran out more than a decade ago. Today the pit serves as a reservoir of water for the milling plant. The company has affectionately dubbed the reservoir "Lake Wilson." But soon after production began, a much richer deposit called Gunung Bijih Timur, "Ore Mountain East" in Indonesian, was discovered right next to Ertsberg, and in 1988 company geologists found Grasberg, just across Dozy's Carstenszweide from Ertsberg. Grasberg—again the name, meaning "Grass Mountain," comes from Dozy's 1936 notes—is one of the century's most important mineral discoveries. It is a copper-gold porphyry and, among the world's mines, ranks third in the size of its copper reserves, and first in its reserves of gold. Depending on the prices of these two metals, estimates of the deposit's value hover between $50 and $70 billion.

Before the discovery of Grasberg, Freeport was considering pulling out of Irian Jaya. After a drill core came up with an intercept of 1.7 percent copper and 1.8 percent gold that continued for more than half a kilometer, the company changed its mind, and instead of leaving underwent a billion-dollar expansion. In 1997 the Freeport mill processed more than 200,000 metric tons of ore each day, and more than 17,000 people worked for the company or one of its contractors in Irian Jaya. That same year P.T. Freeport Indonesia grossed $1.6 billion, and it has regularly been the Republic of Indonesia's biggest taxpayer. The company predicts a mine life of as much as forty years.

A Freeport employee in Irian Jaya, particularly one working up at the mine, makes a very good living. With the company's performance bonus system, a truck driver in the Grasberg pit or a member of a drilling crew could earn in excess of $1,000 a month, which is more than fifteen times the province's average per-capita income. Although there are a few women working as secretaries, only men work at the mine. The lucky one who lands one of these positions will typically work hard for about five years, saving every rupiah—the company provides room and board—and then head back to Java, Manado, Ambon or wherever else he came from. Hard-rock mining in the cold and fog and altitude of the Carstensz mountains is not something one wants to do for life, and a stint with Freeport is treated like military service, a temporary job for a young and healthy man. The nest egg these men bring back will usually be converted to a nice house, a small store or other modest business, and perhaps an education fund for their children.

Very few native Irianese land these jobs, and the ones that do are mostly from Biak and the larger cities of northern Irian Jaya, not the local Kamoro and Amungme. Indonesia doesn't have a history of affirmative action programs like the ones the United States is now so busy dismantling, and mine jobs are so desirable that one imagines that at least some regional or ethnic favoritism plays a part in hiring and promotion. And the people doing the hiring are from Java and elsewhere in western Indonesia. But with such fierce competition for jobs, the biggest handicap faced by Irianese applicants is that, as a group, they lack the education and language skills of candidates from western Indonesia.

The company recognizes this, and recently began a five-month course in basic skills training for Irianese who are seeking jobs with Freeport. Basic skills, in this case, mean such things as learning to punch a clock on time, how to dress properly for work, and rudimentary literacy. But education and training, even with the best intentions behind them, are gradual processes. So far, for example, twenty-four Kamoro have graduated from Freeport's basic skills program. Company statistics from 1997 show a total of seventy-three Kamoro employees, of whom thirty-one are day laborers.

One reason this figure is low is that the Freeport company itself concentrates chiefly on running the mine in the highlands, and manages few operations in the lowlands where the Kamoro live. Of the more than 17,000 people with mine-related jobs, only about one-quarter of these receive a paycheck from Freeport. The rest work for various contractors. Hiring statistics from the contractors are hard to come by, but it is probably accurate to say that with the exception of a few of the construction outfits, most hire Irianese only as menial day laborers.

THE MOST POLITICALLY prominent Kamoro is Titus Potereyauw, the head of the new Kabupaten Mimika. The growth of Timika has been so dramatic that the Indonesian government decided to create a new district from the eastern half of the old Kabupaten Fakfak, with Timika as its *ibu kota*—literally "mother city"—or capital. This makes sense, as the population of Timika has now surpassed that of Fakfak, which also is located more than five hundred kilometers away.

PASIR HITAM.
This settlement, near the mouth of the Muamiua River, gets its name,
which means 'Black Sand,' from the humic acid–stained beach.

TITUS O. POTEREYAUW, TIMIKA PANTAI.
The *bupati* of Kabupaten Mimika.

The *bupati* is acutely aware of the disadvantage the Kamoro people face, not just in finding work at the mine, but competing in general for jobs and opportunities in Timika. As the most visible and powerful Kamoro man in the Indonesian government, he has made it one of his goals to better the socioeconomic position of his community.

Titus Potereyauw is a hale and barrel-chested fifty-nine years old and has the easy, open manner of someone who is used to being respected. He seems to wear the mantle of his office lightly, and he displays none of the pettiness of lesser politicians. There is nothing soft about him, however. I'm sure when he gives an order, it is only once. He struck me as the kind of a man who would know exactly how to discipline a twelve-year-old boy who had just thrown a rock through a neighbor's window. He and Apollo are good friends and share many of the same opinions, and he was relaxed and jovial during our interview.

I asked him why it was that so few Kamoro seem to succeed in the new economic climate of Timika. The root of the problem, he said, smiling, is that "nature is too generous here."

"For the Kamoro, nature has everything ready for them," he said. "There is plenty of sago, and the rivers are full of fish. It is an easy life. The old people, particularly, don't believe in schools. They take their families with them inland to pound sago, or to go fishing on the river."

The *bupati* drew a sharp contrast between the material conditions faced by the Kamoro, and those faced by the Amungme and others in the highlands.

"For the Amungme, the situation is very different. It is difficult to find food in the mountains. They have to work harder just to get by. They plant gardens, send their children to school—whatever they need to do to survive. This is why they are faster to develop."

I don't think the *bupati* was trying to pass moral judgment on traditional Kamoro culture, and being Kamoro himself I am sure he was not hinting, as many Indonesians would, that the basic problem faced by the Kamoro is simply that they are inherently lazy. But Titus is a pragmatist, and has an urban and educated man's standards of what constitutes a modern Indonesia. He knows that the opportunities now available in Timika are opportunities created by a capitalist economy, and that concepts like rent and wage labor and investment are far less abstract to a highland farmer than they are to a Kamoro. The only way to make it possible for the Kamoro to participate in the new economy of Irian Jaya, he said, is to get the children out of the villages and into school.

TIMIKA.
In the foreground is the Aikwa River, now bordered by levees to create a tailings plain.

"They can't learn if they're in the villages," he said. "The atmosphere is no good. Their parents are too quick to take them out of school to go gather sago, or go fishing. The children must go to school: primary, junior high, high school and university, even international universities. Some children, they might stay in Jakarta or other cities. But a few will come back."

The *bupati* himself left Keakwa as a young man, and served as a government official in the Merauke area while the province was still under Dutch rule. After a period of study in Jakarta, he served as the *camat*—roughly equivalent to mayor—of Agats, and then Babo, and after finishing up his university education in Jakarta, in 1978, became *camat* of Manokwari, a city a bit bigger than Timika on the northeast coast of the Bird's Head. After four years as *camat,* he ran the tax and revenue department of first Manokwari, then Biak, until moving to Timika last year to take over as *bupati.*

"If I stayed in my village," he stated flatly, "I would not be where I am now."

After translating this statement, Apollo quickly added: "This, David, is true for me as well."

The *bupati* outlined a number of programs—cooperatives to store and market fish, vegetable and fruit planting programs, and health care programs—that he thought would help the Kamoro. He recalled that the Dutch had forced the villages to plant vegetables, whereas the Indonesian government simply recommends that they do. "Maybe," he said with a smile, "we need to go back to the Dutch way." But of all these programs, education is the most important, he said. Boarding schools with a place for every child, and a scholarship program to eventually send them on to university, will make the biggest difference.

BEFORE THE DUTCH arrived, the Kamoro lived a semi-nomadic existence, drifting between their upriver sago and hunting grounds and their fishing and shellfish gathering areas along the sandy shores of the coast. Villages were social, rather than geographical, entities. To the extent that a village could be said to have a location at all, it tended to be further upriver than the villages today, or put another way, closer to the sago and further from the fish.

When the Dutch began administering the Kamoro area in the nineteen twenties and thirties, this began to change. Nomadic subjects are the bane of a colonial administration—they are, at the very least, difficult to count and keep track of—and the Dutch, wherever possible, moved the Kamoro to permanent villages on the coast. Their reasons for this were usually stated in

81

INDEPENDENCE DAY DECORATIONS, TIMIKA.
A gateway in the Sempan Barat neighborhood displayed this somewhat ambiguous painting during the August 17, 1997 celebrations.

terms of hygiene and health, and it is true that the groundwater tends to be better along the coast, and that the ravages of malarial mosquitoes are greatly reduced by the saltwater and sea breeze. But fundamentally the Dutch, like every other government in the world, believed that a fixed address was a requisite condition for a people to be considered civilized.

It is one of the world's hoariest truisms that settled farming communities represent an advancement over nomadic or semi-nomadic hunting and gathering communities. It was settling down in one place and planting crops, the argument goes, that led to a reliable source of food, which in turn allowed for the growth of high population densities, which in turn allowed for the development of complex forms of social organization. In short, the person who took the first step toward civilization was a farmer. According to this logic a semi-nomadic hunting and gathering group like the Kamoro is an atavism, an embarrassing throwback to an earlier, more primitive form of social organization.

Today most anthropologists reject this history. For example, analysis of the size and density of fossil human bones has shown conclusively that we all took a step backward in terms of health when we first gave up the hunter-gatherer's varied diet for a single, planted crop. And the world has seen far too many

complex, highly developed nomadic societies to suggest that farmers have an advantage in terms of cultural sophistication. But the popular imagination still associates farmer with advanced, and hunter-gatherer with backward. The only difference today is the delicacy of the language used. One usually hears euphemisms such as "dynamic" and "non-dynamic," (since "static," the obvious partner, seems still a bit too negative), or even more vaguely, "traditional."

One of the most interesting champions of nomadism was British author Bruce Chatwin, whose graceful and original travel writings continually teased at the hypocrisy of the classic settler myth. The murder of Abel, the nomad, by Cain, the planter and builder of the first city, was to Chatwin the symbol of a kind of cancer at the heart of Judeo-Christian society. He had been preparing a book tentatively titled "The Nomadic Alternative" when he died in 1989, and in the introduction, the only fragment that remains, he writes:

"The word 'civilisation' is charged with moral and ethical overtones, the accumulated inheritance of our own self-esteem. We contrast it with barbarism, savagery, and even bestiality, whereas it means nothing more than 'living in cities.'"

It seems clear that the real reason the Europeans thought more highly of the settled farmers they encountered in their colonies than of the hunter-gatherers was that to think this flattered their own history. A northern European, whose distant relatives died young clearing boulders from a barley field, sees hope and determination and other noble human qualities in a farmer's struggle to raise a crop. Chopping down a sago tree every once in a while, wrapping up the starch, smoking a cigarette, and going home, just doesn't communicate the same sense of heroic effort. And the Indonesian government, run by people who come from a tradition of farming irrigated rice—a particularly laborious crop—has at least as much trouble as did the Dutch understanding a semi-nomadic hunting and gathering society like the Kamoro.

"RIGHT THERE," ALO said, pointing out the window of our car, "is the best place to hunt crocodiles near Timika." His finger indicated a bizarre wasteland of dead trees standing in a wet, silty plain. Alo should know. During the hard times in the 1980s, between jobs, he was forced to hunt these animals just to put food on his table. Both species of crocodiles found in Irian Jaya have been protected since 1980, but there are still plenty of people willing to buy the salted belly flats, and when your kids are hungry you do what you have to.

Crocodiles make Alo nervous. One hot, muggy afternoon we were standing near the boat landing at one of the western Kamoro villages and Kal and I decided, spontaneously, to go for a swim. Alo demurred. At first we thought he was being modest, so we teased him, but he just sat on the shore with his cigarette. We were hot, so we shrugged our shoulders and ran into the water. When we were about to get out, he finally got in briefly, but he never looked comfortable. Afterward he told me he was worried about crocodiles. I think he's afraid of the bad karma he accumulated during his hunting days.

When Alo pointed out the spot—a still, slightly murky lake among the dead trees—we were driving south on Freeport's East Levee, about ten kilometers southeast of Timika. Sure enough, although it was the middle of the day, we saw one, floating, in the way crocodiles have, with the patience of something that is already dead. Eyes less trained than Alo's would have registered it as a log. It was the southern variant of *Crocodylus novaeguineae,* the New Guinea freshwater crocodile.* The New Guinea crocodile is smaller than the saltwater crocodile, *Crocodylus porosus,* which lives closer to the sea and is much more feared. The specimen Alo pointed out was still a juvenile, and only about as big as a ten-year-old boy.

The surreal landscape is the result of a freak flood in 1990, which dumped so much water into the Aikwa River that the very ground around it became fluid,

*Many scientists say this is a distinct species. It has not yet been named, in part because of the paperwork needed to maintain the legal protection it now enjoys under the name *C. novaeguineae.*

and in a great, viscous sheet, flowed some four kilometers east to the next drainage, the Uamiua River. Freeport's soil engineers call this "the sheet-flow event." When the rains stopped, about thirty square kilometers of lowland forest were covered in a thick layer of mud. With the oxygen supply cut off from their roots, the trees slowly died, leaving the driftwood forest that

Fig. 3.1 CROCODYLUS.

remains today. When the light is right, this landscape has its own abstract beauty, like the saline flats west of Salt Lake City, or the saguaro deserts of Arizona. But at high noon the scene is one of raw desolation, and it makes a perfect poster for the mine's critics.

This area of scarred forest falls inside a thirty-kilometer-long levee system designed to contain the silty residue from the ore grinding and concentrating operations up near the mine. The Aikwa receives these milltails or tailings, as they are called, and the two levees, approximately parallel and three to five kilometers apart, have created an artificial floodplain for them to settle in.

In essence, this area of lowland rainforest is being sacrificed. By the time Grasberg has been fully mined, perhaps thirty years from now, the area between the levees will have been filled with a billion tons of silt. The company has set up demonstration plots showing that a wide variety of plants grow quite readily in the tailings, and the results improve with green manure crops. Eventually this area will become a wide, flat plain of farmable soil. Unfortunately, at the southern end of this plain, buried under several meters of tailings, will be the sago groves of the Nawaripi Kamoro.

The Nawaripi, sometimes called the Koperapoka, have traditionally lived along the Uamiua watershed, the next river system east of the Aikwa. At the time of my visit, Freeport was working with the leaders of the Nawaripi on an agreement for the release of this land. The terms of this were not yet clear, but would probably involve a financial settlement and a Freeport-funded relocation of the people still living in the area to a suitable site to the east, away from the tailings plain. The mining company had given a grant to the Jakarta-based Sejati Foundation to provide assistance to the Nawaripi during this process, and had hired anthropologist Todd Harple to provide it with some historical and social background on the Nawaripi, as well as the other Kamoro living in the area.

Todd enjoys working with the Nawaripi people, who are known in the area as a particularly boisterous and lively group. Theirs is one of the most different of the several Kamoro dialects, with distinctly rounded consonants. For example, the Koperapoka River, to the Nawaripi, is the Operapoa—"*Oh*-prah-poh-ah." The Aikwa River is the Ayua, pronounced "*Eye*-wah." Aikwa—"*Eye*-kwah"—is a Tipuka pronunciation, and in Apollo's dialect from further west the river would be called the Aika, "*Eye*-kah." The difference is marked enough that Apollo almost always used Indonesian when we were talking to the Nawaripi.

Twenty years ago, these people lived in a pair of villages on the Muamiua River, about fifteen kilometers from the sea. These two villages—Naikeripi and Waonaripi—enjoyed a complex relationship that Todd is still trying to work out. The two major *taparu* groups living in Naikeripi, and the four or five *taparu* groups living in Waonaripi, married only among themselves, yet the two villages shared a sense of identity, and were located just across the river from one another.

The name "Nawaripi," now used generically to refer to members of both these groups, is simply an acronymic combination of Naikeripi and Waonaripi. The name "Koperapoka" dates from the very early seventies, when the government—for the purposes of appointing a village head and keeping statistics—consolidated both Naikeripi and Waonaripi into a single unit, Desa Koperapoka.

In 1977, a tense period in the province, the Indonesian military evacuated Desa Koperapoka and moved the people to Timika, into a neighborhood still known as Koperapoka. Gradually, some of these families filtered back to their old sago and hunting grounds, and a few years ago the government, with financial assistance from Freeport, built a settlement of fifty houses just south of Timika to give them a place to live closer to town. This village is called Nawaripi, or sometimes Nawaripi Baru, "New Nawaripi."

About four hundred and fifty Nawaripi Kamoro live in the Koperapoka neighborhood of Timika or in Nawaripi. But their sago fields, and the land and rivers to which they have hereditary hunting and fishing rights, are across the tailings plain on the Uamiua watershed. From Timika, this requires a very roundabout trip north out of town, across the Otomona bridge, then south along the East Levee—about forty kilometers to end up just seven kilometers away as the cockatoo flies.

Todd told me he has heard complaints that since transportation to their sago groves is so time consuming, and only intermittently available, some of the Nawaripi people in Timika are now collecting sago nearby, from groves that belong to the Hiripau and Tipuka people. If this continues, he fears, it is certain to produce conflict. In the past, he said, something like this could easily start a war. The people stealing this sago, interestingly, were selling it at market, using the money they earn to buy food, and in particular, sago. Although circumstances may have forced them to steal, Todd said, they certainly weren't going to *eat* any of the sago that they hadn't come by honestly.

Over the last few years, several small Nawaripi settlements have sprung up along the East Levee. One reason people have moved here is the difficulty in getting back and forth from Timika to their sago fields. Another, Todd said, has to do with a replay of the twinned nature of the original Nawaripi villages. In many ways the new villages—Nawaripi and the Koperapoka neighborhood of Timika—have recapitulated the original relationship between Naikeripi and Waonaripi. Nawaripi village is almost entirely populated by Naikeripi; the Nawaripi Kamoro living in Koperapoka are almost all Waonaripi.

The Koperapoka neighborhood, according to 1996 statistics, has a population of 7,687 people, only a few hundred of whom are Nawaripi Kamoro. Koperapoka is right in the heart of Timika, and housing pressures and the rising cost of living are driving the Kamoro out. Nawaripi village was built especially to accommodate the Nawaripi Kamoro, but since it has become the new Naikeripi village, the Waonaripi don't feel comfortable there. Had the people who planned Nawaripi done their homework, they would have built two villages—and, as long as I am on the subject, they would also have located the villages on a river. In the meantime, the Waonaripi being priced out of Timika are moving to the East Levee.*

D RIVING SOUTH ON the East Levee, our car passed an area of mixed lowland rainforest and, as we got closer to the coast, freshwater swamp forest and scattered lowland peat swamp. This levee intersects one of the richest and most productive wildlife habitats on earth. For the Kamoro, the drier inland edge of this habitat provides the best hunting: wild pigs, tree kangaroos, cuscus, and particularly, the southern cassowary.

Two hundred or so people now live in four small settlements on the East Levee, and they make the mining company nervous. There is nothing wrong with their living along the levee for now, but as the tailings plain fills, these villages will be vulnerable to what the company's engineers and meteorologists call a "hundred-year event." This is a large-scale flood with a once every hundred years probability, which might overflow the levee, producing disastrous consequences for anyone living there.

These settlements are on the Uamiua River, just east of the levee. The Uamiua, pronounced "*Wah-mee-wah*," is almost never called by its original name. The pronounciation of this word is just too counterintuitive to an Indonesian or English speaker, and the river has been dubbed Kali Kopi, the "Coffee River." At first this name doesn't appear particularly helpful in a place where all of the lowland rivers are brown with fresh sediment, and in fact the Kopi is clearer than most, because its tributaries do not reach so far up into the highlands. But the Kopi is what is called a blackwater river, with water stained dark by humic acids leached from the decaying material in the peat bogs it passes through. It actually looks less like coffee than tea, but Kali Teh doesn't have the same ring.

* Since my visit, Freeport, in exchange for Nawaripi land in the tailings area, built a proper settlement east of the levee called Nayaro.

MOSES YAWA, PASIR HITAM.
Moses is the head of traditions for the Kaogapu community.

We stopped first at the northernmost settlement, called Upper Kali Kopi. It consists of nothing more than a few rough wooden houses, set on the edge of an old gravel borrow pit used during the levee construction. The houses were built away from the trees, and the sun was merciless. You could throw a stone from the houses to the edge of the Kopi River.

The place looked deserted, but soon we were met by Mickael Pomsaru, a man from Sorong who moved here and married a Kamoro woman. Mickael assured me that some forty people live here, although at the time they were all out hunting and fishing. This, he said, is why they moved here.

"We call this 'the land of the cassowary,'" Mickael said, and added that the drylands east of the Uamiua River here were perhaps the very best place in the area to hunt this large, ill-tempered flightless bird.

The cuscus, a cat-sized marsupial an Australian would call a possum and a scientist a phalanger, is the easiest prey. These cute, big-eyed animals are sluggish enough that a skillful hunter can grab one off a branch by hand. Wild pigs, which are run down by dogs and speared, are perhaps the most profitable, and Mickael said that their meat fetches Rp 2,500 to Rp 3,000 (a bit more than $1) a kilo in Timika.

The two most marketable species of fish caught here are *ikan lele* and *ikan sembilang,* the fork-tailed ariid catfish and the eel-tailed plotosid catfish. A good-sized fork-tailed catfish is worth about Rp 1,000; the eel-tailed catfish, said to have sweeter flesh, is worth three times this, Mickael said. A little further south, the freshwater shrimp can reach the size of an ear of corn, and these sell for as much as Rp 2,000 apiece in the Timika market.

As we continued south, big white cockatoos and mobs of screaming red and black lories burst through the trees overhead. The vegetation gradually began to change, and here and there a clump of pandanus appeared, their thin trunks propped up by a tangle of aerial roots. "You can tell a peat bog when you see pandanus," Freeport's head of lowland road and levee construction once told me, "especially when you see Ol' Hundred Legs." These scattered bogs are the bane of road construction in the area. "Ol' Hundred Legs" has its limbs for a reason, and the soil consistency in these areas has been described as "like grease." Whenever possible road builders survey around pandanus.

Central Kali Kopi, five kilometers further south, is the largest of the levee settlements, with more than a dozen houses arranged in two neat rows. The houses, compared to those of Upper Kali Kopi, seem to have been built with permanence in mind. This little village has a church, a volleyball court and, when we visited in the summer of 1997, a brand new grade school.

The teacher is Pak Sutrikman, a young Javanese man working for the Sejati Foundation. Pak Sutrikman said he had about seventy-five students, from seven to fifteen years old, and all but one were in grades one through three. The school is a simple wooden building, with large windows on all sides to let in what little breeze can be found. There is a single large classroom with benches and writing tables for the students at one end of the building, and a small, separate teacher's quarters at the other. School was not in session when we arrived, but the chalkboard showed basic addition and subtraction problems, using groups of circles, triangles, and squares instead of numerals.

Before the school was built, some of the families living along the Kopi River left their children behind in Timika to go to school, but those who didn't want to be separated from them, or didn't have family in Koperapoka or Nawaripi where they could stay, took their children out of school. When we met, Pak Sutrikman had only been on the job for two weeks, and he looked a little worn. The Kali Kopi is a long way from Jakarta, and it must be a difficult adjustment for him. Not just to the climate, isolation, and living conditions, but also to the task of teaching simple addition to teenagers using circles and triangles.

ALO PUT HIS hands together, palm to palm, and then opened them. "It's like a clam shell—*aopao.*"

We were talking about the central and perhaps defining concept of Kamoro society, *aopao,* a term that translates as something like "balance" or "reciprocity." The etymology of the word comes from the word for a type of clam, Alo said, which provided his visual metaphor. The two halves of a clamshell are equal and balanced, and perhaps more importantly, neither is of any use to the clam without the other. The most literal meaning of *aopao* in the Kamoro language is "to exchange food," but the term refers generally to a reciprocal exchange of any kind.

When a Kamoro man marries, he provides his bride's family with a canoe, clothing, and other goods. Although outsiders sometimes loosely call this a "bride price," the man is not "buying" a wife. He is redistributing goods and labor to bring the relationship between his family and his wife's family back into balance. This is *aopao.** If a village's sago groves are afflicted by drought, not an unusual occurrence, the people may go to another village to harvest sago. The visitors will then split this harvest with the village that controls the fields, as well as supply them with canoes or other goods. They are not, in this way, "buying" sago. They are redistributing goods and labor to bring the relationship of the two villages back into balance. This, again, is *aopao.*

Traditionally, the Kamoro could be thought of as organized into villages only if one understood "village" to mean the people, not the physical place.

* The specific term for exchange by marriage is *ayapao,* which is also the name of the clam. But *aopao* is the generic term for an exchange of any kind.

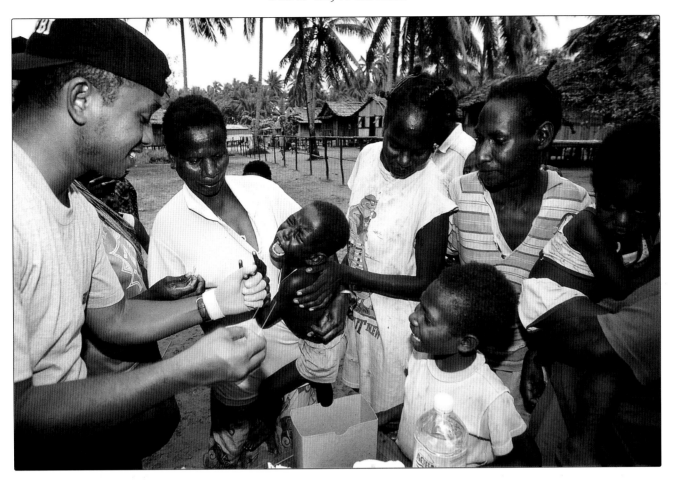

TESTING FOR MALARIA, KEAKWA.
Benediktus Ankus, Bernarda Mutiyu holding her alarmed son, Kansius, Agustina Pauta, Sopia Amareyau,
her mother Yohana Amareyau, and Petrus Mutiyu, next in line after his brother for a finger prick.

Anthropologist Jan Pouwer uses the word "tribe." The locations of the settlements of these tribes moved frequently, and—sometimes temporarily—two or more tribes might combine into one settlement, or a single tribe might split into two or more settlements. Today, a village—in the orthodox sense—is a creation of the Indonesian government, in most cases following Dutch practice.

For example, the people traditionally belonging to the tribe of Utaka'a currently live in the villages—"Desa" in Indonesian—of Tapormai and Umar. The provincial government records population figures, locations, and other statistics for Desa Tapormai and Desa Umar, but for the Kamoro the most relevant factor is that the people are Utaka'a. Today these *desa*s can be like Aika-Wapuka, made up of the Aikawe and Wapukawe tribes, or like Potowai-Buru, made up of people of the Emowai tribe who used to live separately in Potowai and in Buru (which was traditionally called Pura).

Beneath both the traditional level of tribe and the new government level of *desa* is the *kampung*, which is usually translated as "hamlet." Through most of Indonesia a *kampung* is a logical sub-unit of a *desa*, but in the Kamoro area the difficulty of assigning traditionally semi-nomadic social groups to villages has led to some confusion. For example, Desa Tapormai is rational in both the government and traditional systems, and is called "Tapormai." But Desa Umar is almost always called "Ararao." The government considers this a *kampung* name, but it refers to exactly the same unit as Desa Umar. The old Desa Koperapoka was more logical, having been made up of two sub-units: Kampung Naikeripi and Kampung Waonaripi.

Finally, beneath the blurred and somewhat confusing Desa and Kampung levels is the basic unit of Kamoro society: the *taparu*. A *taparu*, a very long time ago, represented a single longhouse group, and all the families in it lived under the same roof. Pouwer counted one hundred and sixty *taparu* in the Kamoro area and fifty tribes.

The *taparu* is famously difficult for an outsider to understand. The word comes from *taparé*, "a tract of land," and Apollo and Alo told me that the most useful definition is the group of people who have rights to gather sago and hunt on a given tract of land. In one sense, *taparu* is something a person is born into, following matrilineal descent and kinship, which chiefly pass down through the mother's side and across through sister ties. But since the arrival of the Dutch and the Catholic Church, Apollo and Alo told me, the father's side has been followed as well. And if a family

87

moves, the children will usually be included in the *taparu* of the new residence, not that of their mother or father. When Pouwer did his research in the 1950s, he concluded that overlapping sets of social, political and economic factors exerted more of a defining influence on *taparu* than descent.

In a way, trying to formulate complicated rules of *taparu* membership based on inheritance and locality misses the point. The membership of a *taparu* is simply the physical manifestation of a network of *aopao* obligations. The reciprocity relations of *aopao* are not the glue that holds Kamoro society together; rather the structure of Kamoro society is a product of the shaping forces of *aopao*.

The centrality of this concept to Kamoro society complicates its encounters with western—and western Indonesian—capitalism. A capitalist society's "rich" and "poor" do not have the same meaning in a society controlled by the logic of *aopao*. Since the real value of an exchange within traditional Kamoro society is the balancing effect it has on the relationship between two parties, the accumulation of goods cannot take place in the same way. Certainly there were people in traditional Kamoro society who enjoy elevated status. But these people were "rich" only in the sense that they could control large movements of goods and services. In other words, where most people could write and deposit ten-dollar checks, these people could write and deposit million-dollar checks. But in both cases, because of the force of *aopao*, their average account balance was the same: zero.

Things are changing on the south coast of Irian Jaya, and capitalist notions of ownership are becoming part of the fabric of Kamoro society. But deep-seated values like *aopao* change slowly, and some aspects of Kamoro society not only fit poorly within the logic of capitalism, but perhaps even oppose it.

For example, the Freeport company wants to include a section of the sago fields of the Nawaripi people in its tailings plain. In a capitalist society, the two parties would sit down, negotiate a mutually agreeable value, and then Freeport would purchase the title to the land. Traditional Kamoro culture, however, allows no means for alienating land. Sago can be sold or traded, fish or game can be sold or traded, but there is no precedent for trading or selling the land or rivers these products come from. The Kamoro—and to a Californian this is at the same time both wonderful and inconceivable—have no real estate agents.

Fortunately for the mining company, however, land use is recognized by traditional Kamoro society, and in accordance with the principle of *aopao* the Nawaripi can give Freeport the right to use their land, in exchange for an appropriate package of goods and services. The sago fields, even after they are buried under several meters of tailings, will always be on Nawaripi land. But at the same time, as long as the exchange remains in balance, Freeport can go on using them.

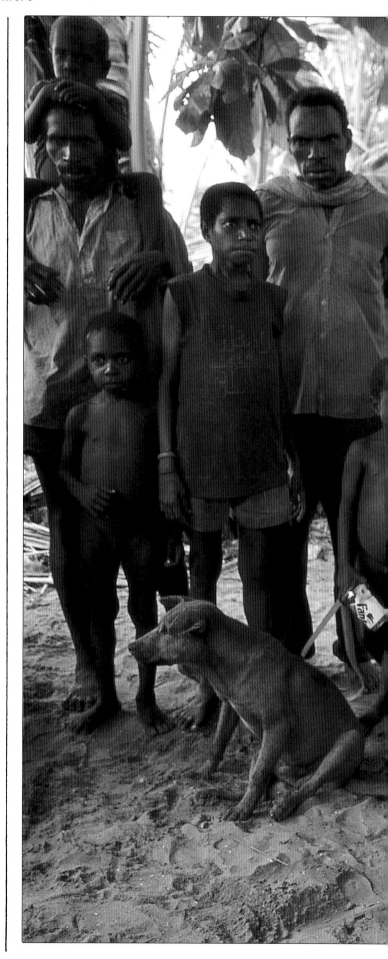

FRESHLY KILLED CROCODILE, PASIR HITAM.

RAISING THE MBITORO, HIRIPAU.

ALO AND APOLLO are as fond of a cold beer as Kal and I, and at the end of a hot day running around Timika the four of us often retreated to a cool watering hole to talk about the day's events and plan the next. Our favorite quickly became a place formally called Komoro Tame. "Tame" is the Sempan variant of the Kamoro *kame*—"house"—and "Komoro" is, well, a mistake. The sign blew down in a storm some time ago, perhaps fortunately given the misspelling, and in any case everybody calls the place "gay-ess-bay-jay." GSBJ—Graha Sarana Buana Jaya—is one of Freeport's contractors, fielding teams of carpenters to build helicopter pads, walkways, and drill platforms for the company's exploration teams.

The bar, and a small hotel with a swimming pool to which it is attached, was built by the contractor to give its workers a place to unwind between demanding stints in the highlands. GSBJ is one of the handful of contractors that hires a significant number of Irianese workers—in fact, a majority of its carpenters are Irianese, mostly highlanders, because that is where the exploration work is taking place. Eddy Taylor, the head of GSBJ's field operations, told me that these men handle a chainsaw better than anyone he has ever worked with. They have developed an unusual technique to rip logs into planks—they take the kick-back guard off and plunge the saw downward, cutting forward against the top of the bar. The manufacturer's legal department might not approve, but using the tool this way the men can hold a line to a few millimeters over a two-meter cut, Eddy said, and they're fast.

At GSBJ the beer is cold, the bartendresses are quick to replenish the fried peanuts, and the atmosphere is jovial and tolerant. It is probably the most integrated bar in town. Expatriates with a weekend off frolic in the pool with their busty companions. A taxi driver quietly nurses a beer at one end of the long, oval bar, taking a temporary break from the demands of Islam. A group of regulars, all Kamoro men, hold down the other end, cheering the band. When the mood comes over them, they shuffle solo out onto the dance floor to perform quirky, self-absorbed versions of the twist. The band alternates between rock-and-roll classics and cloying ballads, never completely mangling either. The Ambonese lead singer, in her enthusiasm, occasionally attempts a note in a range where her voice has no business going, but this aside, she and the band provide an enjoyable performance.

We were talking about Kamoro woodcarving, a conversation that started with a remarkable sculpture decorating the GSBJ pool. I suppose it is a kind of *mbitoro,* but quite unlike any I had ever seen. The lowest and largest figure is a woman nursing a child, with at least three male figures standing on her head. For reasons that were not apparent, two large nails had been driven into the head of the topmost figure, giving him the appearance of Tintin. Since the main figures in Kamoro *mbitoro* are always men, I specu-

lated that perhaps the artist intended this one, with its strong image of a woman burdened with both a child and three generations of men, as an ironic, feminist reinterpretation of the genre. But then, noticing the turtle at the very base, I decided that despite the protruding *tokae* and general form, this was not a *mbitoro* at all, but rather a very unconventional version of a Balinese *padmasana*, the symbolic representation of the three-part universe resting on Bedawang Nala, the world turtle. (Actually, Kal later discovered, it was carved by an Asmat artist, and it is neither a *mbitoro* nor a *padmasana*—nor, for that matter, an Asmat *mbisj.*)

The oldest and finest Kamoro woodcarvings are held in two ethnographic museums in England and four in Holland. The British collections were obtained during a 1910–1911 expedition sponsored by the British Ornithologists' Union. The Dutch collections are more extensive, and the oldest pieces, consisting of bamboo penis cases and a few body ornaments, were collected by Salomon Müller in Mupuruka during the 1828 *Triton* expedition. Only one survey of Kamoro art has been published, by Simon Kooijman of the Rijksmuseum voor Volkenkunde in Leiden, a museum with arguably the single most extensive collection of Kamoro art.

The best Kamoro sculptures are abstracted into bold and unlikely shapes, and they are true masterpieces, displaying all of the spirit and artistry that first attracted European modernists to the art of New Guinea and Oceania. A Kamoro artist rejects all rules of proportion and dimensionality, obeying only his imagination. A man is stripped of his arms, and his torso is carved into a flat lattice producing a kind of eerie visage. A woman, her arms and legs covered with chiseled tattoos, is carved in three dimensions until the artist reaches her face, which is suddenly split and rendered as two separate, flat faces. A shield-like panel sprouts, at random, two withered legs. A squatting figure on the back of a canoe paddle is abstracted to a few simple, disconnected scribbles—a face, genitals, the points of contact between elbows and knees. The forms are powerful, even a little frightening, and always surprising.

But Kamoro art, despite its high quality, is almost unknown outside of a few specialists in Holland. The reason for this is the long shadow cast by the Kamoro's neighbors, the Asmat. Probably a dozen or more books have been written on Asmat art, of which at least half are still in print. These are, for the most part, full-color, oversized, lavishly produced art books. By contrast,

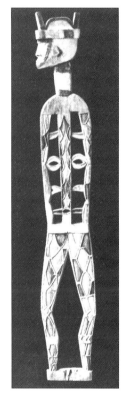

Fig. 3.2 CARVING. In the Etnografisch Museum, Antwerp. Acquired in 1956 by J. Hoogerbrugge. Origin listed as 'Mimika.' 170 cm.

Kooijman's 1984 *Art, Art Objects, and Ritual in the Mimika Culture* was produced in a trade paperback format, and the publisher's sales goals for the volume were so modest that the budget did not even accommodate color plates. This is a shame.

I am a great fan of Asmat art, and the reputation of Asmat woodcarvers is certainly well deserved. But to my eyes, the best of the old Kamoro pieces are even more imaginative than those of the Asmat. An Asmat war shield or *yames*—"jamasj," in the Dutch romanization—is a stunning and colorful sculpture with a great variety of treatment of the motifs, but its basic shape is relatively fixed. In contrast, the old Kamoro *yamate* in the collection of the Rijksmuseum bend and perforate their subjects—hornbills, people, giant lizards—into an endless variety of jagged and startling shapes.

Today an Asmat carver can earn a steady income shaping openwork panels, small shields, or little dioramas of traditional life: sago making, fishing, men paddling a canoe. Some of these are sold to the steady trickle of tourists who reach Agats, the capital of the region, and many more are shipped out to Wamena in the highlands, which sees far more tourists than Agats, and even to Bali. Asmat *mbis,* roughly the equivalent of the Kamoro *mbitoro,* sell in art shops in Kuta, Bali for $800 and up. Some Asmat carvings reach Europe, and a few even make it to the United States and Japan.

The Catholic mission has for many years now been a great supporter of the Asmat carving tradition, and in August 1973 opened a small museum in Agats. The Asmat Museum of Culture and Progress has built up an admirable collection, and it is refreshing to see a museum of traditional art located where the Asmat people and artists themselves can visit. Once a year, in the fall, the mission sponsors an auction of Asmat art, and collectors come from Jakarta, Europe, the United States, and Japan to bid on the best recent work.

One of the reasons Kamoro art does not enjoy the same reputation as Asmat art is that the quality of the few contemporary pieces available for sale ranges, frankly, from merely bad to truly awful. Kamoro art—like Asmat art, before the Crosier mission stepped in—was almost always produced as part of the ritual cycle, and when the Dutch colonial government and Catholic missionaries stopped the traditional cycle, the art stopped being produced as well. With the exception of a few of the *mbitoro,* in all our time in the Kamoro area, neither Kal nor I once saw artwork of the quality in the collections of the Dutch and British museums.*

Although a few shops in town sell woodcarvings, Timika does not get even the small volume of tourist traffic that passes through Agats. Currently the biggest patron of Kamoro carvers is Freeport, which

FIGURE CARVING, PECE.

commissioned monumental carvings to decorate the Sheraton Hotel, and more recently, the new company town of Kuala Kencana. The company also set up a carving center in Timika, the Gedung Seni Kamoro, where most of these large sculptures are produced.

I had been looking forward to visiting this center and we finally got a chance to stop by. We stayed about ten minutes. Scattered around the room were a dozen or so carvings, in various stages of completion, and they were ugly enough to make even a layperson cringe. I didn't know what to say. Kal, who is a connoisseur of Oceanic and African art—in the sixties he collected and sold African and New Hebridean carvings that are now displayed in museums—couldn't even bear to look at them, and quickly stepped outside. The carvings were miniature *mbitoro,* tiny *karapao,* toy canoes, and the like. They were crudely carved, poorly finished, and utterly without aesthetic virtue. Kal, if I recall correctly, used the term "firewood." The carvings looked like they had been made by a bored and unskilled child, under duress, as a gift for his least favorite auntie.

I subsequently discovered that these items, commissioned by Freeport for a new display in the upstairs conference room of the Sheraton Hotel, probably *were* carved by bored and unskilled children. The head

* One ray of hope is an annual Kamoro art auction, patterned after the Asmat auction in Agats, which is held every April in Pigapu, in the Timika area. This project, in its third year as this book goes to press, is organized by Kal, and funded by Freeport. Carvers come from all along the Kamoro Coast, and the quality of the best pieces—which fetch several hundred dollars at auction—is excellent.

carver at the center, busy with lucrative commissions for larger outdoor sculptures—standard rate, $200 per two-meter hardwood sculpture—said he had assigned at least some of the work on the conference room job to his young "apprentices." I don't know what Freeport had to pay for these abominations, but hopefully by now they have done the right thing and buried the lot in the forest.

I was beginning to despair of finding any good carvers in Timika when Alo mentioned that his brother-in-law was a woodcarver. In fact, Alo said, he worked on the largest of the three monumental carvings that stand guard in front of the Sheraton Inn. Although this carving, which looks something like a totem pole, is a modern interpretation of a *mbitoro,* its artistry has always impressed us, and we decided to look up Paskalis Wepumi.

PASKALIS AND HIS family live in Pulau Pisang, a Kamoro settlement on the eastern edge of Timika, just across from a gravel lot where a bus for the roadwork contractor Petrosea drops off and picks up workers. The settlement, with about fifteen very modest plywood-sided houses, is more than a squatter's camp, but less than a small village. The houses are roofed variously in galvanized steel, plastic tarp, or thatch—sometimes a bit of each. Outsiders sometimes want to call it Kampung Pisang, "Banana Hamlet," but the Kamoro always stick to *pulau,* or "island." The site of this settlement was at one time a sandbar island on the braided Aikwa River, but it now lies on the dry side of the West Levee. *Pulau* still applies, however, because when you are driving down the levee road, the settlement stands out as an island of green banana leaves surrounded by dusty grass.

We caused quite a stir rolling into Banana Island, chiefly because we came by car. The settlement is cut off from Timika by the Freeport company road and access to the village itself is a dirt footpath. The Freeport road was temporarily open because of construction on a new power line, however, and our driver prided himself on his ability to negotiate anything even remotely resembling a road. Despite our efforts to curb his enthusiasm, he came barreling into the little settlement with such a fury that we were afraid he was going to drive right into Paskalis's little plywood house.

The afternoon light was soft through the banana leaves, and the rise of the former island encourages a slight breeze. The walls of Paskalis's house were bare, and in order to have two benches and a table around which to talk, one bench and the table had to be borrowed from the neighbors.

Paskalis is a handsome man in his late forties, and although he has the body of a twenty-five-year-old, his eyes are well into middle age. He is shy to the point of seeming forlorn, and when answering a question, he takes his time and chooses his words with care.

MBITORO, ATUKA.
The face rendered is that of Maora Utakapeya.

Paskalis is Asmat on his mother's side, and Kamoro on his father's. His father, Hendrikus Wepumi, is from Kokonao, and met his future wife Emiliana Namoreb while working as a mission teacher in Ayam, a few hours upriver from Agats.

Alo is Paskalis's greatest promoter, to the point of visibly embarrassing his brother-in-law. ("You'll see, David, he can do anything, carvings of men in canoes, fishermen, anything. Right, Paskalis?") Alo's theory is that his brother-in-law's special talent comes from his Asmat blood. Even among the Kamoro, "Asmat" has a special cachet when it comes to artistry. Paskalis himself said that although he feels both influences, Asmat and Kamoro, he doesn't think either one is more important. If his carving ability has a source, he said, it is probably the years he spent watching the work of his maternal grandfather, a famous carver in Ayam.

Paskalis takes his talent seriously. For example, he prefers to work in hardwood because of the permanence of the carvings that result. He considers it very important that the spirit and shape of the raw wood be allowed to influence, perhaps even determine, the form of the carving. He scorned the expedient of first sketching a design on the wood in pencil or chalk, and implied that this kind of thing was strictly the province of dilettantes and hacks.

Fig. 3.3 YAMATE.
In the Rijksmuseum
voor Volkenkunde's
Justinus van Nassau
collection in Breda.
Acquired in 1910 by
J.J. van der Bie.
Otakwa River.
191 cm.

"For me, the carving comes straight from here," he said, pointing to his head, "and from here," pointing to his heart. In the past Paskalis has carved in the Asmat style, but since moving to the Timika area he has concentrated on Kamoro motifs. He does not really prefer one over the other, he said, but it makes more sense to him in his current cultural surroundings to work in the Kamoro idiom.

Paskalis and his family are poor. Quite a few people live under his simple roof, including Alo's mother. When we met he no longer even owned any carving tools, as one by one his chisels, hatchet, and saws had been "lost" (a polite way of saying that they had been bartered off). Kal and I decided to commission some carvings from Paskalis. We were interested in witnessing the carving process, and were happy that our interest might also improve the economy of his struggling household.

With the arrival of a tourist market, however small, art styles have changed in Southwest New Guinea. The Asmat now regularly produce a type of carving texts call "ajour," which are flat panels of open-work carvings, often representing many human figures entwined together. (The name is not Asmat, but French, meaning "openwork.") This style is said to have begun in 1960, in Atsy, when a missionary gave local carvers cutoffs from the iron-wood planks being produced at the village's newly opened sawmill. The Asmat had also noted that Europeans would buy entire canoes just for the latticework prow ornament, which they would cut off. To the Asmat it seemed less wasteful—and a whole lot less work—to make only the ornament in the first place.

Ajour can be very fine pieces, but the most common modern productions, by both Asmat and Kamoro carvers, are artless and unpleasant little dioramas of everyday life—fishermen in a canoe, women pounding sago, and the like—in a style I call "suitcase pastoral." These carvings are cheap enough to be treated as disposable trinkets, and small enough to fit in a tourist's bag. But they are ugly little homunculi, and although they have at times out of necessity been Paskalis's stock in trade, we asked him instead to interpret two traditional items: a *yamate* and a *wemawe*.

The *yamate,* pronounced "*yah*-mah-tay," has always puzzled art collectors. Superficially it appears to be a rectangular, decorated shield, but unlike the apparently similar Asmat *yames,* it has no handle. Alfred Court Haddon and J.W. Layard, reporting in 1916 on a group of Kamoro artifacts collected on the Otakwa River by the Wollaston expedition in 1912–1913, called the *yamate* "ceremonial tablets." Kooijman, in his *Art,*

Art Objects, and Ritual in the Mimika Culture, calls *yamate* "ornamented shield-shaped and oblong objects with a ceremonial function."

Kooijman is dissatisfied with this definition, however, and speculates that the *yamate* has evolved from a functional shield to something more purely decorative. Elements of Kamoro ritual, he writes, hint strongly of a time when the culture was more violent.

> This suggests that the *yamate*—which in the cultural context we know something about had an exclusively ceremonial function—developed from war shields; and this is made even more likely by the similarity between the word *yamate* and the Asmat word for shield, *yames.*

According to Apollo and Alo, Kooijman's speculations are correct. Both insisted that the *yamate* originally had a martial purpose. The big ones, which can reach two meters in length, were used in warfare. The smaller ones, Apollo said, were used for "fighting in the village."

"You mean boys, play fighting?" I said.

"Oh no," Apollo said, "*fighting.*"

The *yamate* also have a ceremonial purpose, they said, and sometimes, especially nowadays, a person might hang one on his wall just for decoration.

The word "yamate," Apollo said, can also refer to a specific motif, which is a variety of *uku,* a type of shell. The *yamate* motif, which shows up on *mbitoro* and other traditional carvings, looks like a heavily stylized interpretation of a group of upside-down cowrie shells and is, logically enough, common on *yamate.*

The *wemawe* is a genre of figure sculpture, and at least in an approximate sense, Apollo said, can be considered the female equivalent of the *mbitoro.* The traditional style was a meter or two high, and served a ceremonial purpose. It always represents a woman, and she is usually pregnant. These carvings, Apollo said, were produced only in the area between the Otakwa and Kamora rivers, and never in his own village of Paripi or the other western villages.

It has been a long time since Apollo or anyone else has seen or heard of a *wemawe.* Only seven exist in collections in Europe—in the Rijksmuseum in Leiden, and in the Rijksmuseum's Justinus van Nassau collection in Breda. Kooijman calls them "female figures," and notes that they were all collected by the Dutch military expeditions in 1913. Pouwer suggests they served a function in the *kiawa* ceremony, which is an eastern variant of a ceremony called *emakame.*

Both Apollo and Paskalis said that small hardwood figures, not necessarily *wemawe,* were sometimes kept in the house for decoration, but both thought that this might be a recent phenomenon.

O UR FIRST STOP would have to be the hardware store, to get Paskalis some tools. We looked at chisels first, and he picked two wooden-handled framing chisels for the main carving work,

MODERN WEMAWE, PULAU PISANG.
Paskalis Wepumi carves a small sculpture commissioned by the author and photographer.

PASKALIS WEPUMI, ATUKA.

having—under the rather disdainful eye of the proprietor—examined the entire stock before making his selection. He also selected a keyhole saw, a small hatchet, a plane iron, and finally a file and stone to keep everything sharp. Next we needed some wood.

According to Paskalis, there are only a handful of hardwoods regularly used in carving. His favorite is *kayu besi*. *Kayu besi* literally means "ironwood," but the term is almost meaningless because it refers to any of at least a dozen species of relatively dense, straight-grained hardwoods. The wood called *kayu besi* in Timika seems to me to be from one of the *Intsia* species. Elsewhere I have heard it called "redwood" for its rich color.

We decided to round up some *kayu besi* while we still had our taxi. In the past, wood for carving would have been gathered in the forest, although *kayu besi* is not a traditional material. This wood is commonly used for framing lumber in Irian Jaya, and it still gives me a shock to see this beautiful ruddy wood, which looks something like mahogany, used for studs and joisting. In the United States a wood like this would be sold by the pound.

Aggressive logging in the nearby forests has stripped the local supply of *kayu besi*. Further east in the unlogged Lorentz Park, Alo said, the trees can be found growing quite close to the coast, but in the Timika area one would now have to go far inland to find any.

Rather than cut our own tree, we decided to visit a construction site in Sempan Barat. Although smaller boards are dimensioned at the mill, in Timika the larger beams and posts are ripped on site from logs, and Paskalis picked through a pile of the leftover stumps for suitable pieces for our carvings. The foreman at the site said Rp5,000 per stump would suit him, as well it should, since the Rp10,000 went straight into his pocket. After setting Paskalis up with tools and wood, we left, promising to come back the next day to see how the carving was coming along.

When we arrived late the next morning, Paskalis was irritable, and had done little beyond stripping the bark off one of the stumps. He said he had gotten started late, and apologized profusely for not being further along. "There was too much noise around here last night," he said. He didn't have to elaborate, as we had already noticed his father and a friend, sitting on the old Aikwa River gravel behind the house, smoking cigarettes, talking, and occasionally bursting into song. Every now and then Hendrikus took a sip from an old plastic soda bottle, full of a clear liquid that I don't think was water. I told Paskalis not to worry. It had probably been a while since money had come into this household (we gave him an advance for the carvings) and I wouldn't deny my own father some cigarettes—and a bottle of *arak,* if that's what he wanted.

Paskalis began carving professionally when he was sixteen years old and living in Syuru, a small Asmat village adjacent to Agats. He produced trinkety tourist items in the Asmat style of suitcase pastoral, which were sold at shops in Agats. In 1971, he moved to Atuka, and eventually to Timika. In Timika he continued to carve the same types of souvenir items, which he sold for very low prices to the Bugis-run art shops in town. The most popular, he said, were nautical scenes, or scenes of a man and a woman, in Apollo's polite translation, "playing love." Paskalis remembers European tourists, particularly the French and Germans, liking these latter items the best.

Every few days over the next two weeks we stopped at Pulau Pisang to see how the work was progressing. The *wemawe* Paskalis was carving for us eventually took a traditional, but somewhat grisly shape: a snake eating a pregnant woman. This snake is the giant, mythical python called Biroko or, in the western dialect, Miroko. Biroko plays a role in a famous story by eating a woman and her sisters while they are out pounding sago. Biroko then adopts the son of the eldest sister and calls him Birokoteyau, "Son of the Python." Birokoteyau eventually discovers what happened and kills the python Biroko, chopping its body into small pieces. This is a female story of generation, and the pieces of the snake, like seeds, sprout into people. The tale provides the script for the *kiawa* festival.

Like most Kamoro stories, this one has more than one version. In the west, the Snakewoman's son slays not her but the *wou,* a huge, mythical varanid, or monitor lizard. The *wou* is also commonly featured in Kamoro carvings. Once, while Paskalis, Apollo, and I were talking, Kal wandered off around Pulau Pisang to take some pictures, and ended up buying a small wooden statue carved by one of Paskalis's neighbors, Kaspar Nawatipia. This sculpture showed a Godzilla-like lizard—the *wou*—holding a fish.

I HAVE ALWAYS been fascinated by the terrible animals that populate human nightmares and myths, and am tempted to believe that sometime, in a distant but real past, these were living animals that coexisted with humankind. Like the wonderfully named dire wolves and saber-toothed tigers of Pleistocene North America. As soon as Apollo described it to me I thought the *wou* belonged in the same category.

The *wou,* Apollo said, now thankfully lives on only in myth. It was a very, very large lizard, something like an oversized Salvator's monitor, a savvy beast widely distributed in Southeast Asia that, like the raccoon in North America, is just as happy prowling backyards as the forest. But the most similar animal to the *wou* still extant is the Komodo dragon, a three-meter-long varanid that is the largest lizard in the world. Although it looked a lot like the Komodo dragon, Apollo said, the *wou* had a spiny ridge down its back, and it was much bigger. "And of course," he added, "it could eat entire villages."

In 1858, the English anatomist Sir Richard Owen identified the fossil remains of a giant varanid (a goanna to an Australian) that roamed Pleistocene Australia and New Guinea. He called this "gigantic land-lizard" *Megalania prisca.* Owen based his identification on three vertebrae found in Queensland, and since then only a scattered few fossils have added to our knowledge of this enigmatic creature: a few more vertebrae, and some jaw and leg bones. With this relatively scanty evidence,

Fig. 3.4 MEGALANIA PRISCA
This drawing is of a 1974 reconstruction by the National Museum of Victoria in Australia. The bones in black are actual fossil material. At this scale, an average person would be about the height of the word "Megalania" above, turned on end.

the National Museum of Victoria in Melbourne, Australia reconstructed *Megalania* in 1974. The skeleton that resulted measures five-and-one-half meters. The maximum length of *Megalania* that can be inferred from fossil material is seven meters, and an animal this size may have weighed as much as a small automobile.

Australian zoologist Tim Flannery, in his 1990 *The Future Eaters,* describes this monster:

> [*Megalania*] was about the size of a medium-sized *Allosaurus* and, if the agility, intelligence and rapacity of living goannas is any guide, must have been a terrifying predator.

It is now common knowledge, at least among American schoolchildren, that human beings and dinosaurs never coexisted. But despite its size, *Megalania* was not a dinosaur. The Cretaceous Period, the golden age of the dinosaurs, ended sixty-five million years ago, while the Pleistocene Epoch lasted until just ten thousand years ago.

The few *Megalania* fossils so far discovered have been dated to 19,000–26,000 years ago. Since human beings have lived on New Guinea and Australia for at least forty thousand years, it seems certain that people and *Megalania* once coexisted. And the evidence of the giant varanids of Komodo, marooned on a few dry islands west of Flores, makes it at least possible that a relict population of *Megalania* survived until much more recently.

The fossil remains of another large Pleistocene reptile have been found in southern Australia—*Wonambi narracoortensis,* a fat, python-like snake. *Wonambi,* it has been estimated, reached six meters in length. With the evidence available I can't help thinking that it was *Megalania,* under its alias *wou,* and *Wonambi,* under the alias *biroko,* who first taught the Kamoro the meaning of terror. In fact, I am tempted to write to the Victoria museum—in their reconstruction, they forgot to include the *wou*'s dorsal crest.

97

CHAPTER FOUR

Looking for a Mask

The Rhythm of Life in Paripi Village

N THE AUGUST morning we were to leave on our long boat trip to the western edge of the Kamoro area, Kal and I sat in a dusty little coffee shop in Hiripau, twenty-five kilometers south of Timika. The nine o'clock sun, already fierce, streamed in through chicken wire windows. The coffee in our pink and blue plastic cups had long been reduced to a residue of sweet mud. In silence, we watched the flies copulate on the hot concrete floor. Our waiter, curiously androgyne in makeup and a blouse, brought us another plate of oily doughnuts covered with multicolored candy sprinkles. Nobody is afraid of sugar in the tropics. The chili *sambal* we ordered for our trip, a specialty of the house, had leaked through its plastic bag and was slowly staining the counter Mercurochrome orange.

Alo was out behind the cafe, down on the bank of the Wania River, checking on our boat, which rocked gently at the end of its painter. Stuffed into the long dugout were three green two hundred-liter drums of kerosene, five twenty-liter plastic jerrycans of gasoline, and three twenty-liter cans of Shell two-stroke oil—enough fuel to reach Australia. Our gear bags were stowed amidships, covered in plastic and securely tied. A blue tarpaulin to repel rain, spray, and the relentless sun, had been rigged in a canopy over the middle third of the boat. A brand-new forty-horsepower Yamaha outboard was clamped to the rear. Our driver, a handsome young Kamoro man from Mwapi named Tobias, leaned back on our plastic-wrapped bags and smoked a cigarette. His teenage assistant was already sound asleep.

Kal stood up, looked outside, and made an obscene gesture with his right hand, miming the male autostimulant act. It is Kal's code for the frustration of those times when plans fall through and we find ourselves with an unscheduled three or four hours of waiting.

ALBERT OROKAI, PARIPI. Burning a new canoe, which seals it and gives it shape, is the most dramatic stage in its construction. It is also uncomfortable, and here Albert suffers from the heat.

TEODORUS TUKANI, YARAYA. This portrait was taken in front of the woodcarver's house. Kal bought a fine *yamate* from him.

His patience had worn thin. He had wrung all the photographic inspiration he could from the dusty streets and zinc roofs of Timika, and wanted out badly.

For two weeks we had been trying to get out of Timika, but had been thwarted at every turn. There are no telephones beyond the Timika area, and despite many messages sent through the mission radio system, our scheduled boat never showed up. Finally, we gave up, and looked for another. By the time we had made the arrangements, Indonesian Independence Day celebrations were in full swing, which not only brought social and family obligations for Alo and Apollo, but also meant that most of the people in the villages we planned to visit would be gathered in Kokonao, or would even have come to Timika.

Finally, a few days after the Independence Day celebrations, we were all set to leave. Our ambitious plan had been to get up before dawn, gather up Apollo and Alo, meet our boat at Hiripau, and motor down the Wania and up the coast to Paripi, Apollo's home village. Paripi, in approximately the middle of the Kamoro area, was where we intended to begin our exploration of the western Kamoro heartland. All had gone well until we arrived, just after dawn, at Apollo's house. He had some bad news. Late the night before he learned that his signature was needed on some financial paperwork for the Kamoro foundation LEMASKO, and the bank wouldn't open until eight. This effectively ruined our early start, and could possibly—depending on the tides—prevent us from reaching Paripi as planned.

From inside the coffee shop we heard the crunching of the taxi's tires on the gravel at the same time as Alo's shout. With the team finally in place, we climbed aboard our vessel. At just a few minutes before ten o'clock Tobias fired up the engine, swung the boat in a wide arc out into the Wania River, and pointed us south.

THE WANIA IS the main shipping artery for the seventy thousand people living in Greater Timika. For that, it doesn't really look like much, and in most places you could throw a stone across it. The main Mapuru Jaya dock, which is really in Hiripau and against which we tied up our boat, receives goods from the large wooden Bugis freight ships called *pinisi*. This is as far upriver as the *pinisi* can go, and even then they have to watch the tide. The larger vessels must anchor further south in the deeper channel of the Iwinia River, where they offload their cargo into smaller boats to be brought upstream.

I once watched a small freighter called the *Namlea Star* unload at the main dock in Hiripau. Lined up in rows on its deck were two dozen 100cc Honda step-through motorcycles, each carefully wrapped in a kind of white, woven plastic burlap. In boxes, tied with the ubiquitous Indonesian pink plastic twine, were big cast aluminum woks, garden tools, and green, red, and blue plastic strainers, these latter used to keep the flies off freshly served food.

Our spirits were high, and although it upset the handling of the boat somewhat, all four of us crowded up front in the sunshine. Like a bunch of kids, we waved to every boat we passed. Everyone waved back except for the members of the occasional military patrols tearing up and down the river in their fast fiberglass vee-hulled boats. Even the soldiers seemed like they wanted to wave, and then realized only at the last minute that a response would be undignified. And we even caught out one or two.

The Wania swings through tight, blind curves, and carries so much traffic that occasionally Tobias had to cut the motor suddenly to avoid a collision. His young assistant sat at the bow, keeping a lookout for drifting logs, pieces of plywood, lengths of plastic rope, and other hazards, which are not easy to see in the olive-colored water. In just the first few minutes of travel, I noticed a great variety of colorful flotsam: cigarette packs, an orphaned rubber sandal, several plastic toys, an empty battery carton, a brassiere, and a broken umbrella.

Our boat seemed a perfect vessel for the river. Carved from a single log, it was about eight meters long and beamy enough for two people to sit comfortably side by side. An extra twenty centimeters of lumber had been pegged to the gunwales in an effort to make it more seaworthy. The boat, which was unnamed, was a bit wider at the bow end, and in the calm water of the river, did a good job of throwing the wake out and away. Like all keel-less dugouts, if anyone shifted his weight suddenly the entire boat would rock, but a keel would have make it impossible to swing around snags or through tight bends, maneuvers at which a dugout excels.

Just downstream from Paumako, where the road ends, we passed a place called Tirimuru, which in Kamoro means "Short Sand." I don't recall seeing any sandy strip here, but in any case, this is not why the area is famous. Tirimuru is Timika's Napa Valley, where the palm tree called *enau* grows in great abundance. *Enau,* the sugar palm, is the preferred species to tap for palm wine. We passed several makeshift docks,

each with a white plastic jug hanging out in front. They need no other form of advertising.

"We call Tirimuru 'The Happy Place,'" Alo said.

The *enau* palm, *Arenga pinnata,* looks a bit like a coconut palm and even more like a sago palm, but its fronds appear messy and uncombed, and stand a bit more upright than those of the sago. Its hairy, coir-covered stems attract more epiphytes and creepers than other palms which, combined with the dead fronds hanging down, give the trees a generally unkempt look.

Palm wine, toddy, *tuak, segero*—it has many names—is the slightly fermented sap taken from the flower bud of any of several species of palm trees. In many areas of Indonesia, the fan-leaved *lontar* palm is preferred; in others it is *enau,* and less often the coconut palm. The Kamoro prefer the *enau.* In all cases, the palm toddy is a more or less sweet, slightly frothy drink. It is very unlike grape wine. It's closer to beer, but even that isn't a good comparison.

The famous naturalist and explorer Alfred Russel Wallace, sampling some palm wine in the Seram Laut islands in 1860, writes, "It is really a very nice drink, more like cider than beer, though quite as intoxicating as the latter." The palm wine was "one of the few luxuries" he encountered on the dry limestone island of Uta in the Matabello group, where he was marooned by uncooperative winds.

Segero is gathered by slashing, and sometimes slightly crushing, the male flower bud of the tree, and then hanging a vessel underneath the wound to collect the dripping sap. A bit of a previous batch, or a tuft of coir dipped in the previous batch, is introduced to this vessel, often a cut-down plastic water bottle, to provide the active yeast. The sap begins fermenting as soon as it hits the container, and continues throughout the day.

Palm wine is not a particularly alcoholic drink, but it really depends on the time of day you drink it. When first gathered in the morning it is called young *segero,* and in this form is quite sweet and mild, and probably does not even have the alcohol content of light beer. By afternoon, however, it becomes noticeably stronger. Some vendors stagger their harvests so they always have both a young, sweet batch, and an old, strong batch to sell from. Connoisseurs will sometimes order a kind of half-and-half.

The word "segero," which is thought to come from North Sulawesi, is a corruption of "saguér," or "saguir," words that are themselves corruptions of "sagu air," literally "water of the sago." Despite this etymology, the Kamoro do not tap their sago palms.

Segero from *enau* is the most traditional drink in the Kamoro area, but since the trees tend to grow further upriver than most villages are located, few have a ready supply. A big change in the area's drinking habits came about in the mid-eighties, Alo said, when villages began tapping their coconut trees. This practice was introduced by island people from Biak, Aru, and

LEAVING TIMIKA PANTAI.
The *ku-oko* is designed to be paddled while standing.

Kei, areas where there are no *enau* palms. Since most Kamoro villages are now on the coast, and have plenty of coconut palms, this a much more convenient source of palm wine. We didn't stop to sample the *segero* in Tirimuru, although I have drunk *segero* from both *enau* and *lontar* palms in Bali. *Enau tuak,* which is slightly sweeter, is favored there as well, but my own opinion is that the *lontar* produces the superior libation.

The Dutch government in its day, the Catholic missionaries, the Indonesian government, and development workers today, all consider *segero* drinking among the Kamoro to be at best an irritation, and at worst, a dangerous scourge. Although the vendors at Tirimuru conduct their business quietly behind plain white jugs, in villages further from the urban center of Timika the practice has actually been banned. Most observers estimate that palm wine is an accessory to something like ninety-nine percent of the serious arguments in the Kamoro area.

In all our travels through the region, we saw taps only at Keakwa, and those were in the process of being removed. I'm quite sure that there were taps at some of the other places we stayed, but the village "drinkards"—to make African novelist Amos Tutuola's distinction—must have partaken of their foamy pleasures discreetly, and I never noticed any undue quarreling.

The first outsider to spend considerable time with the Kamoro, and to write eloquently of the experience, was Dr. Alexander F. R. Wollaston, an ornithologist who accompanied two expeditions to the Carstensz mountains in the early part of the century. He stayed in the village of Mimika (he calls it "Wakatimi," a slight corruption of the name of the tribe there, Wakotu-me) which at the time was located much further upriver. Wollaston saw the hardest-drinking men age noticeably in the months he was there, and in at least one case blames a young man's death on his taste for palm wine. He also noted the lighter side of this pastime, and in his 1912 *Pygmies and Papuans,* describes a scene—either comic or pathetic, depending on one's taste—that with few changes could probably be set just about anywhere in the world:

One afternoon one of the principal men of Wakatimi came down to the river bank quite intoxicated and took a canoe, which he paddled out into mid-stream and there moored it. From there he proceeded to shoot arrows vaguely and promiscuously at the village, raving and shouting what sounded to be horrible curses. Some of the arrows fell into the village and some sailed over the palm trees, and now and again he turned round and shot harmlessly into our camp, but nobody took the slightest notice of him except his wife, who went down to the river bank and told him in

ULIFA KUTAKAPEYA, ATUKA.

plain language her opinion of him. This caused him to turn his attention to her, but his aim was wild and the arrows missed their mark, so he desisted and went back to the shore, where the woman broke across her knee the remainder of his bundle of arrows, while he cooled his fevered brow in the river. Then, while she delivered a further lecture, he followed her back to their hut looking like a whipped and ashamed dog.

PAST TIRIMURU, THE vegetation begins to change. Here and there, in sections, the distinctive tight, upright fronds of nipa line the river. The nipa palm is called *awani* in Kamoro, and its fronds are called *kopere.* This latter word is the source of the name of Koperapoka village. In Potowai-Buru, a town near the western frontier of the Kamoro territory, the people know how to make a unique form of palm wine called *bobo* from the nipa, Apollo said. This practice was never common, however, and with the new fashion for tapping coconut trees, may now be extinct.

We also began to pass great clumps of pandanus, which is sometimes, although a bit inexplicably to me, called "screw pine" in English. The pandanus tree has several crowns of long, sharply serrated leaves growing from a crooked, spindly trunk supported by a teepee of aerial prop roots. It looks a lot like a huge, stalked pineapple plant, and nothing like a pine. A thicket of pandanus is simply impossible to walk through, worse in this regard even than a tangle of mangrove roots.

New Guinea is very rich in pandanus species, many of them endemic. Once a year one type of lowland pandanus, *umuku* in Kamoro, produces a large, bright red fruit called *umuku eke.* (The Kamoro language modifies nouns like English—"pandanus fruit"—rather than like Indonesian—"fruit pandanus.") Mixed with sago, the fruit produces a dish that is both tasty and has a festive color: a bright, artificial-looking red like maraschino cherries. The pandanus season, like that of so many other jungle fruits, is frustratingly short, usually lasting less than two weeks.

Continuing downstream, our canoe passed the Piga River, and the old site of Pigapu village. The Piga enters the Wania from the north, and near this junction is a small creek called the Wikiki, where there is a lumber dock. A few families built small shelters nearby, to live in while they earned a little money loading logs. Kal and I stopped there a few months ago, and the men, from Hiripau and Mapuru Jaya, said there hadn't been any work since the lumber company opened a larger dock further upstream.

Pigapu does not appear on contemporary maps of the area, nor does Mware, which used to be located further up the Piga river.* The sago groves that belong to these villages are still here along the Piga, but the people now live in Mwapi (*Mwa*re and *Pi*gapu), a settlement on the main public road between Mapuru Jaya

* About a year after I left, the Pigapu people moved back to their original village site. The Mware, for now, remain in Mwapi.

105

and Timika. Wikiki is the last settlement on the river, and from here the Wania turns south, and within a few kilometers, broadens.

"Thirty years ago," Apollo said, looking out over the wide river, "this was the best place in the area to catch sawfish and sharks. You could even see whales here sometimes."

This puzzled me, because as far as I could tell we were still in the forest, and according to the map, at least fifteen kilometers from the sea. I asked him what a whale would be doing so far upriver.

"This is all new," he said, pointing to the forest lining both sides of the river. "When I was a boy you could see all the way to the coast."

Today you wouldn't even be able to see to Wikiki. Not with a thick forest of thirty-meter trees in the way. What had just four decades ago been an open area of thinly vegetated sandbars and river banks, covered with low-growing strand plants and bushy mangroves, had evolved into a lowland forest.

Irian Jaya's mountains are quite young, and still relatively unweathered. The amount of sediment the rivers carry to the south coast is staggering, and it seems quite possible that this could literally change the map in thirty or forty years. I have compared World War II–era Dutch maps of the coast here with contemporary satellite images, and the difference is in some areas striking. While the area through which we were passing seems to be building up, in areas further to the west, particularly around the village of Umar, the coastline seems to be eroding.

Soon we left the Wania and entered the narrow Waya River, a shortcut to the coast. Within minutes Tobias cut the engine. We had suddenly come upon a logjam, a clump of branches and uprooted trees several meters high and four times as wide. The existence of this obstacle was a mystery until I looked at the map and saw that this point marked one of the several outlets of the mighty Kamora River. Although it hadn't rained on the coast in weeks, heavy rains had fallen in the highlands, and the Kamora, overflowing its banks, had uprooted trees and carried them seventy kilometers downstream.

Thankfully, a dugout is an excellent vehicle for navigating through or around this kind of obstruction, and soon we were able to thread past the logs. When the Waya River opened up into the broad Apiriyuwahu River, I trailed my finger in the water and for the first time could taste salt.

The estuary of the Apiriyuwahu is almost two kilometers wide. The surface was quiet, and we could see the pounding surf in the distance. I was surprised when Tobias slowed the boat to a crawl. When you look out over this huge, calm body of water, you think your pilot should just point the canoe where you want to go and twist open the throttle. This would be a foolhardy act, however, and would put the boat on a sandbar in seconds.

Even at high tide most of the river mouths have to be negotiated in an improbable series of zigs and zags, following the tiny channels disguised by the calm, unreadable surface. It is not the narrow, twisting creeks where pilots get their boats into trouble, but the estuaries. Sometimes a previous navigator has thoughtfully marked the channel with a thin stick or two, but this is not common. More than once I noticed that the serendipitous appearance of a wading bird, alighting in an area that looked like deep water and then standing there, with its knees dry, would cause Tobias to change course suddenly.

In traversing the estuary of the Apiriyuwahu we had to get out and push our boat no more than five or six times, which isn't considered bad at all. Just before we reached the sea, we turned sharply west into a little tidal creek with a perfect name: Kumako, literally "the way of the canoe." Since the mouth of the Apiriyuwahyu is guarded by shifting sandbars and a frightening line of breakers, everybody takes the Kumako.

The tide was still with us, and we followed the small creeks all the way to Kokonao. Just before we reached this large village, which is on an island of the same name, we passed a small dugout so loaded with sand that it looked like you could flick a pebble onto it and it would sink. The man paddling said he was delivering the sand to the village of Keakwa, where it would be mixed with cement for a new concrete well. Keakwa is on the beach, so at first this man might seem to be carrying coals to Newcastle. Beach sand, however, is too salty to use in concrete. This man's cargo came from the sandy banks of the Mimika River. The Mimika's flow is strong enough to beat back the tide, and it stays fresh almost to the sea.

Kokonao is actually a cluster of four separate villages, but they are set right next to each other and appear to be a single small town. Approximately two thousand people live here, and the town boasts an airstrip, the headquarters of the Catholic Mission, and several schools, including the oldest one in the Kamoro region. Kokonao was the Dutch capital of the region, and today is the center of the *kecamatan,* the subdistrict under the *kabupaten.* We stopped briefly to talk to the *camat* and the Catholic father, but it was already afternoon and we wanted to reach Paripi before dark.

When we left Kokonao we headed out to sea. Just before facing the breakers, we came upon a group of people camping on a low sandbar island. These people, from several villages west of Kokonao, had come to town for the August 17th Independence Day celebrations two days before, and they were having too much fun to leave just yet. Alo and I were standing in the bow looking at the sea as we rounded the last clump of mangrove, surprising a small boy in his canoe. At the sight of me he panicked, leaping from his tiny canoe and swimming madly for the protection of the mangroves. I think he jumped right out of his shorts, which

ABEL NANIPIA, NEAR PARIPI.

MARSELUS TAKATI, PARIPI.
Marselus's grandson never did get used to Kal.

were two sizes too big anyway. Alo looked like he was going to go overboard as well.

"I can't believe it!" Alo said, through tears of laughter. "He really thought you were going to cut off his head."

THE SUN HAD set by the time we wearily pulled up to the sheltered spur of sand that serves as a dock for the twin villages of Paripi and Ipiri. It was a good fifteen minutes' walk in the dark to the villages, but since Apollo was born and raised here, we weren't too worried about finding our way.

The last couple of hours had not been particularly comfortable. We quickly discovered that, despite appearances, our craft was not well built for the sea. The awning kept out most of the direct spray, but unseen waves would occasionally strike the side of the boat at just the right angle to slap up between the gunwale and the edge of the tarp. These, without warning, would strike Kal or me, with surprising force, in the face or the crotch. Alo and Apollo preferred to sit near the opening of the tarp which, although it exposed them to a constant light spray, kept them out of the way of these sudden, drenching waves.

The path to the village led through a grove of coconut trees and past a graveyard and ended up at Ipiri village. We walked quickly through Ipiri, and then, in adjoining Paripi, stopped at a traditional wooden house, set a bit inland and away from the main row of houses, just behind a huge, bearded fig tree. This was Apollo's brother's house. We were quickly shown inside, and news of our arrival began to ripple through the village.

Hands appeared to clear a bench and some chairs for us, and somebody quickly lit a couple of oil lamps—tin cans filled with oil and pinched along the top to hold a piece of shoelace for a wick. The water kettle must have been put over the fire on the cooking platform out back, because in a few minutes a tray appeared with glasses of coffee and condensed milk. I heard someone pumping a pressure lantern out back, and when the hissing white light filled the room, I could see our surroundings for the first time.

Pinned to the walls were several yellowed newspaper clippings, so frail that the ink on both sides was equally visible. These were joined by two or three religious pictures, perhaps pages from a calendar. Their colors were still bright. A plastic clock, curling with age, displayed the correct time twice a day. A simple wooden cabinet stood in one corner of the room. On it were two ABC flashlight batteries and an

MONIKA DAOTEYAO, KEAKWA.
The juice of a young coconut is most refreshing on a hot afternoon.

empty tin of Ovaltine. The chairs and bench were nailed together from hand-hewn boards, but there was no risk of a splinter. The surfaces were polished smooth by years of contact with human backsides.

Soon we were not Apollo's brother's only guests. By the time we got our coffee, every square foot of floor space was occupied by the older men of the village. Outside the door, seated on the steps or standing, with faces pressed up against the window, were the rest of the members of the village. Faces could be seen as far as the rays of the lantern reached, and in the darkness beyond, I could see scattered red beacons— cigarettes being drawn.

Marselus Takati is a heavyset man old enough to have earned his light dusting of gray hair. He is not the *kepala desa,* the official village head, but the *kepala desa* is chosen by the government. Marselus does not have a title on paper, and I don't think he would have any use for one. I never saw him hurry. When he's thinking, which is often, he looks slightly angry. He has a habit of standing, arms crossed behind him, while others sit. The first thing he did after we were introduced was to castigate his brother for staying away so long. Apollo hadn't been to Paripi in four years.

Although Marselus is Apollo's brother, they do not have the same mother and father. He and Apollo are brothers according to *paraeko,* which is a group of people in the same generation—both siblings and cousins—who have the same maternal grandmother. Kamoro of the same *paraeko* call each other "brother" and "sister," where an American would distinguish his or her immediate family members from cousins.

Several weeks before, in Timika, Kal and I and Apollo were sitting in my hotel room talking about an article by anthropologist Jan Pouwer called "A Masquerade in Mimika." The article appeared in 1956 in the journal *Antiquity and Survival,* and describes a 1954 funeral celebration in Kokonao. It contained no photographs of the celebration, but one line drawing, which caught Kal's eye, showed two dramatically costumed figures, each wearing strange, pointed masks.

"Are these masks still used?" he asked Apollo.

"I only know of one."

"And where is that?"

"In Paripi," he said. "It's *that* one"—pointing to the righthand figure in the drawing—"It belongs to my brother."

At that moment, Paripi became our principle destination. We planned to visit a number of villages all the way to Etna Bay, the westernmost frontier of Kamoro land. But we also wanted to spend a more lengthy amount of time, at least a week, in one place. That

MBI-KAO, PARIPI.
Manu Waremani wears the mask, a likeness of Miminareyau, during the *ku-kaware*.

place, Kal decided, would be Paripi. He also decided we would arrange to have the people of Paripi stage for us a *ku-kaware,* a canoe-building ceremony in which the mask traditionally appears.

None of the other ceremonies and events we saw and photographed for this book were staged for our benefit, and at first I thought it would be a bit silly for us to do so for the *kaware.* But the needs of a writer and the needs of a photographer are different. Candlelight and conversation are enough to keep a writer busy, but a photographer requires action, daylight, and color.

I asked Apollo what he thought of Kal's idea. At first he didn't follow my question, as he was already calculating how long it would take to cut the tree, perform the ceremony, and carve the canoe, and thinking about where we would stay in Paripi. When I made myself more clear, he smiled. He couldn't comment on any ethical objection I might be harboring, he said, but he was sure of one thing: The people of Paripi were going to love this.

Marselus Takati had to think for a while before he could remember when the village last staged a *ku-kaware.* He conferred with some of the older men, and realized it must have been in the early 1970s, which surprised even him. The mask is as old. It is a representation of Miminareayau, and is called *mamokoro* or *mbi-kao,* pronounced "*bee*-cow." Marselus's son Gerardus brought it out from the back room. It was a shrunken, brownish tangle of twine, like a crocheted potholder somebody stuck in a drawer twenty years ago. Holding it in my hand, it seemed too small for a grown man to fit over his head.

Marselus is the leader of *taparu* Baukaripiti, and is thus the "owner" of the mask, as well as the man who can decide whether or not a *ku-kaware* should be held. Although he is the mask's owner, he didn't make it. The mask was constructed by his father, Teodorus "Teo" Takati. Teo is now dead, and Marselus does not know how to make a *mbi-kao.* He never sat down with Teo long enough to learn.

Marselus's son Gerardus, now in his twenties, did however, and he has made two masks so far. Neither still exists, an unfortunate circumstance for which I heard two contradictory explanations. According to one, a couple of years ago the masks were loaned to the people of Amar village to use in a ceremony, since there is no one left in Amar who knows how to make such a mask. The people of Amar never returned the masks, and they were subsequently lost. (The definition of "lost," in this case, seems to be that the masks were sold to one of the art shops in Timika.) Then Gerardus's father provided a rather different explanation.

"The masks he makes are no good," Marselus said. "They fall apart almost immediately." Gerardus, who is a bit shy, did not try to defend himself against this charge, and he looked so forlorn that I didn't have the heart to keep pressing with my questions. In my notes I wrote "stolen and/or fell apart" and left it at that.

I asked Marselus why it has been so long since Paripi held a *ku-kaware.* The biggest problem, he said, has been time. The traditional *kaware* cycle lasted two to three months, and it has been a while since his village could spare this amount of time.

"The people of this village have been too busy," he said. "When you had three months of free time, like in the old days, you could do it. Today we can't."

I know that the Indonesian village government, and the Dutch government before it, keeps the people busy with collective work, called *gotong royong.* This involves building wells and fences, improving houses, digging gardens, and so on. And I also know that most families, if only in a relatively modest way, are now involved in the cash economy, and that most want their children to go to school. But I still could not see how this would preclude holding a ceremony. Although a traditional ceremony might last three months, there are plenty of stops and starts. Four or five days of activity, then nothing for a

Fig. 4.1 MBI-KAO IN KOKONAO.
A reproduction of Henk H. Peeters's drawing in the 1956 issue of the journal *Antiquity and Survival* that led us to the old *mbi-kao* mask in Paripi.

month. Then a week, then nothing for three weeks. I found Marselus's explanation unsatisfying, and said so. Apollo answered for him.

"I guess the government doesn't like the ceremonies," Apollo said, "because it wants the people to focus on government programs. Also, the children stay home from school to watch the ceremony."

Apollo is an extremely knowledgeable man. There was almost never a question I asked him for which he didn't have an intelligent answer. At times, however, he can be frustratingly fair-minded. He is, after all, a high school teacher. At these times I turned to Alo, who could be depended on to get right to the point.

"They say, 'That *adat* isn't any good,' but the truth is the government and the Catholic Church are *afraid* of the traditional ceremonies," Alo said. "They are afraid of two things. The first is sex. They think maybe a woman will go off with a man who is not her husband. The second is religion. They think maybe the people will stop believing in God, and go back to animism."

From the time of their arrival in the early 20th century, Catholic missionaries and representatives of the Dutch colonial government tried to discourage traditional Kamoro ceremonies. But it was only in the late fifties, when the Dutch stepped up their efforts to govern what was then their last East Indies colony, that they had the influence and organization to ban ceremonies outright, and they did their best to do so. When Indonesia consolidated political control over the region in the late sixties, they continued the policy of the Dutch.

However there was a brief period, after the United Nations stepped in to hand over the region to Indonesia in 1962 and before political control was consolidated by Jakarta, when there was nobody to stop the Kamoro from holding *karapao, kaware,* and other festivals, Alo said. This period offered a kind of breathing space, during which ceremonies could again flourish.

The last *kaware* Alo saw was in 1968, in the neighboring village of Ipiri. That same year, while he was in boarding school in Kokonao, the Indonesian government, police, and military began cracking down in earnest on traditional ceremonies. Beginning again at that time, a village once again could no longer openly build a *karapao* or erect a *mbitoro.*

Thirty years later, things have changed. No single event seems to have precipitated this change; it was gradual, and may simply reflect the increasingly tolerant and understanding attitudes of the new generations staffing the government, military, and clergy. Apollo outlined the current, government-sanctioned approach to ceremonies:

"A *kaware* that lasts two or three months? Well, you can't do that. But one that lasts a few weeks is no problem. As long as you pick a good time, for example school holidays, so the children won't miss school."

Marselus said he and the other village men would discuss holding a *kaware* for us, and he would let us know the result in the morning. Although he showed very little emotion himself, the other men were visibly excited. We had unpacked one of the cartons of pouch tobacco, a necessary precursor for any ceremony. The men were happily chatting and smoking fat, tapered joints of shag *tembakau.* Apollo and Alo stayed awake to catch up on all the news, but Kal and I were exhausted. We went to bed without any worries about what the result would be.

P ARIPI, LIKE ALL villages in the rural tropics, wakes early. Or at least half of Paripi does. Even before the sky was fully bright, I could hear the sounds of women chopping wood as they prepared their breakfast fires. Once these were lit they took bundles of palm ribs, like a broom without a broomstick, and swept the sand around their houses free of leaf litter and cigarette butts. Paripi, like the other coastal Kamoro villages, is built on a strip of clean, white sand. White, of course, shows every crumb.

Very hospitably the *kepala dusun,* Ladislaus Yaota, offered us his house to stay in. The *kepala dusun* is a leadership position ranking under the *kepala desa.* Other than the small wooden plaque bearing his title that has been mounted to the right of the door, Ladislaus's house is the same as the others in the village, and is a typical example of Kamoro village architecture.

The house is of post-and-beam construction, with the load-bearing members being sturdy, hand-hewn lengths of local hardwood. It has only a single story, and is raised about a meter off the sand on posts as insurance against the occasional freak high tide. The entire structure is maybe nine meters long and four meters deep, with a kitchen area, two meters wide, extending another three or four meters out the back. The kitchen has a roof, but no walls. The fire pit is at the end of this extension furthest from the house.

The walls are made from the stiff ribs of palm fronds, stacked vertically and packed tightly together. The material looks like split bamboo, but without the knuckles, and makes a remarkably light-tight wall. The floors are joisted with sapling tree trunks, and the flooring itself is made of bark, split and pounded flat into strips. No attempt is made either to fasten or join the strips of flooring. A dropped pen or cigarette lighter quickly falls through, and occasionally the leg of one of the benches would get caught between the strips, and teeter wildly. The benefits of this springy, comfortable surface far outweigh these small inconveniences, however. A woven mat or two thrown over this floor makes a perfectly fine surface for sleeping, and was a real comfort compared to the concrete or hardwood floors in the more "modern" buildings where we often stayed.

Ladislaus's house had no distinct rooms, but a kind of partial divider of the same material as the walls separated the sleeping areas, which made it easier to fall asleep with the pressure lantern still burning in the main area. One main door opened to the front of the house and, shotgun shack style, another opened to the kitchen behind. Leading up to the front door was a short staircase or stoop of four broad planks. This stoop was a popular place to sit and talk during our stay, and particularly after dinner, when our pressure lantern created an oasis of light around it, the front stoop was always occupied.

Unfortunately, the penultimate plank was not well fastened. We soon learned to sit gingerly upon it, but visitors had to learn on their own. At least once a night, while we were inside eating or talking, we would hear a great crash, followed by at least two minutes of laughter. I once asked Alo to help me find a couple of nails so I could fix the damn thing, but he didn't think it was worth bothering with. Secretly, I think he didn't want to spoil such a reliable source of comedy.

About two-thirds of Ladislaus's house is roofed in corrugated sheets of galvanized steel, the other third in traditional sago thatch. Some houses in the village are all thatch, and others all steel. Steel roofing is provided by subsidy from the district government. When and if the roofing arrives, and how much is delivered, seem to be based on a complex calculus of population, village performance in public works and election mat-

KARAPAO BUILDING, HIRIPAU.
The village is close enough to Timika that most of its roofs are steel. In the background is the Wania River.

ters, personal connections, and perhaps just luck. Stacked next to the house of the *kepala desa* of Ipiri, Paripi's neighboring village, were about a dozen sheets of the material. He was expecting a rather larger delivery. Since twelve sheets weren't enough to roof even a single house, they sat there on the sand while he tried to figure out what to do with them. The material was of an extremely low grade, and the steel seemed not much thicker than oven foil. There could not have been a lot of zinc on them either, as the first tiny patches of rust were already showing up, and the roofing had only been sitting there a few weeks.

Galvanized roofing is one of the great irritations in Kal's life. In the twenty years he has been working in rural Indonesia, he has seen more and more of the material creep into his photographs. I have to agree with him that aesthetically, the material does seem to have the power to turn a neat and attractive little village into something more like a shantytown. Home-owners like steel, however, because like aluminum siding in the United States of the fifties, it promises to be a permanent solution. No more replacing the thatch every few years. There is nothing permanent about the thin gauge steel, however, and my guess is that the worst of it wouldn't even last as long as good thatch.

Steel roofs are also considered a sign of progress or prestige. One often hears that they are more sanitary than "insect-ridden" thatch. However, some develop-ment experts say that thatch, which is stripped and discarded or burned every few years, is actually more sanitary than steel, because the disease vectors are regularly destroyed. In areas where rainwater is col-lected for drinking, quality steel roofing has a definite advantage over thatch, but most of the Kamoro get their water from wells. And if you ever try to have a conversation under a steel roof during a pelting rain-storm, or try to nap under one on a hot afternoon, you quickly wish that your host had opted for thatch.

At the time of our visit, three hundred and eleven people lived in Paripi. Population figures are kept religiously by the village secretary, and the one piece of information every *kepala desa* knows is the official head count for his village. Paripi's population is about average for a Kamoro village.

Paripi is adjacent to Ipiri (pop. 322), and the "main street" of both villages is a continuous strip of sand. A bit over a kilometer from Paripi, along a path through the coconut groves, is another village, Yaraya (pop. 285). These three villages, though distinct, constitute a village cluster called Ipaya. This is a particularly nice acronym because it recapitulates the actual geography of the villages: in the west, or left, *I*piri, then *Pa*ripi, and finally, *Ya* raya. Apollo said he came up with "Ipaya" himself some years ago.

A VILLAGE LIKE PARIPI, although full of clean, well-built houses and with a healthy, close-knit population that has plenty of sago and fish to eat, would show up in any government's statistics as impoverished. As a province, Irian Jaya is not the nation's poorest, with a per capita income 35–40 percent higher than that for for Indonesia overall. This kind of comparison is not always useful, however. In Irian Jaya there is a marked disparity between urban and rural incomes, and Indonesian government statistics rate 78 percent of the province's villages as "poor." These are chiefly the smallest villages.

Nobody keeps income statistics at the village level, but a seat-of-the-pants estimate by Alo of the average monthly cash income of a family head in Paripi, or any of the other coastal villages, was Rp 25,000 to Rp 30,000, or a bit more than a hundred dollars a year. This is poverty, of course, but it takes a form very different from what one sees in Jakarta or in New York City. Money is something that is not absolutely essential here. The basic needs of the villagers in Paripi are provided by the sago orchards, the village gardens of manioc and vegetables, and the rich rivers and inland forest. Cash is used to buy treats like tobacco, sugar, and coffee, clothing, and the occasional tool, such as an axe or a wok.

Paripi villagers earn money by taking products to the market in Kokonao. The shopkeepers there will buy dried sharkfins for Rp 8,000–Rp 10,000 a kilo, depending on quality, as well as some dried and salted fish. Fresh sago sells well in the morning market at Kokonao, with its relatively large population of schoolteachers and other immigrants, who have no local sago collecting rights of their own, as do crabs (Rp 500 per crab) and lobsters (even more, depending on size). Government officials and the Catholic Church—which supplies its staff and students in boarding school—are also good customers.

Once in a while, a family or a group of families from Paripi will take a load of live crabs or other produce to Kokonao, sell it, and spend a couple of days shopping in the little stores there. There is no store, or even a *kios* ("kiosk") in Paripi. This is true of most villages, although it is not uncommon for a village schoolteacher, who travels regularly to Kokonao to pick up his government paycheck, to keep a little shelf of treats for sale. The Ekagi schoolteacher living in Paripi sells sugar, coffee, and student items like pencils and pads of paper.

When Apollo was still a boy, the area enjoyed a lively trade in the plumes of the greater bird of paradise, *Paradisaea apoda.* During a relatively short, yearly mating season, the males of these spectacular

Fig. 4.2
BIRD OF PARADISE. Prepared skin and plumes of *Paradisaea apoda.*

birds, which live only in New Guinea, grow beautiful white and yellow nuptial plumes behind their wings. It is in this form that they were sought for their skins. The dealers were Chinese, from Kaimana or Dobo, in the Aru Islands, and would regularly stop at the larger villages of the Kamoro coast to buy the skins. Apollo's father, as a way to see the world, sometimes accompanied a friend who was a dealer in the skins, sailing with him as far as Kaimana.

Plumes and dried skins from paradise birds have been an important trade product from the region for at least five hundred years. Historian Pamela Swadling, in her 1996 *Plumes from Paradise,* argues that the trade is in fact much older. Taking as evidence the appearance in New Guinea of pottery and betel, Swadling argues that the plumes were traded even 6,000 years ago. The earliest buyers were the wealthy courts of Asia, but by the 19th century the plumes became an important product in Europe and the United States, thanks to the demands of the millinery trade.

Today, when even a farmed mink coat may get its owner tagged with spray paint, wearing a hat made of the showy plumes of a very rare and highly protected bird seems almost impossible to imagine. It is also difficult to conceive of just how valuable these feathers were. Plume hunters, at the height of the feather craze, were seeking a product no less valuable than gold or gemstones. According to Swadling, the wholesale price of first-quality greater bird of paradise plumes in London was $21.00 to $24.60 a plume, depending on color. This was a great deal of money in 1913. The demand peaked between 1905 and 1915, and Swadling estimates that during this period thirty to eighty thousand dried bird of paradise skins reached the feather auctions of Paris, London and Amsterdam.

A movement to protect the birds began even in the mid-19th century, and the history of today's conservation movement began with the chiefly upper-class protest against killing birds for feathered hats. The profits were great, however, and most European governments resisted legislation until demand tapered off after World War I. The Dutch ban on paradise bird hunting in Netherlands New Guinea came about in 1924, and this protection has been continued by the Indonesian government. The legislation has ended large-scale legal bird hunting, but skins and even live specimens continue to be sold, chiefly in the domestic market. A stuffed *Paradisaea apoda,* perched on a branch, is a common souvenir for a visitor to bring back to western Indonesia, although the shops are getting a little less bold about displaying such items.

In the past, crocodile skins were another source of village income, again despite their legal protection, although the population crashed in the mid-eighties, making them not worth the effort to hunt. In 1960 Dutch New Guinea exported $527,000 worth of dried crocodile belly flats; in 1980 just $50,000 in skin exports were reported for Irian Jaya. Today, in the

Engel Mayaraiku and his daughter, Paripi.

KASPAR MATAKEYAU, ATUKA.
The coconuts at Atuka were planted with the encouragement of the Dutch colonial government.

Kamoro area at least, the crocodile population seems to be rebounding. This was helped by a very high tide in spring 1997 that flooded part of Kokonao, including a crocodile farm one of the village merchants had established there. He kept hundreds of juvenile and adult crocodiles, many of which escaped in the high water.

Coconut trees line the narrow path from Paripi to Yaraya, planted in neat rows about six or eight trees deep. These belong to the people of Paripi. The bark of the first tree in each row has been cut slightly with a *parang,* and a banner of coconut frond tucked into the nick. Each of these bits of frond are cut in a slightly different way to identify the person who owns the row. Coconuts are almost never stolen, and to do so would be a major transgression. Fresh coconut, either the sweet water of a young nut, or the soft meat of a slightly older one, is eaten daily in Paripi. The coconuts are also left to mature, and then the meat is dried to yield a product called copra, from which coconut oil is extracted.

In 1885 Lever Brothers discovered that copra could replace tallow—animal fat—in the making of soap, and produced their first coconut-based product, Sunlight soap. This innovation, writes Swadling, led to a new demand for copra worldwide. Estate farming of coconuts began on the Dutch side of New Guinea in 1919 when the Maatschappij Kelapa, the Coconut Society, took out a lease near Merauke. This was the first Dutch business in their New Guinea colony. Around the same time Chinese merchants, who had made money trading in birds of paradise and other forest products, began to lease land for coconut plantations in the Fakfak area.

Later, when the colonial government became established, representatives encouraged each village to plant coconuts. The seedlings came from a government plantation on Kilimala, a small island just in front of Kaimana. Paripi's coconut groves from this period were near the village's former location on the other side of the river, and were cut down some years ago. But at Alo's village of Atuka, he said, the coconut plantation is still called "Kilimala" because of the source of its seedlings.

The price of copra collapsed in the 1950s, and although prices rise on occasion, they are currently low enough to make it hardly worth the effort of harvesting and drying the nuts. During my entire visit in the Kamoro area, I saw drying copra on only two occasions, and these were very small quantities.

WHEN WE FIRST arrived at Paripi, we found the beach full of families living in small *pondoks*, or lean-to shelters. These families, I was surprised to learn, were from Paripi and Ipiri, and their permanent houses were just a few minute's walk from the *pondoks*. Why, I asked Alo, are they living on the beach? "They're still on holiday," he said.

These were the families that had gone to Kokonao for the Indonesian Independence Day festivities, where they had camped on the sandbar just inside the river mouth. Apparently, they had had such a good time camping that even though they had since returned home, they decided to keep sleeping out on the beach. Since the weather was unseasonably dry, and there were almost no mosquitoes around, I could see their point. Still, it seemed about the same as setting up a tent in your own backyard. By the end of a week, everyone had trickled back to regular village life and the *pondoks* had been dismantled.

Many of the families out on the beach were working on new canoes. These are dugouts, usually about five meters long, and just wide enough to comfortably accommodate a seated adult. The new vessels were in various stages of completion—some merely roughed out, others smoothed to a thin shell, and still others, already burned black, with just a bit of whitewashing and some finish carving around the prowhead to complete. One canoe, newly carved, had already acquired a serious crack along the bottom. The owner was carefully stapling this tight using nails hammered into the shape of a "U." The new wood is particularly prone to cracking as it dries, and the men keep their canoes covered with coconut fronds and leafy branches during the hottest part of the day.

In time all the canoes crack, and some of the older ones seem to be kept afloat more by their patches than the original wood. Bits of cloth, wadded up and mixed with sap, are pressed into the larger injuries and thin cracks are sutured with handmade staples. Extensive repairs are shielded from further damage by tacking on a bit of sheet steel or even plastic. Some of the vessels have been repaired so often that they look twenty years old. In fact, these warhorses are probably just two or three years old, and most families replace their canoe every year.

The canoes being carved in Paripi are a style called *torupa* ("*tor*-pah"). This design accommodates seated paddlers, and the points of the prow and stern finish with a raised decoration, an abstraction of a man's head. This ornament, called *utiriumi,* represents the man in profile, facing inward toward the passengers rather than outward. His nose, like in the old days, is pierced. Because one sits down to row this canoe, small ledges are carved into the inside to take seats. Also, at the bottom of the canoe under the first seat from the front, a round mortise is carved to take a mast for a small sail. This has the special name *moporo,* literally the vessel's "belly button."

The *torupa* canoes are associated with the western Kamoro areas. Another style, associated with the east, is the *ku-oko* ("*kwoh*-koh"). This canoe, designed to take standing paddlers, has no seats, and each of the sharp ends terminates in a flat, carved "duckbill."

Unlike the short, plain paddles used in the *torupa,* the paddles used in the *ku-oko* are embellished with

CANOE PADDLE, ATUKA.
This appears to be a woman's paddle.

carvings, and gendered. These paddles are long, with a slightly spoon-like blade. A woman's paddle is decorated on the concave side, and she paddles against the convex side, using short, shallow strokes. A man's paddle is decorated on the convex side, and he paddles against the concave side, using long, deep strokes.

Strangely, although the *torupa* is now a western style and the *ku-oko* eastern, the Kamoro insist that the origins of these designs is just the opposite. The story begins, Apollo told me, with two sisters.

One sister lived in the west, and the other in the east. The one from the west paddled her canoe, a *ku-oko,* to the east, where she joined her sister and the other women of the village to collect sago. She spent a few days pounding sago, and then was ready to return. She liked her sister's canoe, which was *torupa,* and decided to steal it. While the other women were sleeping, she crept away from the village, and paddled home in her sister's *torupa,* leaving her *ku-oko* behind. In the morning the women saw what she had done, but they had also been coveting her *ku-oko.* From this point on, the westerners made *torupa,* and the easterners, *ku-oko.*

It is unclear exactly when this original switch took place, but over the last century and a half, the *torupa* style has become increasingly popular, and its use has been moving further and further east. The first pho-

tographs of the Kamoro, taken by the 1828 Dutch *Triton* expedition, show a group of canoes at "Utanata," now the dual villages of Uta and Mupuruka. All of the canoes are *ku-oko,* the eastern style.

By the time Alo and Apollo were boys in the 1950s, they said, the *torupa* dominated from Lakahia Bay to Uta. Uta to Kokonao, which includes Paripi, was a kind of transition area, with both styles being built. From Kokonao eastward, the standing *ku-oko* style dominated. Today the *torupa* has made even more progress, and I did not see a single *ku-oko* west of Kokonao. The transition area seems now to be around Timika Pantai and Atuka, where the *torupa* is continuing to make inroads.

Pouwer reports that the spread of the seated style canoe was helped just after the turn of the century by a sago shortage among the western villages. The band of land suitable for sago is much narrower in the west, and the really broad alluvial plain doesn't start until about Uta. In exchange for rights to collect sago in the rich stands belonging to the villages of the east, the people of the west built canoes for them. These, of course, were *torupa.* These kinds of *aopao* exchanges still go on today. Alo was in Ipiri in 1968 and remembers that nobody in the village had to build their own canoes that year. They got them from Porauka, in exchange for sago gathering rights.

THE MOST DRAMATIC stage in making a dugout canoe is when it is burned. Burning helps seal the outside of the canoe and, with the addition of some water, steams the wood so it becomes flexible enough to be propped open without cracking. Kal wanted to get some photographs, so we arranged with a man on the beach to observe him burning his canoe. He intended to burn his canoe later in the afternoon when the wind died down, and said he would come get us when he was ready to begin.

Around four o'clock the man came and rounded us up, and we followed him out to the beach. His canoe, however, had already been burned. It had opened up nicely, and was straight and perfectly shaped. This, he said, was thanks to the use of a special small leaf, which he called an "anti-Setan." Satan certainly seemed not to have botched his effort, and I didn't see a single crack. The canoe next to it, which had been burned two days before, displayed a nasty, meter-long crack down its side. This was a source of great chagrin to its owner, who for the past two days had been trying to figure out how to repair such a major flaw.

Our friend apologized for the "misunderstanding" that caused us to miss the event of the burning. I am convinced that, upon thinking it over, he decided not to risk jinxing his efforts by having an audience for the burning. I don't blame him, either. If I had spent a week of hard work hacking out this log, I wouldn't do anything to endanger the final, most delicate operation. I'd throw some salt over my shoulder, knock wood, and toss a bit of anti-Setan in there as well.

A bit later we found someone else ready to burn a canoe, and he and his helpers were happy to perform for the camera. A canoe-burning always attracts a few onlookers, but with Kal's flash popping off, and Alo feeding him cameras and lenses and fresh film, and Apollo explaining the details to me while I scribbled in my notebook, and with our usual entourage of about two dozen children, we created a respectable little crowd as soon as we arrived. Nothing attracts attention like a crowd, of course, and pretty soon a simple canoe-burning began to look more like a Hollywood opening.

Despite the late hour, a bit of wind was still coming off the water, which worried the men enough that they moved the canoe back off the beach and erected a small windbreak of coconut fronds.

The first step in burning a canoe is to boil some water, using the canoe as the vessel. The inside of the canoe is filled with dry fronds and branches—a huge stack of these is prepared earlier—and set on fire. Once the fire gets good and hot, water is poured in, unleashing great plumes of steam. The now hot water, to which some mud is often added, is swirled around the inside of the canoe with branches to soften the wood.

Once the inside has been softened, dry fronds and branches are stacked along the outside edges and set ablaze. The heat from this fire dries the outer layer of wood, causing it to tighten up a bit relative to the steamed inside layer, and if all goes well, the sides of the canoe spread gently apart. Sometimes the process has to be repeated. Once the men decide that the canoe is as open as it will get, they prop it into position with stakes and allow it to cool down.

Unfortunately, all did not go according to plan with the canoe-burning we watched in Paripi. The inside heated up nicely, and when the water was good and hot, the outside was lit. As it heated up, the wood hissed and creaked, and, like some kind of live thing, the canoe twisted itself into a shape that first looked like a peanut, and then later seemed to settle into something more like an "S." The men kept adding water and re-lighting the sides, so many times in fact that they started getting live coals on the side of the canoe. I felt bad for them, and I think they may have been a bit embarrassed to have had such a poor result in front of so many spectators.

Eventually they gave up on the fire and the owner, a man with great ropy muscles in his arms and chest, called for some stakes and his axe. Grabbing the still smoldering wood with his bare hands, he began pulling and propping and staking and hammering the reluctant wood into shape. He was still working as darkness fell and we all drifted home to dinner.

The next morning the canoe really didn't look too bad. But sitting there, on dry ground, I couldn't help thinking that it was somehow under tension, like a great wooden spring. I imagined it hitting the water

SHAPING A CANOE, TIMIKA PANTAI.
Moses Tiriyu and Gabriel Yauniyuta, behind Moses, are working.

and immediately snapping back into that first crooked shape.

THE MORNING AFTER our arrival in Paripi, as we had hoped, Marselus said that he and the other leaders would be happy to stage a *ku-kaware* for us. The only complication, and it wasn't a major one, was that they would need a few days to go gather sago, so there would be plenty of food during the activities. This was perfect for us, because after a few more days in Paripi we planned to head west to Lakahia, the furthest edge of Kamoro territory. By the time we returned, the men would have gathered all the sago they needed. We gave the men a case of tobacco, an important symbolic token of the initiation of a ceremonial cycle as well as a real treat, and a couple of kilos of sugar and coffee. Smokes, coffee, and sugar—the universal trinity of the working man.

Since coming to the Kamoro area, one of the things I had been trying to understand was the nature of traditional leadership here. The men of Paripi who made the decision about whether or not to hold a *ku-kaware* for us were, in some cases, traditional leaders. These are men whose advice would be sought on important matters, and whose instructions would be followed without question. Every village has a *kepala desa,* or

EDMUNDUS MINAYAU AND HIS SON, GABRIEL, AT A CAMP NEAR ATUKA.

village head, but the man who holds this position is chosen by the head of the regional government. *Kepala desa*s aren't necessarily traditional leaders, and in most cases they are not.

Anthropologists and other western commentators call traditional leaders in Melanesia and New Guinea "Big Men." Although it probably comes straight from pidgin, I have never liked this term, which sounds to me like academic baby talk. More recently anthropologist Maurice Godelier has suggested a distinction between Big Men and what he calls "Great Men," the latter being leaders in systems where exchange is less competitive and more equivalent than in so-called Big Men societies. Whether one calls them Big Men or Great Men—and Kamoro society, it seems to me, shows elements of both poles of Godelier's typology—the salient point is that these individuals hold their position by force of character rather than by winning some kind of election, or through hereditary right. The Kamoro call men like this *weyaiku-we;* or, in the singular, a *we weyaiku.*

"A *we weyaiku* is a social leader; he must get along with the people," Alo said. "He is like the godfather in the movie. He has a lot of power, but he also has to be generous, and give away things. The position is not inherited. There can be many in a village, or there can be none. It can also be a very temporary position."

In the earliest period of Dutch colonialism, the officers had very little understanding of traditional leadership structures in western New Guinea. At the few villages where the government had any presence, the Dutch chose men who had some relationship with traders—and thus spoke a bit of the Malay language—for their representatives. These were rarely *weyaiku-we.* In the period following World War II, particularly after the efforts of anthropologists like Pouwer, indigenous leadership structures became better understood, and the Dutch tried to pick a *we weyaiku* for village head. When Indonesia took over the governing of the region in the 1960s, this knowledge was forgotten, and village leaders were chosen through political party channels and other government systems of patronage.

What Alo and Apollo call the "true" *we weyaiku* is today almost extinct. Maybe three men in all of the Kamoro area, they said, still deserve the title: Yohanes Kapiyau in Kaokonao; Paulus Weyatoa Takati in Poraoka; and Yosef Tanama in Potowai-Buru. The introduction of the Indonesian government leadership structure, the opportunities presented by education to work in other cities and provinces, and the new cash economy—which has created a type of *nouveau riche* leader—have all contributed to the decline of the *we weyaiku.*

"All the famous ones are dead," Alo said. "This is why the Kamoro don't retain the discipline of traditional life."

Plenty of men still call themselves *we weyaiku.* They may even be leaders, but always with a limited and local reputation. A true leader, of course, doesn't have to call attention to the fact, and while self-promoting imposters are tolerated, they certainly aren't respected. The term can also have a more generic, or limited meaning, a kind of lowercase *we weyaiku.*

"You didn't notice," Apollo said, "but when we first came to Paripi and talked to my brother about the *ku-kaware,* people in the crowd were holding up their thumbs and whispering, 'Ah, new *weyaiku-we.*' This was because of all the attention we were giving the people, and the cigarettes and coffee and such that we were giving away."

But a real *we weyaiku,* Alo said, has a reputation among all Kamoro. He listed some men who were *we weyaiku* in the old mold, all of whom have been dead twenty or thirty years: Pius Nanipia from Paripi; Wameta from Ipiri; Tai from Keakwa; Mamo from Timika Pantai; and Tamatipia from Atuka.

"If you go to Potowai-Buru, far in the west, and ask the first man you meet, 'Do you know of Tamatipia?' he will say, 'Yes, of course,'" Alo said. "Tamatipia was from Atuka, almost two hundred kilometers from Potowai, and he died thirty years ago. Now *that's* a *we weyaiku.*"

EVEN ON OUR second day in Paripi it became noticeable that our presence there was causing some tension with the neighboring village of Ipiri. It was quite obvious to the leaders of Ipiri that we should be staying in their village. Basically, they felt insulted—or jealous—that we chose Paripi instead. Paripi, in their minds, is a latecomer. Ipiri is the original, or "true" village here, and has the more senior sago ownership. The leaders of Paripi, of course, hold a somewhat different opinion.

We decided on Paripi because it was Apollo's home village, and because the people of Paripi still have the knowledge and materials (Marselus's *mbi-kao* mask) to hold the *ku-kaware.* Although Ipiri is a perfectly nice village, there is no *mbi-kao* mask there. Since Alo has some friends and a cousin in Ipiri, with whom he would visit for an hour or so each night, he had to listen to most of this grumbling.

The main path through Ipiri village is a good four meters narrower than the same path when it reaches Paripi. Once, as Apollo and I were walking through Ipiri, I joked that the houses there must be closer together than those of Paripi because the people of Ipiri like each other better.

"Oh no," he said, smiling. "It's because they're afraid."

"What do you mean, 'afraid?'"

It seems, Apollo told me, that a ghost regularly appears at night at the westernmost end of Ipiri village. It has been showing up there for a long time, usually in a little clearing just at the beginning of the coconut groves and, perhaps appropriately, not very far from the village cemetery.

One night the village policeman saw a man he didn't recognize standing in the clearing. He called out to him and asked him to identify himself. The man answered, "Lun." The policeman approached him, to find out why he was there, but without any apparent movement of his legs, the stranger drifted back exactly the distance the policeman moved forward. The policeman shouted at him to stay put, but his efforts to approach continued to be thwarted. Finally, in frustration, he drew his gun and shot him. The bullet, of course, had no effect on a spirit. Seeing this, the policeman quickly returned to the village. He spoke with the Kei Islander teacher, and told him to tell the people there is a spirit in the grove, and its name is "Lun."

Apollo insists that he doesn't believe a word of this story and Alo, if pressed, would say it's folklore as well. Still, Alo in particular is not keen on these sorts of discussions. "It's not healthy," is how he put it. Especially, I suppose, if the subject is raised while you are walking along that very same path, well after dusk has faded to night, just after you have passed the village graveyard.

A variety of spirits occupy the Kamoro world, and they can be assigned to two broad categories: the *roh nener,* or "family spirits" and the *roh umum,* "general," or in some sense, "public" spirits. These are Indonesian language terms; the Kamoro language tends to be quite specific when referring to spirits, and doesn't offer broad categories. The man who applied the anti-Setan to his canoe before burning it was actually appeasing, or trying to be respectful of, the family spirits called *ku we. Ku we* means nothing more than canoe (*ku*) people (*we*). The linguistic convention of calling spirits "people," Apollo said, is a form of respect. For example, the *ameta we* are the spirits that look after the health of the sago groves. Nobody imagines that they have the materiality of a human being, but they are considered to be alive, like a person, and are therefore euphemized as the "sago people."

To Alo and Apollo, both Catholic, both very well educated, and both culturally fluent in the cosmopolitan world of Timika, these spirits, while not exactly meaningless superstition, act at a very low and unthreatening level. Like making a wish on a birthday cake, carrying a lucky charm, or picking a lottery number based on the birth dates of your children. Alo and Apollo certainly understand the place of spirits in the larger web of Kamoro culture, but I think both men, who don't get out into the villages much anymore, were surprised by just how strong these beliefs remain.

A single well serves both Ipiri and Paripi, and it is located right on the border between the two villages. Technically it is in neither village, which seems like a wise form of insurance against any potential quarrels. The water is clear and fresh, and appears less than two meters down. Even so, most of the women in both

YULIANA APAREYAU, TIMIKA PANTAI.
Preparing offerings for the second stage of the *karapao* ceremony.

villages once in a while feel the need to leave a small offering—a bit of tobacco, a bit of food—to the *roh umum* of the well in order to ward off *kadas*. This stubborn and disfiguring disease, a fungus called *Tinea versicolor,* causes its victims to develop scaly white skin. It is not uncommon in the Kamoro villages, and some cases are so bad that just looking at the poor person can make your own skin itch. (Despite appearances, however, it seldom makes its victims itch.) Now that I think of it, I don't remember seeing any cases of tinea in Paripi.

At one point, after we had been in Paripi for a while, Apollo told me that some of the older people in the village thought that Kal and I were ancestral spirits that had returned. At first I thought he was teasing me, and I scoffed.

"Oh no, it's a little bit true, that's what they say," he said. "It's like a 'cargo cult,' I guess."

It seems that when the ancestral spirits, called *maitemiwe,* return, they bring goods of some kind, and perhaps even our seemingly modest largess—tobacco, coffee, sugar, money for our lodging and food—was enough to convince some of the older people that we were these spirits. Apollo also speculated that the reason we were thus mistaken was because we ate Kamoro food—sago, crabs, and fish. Since nobody could recall other human outsiders doing that, the only category left for us was returning ancestors. Must be the reason we're so light-skinned, I said, is that we've been out of the sun for so long.

"I know it's funny," Apollo said, "but I'm not joking."

Once when Alo and I were walking through Ipiri, an old woman who had known him as a child came up to him. They embraced, and spoke for a bit. The woman didn't address me, or even look at me, which seemed strange. As we walked on, Alo looked at the ground and shook his head slowly.

"Do you know what she said? She said, 'How is your father?' She meant *you!* She knows my father is dead. She thinks you're my father come back."

"But Alo, I'm obviously too young to be your father."

"No, no. You don't understand. If my father's going to come back, he's going to come back as his younger self. Wouldn't you?"

We tried to joke about it, but finally were unsuccessful. The encounter was unnerving. As if a fortune teller, without making eye contact, had instructed me to look after my health. Or as if a stranger, his face bright with recognition, ran up to me on the street, only to turn away at the last minute, suddenly afraid.

123

CHAPTER FIVE

Bread from a Tree

Marvelous, Maligned Sago

NE OF THE things that surprised me most upon leaving Timika was how much the quality of the food improved. Scattered small restaurants in town do an adequate job with basics like fried rice, but even at the restaurant of the four-star Sheraton Inn, the food is no better than mediocre. But when we were out in the Kamoro villages, more often than not, we ate like kings. Great plates of steaming mangrove crabs. Crispy slabs of fatty catfish. Oysters. Clams. Tangy fried manioc leaf. And lots of fresh, chewy sago.

Before he died, the great Irish humorist Brian O'Nolan began writing a book in which a philanthropic American woman decides to solve Ireland's problems by introducing an exotic crop, one that promises to be more reliable than the potato, which had so famously let Hibernia down a century before. Actually, since this is a book by O'Nolan—writing, as usual, under the name Flann O'Brien—it quickly transpires that this woman's philanthropy is of a curious type. Her interest, as she puts it, is in "American health, liberty and social cleanliness," and she cares less about helping the Irish than about helping the Irish stay in Ireland. The crop with which she proposes to do this is the sago tree.

I don't know why O'Nolan never finished *Slattery's Sago Saga*, but my instincts suggest that when he began quoting Marco Polo at length on this curious tree he realized that he had struck what for the humorist can only be poison—something already so perfectly strange that there is, alas, no oxygen left for irony.

"And I will tell you another great marvel," writes Rustichello, in Henry Yule's edition of Marco Polo's travels. "They have a kind of trees that produce flour, and excellent flour it is for food. These trees are very tall and thick, but have a very thin bark, and inside the bark they are crammed with flour. And I tell you that

MARY LUISA MIYAMERO, EPENAUPO. While the others pound the pith, Mary washes out the starch. Her trough is made from the flanged lower section of a sago palm leaf base.

TIMIKA PANTAI. As the staple of life for the Kamoro, sago is of great ritual importance. During the *karapao*, this crate of sago starch will be flamboyantly chopped open and distributed.

Messer Marco Polo, who witnessed all this, related how he and his party did sundry times partake of this flour made into bread, and found it excellent."

There is something fantastical, particularly to a European used to temperate hardwood forests, about eating a tree. For Marco Polo, the sago trees he found in Sumatra, or "The Island of the Lesser Java," ranked with the Teeth of Buddha and men with tails as one of the "marvels" he encountered during his famous travels to the East in the last few decades of the 13th century.

But sago, for reasons that are not immediately apparent to me, is also the world's most frequently reviled staple food. Few visitors since have been as kind in their reports as was Marco Polo. "Tasteless," "gummy," "bland," "insipid," "gritty"—these adjectives appear over and over again in the accounts of travelers, explorers, and naturalists. Australian journalist John Ryan, describing Boven Digoel in his 1970 *The Hot Land,* can think of no better way to communicate the horror of conditions at this infamous Dutch colonial prison camp than by noting, "Some [prisoners], too lazy or disheartened, were even eating sago, the rubbery tasteless food of the native swamp-dweller."

To me, an unpleasant staple food is something like the bitter forms of manioc grown in the worst parts of the African thornscrub. No other crops will grow there. Sweet manioc or cassava, called *kasbi* in Irian Jaya, *singkong* in western Indonesia, and tapioca in the United States, is a nice enough thing to eat, like a white potato but, pleasantly, a little more chewy. Bitter manioc is very different. This plant produces tubers that are so full of cyanogenetic glucosides—cyanide, essentially—that not even a starving pig will eat them.

Before bitter manioc can be safely cooked and eaten, the roots must be peeled, crushed and then left to ferment for three days, or alternately, soaked for three days in several changes of water. When the rains are late, and the children are silent with hunger, some village women rush the preparation of their manioc porridge, with disastrous results. The effects of the poisoning begin with a strange twitching in their legs, and then paralysis sets in. The malady is called *konzo*. In Africa there are children, their legs spindly and twisted, who walk with a cane because of permanent neuromotor damage caused by improperly prepared manioc. That, to me, is an unpleasant staple.

Food has always been more than just something to eat. To the people who depend on it for their livelihood, a staple crop often becomes the center of a mythological narrative, such as the rice cults of Southeast Asia, or America's own powerfully symbolic "amber waves of grain." Outsiders also find food to be a convenient way to mock other nations and cultures, which explains the persistence of such terms as "Limeys" and "Frogs." Food can also be used to position other cultures on an imaginary ladder of advancing civilization. In the United States, the land of wheat and beef, some commentators a few decades back held the rice diet of the Chinese responsible for what they saw as a variety of political, social, and moral lapses. In the land of rice, sago can play the same role.

"One thing is certain," writes John Crawfurd in the entry on sago in his often cited *A Descriptive Dictionary of the Indian Islands & Adjacent Countries*, "that no nation of the Archipelago, of whom it has been the chief vegetable diet, has ever acquired any respectable amount of civilisation."

Crawfurd's *Dictionary* was published in 1856, but things are little different today. While researching this book, I had the following conversation with a young medical field worker from South Sumatra:

"Have you tried sago?" he asked.

"Yes, of course."

"Do you like it?"

"Oh, very much. And you?"

"Uh, I don't know. I haven't tried it."

I was shocked. We were in Keakwa, where he was on a monthly visit to test and treat the people for malaria. He had been working in the Kamoro area for almost two years, and had never once eaten sago. He actually said "belum," which literally means "not yet," but this word is nothing more than a kind of linguistic politesse. If you asked a polite Indonesian if he'd been to the moon, he'd say, "Belum." After a pause to shape his thoughts accurately into English, he said, rather seriously:

"The Kamoro are advancing. Now they want to eat rice."

I am sure this statement was made with only the best intentions. I spent a day and a half with him and the other members of the malaria control team, and as far as I could tell they all enjoy their work, and have a genuine sympathy for their Kamoro patients. I saw no other signs of a judgmental or paternalistic attitude on his part. But I think to him, a western Indonesian raised on rice, eating sago is a bit like testing positive for the *Plasmodium* parasite—an unfortunate, but treatable condition.

Perhaps it is easier for an American or European, used to eating wheat bread, to appreciate sago. One reason its reputation suffers so much in these parts is that the comparison is always made to rice. The most rice-like version of sago, in which grated and moistened sago flour is tossed in a hot pan to produce small "grains" of cooked sago, is frankly a weak dish. Sago should properly be considered a "loaf" or "cake." Although rice cake or *lontong*—a kind of sticky rice packed into a tube and cooked until it is chewy—might be usefully compared to it, sago is really a type of bread.

The single most common criticism of sago is that it has no discernable taste. This is not strictly true. Fresh, properly cooked sago does have a faint taste, but it is difficult to describe, and very subtle. It is more a scent, something like the clean, botanical essence that comes from a green leaf snapped in two. Only in the best and freshest sago will this be noticed, and more commonly sago tastes slightly sour, even unpleasantly so if the sago is very old. But a discussion of the flavor of sago misses the point, because fundamentally sago is an investigation of texture.

Sago gives the cook a remarkable range of consistencies to work with, from something as viscous as glue to something as dry and hard as pressed cinder. The savvy cook will know how, and under what circumstances, to use heat and water to release these textures. If she is really skilled, she will know how to combine them.

One of my favorite early descriptions of sago comes from Captain Thomas Forrest. In the late 18th century, Forrest, working for the British East Indies company, captained a small ship called the *Tartar Galley* on a clandestine mission to look for sources of spices outside of Dutch control, particularly in the Raja Ampat islands and the Bird's Head of New Guinea. Forrest never found spices in any appreciable quantity, but the maps and descriptions he left behind are excellent, and proved valuable for explorers and navigators for at least the next hundred years. Forrest personally liked sago very much, and the following passage from his 1779 *A Voyage to New Guinea* makes it clear he understood that the key to this wonderful food is its texture.

> The sago bread, fresh from the oven, eats just like hot rolls. I grew very fond of it, as did both my officers. If the baker hits his time, the cakes will be nicely browned on each side. If the heat be too great, the corners of the cakes will melt into a jelly, which, when kept, becomes hard and horny; and, if eat fresh, proves insipid. When properly baked, it is in a kind of middle state, between raw and jellied.
>
> A sago cake, when hard, requires to be soaked in water, before it be eaten, it then softens and swells into a curd, like biscuit soaked; but, if eat without soaking (unless fresh from the oven) it feels disagreeable, like sand in the mouth.

In reading early accounts by explorers to New Guinea, I have always used whether or not the author genuinely liked to eat sago as a kind of litmus test to judge the accuracy and sympathy of his or her account. Forrest, who writes, "From experience, I equal the fresh baked sago bread to our wheatbread," certainly passes this test, and the rest of his account confirms his

ADRIANA UNUMPARE, PARIPI.
Tossing moistened sago in a hot, dry wok produces a dish something like a chewier form of grits.

powers of observation. Naturalist Alfred Russel Wallace, who was never a morning in Eastern Maluku or New Guinea without sago cakes to dip in his coffee, also passes the test, and he produced *The Malay Archipelago,* which has more than once been called the finest and most accurate travel account ever written.

LIKE RICE, SAGO is generally quite simple to prepare. The starch is first grated and mixed with a little water into a kind of dough, and then cooked in any of a variety of ways:

❡ Pressed into the bottom of a dry pan, and heated on both sides, to yield a kind of pancake. This can be thin, like a French crêpe, or thick, like Italian focaccia. If a waffle iron is used instead of a pan, the result is a sago waffle, and the irons typically stamp a cheerful little imprint of a flower or a heart in each quadrant.

❡ Tossed in a dry pan over the fire, which yields a kind of sago meal, or sago grits. A common, and much tastier, interpretation of this method is to mix in fresh grated coconut and a bit of salt.

❡ Pressed into "ingots" in a specially heated sago oven. This device looks like a multi-slice toaster, albeit one made of earthenware. The oven is first heated, and then moist dough is pressed into the hot slots. The sago cooks in just a couple of minutes, and the retained heat of the oven is good for a few rounds before it has to be returned to the fire.

❡ Roughly shaped into a ball or patty and set on the coals of the fire. This, of course, is the most traditional method, and goes back to the days when cooking utensils were nonexistent. Nobody would now cook their sago this way in the village, but when out hunting, gardening, or working in the sago orchards, this is the preferred method. To make adjustments to the cooking sago, the men fabricate a pair of tongs by skinning a bit of flexible bark and then folding it.

❡ Mixed with a lot of water and cooked down into a very viscous, almost transparent porridge or soup. This dish is unique. I am at a loss to think of anything remotely similar in the world of food, although an accurate, and very unflattering comparison to a certain bodily secretion could easily be made. Sampling this dish on Buru Island in the mid-eighteenth century, the French explorer Louis de Bougainville called it "abominable." Sago porridge is exceedingly difficult to serve, because once you spoon some into your bowl, the rest wants to follow.

My personal favorite is the pancake style, mixed with maybe a touch too much water and pressed thickly and not too evenly into the bottom of the pan. Straight from the heat, this yields a wonderful, chewy

129

EPENAUPO.
The pith of a sago tree, though fibrous, is not much harder than an unripe apple, and felling one is short work.

item that has no real equivalent in the world of starches. It has a crunchy, granular outside, and a gummy, almost transparent inside.

The most common style is probably the ingots, or I guess "loaves" or "biscuits" would be more flattering. These are baked in the oven, and are rectangular slabs, with a slight taper to the sides, to make them easier to extract. Forrest was describing sago loaves in the passage above, and later suggests that the best size to insure correct baking is that of "an ordinary octavo volume." This slightly archaic terminology refers to a book the size of a standard trade paperback. Tastes must have changed in the past two hundred years, because I didn't see any loaves of sago this large. The ones I encountered were the size of a sextodecimo volume—a little smaller, but a lot thicker, than a slice of toast. One of the most common sights in a Kamoro village is a child clutching a sago biscuit with a chunk of charred catfish on top.

Fig. 5.1 SAGO OVEN.

The loaves keep better than sago cooked any other way. When we left a village, we would have the flat style for breakfast, but would take loaves along to eat later for lunch. Even after several days they're still fine, although by then they are quite dry and consequently a bit of a burden to eat.

The literature makes much of how well sago keeps, but there seems to be a lot of misinformation on this point. Some commentators blithely suggest storage times of six months, and even years. Cooked and thoroughly dry sago, such as hard loaves or the pearled sago used in Chinese and Southeast Asian desserts, will certainly keep a very long time, but freshly harvested and cooked sago is a treat, like freshly baked bread, that doesn't travel well. Most Kamoro consider week-old sago to be past its prime. The dried or cooked and stored forms receive exactly the same consideration an American gives to a box of stale corn flakes in the cupboard, or a western Indonesian gives to government warehouse rice.

NUTRITIONALLY, SAGO SUFFERS in comparison to staple grains such as wheat or rice, and even to tubers like sweet potatoes, taro, or manioc. Though mostly starch, these other foodstuffs contain significant protein and vitamins. Sago, on the other hand, is almost laboratory pure carbohydrate. One hundred grams of dry sago yields 355 calories and contains, on average, 94 grams of carbohydrate, .2 grams of protein, .5 grams of dietary fiber, and a negligible amount of fat. This same one hundred grams, which when cooked yields a loaf about the size of two thick slices of bread, contains a bit of calcium (10 mg) and a small amount of iron (1.2 mg), but vitamins such as carotene, thiamine, and ascorbic acid are present in such small amounts as to be essentially unmeasurable.

A loaf of bread of a size yielding the same calories would contain, in addition, a reasonable amount of nutrition: 11.5 grams of protein, 3.1 grams of dietary fiber, and 3.1 grams of fat, as well as a number of important vitamins and minerals (See Fig. 5.2 below.)

Agronomists routinely become alarmed at the diets of traditional people who depend on low-protein staples like manioc and sago, calling them inadequate, or "poor man's diets." But if sufficient additional sources of protein are available, and in the rich waters and forest of the Kamoro lands they certainly are, sago is in no way a substandard staple.

Sago is, for example, a very energy rich food. In his

FOOD VALUE PER 100 g

	Water g	Energy cal	Protein g	Fat g	CARBOHYDRATE Total g	Starch g	Sugar g	FIBER Total g	NSP g
Sago DRIED	12.6	355	0.2	0.2	94.0	94.0	*tr.*	NA	0.5
Sweet potato ORANGE VARIETY	73.7	87	1.2	0.3	21.3	15.6	5.7	2.3	2.4
Manioc RAW	64.5	142	0.6	0.2	36.8	35.3	1.5	1.7	1.6
Rice POLISHED WHITE	11.7	361	6.5	1.0	86.8	86.8	*tr.*	2.2	0.5
Wheat FLOUR, WHITE	14.0	347	11.5	1.4	75.3	73.9	1.4	3.7	3.1

NUTRIENTS PER 100 g

	MINERALS Na mg	K mg	Ca mg	Fe mg	VITAMINS Carotene µg	E mg	B1 mg	B2 mg	C mg	Folate µg
Sago DRIED	3	5	10	1.2	0	*tr.*	*tr.*	*tr.*	0	*tr.*
Sweet potato ORANGE VARIETY	40	370	24	0.7	3,930*	4.6	.17	*tr.*	23	17
Manioc RAW	5	330	18	0.5	*tr.*	NA	.06	.02	31	19
Rice POLISHED WHITE	6	110	4	0.5	0	0.1	.08	[.02]	0	20
Wheat FLOUR, WHITE	3	130	140	2.1	0	0.3	.32	.03	0	31

* Carotene content of sweet potatoes: 1,820–16,000 µg/100g orange; 69 µg/100g white.

NSP, non starch polysaccharides; tr., traces only; NA, present but no data available; [ ], estimate; Na, sodium; K, potassium; Ca, calcium; Fe, iron; Carotene, β-carotene equivalent.

After J.G. Vaughan and C. A. Geissler, *The New Oxford Book of Food Plants*, 1997. Sources: Royal Society of Chemistry/MAFF (1991) and supplements (1988–1994).

Fig. 5.2 ANALYSIS OF FIVE STAPLES.

report to the Second International Sago Symposium in 1979, Lie Goan-Hong cites research in Papua New Guinea that found the daily calorie intake of an average adult male sago eater to be 3,600. This is more food energy than the average adult fish-and-chips-eating Englishman gets (3,317 calories), and the British don't seem to be starving. In fact most nutritionists, who suggest we eat 1,500 to 3,000 calories a day depending on our activity level, would say the British eat at least 1,000 calories a day too many.

The composition of one's entire diet matters much more than an isolated analysis of the staple. One would

PAULINUS MAPUWARIPI, EPENAUPO.

be much better off eating a well-balanced, 3,600-calorie diet based on sago, fish, and the occasional bit of vegetable than a diet based almost entirely on white rice (not uncommon among the urban poor in Southeast Asia), no matter how much more protein and nutrition the rice contains.

In his report, Lie notes that the differences between diets based on low-protein staples can be "striking," and that in particular the diet reported from New Guinea was well-balanced. But in general, like so many others, he seems to be arguing for rice. And his argument, tellingly, is not limited to nutrition. Toward the end of his report, Lie cites researcher R. Ohtsuka, who gathered information on sago in the Oriomo plateau of Papua New Guinea:

> Also noted is that it is impossible for peoples depending on sago, wild or planted, to migrate out of the low, swampy land, unless they change their staple food. Although the subsistence system dependent on sago is stable if some animal resources are available, the environment is a severely restrictive swamp.

The "low, swampy land"? A "severely restrictive swamp"? Clearly the scientists don't like this particular type of real estate, but why is it automatically assumed to be a hardship to be a "swamp-dweller"? For the record, the Kamoro don't live in their sago groves. The villages I visited were sandy and breezy, and a whole lot more comfortable than, say, downtown New York in August—or downtown Jakarta any time of year.

On a hot, sunny morning in late January, Kal, Apollo, and I waited for Tony Rahawarin, who was going to take us to meet some Nawaripi families who would be going out to gather sago at the southern end of the East Levee.

Tony drove up in a white Toyota. Everybody who works for Freeport drives a white Toyota. The company decided a long time ago to order all of its fleet cars in the same color, and white makes good sense in the heat of the tropics. This decision both simplifies procurement and, according to the same logic that applies in schools that require uniforms, minimizes jealousies and competition among the workers.

The Toyotas, however, come in several different models. The most desirable are built on a large, sleek chassis, powered by supercharged diesel engines. Some of these are used up at the mine, where the altitude and steep conditions require strong engines and sturdy suspensions. Others have an easier life in the lowlands, where the heads of major departments and other employees with enough clout to command one appreciate them more for their generous leg room, electric windows, and smooth ride. Tony's white Toyota was not one of these. It was a tiny square-sided vehicle, as if the body panels had been riveted together from sheet steel to save the cost of building a stamping die. Its engine was a breathless four-cylinder.

Our plan was to meet a half a dozen families from Paopau, the southernmost settlement on the levee. Paopau, now usually called Lower Kali Kopi, is a good eight or nine kilometers from the sago groves, and Tony had sent a truck earlier to give the people a lift. We didn't plan on stopping at Paopau, but when we saw the crowd out by the side of the road, we pulled to a halt. The truck, it quickly became apparent, had never arrived. The sun was already high in the sky, and although pounding sago is never easy work, it's a lot more enjoyable at nine in the morning than it is at noon. The people of Paopau were not happy.

Tony said he had an idea of where he could find the driver, a predictably unreliable character named Moses. At the time, the thrice-weekly truck driven by Moses was the only source of transportation for the people living on the levee. The program was run by Tony's office, and Moses was the classic problem employee. He was about as popular with the people on the levee as cerebral malaria. Just the mention of his name was enough to get the whole crowd grumbling and kicking at the dirt.

Once he realized what happened, Tony quickly devised a Plan B. By carefully arranging our limbs and breathing shallowly, we fit another three passengers in the tiny truck. We would drop them off at the sago grove to begin looking for suitable trees, and then we would go find Moses and send him back for the others. If we couldn't find him, Tony promised, he would shuttle back and forth in his little vehicle until everyone was there. Packed like sardines, we headed south, and about two kilometers from the end of the levee, reached the first sago tree.

At least fourteen palms in eight genera yield edible starch, although in the old world only *Metroxylon* (and to a lesser extent, *Arenga*) are important other than as occasional use or emergency foods. Palms of the genus *Metroxylon* are the source of true sago, and can be found from the southernmost part of Thailand and the Malay Peninsula all the way to Polynesia.

Two species have traditionally been distinguished, the smooth sago (*M. sagu*), said to inhabit the more westerly part of the *Metroxylon* range, and the thorny sago (*M. rumphii*), said to be found in Maluku and points east. Recently, however, the Dutch palm taxonomist Jan B. Rauwerdink has shown this to be incorrect. Using electron microscopy of pollen grains, chromosome analysis, and field study, he identified five true species of *Metroxylon,* but the trees found in Irian Jaya and Western Indonesia are all *M. sagu.* In keeping with the tradition of identifying sago by its degree of spininess, Rauwerdink has listed four distinct growth forms of *M. sagu,* ranging from trees with leaf bases and petioles that are spineless (forma sagu) to those bearing fierce spines four to twenty centimeters long (forma longispinum).

Most of the sago in the Kamoro area is forma longispinum, but I am told there is a nice stand of forma sagu near Timika, on Hiripau land. This variety is rare enough in the area that it is sometimes called "Satan's sago." The Kamoro call the more typical spiny variety *ametaoko,* literally "true sago." Satan's sago yields more starch, however, and there is no discernable difference in the taste. Its obvious advantage is that it is much more pleasant to work with.

Rauwerdink uses "forma" because the genetic difference between the palms is not marked enough to warrant "variety," or even "subvariety." A spiny plant can give rise to spineless offspring from the same flower, and vice versa. In general, the spiniest form is the most common in the wild, and the more or less spineless forms are common only under domestication.

One sad, but unintentional, result of Rauwerdink's taxonomic reorganization, published in 1986 in *Principes,* the journal of the International Palm Society, is that the name of Georg Everardt Rumph, or Rumphius, the famous 17th century naturalist of the Dutch Indies, is now no longer associated with the sago palm. Rumphius, stationed on Ambon island, was one of the first scientists to investigate sago, and he even taught the Ambonese more efficient methods of extracting the starch.

A mature *Metroxylon* palm stands eight to twenty meters high, a thick, straight bole with a crown of fronds. The fronds are up to seven meters long and pinnate, like a coconut palm, rather than palmate or fan-shaped, like a palmyra or the common palmetto of the American South. The young trees are slow to produce a bole (with palms this really should not be called a "trunk") and for three to four years the crown of fronds rises out of the ground like a huge fern. When mature the bole can reach sixty centimeters in diameter. Sago is not very long-lived and, perhaps appropriately, behaves more like a vegetable than a tree. It is hapaxanthic, which means that when it is ready, usually after ten to fifteen years, the tree flowers, and then dies. Like a banana plant, when the main stem dies it leaves behind at its base one or more new suckers ("soboles," to be technical) to take over.

Sago is choosy about where it grows. It needs a lot of water, but it must be sweet (and if it is too wet the palms stay in their juvenile, giant fern stage, and don't produce starch). The trees grow best just inland of the last of the true salt-tolerant mangrove community plants. Working from an an aerial photograph, you can often draw the line marking the limit of the tidal influence just by looking for the distinctive crowns of the sago palms. Scientists have estimated there are six million hectares of wild sago growing in the *Metroxylon* range, and most of this is in New Guinea.

When we reached an area where both sides of the levee were thick with mature sago trees, the men told Tony to stop, and we dropped them off. We continued south to find Moses, and caught up with him about two kilometers further on, at the very end of the levee. At first all we saw was the truck. After some very

vigorous rapping on the front door, the reclining shape in the front seat got up and rubbed its eyes.

"Moses?"

"Yes, Mr. Tony?"

"What time is it?"

"My watch won't work, Mr. Tony." Moses rummaged a bit under the front seat and produced the offending item. He shook it a bit. "See, it's broken."

"I see that." Tony smiled slightly. "Moses, you've got to go and pick up the people at Kali Kopi Bawah."

"Okay Mr. Tony," he said, and got out of the car. He paused, looking at the ground. "I have to get my net, though."

"Your *net*?"

It turns out Moses was not just napping. At the very end of the levee a tea-colored stream swings east and disappears into the swamp forest through a narrow copse. Apparently when Moses found this perfect rivulet—clear, narrow but still deep enough, and with sturdy trees on either side—he couldn't resist the urge to set a net there. It became even more difficult, he said, when he saw a giant catfish here last week.

"Really?" Tony said. "How big was it?"

A fish of the size Moses indicated would probably best be baited with a whole chicken.

Tony didn't ask him how he happened to be down here in the first place, since his regular route never came this far south. He just told him to pack the net up and go get the people at Paopau, and we drove back to the sago groves.

THE SAGO AREA being worked that day is called Epenaupo, from *epe,* a type of pandanus with leaves that can be woven into rainproof mats. Because of our late start, the people of Paopau decided to save time by cutting trees right next to the levee, rather than hiking further back into the swamp. Somewhat unexpectedly, this proved to be a real boon for Kal's photography. By standing on the levee he could get just about any angle he desired, without the usual forest problems of trees in the way and dappled sunlight that wreaks havoc with contrast control.

In harvesting sago, the first task is to find a suitable tree. Any tree will have some starch in it, but the tree is best when it is fully mature, but hasn't yet begun to flower. Finding such a specimen is something of an art, because the band is fairly narrow between a tree that is too young, and has little starch, and one that is too old, and already has begun converting its starch to sugar to fuel flower growth. There are some signs, however. Sago trees carry their fronds in a rather upright fashion, more upright, for example, than a coconut palm. A sago palm ready to harvest, however, will slouch a bit in this regard. It is a subtle difference, but if you look at enough of the trees you start to notice it. Also, the stems of the fronds at this time begin to display distinctive, silvery barring, like an aging man with streaks of gray in his beard.

VICTORIA AMAYI, EPENAUPO.

When the men spotted a good candidate—and it was men who did the cutting at Epenaupo—they tested the tree first to see if it was worth felling. A tree is tested by trimming away the outer bark, then sinking an axe into the pith and withdrawing it. If the steel comes out covered with a fine dusting of starch, you've probably found a good tree. Usually the axe was passed around and there was a bit of discussion before the decision was made. When everyone agreed, a few men started clearing brush and small trees from the path that was chosen for the tree to fall, and one man stepped up to the tree.

It doesn't take more than a few minutes to chop down a sago tree. The outer layer is tough, but only a few centimeters thick, and once the axe reaches the pith the going is easy. With the final stroke, the tree begins slowly to tip, and the axeman walks nonchalantly out of the way. I have never seen the Kamoro fell a tree of any kind that landed even an arm's length from the area that had been prepared for it.

The tree hits the ground with a tremendous, muffled thump that is more vibration than sound. *Metroxylon* is not a particularly attractive plant, unlike the beautiful, red-skinned sealing-wax palm, or the stately royal palms that decorate gardens or line roadways in the tropics. It is a sloppy-looking tree, and when it hits the ground one can see why: its thick husk is a mess of ferns, mosses, and creepers of all kinds. Before the starch can be harvested, this aerial garden has to be hacked away, as do the leaves, the stalks of which are armored with ferocious spines. (The trees at Epenaupo were definitely forma longispinum.)

The women do most of this work with *parang*s, the Indonesian machete, and in a short time the stem has been stripped of vegetation, and the fronds have been cut off, de-thorned (a quick swipe of the *parang* against the axis of the spines), and laid out to provide stable footing in the swampy ground. Once in a while a woman would frown, reach down, and pull a spine out of her bare foot, but it didn't happen as often as I would have guessed.

It is taboo to walk on the stem of the fallen sago tree during the course of this work. Since the bole offers the only stable footing on the swampy ground, this is a real hardship. But if anyone should be so foolish or arrogant as to ignore the taboo, I was told, when the bark is pulled back the pith of the tree will be revealed to be barren of starch.

Once the tree is felled and stripped, the hardest work begins—pounding the pith. In the past, this was strictly women's work, but the Nawaripi people mostly worked in couples, with both husband and wife taking turns. Alfred Russel Wallace describes the pith of the sago tree as "about as hard as a dry apple, but with woody fibres running through it about a quarter of an inch apart." His description, as always, is sound. It's the "woody fibres" that make the job so much work.

By the time the pounding began it was about eleven o'clock, and the temperature was probably close to ninety degrees in the shade. Only we were right next to the levee, so there wasn't much shade. It is hard to estimate the temperature in the full sun, but the gravel of the road was hot enough that I could feel it coming through the soles of my shoes. The Nawaripi people were not wearing shoes.

Late morning also brought out the day-biting *Aedes* mosquitoes. These are big for a mosquito, and are actually beautiful insects, striped like zebras in white on velvety black. When you swat them they leave a smear of powder, like a butterfly. And, if you haven't been paying attention, a spot of red. It is when you have acquired a few red spots that you remember that *Aedes* is the vector for dengue fever. The mosquitoes disappeared by early afternoon, leaving only the flies and sweat bees. The humidity, since the people were working in mud and water up to their ankles, was probably at saturation.

Despite these conditions nobody seemed the least bit tired or irritated. There was so much laughing and joking going on that if I didn't know what I was looking at, I might have thought that they were chopping down these trees for fun. This, to a large degree, was because of Paulinus Mapuwaripi.

"High spirits are very necessary when you work hard," Paulinus told me. "This," he said, winking at Apollo, "is the difference between the Nawaripi and the western Kamoro—we have SPIRIT!" With this, Paulinus began to whoop and yell, until everybody on both sides of the levee joined in. Throughout the day, he kept his eye on everyone, and if he saw their spirits flagging, he would run over and start pounding their sago for a while, or hurl an insult from across the levee, forcing everyone to double over with laughter.

Once I watched Paulinus, a wiry man probably in his late thirties, shout something at an old woman. Then he ran over to her, seized her pounder and begin chopping her section. The woman was laughing, as was Apollo, who was standing next to me.

"What did he say?"

"He said, 'You pound like an old woman,'" Apollo told me, shaking his head in mirth.

It was impossible not to be charmed by this man. Paulinus was also very indulgent of my ignorance of the various aspects of sago gathering, and provided me with much information on the fine points of pounding and washing sago.

Paulinus and his wife Victoria Amayi set up their operation on the west side of the levee, inside the area that would become the future tailings plain. No silt had yet made it down this far, and the surface water was clear and just a little tannin-stained, with the color of weak tea. In fact the water was cleaner and more plentiful on this side than it was on the other, which is why, Paulinus said with a wink, he and his wife chose this spot for their washing operation.

More than any other factor, the taste of the sago

PAULINA MAOPEYAUTA, NEAR PAUMAKO.
Squeezing and washing the starch is always the work of women.

depends on the quality of the water used in washing, Paulinus said. During the height of the dry season, you have to dig a well to get access to groundwater for washing, and the dirt in the water spoils the taste of the sago. January is technically the dry season, but this year has been wet and at Epenaupo there was still plenty of water on the ground, a condition for which Paulinus thanks the Freeport mine.

The sago pounder or chopper, called *tai*, looks a bit like a pickaxe, but the working end is cylindrical and slightly concave, a bit bigger in diameter than a Kennedy half-dollar, or an old-style Rp 100 coin. Each time the *tai* falls it takes a small, rounded "bite" of pith. In the past, this tool relied on the strength of the ironwood alone, but for the last ten or twenty years, an innovation has been adopted to make the *tai* cut faster and last longer: an iron band around the cutting tip. No one could be sure where this new technology came from, but Paulinus speculated that it was from Maluku.

Paulinus did most of the pounding, while Victoria did the washing. But sometimes he would get distracted by his morale-raising duties, or the questions of a visiting writer, and Victoria would have to take a spell with the *tai*. Their young son Agustinus also helped, although he seemed more efficient at bringing armloads of pounded sago to his mother for washing than in swinging the *tai*.

Pounding breaks up the pith into a dry pulp. This pulp, when washed, yields the sago starch. The apparatus employed in the washing operation is a marvel of hydraulic engineering. Two sections of the sheathing leaf base of the sago fronds—one laid out in a trough, the other propped at an angle, feeding the trough—constitute the basic assembly. At various points in this assembly woven mats, plugs, and pinned flaps serve as filters, dams, and weirs to control the washing and settling operation. The women bring only a *parang*, a plastic bucket for water, and their main washing mat; they make everything else on the spot from the sago tree. The women's knowledge and skill at this construction is such that the pieces are cut with single, perfectly aimed strokes of the *parang*.

The women extract starch by pouring water over the pulp, and squeezing the wet mixture to yield a stream of starchy water, which runs down to the settling trough. As the pulp is exhausted, they cast it aside and replace it with more. After a few hours, the basin fills with sago starch. Rust-red foam sometimes appears in the trough, and the finished sago can have a reddish, pink, or peach-colored tint, or be pure white. The color seems to have no effect on the taste.

137

As the workers became hungry, somebody would occasionally wander off to find a "millionaire's salad." This is the crispy, slightly sweet vegetable that lurks at the growing tip of a tall, skinny palm. It has this name, I suppose, because it seems an incredible extravagance to fell a ten-meter tree just for a bit of edible vegetable the size of a small bunch of celery. A sago tree that has already flowered also yields a sweet snack called *awate*. Flowering causes the starchy pith to go to sugar, particularly near the crown of the tree, and this is cut out in pink chunks and eaten like sugar cane. Paulinus's son Agus was a big fan of *awate*. If they have gotten an early start and there is still time left after pounding the sago, the people might also go look for breadfruit trees or any forest fruits that might be in season.

By early afternoon, most of the teams had accumulated enough sago to cook for lunch. Paulinus built a small fire, took a bit of the sago that had already settled, patted it into a ball, and placed it on the coals to cook, and most of the others did the same. One man had brought along a piece of dried meat to eat with his sago. When I first saw it sitting on a stump next to his *parang* and other effects, I had no idea what it was. It was a shiny black cylinder, covered with flies, and I was about to ask if it were some kind of a charm, like a rabbit's foot, when Apollo saw me studying it and said, "His lunch." Then I recognized it: a turtle's head.

ONE OF THE most celebrated forest delicacies in southern Irian Jaya is the larva of the sago beetle. Since I had never seen or eaten a sago grub, I asked Apollo to help me find some.

There are actually two varieties, he said: one is called *kowri;* the other, *ko'o.* The *kowri* is by far the larger of the two, and favors trees that have flowered and died, but are still standing. These larvae are "dirty," Apollo said, referring to a kind of vestigial black shell that must be removed before they can be eaten. Although it was probably possible, he said, he had never heard of anyone eating one that hadn't been thoroughly cooked. He also could not recall the last time he ate one himself. At this point I suggested the variety we should really be looking for was the *ko'o.*

Fig. 5.3 SAGO GRUB.
The larva of the weevil
Rhynchophorus ferrugineus.
Image is to scale.

This insect is the larvae of a large weevil in the family Rhynchophoridae, probably a regional variant of *Rhynchophorus ferrugineus. Rhynchophorus* is very large for a weevil, about three centimeters, and varies in color from shiny black to a kind of reddish brown. The wing shields have fine ridges like worn corduroy, and the snout, typical of a weevil, is long.

The larvae of this insect are very important to the neighboring Asmat, who gather great quantities of them for ritual feasts. They are a feast food for the Kamoro as well, although this was much more important in the past. Today, Apollo said, *ko'o* chiefly serve as an occasional treat. This beetle lays its eggs in sago trees that have died and fallen down. The Asmat, in fact, often fell sago trees and punch holes in the bark to make them more attractive to the female weevils. We found a fallen tree and, with a borrowed *parang,* hacked through the outer layer of moss and ferns.

Peeling back the dirty outer layer of the trunk revealed dozens of the wriggling grubs. These are fat, white creatures, about the size of a plum, with the shiny brown head of a beetle. A small boy had been following us, and when he saw the larvae, his eyes lit up. He immediately pulled the front of his T-shirt up with his left hand to form a sack, and began filling it with grubs. In just a few minutes he had collected a wriggling mass of perhaps a hundred larvae. He also quickly became rather proprietary about them, and only reluctantly handed over a few for us to sample.

To eat a grub, you hold it by the head and bite off the soft white body, as Apollo quickly demonstrated. The head is hard (it will become the adult beetle's carapace) and is not meant to be eaten. By this point Kal had wandered over, and, misinterpreting my prolonged examination of the larval insect as a failure of nerve, told me to get on with it. The texture and taste were a complete surprise. I was expecting something like a pat of butter, but when the rubbery sack burst in my mouth, it yielded a moist, vaguely grainy material, with a pleasant, neutral taste, even a little sweet. The flavor is mild enough that I can see how people are able to eat so many.

Writers who claim the texture is like mayonnaise are dissembling. It is more like cake batter, though of course not as sweet. The only disconcerting aspect of the experience is the discarded head, which keeps gnashing its jaws long after it has been severed from the body. The sight of a pile of these angry little crabs takes some getting used to.

Although often eaten fresh, for festivals the grubs are usually wrapped in leaves and cooked. Everybody told me that cooking yields the superior dish, although I have yet to sample it. The grubs are quite nutritious, and can be an important dietary component, especially for people living where seafood and game are scarce. Scientists in Australia analyzed the larvae and found each 100 gram serving to yield 181 calories, and to contain 13.1 grams of fat, 9 grams of carbohydrate, and 6.1 grams of protein.

BY MID-AFTERNOON, MOST of the settling troughs were full, and it was time to wrap the sago up into *tumang*s. The *tumang* is a container, its size and shape basically fixed by the inside dimensions of the settling trough. The settled sago is removed in two chunks, placed flat side to flat side to make a tapered cylinder, and then packaged in a con-

Yudas Apewa, Pulau Puriri.
Skills with the *parang* are acquired early.

tainer made from two sago fronds. The fronds are singed in a fire to make them more flexible and to cause their sharp edges to curl harmlessly inward, and then cleverly woven together to form a strong, slightly tapered tube. A *tumang* of wet, freshly packed sago might weigh 25 kilograms or more, but it soon dries down to 15–20 kilograms.

At the time of my visit, a *tumang* of sago fetched Rp 20,000 to Rp 25,000 in the Timika market, about $6. This amount should feed a family for at least a week. In this area, I was told, a tree can yield up to ten *tumang*s, but the average is three to five, or perhaps sixty kilograms of starch. Researchers in other parts of Irian Jaya and Papua New Guinea report yields of from 29 to 206 kilograms of sago per tree, which is quite a large range, considering that the mature trees are the same size everywhere. Commercial production in Malaysia using mechanized grinders is said to approach 300 kilograms per tree; how close to this figure a couple can get pounding and rinsing the pith by hand depends on how hard they want to work.

Pieter Mandobar, who with his wife Mia was working a tree on the same side of the levee as Paulinus's family, said that in Yapen, an island in Cenderawasih Bay in the north of Irian, people get much better yields from each tree, perhaps even six or seven *tumang*s.

Pieter was born and raised in Serui, on Yapen, and only moved to the Kamoro area when he married Mia, a local woman. He added, with a bit of pride, that the reason they get better yields is that the Yapenese were more efficient, and worked harder. The Kamoro, of course, dispute this claim, but it did seem to me that Pieter and Mia were able to squeeze their *tumang* from a very small section of trunk.

One of the great advantages of sago as a staple is its tremendous efficiency in keeping a community fed. Agronomists usually define efficiency in man hours of labor to produce one million calories. Researchers's results vary tremendously, but one gives the following: manioc (Brazil) 146 man hours; wet rice (China) 186 man hours; dry rice (Philippines) 111 man hours; sago (Papua New Guinea) 80 man hours. All studies rate sago very high on the efficiency scale, either beating or matching shifting agriculture of manioc in calories per man hour of work.

Some calculations make this even more clear. Figuring a sago intake of 2,500 calories a day (70 percent of 3,600 calories, based on research in Papua New Guinea) and that sago yields 3,550 calories per kilogram, an average person will need to eat almost 260 kilograms of sago by dry weight every year or, put another way, two to four trees. Since two people working together produced a twenty kilogram *tumang* in about four hours at Epenaupo, I calculate it will take a Kamoro man or woman no more than 103 hours to produce a year's worth of sago for him or herself. (This comes to 113 hours per million calories.)

Two-and-a-half working weeks a year to get all of your starch is not bad. And harvesting is the only labor involved. The trees don't have to be planted or pruned or weeded or otherwise worried about. According to one 1958 report from Dutch New Guinea, a single hectare stand of sago can produce a sustainable harvest of fifty-two trees. This means that each hectare can support seventeen people, or an average village requires less than twenty hectares of healthy sago.

Communities that practice so-called primitive forms of agriculture like sago gathering are often, for that reason, considered less "dynamic," or even "backward." To me, it just looks smart. It also looked smart to Thomas Forrest more than two hundred years ago.

> No wonder then, if agriculture be neglected in a country, where the labour of five men, in felling sago trees, beating the flour, and instantly baking the bread, will maintain a hundred.

His Indonesian crew, raised on rice, still complained, but eventually their bellies were satisfied:

> I must own my crew would have preferred rice; and when my small stock of rice, which I carried from Balambangan, was near expended, I have heard them grumble, and say, *nanti makan roti Papua,* 'we must soon eat Papua bread.' But, as I took all opportunities of baking it fresh, being almost continually in port, they were very well contented.

CHAPTER SIX

The Edge of Maluku

Lakahia, Where the Kamoro Met the Outside World

HE ARAFURA IS a sullen, provincial sea with water the color of tree bark. It is so shallow that it behaves like a huge, windswept lake, lashing out unpredictably at the first sign of bad weather. Daily tides heave the brown water up and down as much as five meters, setting an inviolable schedule for travel. Long, inscrutable sand spits reach out from the coast to confound and harass the sailor. It is an excellent place to wreck a ship.*

We said our goodbyes in Paripi, promising to return in a week or so, loaded our boat and headed west. Our destination was Lakahia Island, a small coral island in a bay of the same name on the south side of the New Guinea bird's neck. Lakahia attracted us because it is the westernmost frontier of Kamoro territory, the last place heading toward the setting sun where the Kamoro language can still be heard. Since cultural influences reached New Guinea from the west, this little island, more than two hundred kilometers from Paripi, also holds a place in history far more important than its modest dimensions might suggest.

The sandbars, shallow rivers, and mangrove forest of the rest of the Kamoro coast stymied earlier European explorers, but the deep, protected channel of Lakahia Bay always provided a reliable anchorage, and the island is mentioned in many of the early European accounts. Even before the Europeans, traders from within the Indonesian archipelago faced the same nautical constraints, and Lakahia became a trade entrepôt, where innovations such as metal tools, cloth, betel, and tobacco were introduced to the Kamoro world, and where local products like resin, aromatic bark, bird skins—and, particularly, slaves—were shipped off. Lakahia was the furthest reach of the trade and political network of Maluku, the famous Spice Islands that first brought Europeans to these waters.

PORTAGE TO THE MATOAPOKA RIVER. Rough weather forced this woman and her children, returning from gathering shellfish on the river, to walk, while her husband poled the canoe just offshore.

HOLLOWING A CANOE, PARIPI. Frans Nawima, Mikael Epatepea, Vincen Imini, and Primus Atiripuku. The woman in back is Peternela Aniri.

West of Paripi the limestone mountains of the Charles Louis Range begin to dip south towards the coast, gradually narrowing the area of mangrove. From Paripi you would have to travel forty-five kilometers due north to reach an elevation of one hundred and fifty meters. From Ararao, about halfway to Lakahia, ten kilometers would get you to the same elevation. At the Nariki Peninsula, just west of Potowai-Buru and almost at Lakahia, you could scramble up to the top of a six-hundred-meter peak right from the shore. Because of this, beyond Paripi we had no choice but to travel by sea, suffering a monotony of spray and drenching waves.

We hired a local pilot named Manu Karuwe to escort us to Lakahia. Manu moved to Paripi to live in his wife's community, but he was born in Yapakopa, near Potowai-Buru and only a few hours from Lakahia. He has made the Paripi to Lakahia trip many times. A guide might seem unnecessary for a coasting route that never leaves sight of the land, but it is just as easy to hang a boat up in the little channels through the sandbars as it is to get lost in the tangle of mangrove creeks. Probably easier, in fact, and the penalty for making a mistake in the breakers is more severe. Manu sat at the bow and almost never spoke, just raising his right or left hand every now and then to direct Tobias through a confusing swirl of surf or away from a hidden sandbar.

We soon learned that Tobias, a river pilot at heart, didn't have much of an instinct for the open sea. Manu's arms were getting a lot more exercise than he had expected. Occasionally he would stare back at the stern and shake his head in disbelief as Tobias, despite

---

* The name of this moody body of water can be traced to the Portuguese *alfuori*, "the outsider," an Arabic-derived word first applied by the Portuguese in India to the people living outside of the influence of their colonial settlements. In the early 16th century the Portuguese brought the word with them to the Spice Islands of Maluku, and even today "alifuru" is used there to refer to the more traditional inland people of Seram and Halmahera (the term functions much as has "kaffir" or "caffre," derived from the Arabic word for "infidel," in Africa). Until at least the middle of the 19th century outsiders thought the alifurus—or "arafuras," as it was often spelled—of New Guinea were a different race from the men they met on the coast, and some Europeans, with characteristic vanity, even speculated they might be white-skinned.

KAOKATURU.
These people, from Ararao and Poraoka, have been encamped at the mouth of the Umari River for a month.

instructions, would once again trap our boat in the rolling trough of the breakers, soaking us all thoroughly and knocking the fuel drums free of their chocks.

Manu wore a black long-sleeved T-shirt and shorts, and other than a camouflage green baseball cap, brought along no protection against the rain or spray. This was one reason he was nonplussed each time Tobias steered us clumsily into a wave. On his arms and legs he wore bracelets of rubber O-rings, a form of jewelry that is not unpopular in urban areas of the United States. I worked in a downtown San Francisco hardware store in the early 1980s, and the head of the plumbing department had to order extra quantities of the larger sizes of sink basin O-rings because people would buy them two dozen at a time to wear on their arms. I identified Manu's arm bracelets as fuel drum bung seals, but I couldn't immediately place the big square-section rubber rings on his legs. Since I didn't want to shout such a silly question up to the bow I asked Alo, who was sitting next to me. He laughed. "Hydraulic seals from a front-end loader," he said, matter-of-factly.

A few hours from Paripi our engine mysteriously began to lose power. For about half an hour Tobias chopped the throttle on and off like a Singapore cab driver, either out of frustration or because he thought

that this might clear some carbon from the engine. Finally he gave up and throttled back, and we proceeded calmly at a walking pace. Unfortunately, we faced the same problem as the early explorers, and several hours passed before we could find a place to pull in safely to have a look at our crippled motor. At this spot, called Irua, a canoe can just slip in past a sandbar to reach a calm inland river called the Matoapoka, which parallels the coast just west of Ararao. This we did, and were happy to dry off and stretch our legs.

FOR ALMOST TEN YEARS, from 1974 to 1983, Irua was the site of Umar village, and judging from the piles of coconut husks and clam shells that littered the ground, it is still visited regularly. A solitary house stood near the shore of the Matoapoka River, and we built our fire in front of it. The thatch roof was in good repair, but the house was empty except for a fishing net full of empty shells from the *poro* clam, which had been saved to make lime. The Matoapoka is famous for its shellfish, particularly oysters. *Matoa* is Kamoro for "oyster," and *poka* means "place of" or literally, "to have."

Tobias removed the spark plug and carburetor from the engine, but neither of these components suggested the source of our troubles. Alo, who trained as a heavy equipment mechanic in the early seventies, saw that Tobias had reached his wit's end and decided to have a look. He quickly determined that the motor was fine. Our problem was with the rubber fuel line, which had been ineptly routed—directly underneath our spare drums of two-stroke oil. The line was sturdy, and the weight of the drums was not in itself enough to cause problems, but the added burden of Tobias's napping assistant eventually caused it to pinch nearly shut. This was very good for our fuel economy, but left our engine with barely enough power to run a ceiling fan.

While Tobias reassembled the outboard, Alo spotted a family fishing across the river, and shouted out to them to see if they had any fresh fish to sell. Although the river is not particularly wide here, a slight breeze carried his voice uselessly downstream. He quickly found a tiny canoe and paddle that had been stowed on our side of the shore and, squeezing himself in, paddled off to negotiate for our lunch with a pocket full of damp rupiah notes.

Apollo and I took a walk along the shore. Near where the river met the sea, I found a whale vertebra lying on the sand, a piece of bleached bone the size and shape of a child's chair. When I reached down to pick it up, Apollo stopped me. "If you touch a whale bone," he said, "it will bring high winds." With the troubles we had been having so far, I decided not to risk it.

The sandy bank separating the river from the sea is less than a hundred meters wide at Irua. It is lightly shaded by a grove of feathery casuarina trees and a row of coconut palms. The afternoon sun made a drink of young coconut water seem tempting, and I half-heartedly suggested we "borrow" a couple. Apollo told me not to even joke about such a thing. Poaching coconuts is taken very seriously here, he said, and the perpetrators of such deeds quickly find themselves the victims of black magic.

In some cultures a lock of hair can be used to wreck havoc on its erstwhile owner. For example, nineteenth-century Russian anthropologist and naturalist Nikolai Miklouho-Maclay was never able to convince the people of Astrolabe Bay in northeastern New Guinea to allow him to take hair samples for his ethnographic collection. They were afraid he planned to use their hair for black magic. In other cultures people are wary of releasing their name to a stranger, because that information is enough to make them vulnerable to spells. The Kamoro, Apollo told me, have to watch out for their footprints.

The owner of a violated coconut tree will exact revenge by taking a bit of sand from one of the thief's footprints, wrapping it in special leaves, and placing the bundle in an ant nest. This will bring its victim great pain, and eventually, death.

"First he will feel something wrong in his feet," Apollo said, "and then it will gradually work its way upward. When it reaches his head, he will die."

Alo soon returned, successful, with a fork-tailed catfish, a mullet, a snapper, and a small jack. All were fresh and glossy-eyed, and we tossed them on the fire. These are all fine eating fish, and with some sago biscuits we brought from Paripi, made a first-rate lunch.

By the time we had solved the problem with the fuel line and eaten our lunch, the wind had come up and turned the Arafura Sea into a field of whitecaps. It won't be possible, Apollo said, to continue by sea. We could continue by the protected Matoapoka River for a few more kilometers west, he said, but once this river ends, at the mouth of the Umari River, we would have to stop for the night.

When we reached the Umari, at a sandy point on the eastern shore called Kaokaturu, we were surprised to find it crowded with people. The map doesn't show a village here, and in fact, there usually isn't one. But when we arrived we found an encampment comprised of most of the people of Ararao, and the entire village of Poraoka, down to the last dog and chicken. Ararao is just fifteen kilometers away by a protected river, but Poraoka is almost fifty kilometers to the west by the open sea. For the past two months, we were told, these people had been living here in lean-to shelters dug into the sand, fishing, gathering oysters along the Matoapoka, and going upriver to hunt and pound sago.

"It makes me happy to see this still happening," Alo said, and as we walked around the temporary settlement, he was buoyant. Imagine a huge, two-month-long picnic. Little boys played with model canoes fabricated from bits of driftwood and pitch, and the girls chased each other through the vines growing along the beach. Dogs snuffled at old crab shells, and chickens pecked at the sea wrack along the high tide line. The women and men sat comfortably around the fire, chatting, smoking, or just staring at the reddening sky.

To settled urbanites like Alo and Apollo, this scene brought on a wave of contentment, a feeling that seemed to combine nostalgic memories of their youth and a sense of pride in the irrepressibility of the nomadic spirit of the Kamoro, a spirit that continues despite eighty years of the best efforts of two governments to get them to stay put. Neither said much as we walked around the encampment at Kaokaturu. I decided not to spoil their reverie with my questions.

The western shore of the Umari River was also temporarily populated, by the people of Aindua, whose permanent village lies less than two hours to the west. They were there for the same reason as the people of Ararao and Poraoka. We motored across the river and talked to them for a bit. They were having as good a time as the people on the other side, and were most happy about their success at hunting in the drylands just upstream. As proof, the village head asked his wife to heat up some sago and proudly produced a thin stew swimming with chunks of wild boar.

This meat is robust and gamey, and tastes surprisingly different from domesticated pork. Some scien-

145

tists consider both domestic and wild pigs in New Guinea to be part of the same gene pool, consisting of a hybrid between the wild boar (*Sus scrofa*) and the Sulawesi wild boar (*Sus celebensis*), and most believe that the pig, like the domestic dog, was brought to New Guinea only about two thousand years ago. Tantalizingly, however, two pig incisors have been found in ten thousand to twelve thousand year old archaeological sites in Papua New Guinea, although this recent discovery is still very controversial.

We returned to the Kaokaturu side to spend the night in the only permanent dwelling in the area, a modern wooden house that had been built as a small military post and quarters. The army officers were gone, and the house was being looked after by Lee Ong, a Chinese trader from Kaimana.

Lee Ong, tall and almost impossibly thin, was shirtless when he met us at the door. He was very friendly and hospitable, and immediately served us tea. We joined a group of Kamoro men who were also sprawled around the room, drinking tea and smoking. Lee's cat had just had kittens, of which one was as exquisitely patterned as a Japanese koi, and they crawled about our feet as we chatted.

Over the years Lee has dealt in many trade products, he said, but at the time of our visit he was in the area to buy grouper, a valuable and relatively new product. These fish are shipped live all the way to Hong Kong, where they end up on businessmen's plates in fancy restaurants. He makes the rounds along the coast every couple of months, checking on how full the holding pens are, fixing or replacing equipment, and generally getting caught up with his teams of fishermen. When it was time for bed, despite our objections, Lee insisted that Kal and I take his and his assistant's cots.

Later in the trip I was to hear Lee spoken of along the coast, always respectfully. He enjoys a very good reputation among the Kamoro with whom he does business. It took me a while to realize that my informants were talking about the man I had met, however, as at first I heard the name as "Leon."

FOR ONCE THE MORNING greeted us with favorable seas, and we packed our gear and motored out the river mouth and headed toward Lakahia. With our engine working again, we foresaw no trouble reaching the island by afternoon, and our spirits were high. I couldn't help thinking how different this would have been even just a century ago, when no outsider could have approached Lakahia with anything other than a feeling of dread.

Historically, the meeting between the outside world and the Kamoro at Lakahia was almost never peaceful and, until well into the twentieth century, frequently resulted in bloodshed. Despite the speculations and generic indictments that appear in early European texts, the Kamoro have never been cannibals. Warfare, however, was common, and from the point of view of the victim it probably doesn't matter much what becomes of the corpse. The Kamoro living in the area of Lakahia, where slave raids were regular and competition for outside goods was fierce, seem to have been even more than typically nervous and prickly. For outsiders, unaware of the local political situation, it was like stepping into a bear trap.

The first recorded European visitors to this low, wooded island were crewmembers from Luis Baéz de Torres's galleon *San Pedro*, who came ashore on October 16, 1606 seeking food and water. Heading north and west after rounding the False Cape of Dolak Island, Lakahia was the first place Torres encountered where he could anchor his ship within reach of shore.

According to the account reproduced in historian and former sailor Brett Hilder's 1980 *The Voyage of Torres*, the houses on Lakahia were located high up in the trees, and at the first sign of the Europeans, the villagers clambered up into them. When they reached shore, Torres's crew saw only women and children peeking out of the houses, and guessed that the men had retreated earlier in their canoes. They saw only one lone man paddling a canoe in the bay, perhaps keeping watch, and he maintained a safe distance.

The landing party found a large pig wandering around, which they speculated had either been left as a kind of peace offering or was simply too heavy to haul up the ladder to one of the tree houses. In any case they decided to take it, as well as some oysters and *Trochus* snails they found along the shore. They departed without meeting the people of Lakahia, and named the island Isla de los Ostiones, the "Island of Oysters." Although history hasn't recorded it, the Lakahians may well have named Torres's men "The White People Who Steal Pigs and Shellfish."

The *San Pedro* and its tender were the remnants of an expedition led by Captain Pedro Fernandez de Quiros from Peru to Manila to discover the Austral Land and, of course, claim its presumed riches for Spain. Quiros's crew mutinied in Vanuatu and returned to Peru, but Torres continued on, in the process becoming the first explorer to pass between New Guinea and Australia, through the strait that now bears his name. The account of this voyage, written by Captain Don Diego de Prado, remained a Spanish state secret for some three hundred years. The information was so well guarded that when Captain James Cook repeated Torres's feat two centuries later by a slightly different route, it was believed he was the first to have done so, and the passage was named "Cook Strait."

Torres's encounter with Lakahia resulted in the theft of a pig and some shellfish, but nobody was killed. In this respect it is very nearly unique in the history of this bay. The Spanish were soon followed by the Dutch, and actually Willem Janszoon, in the Dutch ship *Duyfken*, had six months earlier covered some of the same ground as Torres, although he did

LEANDER MAWAPOKA, TIMIKA PANTAI.

WARIFI.
Copra dries on racks in front of these houses. In the background is the north shore of Lakahia Bay.

not find the strait between New Guinea and Australia. Jansz. touched near Omba, the next Kamoro village to the east, but not Lakahia.

In 1623 the Dutch colonial governor of Ambon in Maluku dispatched Jan Carstenszoon in the *Pera* and the yacht *Arnhem* to investigate this coast for sources of trade products, chiefly aromatic bark and resin. While sailing the Kamoro coast, Carstensz. became the first European to see New Guinea's glaciers. He didn't stop at Lakahia, but on February 11, 1623, he lost Dirck Meliszoon, skipper of the *Arnhem,* and nine other men in an attack by the people of Mupuruka near the Umari River. A few days later Carstensz. saw New Guinea's glaciers from the shore. Carstensz. was the first European to report seeing glaciers in the tropics, and histories routinely report that this was considered so unlikely that his account was not believed for at least another two hundred years. This is doubtful, however, as even by the mid-17th century European maps of New Guinea include Carstensz.'s "Sneeburg," which means "Snow Mountain" in Dutch. They also include "Doodslagers Rivier," his name for the Umari River, which translates as something like "River of the Murdering Butchers."

The first European specifically seeking contact with Lakahia was Hollander Gerrit Pool, who had heard there was coal on the island and, in 1636, sought to buy some to use in forging. Pool never made it to Lakahia, because he was murdered on the way at nearby Namatota. In 1678, Johannes Keyts actually signed a contract for the delivery of coal and aromatic bark from Lakahia, but when he arrived was attacked and lost six men. By the end of the 17th century, the Dutch, perhaps wisely, gave up on this part of New Guinea, and until the 19th century concentrated their commercial efforts on the islands further to the west.

"AS DEAR AS PEPPER," was a common saying in 15th-century Europe, and the popularity and value of spices was the driving force behind the European Age of Exploration. The first ragged bands of European sailors who reached New Guinea and the islands of the East Indies did so not out of a pure spirit of discovery, but to return to the maritime capitals of Europe with a valuable cargo for themselves and their backers. What they filled their holds with were spices. Pepper, originally from India and later transplanted to Sumatra and Java, was certainly valuable, but the real prize was the so-called holy trinity of spices: cloves, nutmeg, and mace.

Cloves are the dried flower buds of the tree *Syzygium aromaticum;* nutmegs, and the lacy red aril of the nutmeg, called mace, both come from the tree *Myristica fragrans*. At the time of the Age of Exploration, both of these trees grew only in the tiny Spice Islands of Maluku, just west of what is now Irian Jaya.

Cloves, nutmeg, and mace had been imported into Europe through the Middle East since at least the days of the Roman Empire, and all three products had myriad uses, both culinary and pharmaceutical. The knowledge of cloves in the Middle East is ancient, and a jar of dried cloves has been discovered at the 3,700-year-old archeological site of Terqa (Ashara), on the Euphrates River in present-day Syria. French historian Fernand Braudel, in his sweeping treatise on the early modern period, quotes *Le Ménagier de Paris* of 1393 and notes numerous recipes calling for cloves and nutmeg. Medieval Europe was carnivorous, and one imagines that the spices must have greatly aided the palatability of meat in an era before refrigeration.

Today, with cloves and nutmeg common baking spices on American grocery store shelves, and with ninety thousand metric tons of cloves going up in smoke each year in Indonesian *kretek* cigarettes, it is almost impossible to imagine how valuable these spices were in medieval and early modern Europe.

According to 17th century Dutch records, cloves were purchased in Maluku for approximately one-tenth their weight in silver, and by the time they reached the entrepôt of Melaka, on the strait between Sumatra and Malaysia, customers could just stack silver guilder coins on the other end of the balance beam. By the time they reached Europe, the buyers would have to start using gold coins.

But it wasn't until the early 16th century that the gold coins were being paid to European merchants. For centuries, spices had been shipped to Europe overland through the Middle East, and later by boat through the Red Sea. The Europeans sought their own route to the Spice Islands not only because of the high cost, but also because the trade was controlled by their religious enemies—the Muslim kingdom of Melaka, the Muslim Gujarati traders of Cambay in India, and the Muslim Mamelukes of Egypt.

The Portuguese led Europe in technologies of navigation and naval warfare, and in 1488, Bartolomeu Dias successfully rounded the Cape of Africa. Ten years later, on May 20th, Vasco da Gama reached Calicut (Kozhikode) on the Malabar Coast of India, and within another decade Portuguese Admiral Afonso de Albuquerque hatched a plan to seize the spice trade from the "Infidels." The Portuguese captured Goa in 1510, Melaka in 1511, and Hormuz in 1515. Aden still resisted, but by the early 16th century the Portuguese had broken the Muslim monopoly.

Although they had captured Melaka, near present-day Singapore, the Portuguese still had not reached the Spice Islands, and Albuquerque immediately dispatched an expedition of three ships under the command of António de Abreu to find them. They soon found the Banda Islands, and after his ship ran aground on the reefs of the Lucipara Islands in early 1512, commander Francisco Serrão and six of his men were met by an envoy from the Sultan of Ternate, and escorted north to the islands of Ternate and Tidore.

Ternate, and its almost identical neighbor Tidore,

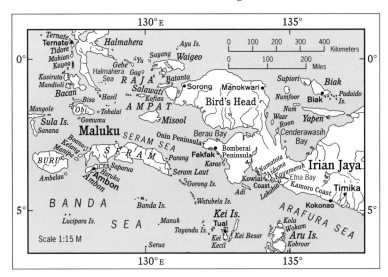

Fig. 6.1 MALUKU AND THE RAJA AMPAT.

are two green volcanic islands, each just five kilometers in diameter, lying just off the west coast of Halmahera's northernmost peninsula, about four hundred kilometers from the tip of the Bird's Head. These tiny specks of land, together with three other small islands immediately south of them—Moti, Makian, and Bacan—were at the time the only place in the world where clove trees had been domesticated. The Banda Islands, the only place the prized round nutmeg then grew, are even smaller, mere motes in the middle of the fifteen-hundred-kilometer-wide Banda Sea.

WHEN THE PORTUGUESE ARRIVED, the sultans of Ternate and Tidore jointly ruled Maluku, a group of scattered islands stretching from Sulawesi in the west to New Guinea in the east, and from Morotai in the north to Tanimbar in the south. "Ruled," however, is not really the correct word. In his 1993 *The World of Maluku,* historian Leonard Andaya suggests that Maluku was less an empire ruled by two competing sultans than a kind of cultural, political, and mercantile network with a symbolic center—incorporating the dualism of the two rulers—located in the two islands.

This status predated the arrival of the Europeans, and also predated the arrival of Islam, which came to Ternate and Tidore in the late 15th century, together with a few words of the Malay language, as a prestige product from the newly dominant entrepôt of Melaka. Ternate's influence extended chiefly to the west; Tidore's influence extended to the east, first through Halmahera's southeastern peninsula, then through Gebe Island, and finally to New Guinea.

In 1526, Captain-designate Dom Jorge de Menese sailed from the Portuguese colony of Goa in India to Ternate, where he planned to take command of Portuguese interests. These were still unfamiliar waters then, and he accidentally overshot his destination and had to stop in a port named "Versija" on the shore of an

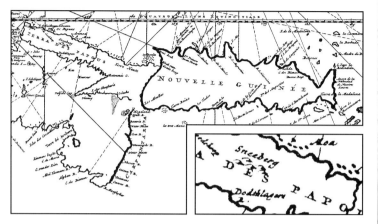

Fig. 6.2 TERRA DES PAPOUS.

Details from a chart in the atlas *Suite du Neptune François,* published in 1700. The cartographer has included Jan Carstensz.'s 'Sneeberg' (Snow Mountain) and 'Dodslagers R.' (River of the Murdering Butchers). It was not until about a half century later that most cartographers had enough information to render Papua and New Guinea as a single island.

unknown island to wait for the season of westerly winds to end. Portuguese charts produced soon after this unplanned sojourn suggest that the island was Biak, although some sources have proposed Waigeo, and still others the Bird's Head. In any case, by this error Menese became the first European to set foot on what is now considered part of New Guinea.*

Menese reached Ternate the following year, whereupon he proceeded to clumsily terrorize the Malukans for three years until he was replaced as the Portuguese captain in charge. Among other outrages, Menese hanged Kaicili Darwis, the uncle of Sultan Kaicili Abu Hayat. Darwis was Ternate's de facto ruler, since the sultan at the time was not yet even a teenager. Menese executed Darwis because he suspected he had called upon the other Malukan kingdoms to band together to oust the Portuguese from Ternate. Among these kingdoms was that of the Raja Ampat.

Raja Ampat means "Four Kings"—*ámpat* being a regional variant of *empát*—and these were Raja Salawati, Raja Waigeo, Raja Misool, and Raja Waigama. The names of three of these are still recorded on the large islands just east of New Guinea's Bird's Head (Raja Waigama was also on Misool Island). This island

* The name "New Guinea" (as Nueva Guinea) was coined by Yñigo Ortíz de Retes almost two decades later, in 1545, and most sources state he arrived at this name because of the resemblance of the Papuans to the people of African Guinea. However New Guinea had also been dubbed "Isla del Oro," the Island of Gold, and one historian has suggested that de Retes's "Guinea"–like Guinea in Africa–was a corruption of *ghana,* an old Arabic word for "riches," and that the explorer was really naming the island "New Land of Riches." "Nova Guinea" first appeared on Mercator's map in 1569.

group is still called the Raja Ampat.

The Raja Ampat were closely allied with the Tidore side of the Malukan center, and European histories generally present this relationship as one between hapless vassals (Raja Ampat) and their spiteful and arbitrary ruler (Tidore), with the former being frequently abused by the latter, particularly by lopsided tribute demands. The Dutch used the term *leen,* or "vassal state," which they would later use to describe the relationship of Ternate and Tidore to Holland.

Andaya argues, convincingly, that this is not an accurate representation. To the parties involved, he writes, the relationship was reciprocal. The Raja Ampat provided Tidore with a tribute of trade goods; in exchange, the Tidorese court granted titles and privilege to the rulers of the Raja Ampat. Thus, on returning home from a tribute-bearing mission to Tidore, the Raja Ampat distributed their own "booty":

> The people gathered and solemnly touched the hands of the leaders of the tribute mission in order to share in the sacred power of the Sultan Tidore while it was still "hot."

A European may not easily understand how this symbolic power could be equal in value to a material tribute of slaves, bird of paradise skins, aromatic bark and ambergris, but to the Raja Ampat it was. And it is worth bearing in mind that to a wealthy ruler of a tiny island five kilometers across who already has one hundred and fifty slaves and dozens of elaborate bird of paradise headdresses, a tribute of a couple slaves and a few bird of paradise skins is no less token a gift than the spoken bestowal of a title.

Many texts describing the relationship between New Guinea and Maluku make much of the punitive expeditions—called *hongi*—in which armed representatives of Tidore riding fast, double-outriggered *kora-kora* ships looted and burned villages in the Raja Ampat islands and along the coast further south. These raids did take place, but only after the Dutch had completely disrupted the traditional relationship between Tidore and its peripheral states. The worst period for *hongi* along the New Guinea coast was the nineteenth century, by which time the expeditions could not properly be considered punitive. They were, instead, simple acts of piracy by a ruler who had long since lost his power to command any tribute at all.

WHEN DOM JORGE de Menese accidentally landed on one of the islands of northwest New Guinea, the name he reported for the people was the "Papuas." The Spanish pilot Martín de Uriarte, exploring the coast of Halmahera in 1526, noted that southeast of the island lay eight large and small islands he called "las islas de las Papuas." Andrés Urdaneta, reporting on Alvaro de Saavedra's stay in the area in 1528, called the same islands "islas de Papuas." And throughout the 16th and 17th centuries, European maps of the area—all based on local charts—distinguished "las Papuas" from "Nova Guinea."

TORUPA ON BEACH, KAOKATURU.

"The Papuas" referred to the Raja Ampat islands, and later, the westernmost extension of the island, approximately what we now call the Bird's Head (although on the 17th century maps it can look like anything from an elephant's trunk to a kind of crab claw). "New Guinea" was reserved for the rest of the island. Some maps even show two islands, the Papuas in the west and New Guinea in the east, divided by a strait.*

By the time the Dutch began to establish their colonial administration in western New Guinea in the 20th century, the term "Papuan Islands" fell from use, and maps and district names used Raja Ampat and Vogelkop for this region of the island. The term "Papuan" did not disappear, however. Anthropologists, linguists, and other scientific commentators still used "Papua" and "Papuan" to refer to the cultures,

languages, and people of New Guinea.

The scientists were using the term neutrally, but increasingly in the 20th century some Dutch officials, and particularly eastern Indonesian petty officials and teachers, began to use "Papuan" in a derogatory sense. As a boy Alo remembers being called "Papuan" by his Dutch teachers, the word spit out as an insult.

Jean Victor de Bruijn, who served as the Dutch district officer or *controleur* in the Paniai Lakes region just before World War II, recalled that the proud highlanders considered "Papuan" to refer to coastal people like the Kamoro, whom they held in something like contempt. Lloyd Rhys, in his biography *Jungle Pimpernel*, recounts an episode De Bruijn reported to him:

> They [the Ekagi or Me] looked upon coastal people more in sorrow than in anger, because they of the mountains were of a superior race. After all, these coastal people were nomadic, without homes or gardens. So superior were the Ekari and Migani [Moni] people that on one occasion they came to the Kontolulle [sic] full of complaint: they were very hurt and angry because some of the police had called them Papuans.
>
> "We will work for you," they said, "but we will not work for your police if they call us Papuans. We are Ekari and Migani people, and have nothing to do with the Papuan (coastal) people, who do not even own a pig and have to work for their own food."

---

* Some of these maps, particularly those of Dutch origin, also confuse the Papuas with the island of Seram. This seems to have begun with the cartography of Petrus Plancius in 1594. Plancius was a minister in the Dutch Reformed Church and instrumental in the creation of the Dutch East Indies company, De Vereenigde Geoctroyeerde Oost-Indische Compagnie (V.O.C.). His maps showed "Ceiram" where the Bird's Head should be, and neglected the real island of Seram altogether. This is unfortunate, but not surprising, at a time when longitude was calculated by dead reckoning and maps still used Marco Polo's names. Carstensz., for example, sailed with a version of Plancius's map, which is why his early account of the "butchers" has them living on Seram.

FIRE-ROASTED PORK, NEAR ATUKA.

The negative connotation of Papua is what led Marcus W. Kaisiepo in 1945 to propose replacing the name with Irian, a word from his native Biak language meaning "to rise," both in a mundane sense like steam rising from a pot, but also metaphorically, like land rising from behind the horizon. "Irian" also has a literary sense, something like "soaring spirit." Marcus Kaisiepo's proposal was placed on record at the Malino Conference in 1947 by delegate Frans Kaisiepo, and when Indonesia took over the province in 1963, both Papua and New Guinea were replaced with Irian.

Today "Irian" and "Papua" have switched senses. Because of the Organisasi Papua Merdeka, and independent Papua New Guinea, "Papua" has come to represent the pride and independence of the native Irianese, while "Irian"–rightly or wrongly–is taken to be an imposed name from Jakarta. Those seeking independence for the province dream of a free "West Papua," not a free "Irian Jaya."

THE ETYMOLOGY OF the word "Papua" has always puzzled me. Every historical text I have read in English that bothers to define the word offers approximately the same etymology, which is, as Gavin Souter writes in his 1963 *New Guinea, The Last Unknown:* "[The word 'Papua' comes] from the Malay term 'orang papuwah' meaning 'fuzzy-haired man'."

The earliest example I have been able to find comes from George Windsor Earl's *The Native Races of the Indian Archipelago, Papuans,* published in London in 1853, and it seems this is the source.

> The Malayan term for crisped or woolly hair is "rambut pua-pua." Hence the term "pua-pua," or "papua" (crisped), has come to be applied to the entire race; and certainly it deserves to be retained, as expressing their most striking peculiarity.

Earl published widely at the time on Papuan and Aboriginal Australian ethnography, although having read some of his work I'm certain it wouldn't be judged very important today. More usefully, he translated the accounts of two of the more significant 19th-century Dutch expeditions to New Guinea. He was also very adept at promoting his ideas. It was Earl, for example, who successfully petitioned the British Admiralty's hydrographer in 1837 to formally name the sea between New Guinea and Australia the "Arafura." This name is far from being of local origin and I have seen no map that used it before Earl. The "Aru Sea" would be a more accurate and conventional name for this body of water.

The problem with Earl's etymology is that I have never found an Indonesian dictionary that contains an entry for "pua-pua," nor have I met an Indonesian speaker who knows what it means.

The most thorough discussion of the term "Papua" occurs in a 1993 article by J.H.F. Sollewijn Gelpke, a historian who had been a Dutch colonial civil servant in the area in the forties and fifties. In "On the origin of the name Papua," Gelpke systematically dismisses Earl and his many successors, including such random and ludicrous etymologies as "papùa" (a local name for papaya, offered because the coiner reckoned there was an inordinate amount of papaya growing in New Guinea), "papoewa" (a local Ambonese term for "tangled," such as a fishing line), and "poea" (a Sundanese word for "ants' nest hanging from a tree").

Gelpke believes that the most plausible source of "Papua" is the Biak phrase "sup i papwa." This was first suggested by Freerk C. Kamma, in a 1954 book on messianic movements on Biak. According to Kamma, *sup i papwa,* which means "the land below the sunset," was occasionally used to refer to the Raja Ampat which, of course, lie west of Biak and Numfoor.

Gelpke and Kamma may be correct, or the term could be a proper noun, coming from the Raja Ampat themselves. What is certain is that "Papua" is not a recent and slightly derogatory loanword from Malay referring to hair texture or some other trivial characteristic of the people of Raja Ampat. Their language and those spoken in Ternate, Tidore, half of nearby Makian, and North Halmahera are all part of the Papuan language family. This linguistic relationship has existed for at least fifteen thousand years, and the term "Papua" may be just as ancient.

THE INFLUENCE OF MALUKU did not reach the Kamoro area directly through the Raja Ampat. The Raja Misool enjoyed trade and tribute relationships with the coastal areas of the Onin Peninsula, where Fakfak is today, but further south the New Guinea coast was controlled by the *raja*s of Seram Laut, a tiny chain of islands off the eastern tip of Seram Island. Seram Laut lies a little more than three hundred kilometers west of Lakahia Bay, and it was with these islands that the Kamoro enjoyed periodic contact with traders.

When the Europeans first arrived in the early 16th century, the Banda Islands were the most important Malukan entrepôt. The winds were more reliable beween Melaka and Banda than they were between Melaka and Ternate or Tidore. From Banda to Melaka and back by sail took six months; the same trip from Ternate took a year. The Bandanese were well-known sailors and merchants, and many transported spice to the west and gathered trade products from New Guinea in the east.

In the early 17th century the Dutch tried to impose their spice monopoly on the Bandanese. Traditional authority structures in Banda were not as hierarchical as those in Ternate and Tidore, however, and the Dutch found it more difficult to control the Bandanese traders. In 1609 they occupied the main island of Banda Niera, built a fort there, and forced the Bandanese to accept a Dutch monopoly on exports of nutmeg and mace.

This proved disastrous to the Bandanese, since not only did the Dutch refuse to bring rice from western Indonesia to trade for the nutmegs—they preferred to fill their ships with cargo having a higher ratio of value to volume—but they also forced the Bandanese to accept heavy velvet and wool cloth in trade. This material was understandably unpopular in the archipelago, and the Bandanese could not use it to buy the sago and rice upon which they depended to live.

Unrest grew among the Bandanese, and this, combined with the threat of a small British presence in the outer Banda islands, convinced the Dutch to send in the infamous Jan Pieterszoon Coen, who in 1621, literally destroyed Banda. Thousands of Bandanese were killed, and thousands more were shipped to Batavia, now Jakarta, as slaves. The population before the massacre stood at fifteen thousand; afterward, it stood at less than fifteen hundred.

The destruction of Banda dramatically altered the trade networks of the eastern islands. Many Bandanese traders fled, settling in the Kei Islands and, particularly, Keffing Island in the Seram Laut group. Some of the newly transplanted Bandanese in Keffing later resettled in Makassar, at the invitation of the ruler of Goa. These merchants soon rebuilt their old trade route, with Seram Laut as the new entrepôt in the eastern archipelago. Slaves, aromatic woods, bird of paradise skins, ambergris, pearls, and smuggled spices came to Seram Laut from the east, to be traded for rice, guns, cloth, pottery, and steel utensils from the west. It has been estimated that from the 17th to the early 19th century, the volume of trade goods moved through Seram Laut at least equalled that handled by the Dutch.

At the same time Seram Laut was becoming the most important trade center in the eastern islands, the actions of the Dutch were further eroding the reciprocal character of relations between Tidore and its traditional peripheral states. In 1683 Ternate formally became a vassal of the Dutch and Tidore informally so. Dutch demands on the areas under the Sultan of Tidore, particularly the extirpation of clove trees and the ending of the slave trade, sparked a short rebellion of the Papuan areas in the early 18th century. Although quelled by the sultan in 1728 with Dutch help, the rebellion was a sign that the Raja Ampat were becoming estranged from Tidore.

In the late 18th century, Seram Laut and the Raja Ampat together lent their support to a charismatic anti-colonial leader named Nuku, who went by the honorific Jou Barakti or "Lord of Fortune." Nuku, with assistance from some independent British traders in the area, led all of Maluku in a rebellion against the Dutch and Dutch-controlled Tidore, and from 1801 until he died in 1805, Nuku sat on the throne of a briefly unified and nearly independent Maluku.

The *raja*s of Seram Laut enjoyed their own peripheral states, with leaders on whom they conferred titles and privilege. These *raja*s were located at various

STEFANUS TAKAYUTA, KEAKWA.

times on the islands of Adi, Namatota, Aiduma, and Lakahia, and they controlled trade on the coast of New Guinea from the southern tip of the Bomberai Peninsula to Lakahia Bay, an area called Kowiai, or in Maclay's phrase, "The Kowiai Coast." The Kowiai language is Austronesian, like those in Western Indonesia, not Papuan, and the Kowiai *raja*s were often of mixed or Seram Laut heritage.

In the 19th century, looting expeditions from the Sultan of Tidore disrupted the balance of power between Seram Laut and the Kowiai *raja*s. With the support of the Dutch, who pressured the sultan to help establish Dutch sovereignty in the area, Tidore directly appointed *raja*s of Aiduma and Namatota, and in 1848 razed the village of Lakahia. In 1874 a looting and slaving raid led by Prince Ali of Tidore again swept through Kowiai, and by the turn of the century, the Raja of Namatota was preeminent in the area.

Namatota's influence extended westward deep into Kamoro territory, through the "Raja" of Kipia. According to anthropologist Jan Pouwer, the Raja of Kipia in 1900 was a famous war leader named Naowo. His influence at the time was said to extend from Uta to Umar, and perhaps even to Lakahia.*

By 1915, the era of the Tidorese- and Seramese-influenced *raja*s in the Kamoro area had ended. The Dutch government and missions were beginning to be established in the region, and trade was taken up by independent Chinese merchants.

ON AUGUST 5, 1894, ornithologist and lepidopterist Captain H. Cayley-Webster, on an expedition to collect birds and butterflies for Baron Walter von Rothschild's museum in Tring, England, finally succeeded against an inclement current in reaching the narrow entrance to Etna Bay, the innermost extension of Lakahia Bay. A dozen Kamoro men cautiously approached in a canoe, and Captain Webster welcomed them on board and offered them a meal of rice and taro. The next morning, several more canoes arrived. But the captain soon began to have misgivings about his new friends, he writes, in his 1898 *Through New Guinea and the Cannibal Countries.*

> I was sorry, however, to see the majority of them had their teeth sharpened to points, resembling the tooth of the shark, this being in my own personal experience a very bad sign in natives. They asked me if I

would like to purchase one or two girls they had for sale. When I asked them what I should do with them, they intimated that of course I should fatten them for a purpose which shall be nameless.

The captain's relations with the people of "Lahabia" were cordial at first, but on August 11 took an ugly turn when, he writes, "my early fears, which I had formed owing to their sharpened teeth, were indeed realised." On this day the men launched a concerted attack against both the captain's boat and a collecting party that had gone ashore. Three among the shore party were killed, and the launch and five rifles were lost.

Captain Webster was not one to take an insult like this without reprisal. He immediately began to lay down a withering fire from a "Krupp gun," a kind of heavy machine gun he had mounted to the deck of his ship. He raked the lines of his Kamoro attackers, whose number he estimated at about three hundred, and the casualties must have been very heavy. Once he had driven back his attackers he ordered their canoes scuttled, and his men took axes to forty of them. Despite these heavy losses, the people of Lakahia, whose village at the time was located on the eastern shore of the bay, not the island, continued to harass Webster for the four days his ship remained becalmed in their territory, and he was regularly forced to rely on his Krupp.

Captain Webster is not a particularly sympathetic character, and he encounters so much "treachery" in his travels—in addition to the attack, someone steals his cigars, a disgruntled carpenter cuts his mast, a rat runs off with a prized chrysalis—that one can't help thinking that he must have earned at least some of it. His text gives the impression of a boorish, judgmental, and clumsy man, whose presence in the area seems to have been a curse unmitigated by insight. But he cannot be blamed for the behavior of the people of Lakahia. Theirs is a history that stretches back at least three hundred years before Webster. In his ignorance, he came seeking butterflies in what was probably the single most dangerous part of western New Guinea.

"These men have been robbed, beaten, and taken away as slaves innumerable times," writes Maclay, who spent a month and a half in the area in early 1874, in his *Travels to New Guinea.* "It is not surprising that everybody appears as an enemy to them. In their turn, they try to pay back in kind anyone who is foolish enough to fall into their hands. It is precisely this place, the coast near Lakahia, that has such a bad reputation."

LAKAHIA IS A LOW ISLAND of sandstone and coral limestone not quite three kilometers long and perhaps a kilometer wide. On a map it appears to sit in the middle of Lakahia Bay, but the deep channel into the bay and good anchorage is west of the island. Huge sandbars reach out from the east, and if you dropped the sea level just a couple of meters the

---

* In J. Modera's account of the Dutch *Triton* expedition of 1828, the lieutenant reports that according to a chief of Uta, the territory from Uta to Lakahia was called "Koyway." Because of this, some commentators, such as Father Petrus Drabbe, have suggested that "Kowiai" referred to the Kamoro. Other than Modera's stray comment, I have not seen evidence to support this conclusion. I think it is more likely that Modera's informant was stating that the village chiefs in this area, through trade relationships and conferred titles—such as the Raja of Kipia—considered themselves part of the prestigious "kingdom" of the Kowiai *raja*s. Since he was speaking to Modera, an important outsider, I think the chief of Uta—who had personally visited Seram Laut and whose village regularly hosted Seram Laut traders—was probably just boasting of his worldliness.

Coal seam, Lakahia.

island would be wholly attached to the Boiya Peninsula by land. As it is, at the lowest tide even a boat as small as ours had to search for the tiny channel that would allow us to pass to the east of the island.

The coastline is a mix of mangrove and sandy beaches, with the beaches seemingly gaining the upper hand. In front of Lakahia village a lone tree stands far out on the sand, a victim of the receding shoreline. Unlike anywhere else in the Kamoro area, Lakahia is ringed with patch reefs of coral and seagrass beds.

Lakahia is the final outpost of the old Meganesian mainland, and eight thousand years ago everything east of this island was dry land. The shallow Arafura Sea ends here. The next bay to the west, Kayumerah, is clear, and the one after that, Triton, is as blue as a postcard. The next equally well protected anchorage a large ship would find sailing east from Lakahia was in Papua New Guinea, which is the main reason Lakahia was the final outpost of trade on this coast.

The formal government name of the village here is Boiya, the same as the cape and small hill that mark Lakahia Bay's eastern shore. The traditional name is Ara, but most people call it Lakahia. The village perches on a flat clearing just above the wide beach fronting the northeastern tip of the island. Although its population of 325 is about average for a Kamoro village, Lakahia looks more prosperous than most, an impression that comes from the concrete block buildings, the galvanized roofs, the generator and satellite television, and the bright clothing. There are five outboard motors here. Many Kamoro villages have one or two, and some do not have any. Five is unusual.

Lakahia's famous coal is impossible to miss. It extends in a broad, black seam right out onto the beach in front of the village, and stands out strikingly against the white coral sand. The coal is soft enough to break off with your hands, and flakes into squarish leaves under slight pressure. The Lakahia villagers don't recall anyone thinking of mining it, but they remembered that an Australian geologist had come to examine the deposit about ten years before. One man had seen the geologist write "75%" in his notebook and asked me if I knew what that meant. I told him I was as much in the dark as he.

The people of Lakahia don't use the coal for cooking, which seemed strange to me until I was told that they do sometimes break off a chunk and light it to keep away mosquitoes. It must be a very low-grade and sulfurous material. Even if Pool and Keyts had been able to buy this coal in the early 17th century, they may not have been happy with their purchase. Alo said when he was visiting Lakahia in 1989 the

ADAM IRAHEWA, OTAKWA.
His catch consists of sharks and fork-tailed catfish.

seam caught on fire, and burned for two weeks before it was finally extinguished by the rain.

The village generator came on at 6:15 in the evening, and one of the men rigged up a fluorescent tube for us at the clinic, a new concrete block building with louvered windows and a few wooden benches. The nurse was in Kiruru, the village at the innermost point of Etna Bay. Since the clinic hadn't been used in a while, there was no water in the bathroom reservoir, and Apollo arranged a place for us to bathe with one of the families he knew.

Kal and I were the most anxious for a bath and, soap and towels in hand, headed across the village to the designated spot. Although there was plenty of clean water and a stool to sit on, the area was completely unsheltered. Only one person was within sight, however, a woman sitting out behind the next house. She seemed studiously to be ignoring us, although I thought I saw a flicker of a smile. Since we had walked all the way over there we figured why not, and began to undress. But when a second woman showed up to join the first, and we noticed she was carrying a chair, Kal and I lost our nerve. We gathered our things and walked back to the clinic.

Apollo saw us return and, assuming we had finished, left with his towel a few minutes later. It was a long time before he returned. "How was your bath?" we asked. He laughed, and said as soon as he saw the situation he hastily arranged to use a more private facility behind his cousin's house.

Much of Lakahia's apparent prosperity comes from a new and quite lucrative trade product—live grouper. In the six-month period before we visited in the summer of 1997, I was told, the village had shipped out three loads of live fish, the first weighing 1 metric ton, the second, 2.5 tons, and the third, 1.7 tons. The total income earned from this was Rp 52 million, about $17,000 at the time, and the five outboard motors and fishing equipment were provided free by the grouper dealer. About half of the adult men in the village now fish for grouper, which means each is earning around $100 a month for his efforts, not bad money here.

The market for these fish is Singapore, Taiwan, and China, especially Hong Kong. By the time a grouper—which an American might call sea bass, and an Australian would call cod—ends up on a diner's plate, it can cost hundreds of dollars. The wholesale prices in Hong Kong for the three species of *Epinephelus* being caught around Lakahia, according to a 1995 report on the live reef fish trade by Robert Johannes and Michael Riepen, range from $20 to $40 a kilogram. The fishermen in Lakahia are paid $2.50–$3.50 a kilogram, depending on the species.

The men set trotlines at night and check them each morning. The live catch is placed in holding nets that have been carefully rigged in the tidal estuaries, and any dead fish are eaten that day. Once a month Lee Ong, who is the broker in this trade, stops to check how many fish the men have caught. When the holding nets are full, he contacts his backers, and a boat with a live well stops at Lakahia, picks up the whole lot, and carries them to Hong Kong.

In the evening, Apollo and I rounded up some coffee and cigarettes and sat down with a couple of the fishermen under our jury-rigged fluorescent light. The work was good, they said, and they much preferred fishing to cutting massoy, an aromatic bark that until recently had been the main trade product of this area, in the sweltering heat of the foothills. The men were well versed in the technical details of grouper fishing and handling, and spoke knowledgeably about the temperature and oxygen content of seawater, the relative abrasiveness of different styles of mesh nets, and the relative merits of different techniques for removing a fish hook. This was the result of Lee Ong's training program, I was told, and it was very impressive.

Grouper, it turns out, is a very sensitive fish in captivity. Mortality in the holding pens is very high: four out of five fish caught don't live to be weighed and loaded on the boat. In the beginning, the men said, it was even worse. The improvement came from locating the nets in areas where the water was cooler, and especially in using a new net material, a kind of a knit that doesn't irritate the fish's sensitive skin as much as the typical knotted mesh. Since the village had shipped out 5.2 tons of live fish—which, given the mortality rate meant something like 26 tons had been caught—I asked if grouper weren't becoming scarce.

"They're not less common," said one fisherman, "but you have to be very careful removing the hook from the little ones"—he said specimens weighing less than a kilogram are thrown back—"because if you are rough and hurt the fish, it will learn and will never bite a hook again. After a while, you won't be able to fish in that area. If you are gentle, it is okay though."

Historically, the most famous and most lucrative product from this area was human slaves. The center of this trade was the coast of the Bomberai Peninsula and the Kowiai Coast, including Lakahia. The first recorded mention of what some historians think is New Guinea occurs in an eighth-century Chinese text by Chan Ju Kua, recording the tribute the emperor had received from the Raja of Sriwijaya, Indonesia's first great maritime empire. Included in this list of valuables is an entry for two slave girls from "Seng-k'i."

Seng-k'i, later also rendered "Tungki" or "Janggi," is though to derive from "Senggaraya," a word for the Bomberai area in Onin, an Austronesian language spoken on the Onin Peninsula near Fakfak. Whether or not this etymology is correct, this seems a singularly inauspicious way to enter written history.

During the Napoleonic Wars in Europe in the early

159

ENCAMPMENT ON BEACH, KAOKATURU.

19th century, the Dutch briefly lost their East Indies colonies to the British, and soon after the restoration, the colonial government sent Dirk Hendrik Kolff to report on conditions in the easternmost extent of their colony. Kolff, in the brig *Dourga,* named after the wife or consort of the Hindu god Siva, visited eastern Maluku and western New Guinea in 1825 and 1826.

In Seram Laut, Kolff found that the slave trade was thriving. Slaves from New Guinea, he reports in the 1840 *Voyages of the Dutch Brig of War* Dourga, "are held in great esteem, so much that their price is higher even than that given for slaves of Bali, Lombok, or Sumbawa." He goes on to note that women from Karas Island, Aiduma Island, and "Koby" (Kowiai?) were considered the most beautiful, and were often sought by the Seram Laut *rajas* as inferior wives.

> The price given for a slave on the coast is usually two pieces of white calico, valued at from eight to ten Spanish dollars, from sixty to seventy rupees (five to six pounds sterling) being obtained by the traders for them in Bali, and other places in that direction.

Kolff, like so many other Europeans before him, met an unfriendly reception on Lakahia. Stopping just off the island on May 19, 1826, he entertained three chiefs of the village with food and palm whiskey, and all seemed well. But the next day, when he sent a party ashore to fill the *Dourga*'s water casks, the men were attacked with spears and arrows, and one sailor died. In retribution, Kolff had his men cut down the island's coconut palms, a harsh punishment in an area with few such trees, and tear down some huts, the latter in Kayumerah Bay, and perhaps not even Lakahian.*

When the Dutch abolished slavery in Ternate and Tidore in 1879, they made an exception for Tidore's "possessions" in western New Guinea. Slavery here did not became officially illegal until the late 1930s.

Although the most valuable, slaves were not the only trade items to come out of western New Guinea. Bird of paradise skins, some low-grade oval nutmegs, and reef products like dried sea cucumber and *Trochus* were also important. In the Kowiai and Kamoro areas the most lucrative trade products, after slaves, were copal or dammar resin from the New Guinea kauri tree *Agathis labillardieri,* used in varnishes and laquers, and an aromatic bark called massoy.

Massoy comes from a tree in the laurel family native to New Guinea called *Cryptocarya massoy.* The bark of this tree is a common trade product throughout the

---

* In his English translation of Kolff, Earl notes that two years later, in 1828, the leader of Lakahia told members of the *Triton* expedition that his men had attacked the landing party only after one of the sailors began cutting down one of their precious coconut trees.

archipelago and has a number of uses, chiefly therapeutic. It is used to flavor food and is an ingredient in tonics, particularly to cure stomach ache and diarrhea, and in ointments to heat up the skin. In Java, shavings of massoy are said to have been placed in the stuffing of pillows to promote health. I have read that massoy is used by the batik industry, as well as in making gin. One source from the 1930s states that in Singapore, it was sometimes mixed with tobacco in cigarettes.

In Keakwa I was given a piece of massoy by Robertus Moporteyau. Robertus was familiar with many traditional remedies and kept a variety of barks and other medicinals around his house. When Kal's son Andres acquired a slight sprain in one of his ankles playing soccer on the beach, Robertus offered to fix it. He disappeared to get some materials, and I expected him to return with an elaborate poultice of rare plants. Instead, he brought back a pot of very hot water, and fixed the ankle with this and a bit of judicious rubbing.

Massoy trees are stripped in meter-long sections, and when dry they look like giant cinnamon sticks. The bark is light and spongy, with patches of white on its outer surface. It has a strong, pleasant, camphorous scent, like Tiger Balm or Vick's Vaporub, with a touch of something like cinnamon or nutmeg. Robertus told me to eat a small amount, and it produced a localized numbness in my mouth. The bark contains eugenol, safrol, and traces of other aromatic substances.

In the Kamoro area, two varieties are distinguished—*lawang,* which grows at lower elevations and has rather thick bark, and *mesui,* which grows in the limestone foothills and has thinner bark. These are Indonesian names. Traders pay a bit more for *mesui,* but the Kamoro consider both equally effective, and the Kamoro language does not distinguish between the two—both are called *tarika.* The Kamoro take *tarika* internally for stomach troubles and apply a paste of it externally to ease headache. While we were on the subject of medicinals, Robertus also showed me a sample of what he considered a more powerful wood. Put a sliver of this in your mouth, he said, and you can have the woman of your choice.

The Dutch learned of the trade in massoy in the late 17th century from a report by the famous early naturalist Rumphius, who arrived in the Dutch Indies in 1653 and stayed there until his death in 1702. Rumphius, German by birth, spent most of his life on Ambon Island working for the Dutch colonial government, and more importantly, assembling catalogs of the plants and "curiosities" of the archipelago.

Rumphius reported in 1684 that massoy trees grow best on the limey, well-drained soil of the coastal foothills between Onin on the Bomberai Peninsula and roughly the Omba River in the Kamoro area. Even at this time, overcutting in the Onin area had shifted the center of massoy gathering south, until, by the late 17th century, the trade was centered in Kowiai, which his text renders "Cubiaay." The local

AGUS TANIYU, ATUKA.
Agus has caught a fine Fly River turtle, *Carettochelys insculpta.*

entrepôt was the island of "Saca Iha"—Lakahia.

Actually, the tree grows throughout the Kamoro area, but the collecting was most common in the area Rumphius describes because the limestone foothills massoy prefers are much closer to the sea in Onin and Kowiai. When the Dutch began administering the Kamoro area directly, they taxed their subjects in massoy (and dammar), and the onerous labor the gathering required became very unpopular.

The trade was later picked up by merchants, chiefly Chinese, who recruited Kamoro labor in exchange for axes, knives, tobacco, and betelnut. The market crashed in the late 1950s, although massoy is still occasionally gathered. Kal recently saw stacks of the bark in the area of Lake Yamur, just inland of Etna Bay.

LAKAHIA IS THE FIRST VILLAGE we have visited that is predominantly Protestant, and all but three or four of the families here attend the Indonesian Protestant Church. The large, open-sided building has pride of place in the village. The church bell is an old acetylene cylinder, hanging in a little roofed bell house. The villages from Lakahia Bay to Potowai-Buru are Protestant; the rest of the Kamoro area is Catholic.

The village has not celebrated a *karapao*—the dialect

here is like that of the Nawaripi people, and the word is pronounced "arapao"—since just after World War II, although the villagers insist that the Protestant church does not forbid such rituals. The reason the *karapao* is gone, we were told, is because the old people who knew the traditions all died without training any of the younger generation. Only ritual singing and some dancing remain of the old Kamoro traditions.

Lakahia Bay narrows dramatically about twenty-five kilometers from its mouth, where another thin bay heads due east. This second bay was named "Etna," after a ship used in a 1858 Dutch expedition, but its traditional name is Kiruru Bay. On a trip along both bays in 1996, Kal and I had seen several strange altars or shrines around the point where Lakahia becomes Etna Bay. The shrines were built into natural shelves in the limestone rock that hung out over the water. In them were porcelain plates, bits of cloth, and in each, a weathered old crocodile skull.

"In the old days, when a man killed a crocodile he took the skull and put it at the location where he killed it," said Melkianus Nai, a man from Lakahia who is in his sixties. "This was because he was proud, and everybody who passed by saw the skull and was reminded of the hunter's strength and skill."

Over time, he said, the man's family would place small offerings next to the skull—a bit of cloth, a few coins, a porcelain dish—in honor of the event. This would continue even after the man had died. Kal and I couldn't quite judge the age of the shrines we saw. They could have been twenty years old or a hundred and twenty years old. One shrine also contained a human skull, and in 1874 Maclay found three human skulls in an altar in the same area (which he took for his collection). I didn't get around to the delicate matter of asking about this, but I couldn't help wondering if it had been placed there for the same reason.

WHILE IN LAKAHIA we took our meals with Apollo's cousin, Irene Fidelia Amirbai, and her husband Otniel Pitan. Irene Fidelia, who goes by "Ucin," is an outgoing woman who also serves as the village nurse when the government nurse is visiting other villages (which is most of the time). Ucin served us rice for dinner, and I seemed to touch a nerve when I asked if there were any sago.

"The reason we're eating rice," she said, "is that everyone is so busy chasing grouper that nobody bothers to go to the mainland to pound sago. People prefer sago, but a lot of rice is now eaten in this village."

It has been so long since anybody from Lakahia visited the village's sago grounds that entrepreneurs now bring *tumang*s of fresh sago from Omba and sell them in Lakahia for a good price. The only problem is that they don't come often enough, and competition to buy this sago when it arrives is fierce. "You have to swim to the boat to get any," is how Ucin put it.

At breakfast on our last morning in Lakahia, Ucin had a surprise for us: fresh wheat rolls, something we hadn't seen for weeks. They were lightly sugared and delicious. While we were finishing our coffee, I watched from the window as Ucin gave a roll each to two young boys. That would make a heartwarming photograph, I thought, with the two boys, holding hands, each happy with a roll in his free hand.

As soon as Ucin turned and walked back to the house, a village dog ambled over to one of the boys and, ever so gently, took the roll from his hand. This was done with such impressive grace that I'm sure the boy had no idea what happened. He certainly noticed that his roll wasn't there anymore, however, and began to cry. The nearest adult, hearing this, figured out what had happened in an instant, and tore off after the dog with a stick. But the dog had a head start, and as far as I could tell he got away.

The Kamoro like dogs, and every village is full of them. The breed is sometimes called the New Guinea singing dog, and it doesn't bark at all. This sounds like a wonderful characteristic in a dog, but when they really get going this "singing" (howling, actually) can be very disquieting.

The New Guinea dog is an attractive breed, short-haired and slim in build, and not very large. It looks a lot like an Australian dingo, but smaller. A light yellow-brown seems to be the most typical color, although darker brown or black are also common. I never saw one with a patterned coat, though many have white chests and shins. Scientists once called it Hallstrom's dog, *Canis hallstromi,* but this animal is now considered *Canis familiaris* like every other domestic dog in the world, and was introduced at least two thousand years ago (some say four thousand).

These dogs are not pets. They are valued for their hunting ability, and the very best ones receive a ceremonial burial like that of a man. When Alexander Wollaston was in Kiura (he calls it Parimau) in 1911, he noted that the village's most prized possession was a piece of iron about the size of a chisel. The price of this item, which had been obtained from the village of Mimika, was considered enormous: three good dogs.

The breed lines of the best dogs are watched as carefully as those of a good hound in the United States, and the best are fearless. They have to be, to corner a wild boar and hold it there until the men can approach with their spears. They also handle themselves competently in the water, and have excellent balance in a canoe. They often perch right up on the bow, and when the canoes return, they enthusiastically jump into the water and swim the last ten or twenty meters to the shore.

After breakfast we loaded our canoe, and prepared to head back along the coast. Apollo looked worried: he said he saw "black air" above the sea. We saw it too, and knew that it didn't bode well. Still, we were determined to continue our journey, and didn't much care what the weather thought of our decision.

KORNELIS KAMIPAPEYA, NEAR IWAKA.
A good hunting dog is almost invaluable.

CHAPTER SEVEN

Along the Brown Sea

Visiting the Villages of the Far West

HERE IS A TELEVISION in the clinic at Omba. It worked for two months. Actually, it still works, and the shipping box placed over it protects it nicely from dust. The television, together with a satellite dish and a generator, was provided by the government, but these gifts came with only two months' supply of diesel. After the fuel ran out, more than a year ago, nobody bothered to buy any more.

When we arrived at the clinic, the floor was covered in a layer of gray dust so thick that at first I thought it was sand. Two men swept it for us, but their brooms were too coarse and the sweeping left a pattern of ridges. From these I could tell that Kamoro men aren't used to sweeping. The wall behind the television held a tangle of wires, and since they were of no use to the television, I separated one to string a line for our wet clothes. The thin cord, a few hairs of copper wrapped in yellow insulation, snapped as I tightened it.

The clinic contained a table, a bench, and two steel bed frames, all of these also covered with dust. Although the concrete building looked relatively new, the walls were decaying, as if the contractor had used beach sand in the concrete. In places I could scrape the material away with my finger. When the first splash of water hit the dry bathroom floor, the ammonia fumes knocked me backward. The last time the nurse-practitioner from Kiruru was here was nine months ago, I was told, and he stayed for exactly one day. Nobody could remember the time before that.

We hadn't intended to stop in Omba, which is still quite close to Lakahia, but when we rounded Cape Boiya the Arafura had turned to meringue. We thought about putting in at the mouth of the O'opa River—O'opa is the traditional name for Omba—but the tide was low and Manu didn't like the look of things there. He thought our chances would be better continuing on and cutting up a tidal creek he knew of

***

NEAR THE PORTAGE TO THE MATOAPOKA RIVER. When the Arafura Sea is misbehaving, the only hope for a heavily loaded canoe is to pole it tediously along the boat channel just inside the breakers near shore.

MARGARETA KEMEYAU, ATUKA.

right in front of Omba village. The O'opa River empties into the sea at a small cape, while the creek Manu sought was inside a small bay, protected from the worst of the waves.

Although Manu's choice was surely the right one, the tide was so low by the time we reached the creek that we had to struggle to drag the boat through the breakers. Actually, with three or four people helping, it wouldn't have been a struggle at all. But even though our arrival attracted onlookers, none of them offered to lend a hand. This was the strangest thing about Omba. In every other Kamoro village we had visited, the people were very helpful and interested. But here they just watched suspiciously as we fought with our boat, which was rocking dangerously in the surf as each new wave threatened to swamp it. Apollo and Alo were so shocked by this behavior that they were speechless. When I pressed him on the subject, Alo, still sweating from his labors with the boat, shook his head and muttered something that included the words "backward" and "education."

Once our boat was tucked safely into the slough, two men finally walked over to say hello. Neither was from Omba. The older of the two, a man of about fifty, was from Kipia, and he and Apollo soon realized that they were related in some complicated way. I don't know what it is about Apollo, but he has more relatives than anybody I've ever met. He also has eight children, and if this level of fecundity runs in his family, that's probably explanation enough.

We forded what was left of the creek and then walked toward the village along the part of the bed exposed by the outgoing tide. The sand was damp and hard, and myriad tiny crabs were busy digging their burrows. Fiddler crabs, whose huge right claw made somebody think of a fiddle, preferred the wet, silty mud on the freshwater side, and their excavations resembled worm casings, or a bead of toothpaste extruded by a jittery hand. Ghost crabs, nervous insect-like creatures with pointed eyes, were more numerous, and worked the drier, seaward side of the sandbank. They dug out one cautious little ball of sand at a time, each bigger than buckshot but smaller than a pea, which they cast out in circles from their burrows.

167

Their work, on the grandest scale, yielded something like a pointillist rendering of raindrops striking a pond. The fiddler crab toothpaste felt just like mud, but the pellets of the ghost crabs crunched lightly underfoot.

The village of Omba, formally called Nariki, is divided into two neighborhoods and somehow gives the impression of being new, although it isn't. Kapok trees line the river where it winds through the village, and banana plants stand in thick clumps. Somebody had planted some tobacco, and I was later told that cigarettes rolled from this were very strong, perhaps because the plants were growing so near the hot coast.

Once we reached the village, the people seemed to warm to us somewhat, and a few men introduced themselves. Then they showed us to the clinic and gave it a desultory sweeping. When we asked to tour the village, a large group of men appeared to accompany us. Although the village head and other men politely answered my questions, they still seemed wary, or even guilty, as if there were something going on here they didn't want us to see. Nobody said so, but I got the distinct impression they wished we had stopped somewhere else.

Eyoksi Wau, the *kepala desa,* said the school goes to the fourth grade, but the teacher left two years ago and never returned. Only one child from Omba was currently in school, he said, in the sub-district seat of Kiruru at the innermost point of Etna Bay. Five people from Omba have finished junior high school, but they all chose to return to the village rather than continue.

We were able to buy some smoked catfish which, together with the rice and "kornèd" from our stores, became our dinner. Kal genuinely likes this corned beef, and Apollo and Alo don't mind it. There are not many cows in Irian Jaya and it makes a nice change. I generally like tinned meat, but a wet plate of this lardy material always depressed me. The smell when the seal was cracked on the pyramidal cans was exactly that of the three-cans-for-a-dollar dog food of my youth, which never helped my appetite.

WE LEFT OMBA early in the morning and quickly, with no regrets. Nobody stopped by the clinic to share a cup of coffee with us after dinner, and as soon as the sun went down, the village became a ghost town. The atmosphere was strange enough that we asked Manu, Tobias, and his young assistant to stay with the boat overnight. Just after the dawn mist had cleared, on an outgoing tide, we slipped out along the Taimakea River and headed away from Omba just as rapidly as we could manage.

Rounding the steep point of Cape Nariki, just before we entered the shallows of the Arafura Sea, two whales surfaced from the deep, black water. The Kamoro, it seems, are very superstitious about whales. Or maybe it is just Apollo. When we saw the whales, which are still called Popefish in Indonesia, Apollo said they are very bad luck for a man who has

Omba.
It took this boy fifteen minutes to catch the rooster, then he couldn't decide what to do with it.

been cheating on his wife. If such a man has accepted a token from his lover—a ring, a bit of food, anything—the whale will sense it, and swim over and stop the canoe. It will not let the boat pass until the unfaithful man leaves the canoe and climbs onto the whale's back. The boat will then be free to leave, but the hapless Romeo will be dragged down to his death.

Fig. 7.1 POPEFISH.
A 17th century interpretation by
Matthäus Merian.

"Good thing we didn't sleep with any women in Omba," Apollo said. I told him that the way I understood the story, the lesson wasn't necessarily not to cheat on your wife, but rather to avoid taking gifts if you do.

The Arafura Sea, as usual, was uncooperative. Just after we saw the whales, conditions began to deteriorate, and we began thinking of places to stop. Potowai-Buru was close, but there was no point stopping there, because at Potowai we could slip inland and run parallel to the coast for a good fifteen kilometers on a protected river. The real problem was going to be the next cape to the east, Waratiri, which our boat would not be able to negotiate in such choppy conditions. We settled on Yapakopa, just west of the cape.

We really had no business making such a long trip at this time of year. The best time for travel along this coast is during either of the two periods of relative calm between the monsoons. February through May, the calm period following the west monsoon, and October through December, the calm period following the east monsoon, are probably the best times to travel. Even at the height of the short west monsoon, from mid-December through January, the winds are patchy and travel is not so difficult. The single worst time to be in a boat on the Arafura is during the height of the east monsoon, which brings steady high winds from May to September. Since it was August, we were getting exactly what we deserved.

The tense and unfriendly atmosphere in Omba left us all with bad feelings, but I didn't think any more about it until Apollo brought the subject up a week later, in Paripi. On the morning we left, Apollo said, the older man from Kipia gave him some chilling news. He said the people of Omba thought that Kal and I had come to kill them, and had paid Apollo and Alo a lot of money to guide us there. That's why, Apollo said, the men of the village stayed so close to us as we walked around the village, and why they seemed so guarded and suspicious. He said that evening he and Alo had encountered a group of men with bows and arrows, and when they asked where they were going, the men said they were going to the forest to hunt deer. But they had not gone hunting at all, his friend from Kipia told him the next morning. Instead the armed men spent the night watching the clinic.

"We slept well," Apollo said, "but they didn't."

I noted that it was lucky that the clinic had an indoor bathroom and none of us had to go outside at night to take a leak.

"Omba is just too far from the government," Apollo said, shaking his head. "The people need education."

AN ODD THING HAPPENED as soon as we came ashore in Yapakopa. I was already most of the way up the bank when I heard somebody crying behind me. I turned around and saw our guide Manu, with his trademark camouflage baseball cap barely clinging to his head, bawling like a child.

Apollo filled me in on what I missed. When Manu was about to step off the boat, somebody from the crowd came forward and briefly detained him. He then stepped down, and the stranger rubbed sand on each of his toes. Then Manu began to wail.

Manu is originally from Yapakopa, and his father died here the year before. The wailing was a traditional way to grieve for his father. The stranger put sand on his feet to insure that his father's spirit, sensing Manu's presence, won't come to the village to see him, which it might otherwise be inclined to do.

In the past this was done to all strangers who came to a village, to insure that they wouldn't attract any unwanted spirits. For their part, Apollo said, upon arriving in a strange village strangers should eat a bit of sand to ward off any sickness they might encounter.

The complication in Manu's situation is that he was in Paripi when his father died last year. When this occurs, tradition suggests that he stay away from Yapakopa for at least three years and only then, with his father's spirit safely at rest, return to visit his family. At this stage he should also bring some coffee and tobacco to host a celebration. We weren't planning to stop in Yapakopa, and if we had been Manu probably would not have agreed to come along. But we were caught by the weather, and there was nothing for us to do but stop.

I told Apollo to give Manu some of our coffee and tobacco so he could at least keep part of the bargain. I briefly met his mother and family, who seemed happy to see him. The little ceremony with the sand also seemed to work, and as far as I could tell his father's spirit never appeared while we were in Yapakopa.

The village of Yapakopa was immediately warm and inviting. "We are not strangers here," was how Apollo put it. A friendly crowd met us at the riverside and led us to the house of the head of the village, Sylvester Auti. Yapakopa is not even halfway to Paripi, but with the weather we faced we didn't have any choice about where we stopped. Although the village was very welcoming, Yapakopa, like Omba, does not often get visitors.

We wanted to offer some coffee to Sylvester and our other hosts, but our remaining sugar had been ruined by a combination of bad packing and an errant wave. Since there was a small *kios* in town, Apollo and I walked over to buy some. The storekeeper, apolo-

DRAWING, OMBA.
This chalk figure of, perhaps, a stingray, adorns the front of a small election *karapao* building.

gizing, said he was out of sugar. Apollo asked if he would sell us some from his personal supply. He was reluctant, so Apollo appealed to his sense of familial responsibility—the merchant, as usual, was one of Apollo's distant relatives.

"This man," Apollo said, pointing at me, "is my brother-in-law from Kei. It is my duty, and *your* duty"—he stared sternly at the storekeeper—"to be hospitable to him. We must share."

This lecture did the trick, and the storekeeper parted with half of his own supply. I don't know if he really believed I was a Kei Islander, but Apollo said he did. I think it is just as likely he went along with the fiction because he was entertained by Apollo's performance. In any case he charged us something like two times the going rate for the sugar so, family or not, he was still a businessman.

Yapakopa (pop. 295) is a clean little village of well-built, traditional houses, and Kal was happy to find not a single galvanized roof. The village has an unusual number of fruit trees, most of which appeared to be still young. These included a jackfruit tree, a *salak* palm—its strange fruit looks like a large head of garlic wrapped in snakeskin, with "cloves" that taste both astringent and sweet—a *jambu air,* which tastes like rosewater, and some citrus. In front of Sylvester's

house a fruiting banana was propped up with a stick to keep the stem from breaking under its growing load.

We arrived in the heat of the afternoon, and most of the people in the village were relaxing in the shade with their children. The chickens were still busy, pecking hopefully at anything that looked remotely edible. They were free to roam, but to make sure they eventually would end up in the right pot, each was branded with a piece of colored thread tied to its wing or leg. The dogs were mostly asleep.

One of the village dogs was a razorback, as clearly marked as the famous African lion-hunting breed. It wore a stripe of forward-facing fur down its back, as if someone dipped an index finger in glue and ran it along the animal's spine in the wrong direction. I was told there were a few others in the village, coming from the same bloodlines, and that they are not common. The dog I noticed was said to be a good hunter, and he did seem to carry himself with unusual dignity. New Guinea dogs have heavily lined foreheads, which at first makes you think they are scowling, but it is a permanent feature and has nothing to do with the animal's mood.

As we walked around the village, Apollo pointed out several plants that have special curative powers, including a small ground plant with pinnate leaves, like a mimosa, that is said to strengthen a woman after

171

childbirth. One of the most useful of these was the beach morning glory (*Ipomea pes-caprae*), a very common vine on the strand behind the beach. It has thick stems and waxy, retuse leaves. The Kamoro call it *yakae* and it grows everywhere here.

Yakae, Apollo said, provides the best first aid if you are stung by a catfish. All catfish have spines in their fins, but many of the species in the Kamoro area carry venom. The worst are the plotosids, or eel-tailed catfish, which can deliver a sting that is said to be painful enough to make a victim seriously consider amputating the afflicted limb. If stung, the recommended course of action is to break off a leaf of *yakae* and apply to the injury the drop of white latex that appears at the stem. The best results, Apollo added, come from the variety with the yellowish, not the reddish, stem. The leaves of *yakae* can also be boiled, producing a decoction that eases stomach ache and, as Apollo put it, "washes the inside of your body."

The white sand of Yapakopa village, particularly under the larger trees and in front of the doorways of houses, was marked with red splotches. The westernmost Kamoro area is betel country. In Lakahia, Omba, Potowai-Buru, and Yapakopa, the betel quid is very popular, and it is not uncommon in Ararao. East of Ararao I occasionally saw an old woman with a wad of betel in her cheek, but the younger generation sticks to cigarettes. In the far west, however, betel is popular with both sexes, and even with relatively young people.

The three necessary ingredients of the betel quid are: *sirih,* the leaf of the betel pepper; *pinang,* the nut of the areca palm; and *kapor,* or powdered lime. Except for the lime, these are imported ingredients, although both *sirih* and *pinang* are now planted here. The betel leaf can sometimes be scarce, I was told, in which case the chewers substitute *daun waru,* the young shoot of a beach hibiscus. All aficionados prefer *sirih,* however, and say the quid is even better with the addition of some *gambir,* another imported ingredient.

BETWEEN MY FIRST VISIT to the Kamoro area in January and my second in the summer, the Indonesian government held national elections. This meant that each village erected a small *karapao* building, usually decorated with the Golkar logo. Golkar, from *golongan karya,* literally "functional groups," is the dominant political party in Indonesia, and the only one allowed to organize below the regency level. These "secular" *karapao* are small, with a single *mbitoro* and one door, and are not followed by initiations. They help prop up interest in the elections, and the building and *mbitoro* create a nice backdrop for political speeches.

This practice is now so established that the village party leadership considers a *karapao* essential for a good turnout at the ballots. I liked to call them Golkar-apao, but Kal always corrected me and said they were of course for the *pemilihan umum*—the election—not the

party, but "pemilu-apao" doesn't have the same ring.

Election season *karapao* began in 1971, soon after the formal incorporation of Irian Jaya into Indonesia. Since the elections take place every five years, the activity may have played a positive role in keeping the woodcarving tradition alive. Although the *karapao* themselves seemed a bit frail and jury rigged, the artistic quality of some of the *mbitoro* was very high.

When I returned in early July, another result of the election season was everywhere apparent. It seemed that every single voter along the Kamoro coast had been given a yellow Golkar T-shirt, and at least a third of them were still wearing it when we arrived in July. Kal found this very disheartening, as all of his photographic subjects were now wearing the same clothes. These shirts are not very flattering, especially after three months of wear. The thin yellow fabric turned unpleasantly greenish with age. A stronger color like bright red would have better disguised the cheapness of the cloth, but the political statement made would then be quite different.

Two young men in Yapakopa had customized their Golkar shirts, cutting the sleeves into neat strips and burning a series of holes into them with cigarettes. The holes ran down the sides in two rows, with a pattern of circles around each breast. The results of these modifications, which I had also seen elsewhere, look better than they sound; something like stage costumes in an Elizabethan play.

WE TOOK OUR afternoon coffee in Sylvester Auti's house, with a dozen of the older men of Yapakopa to keep us company. Our tobacco seemed to provide some welcome variety from the betel. As the conversation shifted to woodcarving and tradition, one man slipped off and returned with an unusual stone club.

This weapon, which the men called *miroko,* had a meter-long ironwood handle to which a nasty looking star-shaped stone had been fastened with a bent twenty-penny nail. The business end had five points, although it had originally been shaped, like a Star of David, for six. One had broken off sometime in the distant past. This *miroko* has been in the village as long as anyone can remember, and one sixty-year-old man said it was already old when he was a boy.

When I asked about the shaping of the stone, which appeared to be some form of limestone, the men became confused. It was not carved, they insisted, but found. It came from Boiya Cape and there are others like it there still, they said. Apollo was quick to tell me, sotto voce, that of course it was man-made. He said the clubs were always made secretly in the limestone hills to the east. Perhaps because it has been so long, he said, the people of Yapakopa have forgotten.

This *miroko* is the last one in the village, and the only one we saw on our journey. Apollo said there are surely a few more around, but they are now kept

MIROKO, YAPAKOPA.
This limestone club, owned by Moses Niwa, may be one of the last of its kind.

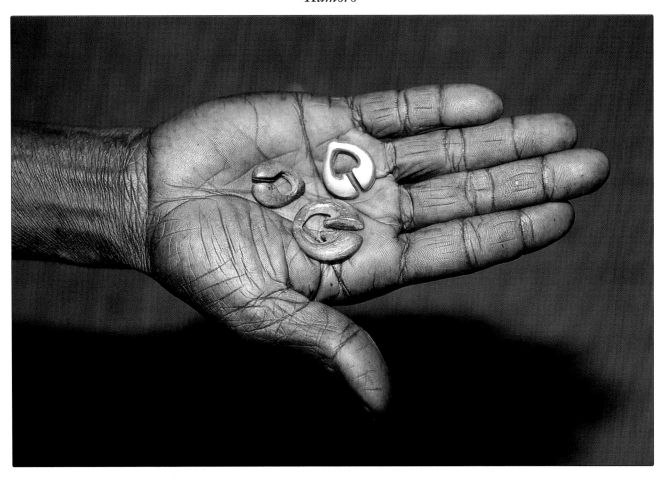

BRIDE PRICE EARRINGS, YAPAKOPA.
Sylvester Auti called the one at left *mamu mame*, the 'eye of the fish'; the other two he called *iriwana*, the 'eye of a whale.'
The earrings, trade products from Nusa Tenggara, are now extremely rare in the Kamoro area.

hidden because the police have forbidden their use. In the old days every family had one. Yapakopa's *miroko* belongs to Moses Niwa, and it was handed down through his family.

In the distant past, clubs like this were used in warfare, but their chief use in more recent years has been to reinforce one's point of view in village arguments. Even today, when people get really heated up, Apollo said, the few clubs that are left will come out. Sometimes they are used by the village leaders to exact judgment against somebody who misbehaved or broke one of the village rules.

One of the men at Sylvester's house, Eferandus Miwa, admitted to having been struck with the weapon some years ago. As soon as he offered this information he regretted it. "So," we all asked in unison, "what was your offense?" Eferandus's memory suddenly failed him, but after considerable coaxing we found out that it involved a young woman. I wasn't able to get a translation of the exact nature of his transgression, because as soon as he started to explain, every Kamoro speaker in the house erupted into laughter.

Miroko, the local term for the club in Yapakopa, is somewhat unusual, Apollo said. In most places it is simply called *nanima,* Kamoro for "club." Miroko is

the name of the hero's mother in a famous story about the killing of the *wou,* the monstrous lizard of Kamoro history. In it, the *wou* is finally dispatched with a *nanima.* When Mirokoteyau succeeded in killing the animal, which had eaten so many members of his family and village, he sang a victory song, a few lines of which Eferandus demonstrated for me: "...u nanioʻo nanima ta oʻo...." In paraphrase, what the hero is saying is: After an encounter with our *nanima* you suddenly don't look so healthy, Mr. Wou.

NOT TO BE OUTDONE by Moses's club, Sylvester brought out three other treasures: his wife's bride price earrings. These were thick and heavy, shaped something like a horseshoe that has the trailing ends pounded in to make it more approximately round. One was made of a metal I was told was "white gold," a heavy, dull-silver material that looked and felt a lot like pewter. The others were bronze.

The smallest earring Sylvester called *mamu mame,* and said it represented the eye of a fish. The others, significantly larger, he called *iriwana,* representing the eye of a whale. Kal scoffed openly at these names. The rings, he said, are identical to those he has seen in the traditional parts of Sumba Island in Indonesia's East Nusa Tenggara province, where they are called *mamuli*

FISHING HARPOON, ATUKA.

and are frankly understood to represent female genitalia or, more abstractly, the womb. "Mamuli" is pretty close to "mamu mame," and even common sense suggests that female genitalia would make a better stylistic theme for a bride price ring than a fish's eye. I doubt that Sylvester was purposely being delicate in his choice of language (and in this regard "fish eye" certainly doesn't work as well as, say, "honey pot") and perhaps the twin distortions of age and foreign origin have combined to produce this unfortunate euphemism.

Traditionally, the earrings are given to the bride by the father of the groom or, in some cases, the sister of the groom. If the groom dies, the bride keeps them only until she remarries, at which time they go back to the giver. Otherwise they keep getting passed along. Sylvester, who is fifty-two, said the two rings are at least three generations old. Since he and his wife have ten grandchildren, there will be no problem finding a home for them.

Mamuli were a traditional trade item throughout the Malukan region, and were brought to the Kamoro area through the Kowiai Coast. Sylvester said the story handed down in his family is that one of the rings was purchased in Bamana, a village in Lakahia Bay, some seventy years ago. It cost an adult pig, a fantastic price, which at the time Sylvester said would have been worth fifty Dutch guilders. Both Apollo and Alo were very interested in the earrings, because they have become extremely rare in the Kamoro area. One can't go to Lakahia or Namatota and buy them anymore, even for the price of a pig, and the only ones left are those that have been handed down.

"In the past they were required, and men sometimes had to go a long way to find them," Apollo said. "Today I don't think even ten percent of the women get earrings. Now we use money."

The earrings are too precious for Sylvester Auti's wife, Wilhelmina Naimu, to wear them very often. When she does, since her ears are not pierced in the old style, she strings them around her waist on a cord.

Bride prices are still paid in the Kamoro area, although the composition has changed. The traditional bride price required heirloom earrings and porcelain, cloth, and for the husband to build a canoe for his wife's family every year. The canoe was the most important part of the exchange, and at least symbolically, still is today. For example, Alo lives in a fairly urban setting, and most of the bride price he provided to his wife's family was in the form of rupiah notes. But he still had to provide at least one canoe (which he bought).

Things are somewhat more traditional further away

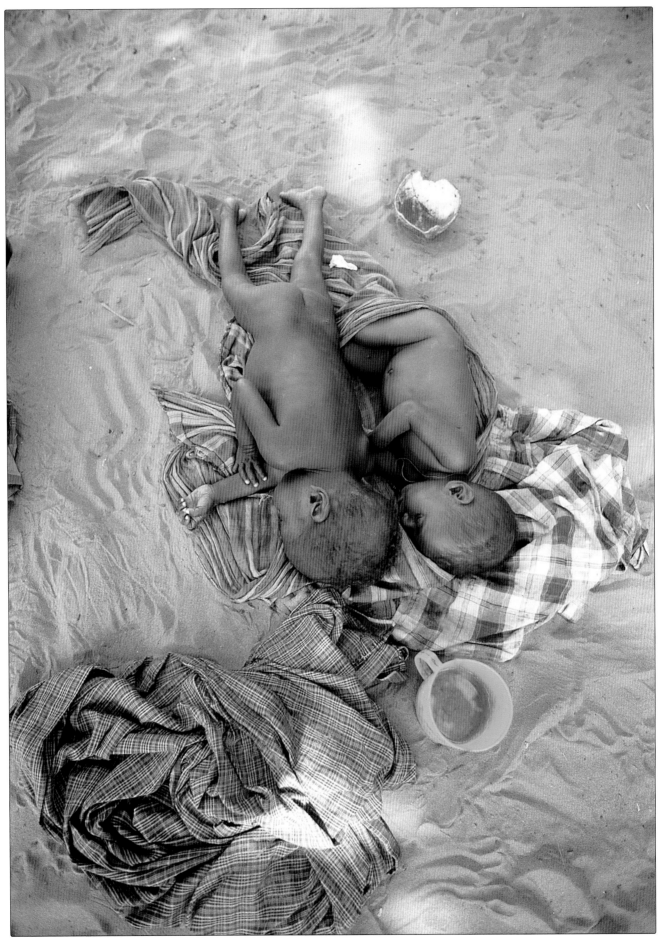

YAPAKOPA.

from Timika. Nikolaus Tukani, from Porauka, married a woman from Yapakopa and moved here about six years ago. His bride price, he said, consisted of a canoe, which he built; four dozen plates and fifteen articles of clothing, which he bought in Kaimana; and one pair of heirloom earrings, which he inherited from his father.

After the wedding, Nikolaus moved into his wife's village, the traditional practice in what is essentially a matriarchal society. Things are changing today, however, and Apollo and Alo say that it is now probably more common for the wife to move to the husband's village. If a potential husband wants to take a woman away from her family, his bride price is higher. Nikolaus, for example, is thinking about moving back to Porauka. If he does, he said, it will certainly cost him another canoe, and perhaps an axe as well.

I found out later that Nikolaus is quite popular in Yapakopa, and the people don't want him to leave. Sylvester gives him every good government job he can to encourage him to stay. But Nikolaus's father is getting old, and he misses his family, so he is still considering moving back.

"WIND FROM BEHIND, waves from the front, okay," Apollo said. "Winds from the front, waves from the front, deadly."
We left Yapakopa at high tide, following the tiny Katiara River east until it met the Aindua River, and finally reached the open sea on the other side of Cape Waratiri. This route gave us about an eight-kilometer respite from the fury of the Arafura. It was at the moment we entered the open sea that Apollo offered the conventional wisdom on small craft travel.

Of course, the latter condition obtained, and the wind conspired with the waves to pound our little boat mercilessly. Within minutes we were all soaked to the bone, and the dugout had shipped water to above the floorboards. We pulled in after less than a half hour, finding ourselves again at Kaokaturu on the mouth of the Umari River.

We waved to our friends still camped on the beach, entered the calm Matoapoka River, and headed east to Irua, where we had eaten our lunch of fresh fish a few days before. At this point, we could not continue by either sea or by the river. We knew Ararao, the main village of Old Umar, was just a few kilometers ahead of us. But the tide had gone out enough to make the Matoapoka too shallow for our boat. The sea, for its part, was still crazy with whitecaps.

We decided to walk. With a lightened boat, Manu and Tobias could motor along the very shallow but protected boat channel that parallels the shore. The rest of us walked the five kilometers along the beach. When we began to see footprints in the sand and a few bright red splats of betel spit, we knew we were close to the village.

Ararao is half of the old village of Umar, and its official name is still Umar according to the government. The other half of the village is at Tapormai, inland on the Umari River where it meets the Tapormai River. This village is near a lumber camp, and most of the Umar people who live there work for Diadiyani Lumber. The coastal village of Ararao (pop. 480) is one of the largest Kamoro villages, but when we arrived we saw no more than a few dozen people. The rest were still back at the mouth of the Umari River, camping and eating fresh wild boar.

Remarkably, however, we found out there was a teacher here, and we were soon escorted to the house of Inosensius Talubun, at the far end of the village. Inosensius, a handsome Kei Islander of about thirty, has been working here for five years. His wife Anita Fatubun, also Kei—they are both from Kei Besar Island—joined him about three years ago. Unsurprisingly, Apollo said Inosensius was his brother-in-law. Of course to Apollo's way of thinking, since his wife is Kei, *all* Kei Islanders are his in-laws.

Inosensius's house had been newly refurbished, and the palm bark and thatch were still bright yellow and green. The inside of the house smelled as sweet as alfalfa hay. Inosensius and Anita had a young boy, a wide-eyed cherub who looked like he was not quite two. Inosensius had rigged up a child-proof gate at the front door, which allowed in the breeze while insuring that the little one didn't accidentally tumble down the stairs—exactly the kind of precaution that would please a nervous American grandmother.

Although I saw school buildings in most of the villages, Inosensius was the first living schoolteacher I had met in the entire Kamoro area outside of Kokonao and Timika. Why, I asked, are teachers such a rare species here?

"Many teachers simply don't have the sense of dedication," he said. "It is not easy to work here. The government wage is not enough to provide food for their families. They must be devoted to the Kamoro people."

Irian Jaya, particularly outside of the few larger cities, is the frontier of Indonesia. The lack of roads, telephones, and even regular boats means that even something as basic as receiving one's salary becomes very difficult. All the teachers working along this coast have to find their own way to Kokonao to get paid. They have to hire a boat, buy fuel, and take time off from teaching to make the trip, which from Ararao takes a full day in ideal conditions, and maybe several days in the kinds of conditions we were facing. More often than not, when the teacher arrives in Kokonao, the bursar is not even there. Typically, Inosensius said, it takes him three or four months, and several fruitless trips, to get paid.

On paper at least, teachers receive a monthly salary from the government, as well as an allowance of rice that amounts to ten kilograms a month per family member. The rice is from government warehouses, and it is by no means considered a quality product.

"There are many different kinds of rice the gov-

177

YUFENSIUS NOKOREYAU, TIMIKA PANTAI.
Yufensius, addressing the crowd at a *karapao,* is the village's chief of traditions.

ernment sends us," joked Apollo, who as a teacher himself also receives a monthly allotment. "Sometimes it is dirty, sometimes it is stale, sometimes it is wet. It can spoil in a month if it gets wet."

The starting salary for a teacher in Irian Jaya is Rp14,750 a day, or about $175 a month at the time of our visit. Every two years a teacher is due for a raise in salary and ranking. Inosensius has been teaching in Ararao for five years. He still makes Rp14,750 a day.

When I asked why he never received a raise, Inosensius said that even though he qualifies for a promotion to the next rank, if he actually wants to receive it he would have to go and make the arrangements himself. First he would have to go to Kokonao and meet with officials there, then he would have to go to Timika to meet with even higher level officials. Finally, after days or weeks of negotiation, he would probably get his raise. If, that is, he provided enough money to grease the wheels of bureaucracy.

"The most dedicated teachers are the ones who are paid the least," he said, "because they don't want to leave their students for weeks to take care of this."

Inosensius admits that difficulties in getting paid and promoted are one of the main reasons teachers here so often become disenchanted and leave, but he insists that a successful community education program requires just two things—that the teacher be dedicated to his community, and that the community be willing to help the teacher. These things, he said, are more important than money.

"The people of Ararao help me and my family," he said. "They give us food when my salary is late, and give us transportation to Kokonao. If there is a good relationship between the community and the teacher, the teacher will stay. Otherwise, he will leave."

This relationship is an example of the kind of reciprocal *aopao* that is so central to Kamoro culture.

"The teachers must be disciplined, and stay in the village," Apollo said. "If they do this, the people will respect them and will provide food—fish and sago. Twenty years ago the education system worked better. There was more discipline then."

Five teachers work at Ararao, although eight have been assigned to the school here. Two Torajans and one Amungme have left. Those who have stayed, other than Inosensius, are two Kamoro men, Agus Tewa and Anaklitus Tiripo, and two Ekagi from the Paniai Lakes. Agus, from Akar village, is a physical education teacher and one of Apollo's former students.

While the *bupati* and Apollo believe that the best education comes from physically removing students from the traditional cycles of village life and placing them in boarding schools, Inosensius is a firm believer in village education.

"You can get just as good an education in the village as you can at the boarding school in Kokonao," he said, adding, with some pride, "just as many of my students get into high school as do students from Kokonao."

The grade school at Ararao has approximately one-hundred and sixty students, and another twenty-five attend an associated grade school at Tapormai. Of Inosensius' graduates, twenty-eight attend junior high in Uta and six at Kokonao. Four former students attend senior high in Timika, and one attends a senior high–level technical school there. One former student attends a college level Catholic theological school in the provincial capital of Jayapura. This is an extremely good record for this area, and Inosensius was visibly proud of it.

There are only three schools outside of Timika, he said, that can boast success rates similar to those of the Ararao and Tapormai schools: The government school at Uta, the Catholic school at Amar, and the Catholic school at Kokonao. The Ararao and Tapormai schools were built by the Catholic Church, and originally the church provided supplies and paid the teacher's salaries as well. But since 1990 the state has taken over the management of the province's parochial schools, and now they are staffed and supplied by the Indonesian government.

K EI ISLANDERS, LIKE Inosensius, have a special relationship with the Kamoro that dates back more than sixty years, to the beginning of Dutch administration of the region just after World War I. At this time, Kei Islanders were brought in by the colonial government as teachers, office workers, policemen, and carpenters. The Catholic Church also relied on Kei Islanders as catechists and teachers. Unlike the Dutch officials and priests, the Kei Islanders actually lived in the Kamoro villages, and they were the first outsiders the Kamoro came to know intimately.

The Kei archipelago is just a bit over two hundred kilometers southwest of Lakahia. There are two main islands, Kei Besar or "Greater Kei," and Kei Kecil or "Lesser Kei." Kei Kecil, together with the smaller Kei Dullah Island adjoining it, is approximately the same size as Kei Besar, but the latter, a long, thin exclamation point on the map, is mountainous, hence the sobriquet "Greater." Perhaps one hundred thousand people live on the Keis, the great majority of them on Kei Kecil. The mountains of Kei Besar are steep and infertile, and the villages there are small and hug the coast. The Kei are the most famous boat-builders in the eastern archipelago.

The meeting of Kei, pronounced "Kay," and Kamoro was not free of misunderstanding. Kei Island society was traditionally stratified into castes, bound together by slavery, indenture, and strict rules of arranged marriage. This is such a deeply ingrained part of Kei culture that it was not something Kei Islanders could easily leave behind when they arrived in Dutch New Guinea. This strict, reified, hierarchical authority was a poor fit with a society like the Kamoro, where authority–such as that held by the *weyaiku-we*–is a shifting product of charisma, wisdom, generosity, and skill, and not a birthright.

Traditionally, Kei society was divided into three castes: the Mel-Mel, the Ren-Ren, and the Iriri. The Mel-Mel began as outsiders, traders from Bali, Sumbawa, and Sumba. Since they controlled access to desirable foreign goods, the traders were treated as patriarchs by the indigenous Kei Islanders, and this is how the caste system is thought to have begun. The traders became Mel-Mel; the indigenous Kei Islanders became Ren-Ren; and the slaves of the Mel-Mel became Iriri.

Like so many casted societies, the Mel-Mel, at the top, consider there to be just three castes, while the Ren-Ren, next in line, are careful to count three subdivisions in their caste: Ren-Ren *sardik,* who are presumed to be heirs to an indigenous, pre–Mel-Mel leadership caste; the common Ren-Ren; and, at the bottom, Ren-Ren who have indentured themselves to the Mel-Mel. There is no division in the Iriri, the former slaves, although there are some villages on Kei Besar with people who are considered Iriri by the Mel-Mel, but who consider themselves to have always been independent of the caste system.

Life as an Iriri or an indentured Ren-Ren on Kei was not particularly pleasant. In addition to the work required, such as carrying the master to his vegetable gardens on a litter or, for a young woman, satisfying him sexually whenever he wished, the position required a constant display of submissive inferiority.

"[The Iriri] were forbidden entry into the master's house except with permission," writes Alphonse Sowada, the Catholic bishop of the area, in a 1971 article on Kei Islanders in southern Irian Jaya. "Once they entered to perform some task, they were required to approach their master in a stooped position and with a shuffling gait. Upon dismissal, they backed away from his presence. They were never allowed to eat at the master's table."

C ATHOLIC MISSION WORK in West New Guinea began in 1894 when a Jesuit named Father Le Coq d'Armandville set up a mission on the Onin Peninsula near Fakfak. D'Armandville died in 1896 on a tour of the south coast, bringing the Church's work to a temporary halt. Then, in 1902, the apostolic prefecture of Nederlandsch-Nieuw Guinea, which included Dutch New Guinea and Maluku, was established at Langgur, near Tual, the largest town in the Kei Islands. Langgur was assigned to the Missionaries of the Sacred Heart, and the Kei

Islands became the center of Catholic mission work in the eastern part of the archipelago. In 1920 this prefecture was elevated to a vicariate.

Kei Islanders began coming to Dutch New Guinea from Tual as teachers in 1905, beginning with the Merauke area, where the government was anxious to quiet the fierce Marind-anim, who were disturbing Dutch–British foreign relations by crossing into British-held territory on their head-hunting raids. By the 1920s, Kei teachers began arriving in the Kamoro area. Many of them were just teenagers at the time, and they were remarkably energetic, building schools and houses, planting huge gardens, and conducting classes with great enthusiasm. They were also, according to many accounts, arrogant, strict, antagonistic to Kamoro tradition, and very demanding.*

The young teachers expected results from their students and their village, and felt personally insulted if these did not come about at the expected rate. A Kei teacher's caste arrogance allowed him to assume his own preeminence over the Kamoro and that, Sowada writes, "he was the person to whom the greatest respect and honor was a matter of village obligation." If he felt that this were not forthcoming, or if the Kamoro did not live up to his expectations, children, and even adults, were sometimes brutally beaten.

It is easy to imagine the Kei Islanders interpreting their arrival on New Guinea in the 1920s as a recapitulation of the original arrival of the Mel-Mel on Kei. And it is tempting to think that some of them, despite their own caste as Ren-Ren or Iriri (no Mel-Mel would have had a reason to leave) used this as a justification to live as did the Mel-Mel back home. The Kei are very secretive about their caste status, and to release such information about a fellow would be a serious breach of protocol. In New Guinea, a lower-caste Ren-Ren could easily get away with giving the impression that he was Mel-Mel.

By the 1950s, relations between the Kei Islanders and the Kamoro were improving. The Church was becoming less strict, the colonial government was becoming more informed, and with a generation of experience together, the Kamoro and Kei Islanders were becoming better aware of their cultural differences. Also, the active role played by the Kei teachers in organizing against the Imperial Navy, and the fact that they suffered alongside the other villagers at the hands of the Japanese, increased their standing with the Kamoro.

In Jan Pouwer's account from the early 1950s, relations between Kei and Kamoro seem more clumsy, or even comic, than brutal. One Kei teacher, who saw Father Gerardus A. Zegwaard squatting and teasing a group of children, sighed loudly and said to Zegwaard: "Father, I would also like to chat with the children like you do, but I can not." The teacher, even though he wanted to, felt it was impossible to put himself in such an undignified position.

"A Dutch official accompanied a Kei teacher on a tour through the village, and put the teacher in an awkward position when he sat among the men of the village," Pouwer writes. "It is impolite for a Kei Islander to stand while his superior (the Dutch official) sits, but it is also against the customs for a Kei Islander to sit among the villagers. The teacher endeavored to compromise, and squatted."

The Church contributed to tensions between the Kei Islanders and Kamoro by regularly demonstrating complete ignorance of both cultures. Pouwer reports that at the time of his visit, Kei teachers had been instructed by the Catholic mission to provide room and board in their own houses for any unmarried village girls above the age of puberty. This, the church thought, would prevent "sexual abuse and adventure."

I don't doubt that the Church's motives were high-minded, and it may be that the Kei Islanders were men of impeccable morals. But it doesn't take much imagination to realize how this arrangement would have looked to the villagers, particularly because, as Pouwer writes, they did not have the faintest notion of the religious motivations behind the rule. This policy, and others like it, did nothing to help relations between the Kei teachers and their host villages.

By World War II, the caste system was dying out on most of the Kei archipelago—or at least its most odious expressions, such as overt slavery and indenture, were dying out. Kei Besar had always been more culturally conservative, however, and as late as the early 1970s Bishop Sowada reports that the Mel-Mel of a half-dozen Kei Besar villages still held slaves.

During the changeover to Indonesian rule in the late 1960s, a tense time in the province, resentment toward the Kei Islanders in the Merauke and Dolak Island areas exploded into open anger, and they were forced out by the Muyu and Kimaam people. This did not take place in the Kamoro area, but many Kei immigrants felt insecure, and some returned to the Keis.

Today, relations between Kei Islanders and the Kamoro seem generally to be based on mutual respect. Inosensius told me that to him, there is no difference between working in the Kamoro area and working on Kei. The climate, the food, and many of the traditions are the same, he said. The one thing Inosensius would not do is trade his current job for one that would require him to live in town—whether that town be Timika or Tual.

"Since the time I was a child, I have lived the simple life," he said. "I *like* village life; I don't want the city."

Inosensius is at least two generations removed from the first Kei Islanders to come to the area. His grandfather came as a teacher to Kokonao before World War II, and lived the rest of his life in West New Guinea, dying in Jayapura. I asked Inosensius what he

---

*In parts of Dutch New Guinea, Kei Islanders, Ambonese, and other immigrants from Maluku were called "Amberi," from Cape Amberi on the Bird's Head via which, historically, they had arrived.

PRIMUS MENAMOYAU, ATUKA.
Primus, uninhibited by gender insecurity, enjoys his morning coffee in comfort.

KONSTAN MIPITAPO, HIRIPAU.
Drumming in a tourist performance of the traditional Nokoro dance.

thought of the arrogance and occasional brutality of the Kei Islanders of his grandfather's generation.

"I've heard from my grandfather, and the older people, that this was the case," he said. "They came to educate the Kamoro, and felt that before they could do this they had to get rid of the rude and backward traditions that existed.

"I am disappointed in what our grandfathers did. The younger, educated generation of teachers does not do this. We don't smack the children. We don't disapprove of Kamoro tradition. In fact we hope, through education, that the Kamoro children will learn to keep the good parts of their traditional life."

THE PEOPLE OF ARARAO, I was told, last held a modest *karapao* celebration in 1994. Although the village looked neat and prosperous, I saw few signs of an active traditional life here. Unlike every other village we visited, there was not even a small election *karapao* building, although I was told this was more out of dissatisfaction with the village Golkar party leadership than anything else. When I brought up the subject of tradition, it immediately yielded controversy. Anaklitus Tiripo, a schoolteacher in his thirties, expressed considerable resentment toward the older generation who, he said, withheld the knowledge of traditional carving, music, and ceremonial life out of self-interest.

"The old people kept the secrets," he said, "and refused to train the young generation. The old men profited from their knowledge. The secrets brought them respect and good food, and they didn't want to share."

During a ceremony, tradition requires that the people of the village bring sago, game, the tastiest fish, shellfish, and cigarettes to the place where the ceremony is held. This is necessary to create the appropriate mood for the ceremony, and to entice the ancestral spirits to participate.

"The food and tobacco is a technique to insure the cooperation of the spirits, true," Anaklitus said, "But of course the old people enjoyed it."

Alo was a bit skeptical, not least because our information was coming from a group of young schoolteachers without any of the older men, who were still camping at the mouth of the Umari River, in the room to defend themselves. Alo didn't think all the blame should be laid at the feet of the older generation.

"It is also true that the young people don't want to sit next to the elders and learn the old stories," he said. "They want to dance the Seka."

This was the second time I had heard about the

ANAKLITUS PANARU AND BERNARDUS MEKAMARUPUKARO, ATUKA.
The two men play handmade guitars.

Seka. The first was when I quizzed Inosensius on what he meant by the "good parts" of traditional life.

"So what are these 'good parts'?"

"Art, dancing, carving."

"And the bad?"

"The Seka."

Although it has its roots in tradition, the Seka, pronounced "*say*-kah," is really a modern innovation. It is, in some sense, a genre of dance music like House, or Disco, but most people, when they are forced to describe it in English, call it "dirty dancing."

The first Seka seems to have been held by junior high school students in Kokonao in the early 1970s, but it was when this generation of students moved on to high school and college in Jayapura that the dance spread. In the provincial capital, Kamoro students mixed with Me students, and with students from all over the province. Following their exams, the students would hold parties in their dormitories. The entertainment at these parties was the Seka.

The word "seka"—which is Indonesian—means something like "to rub." It is, for example, the root of *berseka,* "to rub oneself clean." The dance is not about getting clean, however. Just the opposite, in fact—it is about working up a sweat. Men and women, in pairs, dance in a circle. They do not stand at arms' length.

The music accompanying the dance includes no singing, just guitars and a throbbing electric bass.

"During the dance," Apollo said with a smile, "the partners make an appointment to finish their work."

The dance, I was told, is a hybrid of two traditional Irianese dance and musical forms, *balenggung* and *potao. Balenggung* is from Nabire, on the north coast of Irian in the innermost part of Cenderawasih Bay, and in it young people dance in a circle. It is a sexually charged dance. *Potao* is a traditional Kamoro song sung while rowing a canoe, and in the western Kamoro areas it serves as a complement to a dance called *taori.*

Taori traditionally follows *karapao, kaware,* and funeral celebrations. The *taori* is a wooden pole, wrapped in sago or coconut leaves. Following the ceremony, the young people dance around the *taori,* accompanied by singing and drumming. The symbolism of the pole needs no explanation, and like *balenggung,* the dance is very sexually charged. The young people, inspired by the dance, make appointments to meet later under cover of darkness.

Taori still goes on, and one was held by the young people of Porauka village who were camping on the beach the night we stayed in Kaokaturu. At the time Alo warned me to stay inside, so that I might not fall prey to the attentions of a fevered young woman.

183

The older and more traditional generation of Kamoro do not like the Seka, or the *seka-seka*—more like "rubbing"—as it is sometimes, and somewhat derisively, called by its opponents. To the older men, it is a scourge with no redeeming qualities, and they speak of this dance as if it were some kind of disease.

It is important to realize that this disapproval is not inspired by the sexual aspects of the dance. Some religious leaders and teachers are put off by the sexual contact implicit in the Seka, but the Kamoro elders are a long way from being prudes. *Taori,* which is just as much in the rub-a-dub style as the Seka, is an important and respected part of traditional ceremonies. Basically, the elders don't like the Seka because of the guitars. *Taori* includes traditional singing and drumming; the Seka does not. The lack of the drums, in particular, is unforgivable to the older generation, and reduces Seka in their opinion to cheap entertainment. They shake their heads back and forth with the same incomprehension that older people in the United States must have felt when they first heard Chuck Berry.

Fig. 7.2 Papaya leaves. The leaf on the right is the stronger anti-malarial.

Apollo, perhaps appropriately for someone both old enough to appreciate tradition and young enough to have danced the Seka himself, remains divided on the subject.

"The Seka is both good and bad," he said. "The good is that the dance promotes happiness, and allows people to meet. The bad is that it makes the young generation forget their traditions."

Ever the schoolteacher, he added: "Also they get so tired afterward that they miss school."

Whether for good or ill, the Seka is probably the most significant Kamoro cultural export. It is now danced all over Irian Jaya, and after final exams dormitories from Sorong to Merauke are noisy with the sound of bass guitars—and heavy breathing.

ARARAO IS THE CENTER of Catholic influence in the area, and the village was chosen as a model to demonstrate the Church's gardening program. The banana groves, in particular, are more extensive here than in any other village we visited. We went for a walk to see the famous gardens.

On our way, Apollo and I passed a group of children playing on the sandy, deserted village square. We said hello, and Apollo asked the kids what game it was they were playing.

"Seven Planks," one said, without looking up from the game.

The contest involved a stack of small blocks and a ball, about the size of a softball, that had been shaped from the pith of a palm tree. Both boys and girls were playing. While one child threw the ball at the stack of blocks, another halfheartedly tried to deflect it, which made me think of a form of cricket. After the throw, however, the children began kicking the ball around on the ground, in a wild, free-form version of soccer.

While reflecting on this, I counted up the blocks of wood and got ten. I asked Apollo what he thought of this discrepancy.

"Hey," he said to the kids. "Why do you call it 'Seven Planks' when you have ten? You should call it 'Ten Planks.'"

The children then counted them up themselves, but still looked at us like we were a couple of idiots. To them, Apollo's question was too ridiculous to even warrant a reply, and they went back to their game without saying a word.

The village gardens began when the church delivered an allotment of seedlings to each head of household in Ararao. Today, there is a huge grove of bananas, and extensive mounded plots of taro, several varieties of papayas, at least three types of manioc, and sweet potatoes in at least two varieties. Flowers have been planted throughout the village for no reason other than that they look nice. We even saw a few coffee bushes.

The soil here is said to be richer than that in most villages, and it does look slightly darker than the others. But "soil" is an odd word to use for the substrate upon which Kamoro gardens grow, and it never failed to shock me to see rich gardens growing in what is really just beach sand. This contradicted everything I thought I knew about farming. I never heard of anyone using fertilizer, and the only hypothesis I can offer is that the sediments along the south coast of Irian Jaya are so fresh and undecomposed that they contain significant nutrients in a mineral, rather than an organic, form.

Kamoro gardens are always mounded to promote drainage, and the most successful ones, such as in Ararao, seem to be in those villages where the nearby rivers are strong enough to resist the tidal influx of saltwater. The small creek behind Ararao, for example, runs fresh at all but the highest tide. In areas where the sand is salty, the mounds are built up first, and left fallow for a season or two to let the rain flush out the salt.

Because Ararao's gardens began as an experiment, the variety of plants here is considerable. One plant I had not noticed before was a type of papaya that, rather than having the deeply lobed leaf typical of the species, had broad, unlobed leaves, something like an oversized sugar maple. This variety, Apollo said, does not produce particularly tasty fruit, but its leaves yield a much stronger malaria prophylactic than regular papaya. The gardens held unusual varieties of manioc as well, including some that are better exploited for their leaves, and others that produce larger, and sweeter, tubers. Some of the bitter variety also grew

PETRUS TANIYU, TIMIKA PANTAI.
Having speared a pig the night before, Petrus became a hero to all women. Although for his own part he tried to
remain stoic, his admirers could not resist the powerful aphrodisiacal effect of his hunting prowess.

ERODED MANGROVE, JUST WEST OF PARIPI.

here, and these plants stood as tall as a grown man.

Farming in New Guinea has a very long history, and the island is one of the world's oldest centers of plant domestication. Most archaeologists agree that the earliest farmers lived in the Fertile Crescent of the Tigris and Euphrates Rivers, in today's Syria and Iraq, more than 10,000 years ago. Evidence of farming in New Guinea is almost as ancient. Professor Jack Golson of the Australian National University has found drainage ditches at 1,550 meters in the upper Waghi Valley of Papua New Guinea that are 9,000 years old. Golson's excavations show evidence of soil tilling by 2,000 years ago, and pollen samples show that the casuarina tree had been planted by 1,000–1,200 years ago, which marks the beginning of silviculture at the Waghi site.

The first crops grown in New Guinea were taro (*Colocasia escuelenta*), several types of yams (*Dioscorea* spp.), sago, some types of bananas, sugar cane, and *Pandanus* nut trees. These plants are all native to the island. Today, the most important crop in the highlands is the sweet potato (*Ipomea batatas*), which is of New World origin and may have no more than a four-hundred-year history in New Guinea.

Determining the age of human farming is not an easy task. Golson's evidence shows that, nine thou-sand years ago, a group of people in New Guinea drained a highland swamp and planted taro. But this does not mean that they discovered taro nine thousand years ago. The lowlands people of New Guinea knew about taro for a long time, but it was only nine thousand years ago that the climate had warmed enough to allow them to plant taro in the highland valley Golson has excavated.

Planting a field of wheat or rice is very clearly farming. But the indigenous crops of New Guinea are not grains. Is it farming when someone takes a small satellite corm from a taro plant and puts it back in the hole when the main root is pulled up? Is it farming to separate the suckers of a sago palm that has already flowered and space them apart in the ground so they will have plenty of room to grow? If this is farming, then people around the world have been doing it for something like one hundred thousand years.

Some scientists like to distinguish these technologies from farming by calling them "horticultural" or even "proto-horticultural" rather than "agricultural." To me, this sounds like another instance of privileging grains like wheat and rice over New Guinea's sago and tubers. It is true that no great empires were carved out by people whose bellies were kept full of sago, but this may very well be to its credit.

186

PAULA MAPUPIA, ATUKA.
Kamoro plant their gardens in what seems like nothing more than mounded beach sand, but these beans do not seem to mind.

NEW GUINEA MAY NOT be the home of the world's first farmers, but a growing number of scientists are coming to believe that the island (together with adjoining Australia) and its people represent a crucial stage in the evolution of human history and culture. The interaction of human beings and their environment has become a dominant theme in several recent books: Jared Diamond's 1997 Pulitzer Prize–winning *Guns, Germs, and Steel* and his 1992 *The Third Chimpanzee*; Tim Flannery's 1994 *The Future Eaters;* and Jonathan Kingdon's 1993 *Self-Made Man*. These writers, scientists from the United States, Australia, and England, are physiologists, zoologists, and evolutionists, not anthropologists or archaeologists.

All scientists pretty much agree that modern human beings—*Homo sapiens*—first evolved in Africa, and dispersed from that continent perhaps 120,000 years ago. But what happened between that point and about 10,000 years ago, when the availability of cultural artifacts and other evidence began to allow modern anthropologists to piece together a more accurate history of human movements and achievements, has been mostly a blank.

Kingdon has filled this blank with a hypothesized Banda people, named for the center of their distribution, the Banda Arc of eastern Indonesia. When the first people from Africa reached tropical Southeast Asia 100,000 years ago, he argues, the richest and most suitable environment they would have encountered was the littoral zone, the coastline. There they would have found shellfish and fish, game, and tubers and sago to eat. This environment is what one finds today on the Kamoro coast, or on any other unexploited shoreline of the larger eastern Indonesian islands. In such a salubrious environment, the numbers of the Banda would have increased until they occupied the entire area from peninsular Southeast Asia to Tasmania. The Banda people, Kingdon states, would have settled New Guinea and Australia at least 52,000 years ago, and perhaps 58,000–70,000 years ago.

During the 1970s and 1980s, dates for the first human remains in Australia (and New Guinea and Australia formed a single land mass during the relevant period) ranged from 32,000 to 40,000 years ago. But as Flannery points out in *The Future Eaters*, these dates were arrived at by radiocarbon dating, which determines age based on the percentage of Carbon-14 isotope remaining in the sample. Since ^{14}C has a half-life of 5,730 years, after 40,000 years this isotope represents just one percent of the sample. Even a tiny impurity in a sample older than this will introduce a major error in the date, and because of this, the ^{14}C method is simply not useful for dates older than about 35,000 years. As Flannery notes, a 300-million-year-old piece of coal will also yield an age of 38,000–40,000 years in a radiocarbon test. Work using other methods of dating has resulted in reliable dates of 60,000 years, and further research may push back the arrival of humans in Australia and New Guinea even further.

In *The Third Chimpanzee,* Diamond notes that beginning about 60,000 years ago, human beings underwent a sudden technological advancement, which he calls The Great Leap Forward. Anatomically modern human beings have been around for at least 180,000 years, and simple chipped stone tools were used even by early human ancestors. But 60,000-year-old tools look about the same as 200,000-year-old tools. Then, sometime between 60,000 and 40,000 years ago, there was a great explosion of technological innovation, yielding thin-bladed tools, compound tools, needles, awls, mortars and pestles, nets, barbed harpoons, and fish hooks. And fine art, such as the cave paintings of Europe, appears at this point for the first time. Diamond can find only one plausible explanation for this sudden burst of invention—the development of language.

Flannery finds Diamond's Great Leap convincing, but argues that this date is too recent for it to be accounted for by the development of language. The physical capacity for human speech, he notes, has existed in genus *Homo* for at least 300,000 years. And if language arose as recently as 60,000 years ago, then the world's most isolated people—those of New Guinea, Australia, and Tasmania, who have been isolated for all or most of this time—should have retained some aspect of this primitive language.

> But these people speak languages every bit as complex and advanced as those found in Europe, Africa or the Americas. Indeed, so complex are some New Guinea languages, such as Miyanmin (a non-Austronesian language of the Mountain Ok group of Papua New Guinea) that children are not expected to master them until they are eight or nine years of age. People just laughed when I expressed an interest in learning Miyanmin as an adult.

Instead, Flannery argues that it was the rich and hitherto unexploited environment early humans found in Australia and New Guinea that propelled Diamond's Great Leap Forward.

The pioneers who reached this area 60,000 years ago stumbled upon a veritable Eden of large, lumbering prey animals, including the giant, cassowary-like *Genyornis,* huge wombats and kangaroos, and the diprotodon, a placid marsupial that looked like a long-necked hamster, except that it was the size of a Volkswagen. These animals had evolved in the total absence of large mammalian predators, and like the animals Charles Darwin found on the Galapagos, were likely to have been so unafraid of humans that hunting them may have simply required walking up to them and clubbing them on the head. If this indeed propelled our

Great Leap Forward, then it came at a cost, because these people became what Flannery calls the world's first "future eaters," bringing about the rapid extinction of eighty-six percent of the large animals in New Guinea and Australia.

Although the arguments of all three of these scientists are intriguing, many anthropologists and archaeologists probably remain skeptical, not least because the authors I mention are not anthropologists or archaeologists. Also, the last time the world's seas were as high as they are now was about 120,000 years ago, and any physical evidence for a coastal people in this time period would likely now lie underwater.

Not being a scientist myself, I find these provocative hypotheses easier to accept, and am even tempted to take them a step further. What if all three of these thinkers are correct? What if Kingdon's Banda people reached New Guinea 100,000–60,000 years ago, became the future eaters of Flannery's account, and as a result of these circumstances developed humankind's single greatest innovation—language? There are more than one thousand languages spoken in New Guinea, making this island the most linguistically rich place in the world. A biologist considers the area of greatest genetic diversity to be the geographical source of a strain of plant or animal. What if New Guinea were not an isolated outpost, but rather the original "budding flower" of human language development?

Kingdon hypothesizes that the Banda people became extremely successful in the Southeast Asian archipelago, and even migrated back to Africa, displacing earlier residents of the central, equatorial part of that continent. He notes, for example, that the Banda would have developed a unique evolutionary response to their bright, tropical seashore environment—increased melanin in their skin. They became black-skinned, rather than the medium brown that genetic evidence suggests is the common denominator of the human gene pool, and brought this development with them back to Africa.

The development of language provides a far more powerful argument for the Banda people's success than the technologies of rope-making and boat-building upon which Kingdon's account relies. And Diamond's Great Leap Forward? Although he considers it to have been a worldwide event, he draws most of his evidence from the archaeology of Southern Europe, where data suggests the leap took place 60,000–40,000 years ago. If language followed the Banda people from New Guinea, via Africa, it might reasonably have reached Europe by about this time.

Although some may find this irredeemably speculative, when Yñigo Ortíz de Retes landed near the Bièr River on the north coast on June 20th, 1545, claimed the island for Spain, and named it "Nueva Guinea" because the Papuans reminded him of the people of African Guinea, he may have been right about the "Guinea," but wrong about the "Nueva."

KWARTUS KAMAPU, ATUKA.
A shard of mirror comes in handy when preparing for a festival.

189

CHAPTER EIGHT

The Ku-Kaware

Spirit of a New Canoe

O N THE FINAL LEG of our trip back to Paripi, we once again found ourselves employing the oldest form of human transportation. I don't mind walking, especially on the extravagant, deserted beaches of southern Irian Jaya, but it really is an unusual way to travel the Kamoro coast. When we arrived in Ararao by foot, the first children we met seemed a bit puzzled, even faintly alarmed. I think they were relieved when our boat showed up on the rising tide an hour later.

By the time we left Ararao we were quite used to conditions on the boat. As soon as we saw the approaching breakers of the Arafura Sea, Kal and I would reach behind us, and don the rainsuits we bought in Timika. These suits, from Australia, are issued to the miners up at Grasberg, but a few of them "fell off the truck," as they say in Jersey City, and found their way to the market. Their quality is better than anything made locally, and the shopkeeper drove a very hard bargain—we probably didn't pay more than twice what we would have in Australia. Wearing the jacket backwards seemed to offer the most protection, but the pockets still filled with water when the big waves hit. The only good thing I could say about the constant spray and waves was that they forced me to cut down on my smoking.

By now Kal and I had grown quite tired of our crew's incompetence. For Alo, Apollo, and Manu, the sentiment approached disgust. The heavy seas tossed the boat around, and by this point the bilge was a greasy swill of kerosene, spoiled food, and saltwater. On this particular day, thanks to a carelessly left open can of two-stroke oil, which is dyed the same color as radiator coolant, our filthy ship was filled with bright green foam.

VICTOR UNUMPARE, PARIPI. Victor, entranced, awakened the spirit of the casuarina tree by dancing along its length in a series of sudden, spectacular bursts.

FELIX ERAKIPIA, PARIPI. The *mbi-kao* mask costume is now rare in the Kamoro area. Felix wears it here to act out a stage of the *ku-kaware* called Tukua Kaumare, in which the *mbi-kao* mimes fishing and sago gathering. This is to remind the people that, despite the ceremony, they must not neglect their family's bellies.

We left Ararao at the beginning of the floodtide, and motored steadily while it went to full high, and back again past full low. At the mouth of the Kawarpeau River, a little less than ten kilometers from Paripi, we pulled in. The tide was too low to chance the sandbars lying between us and Paripi with a full boat, and it would be late at night before it would be high enough again. We decided that the best strategy would be for Manu to lead the lightened boat to Paripi, while Alo, Apollo, Kal, and I once again walked.

Just after we disembarked we passed through a mangrove forest that had been reduced to driftwood by the encroaching sea. Some of the trees remained standing, but all that was left of others were spidery prop roots, pounded by the waves and the sand into magnificent sculptures. Under a gray sky, in the mists of the crashing waves, the skeletal forest was haunting and spectacular.

When he was a boy, Apollo said, this was a living mangrove forest, and the people of Paripi came here to catch crabs. Almost at the same time he told me this he spotted one, stranded in a tide pool that had formed around the bole of a dead tree. He snatched it deftly from behind and held it up. Mangrove crabs are both fierce and clever, and an inexperienced handler will quickly find himself severely punished. Apollo was not an inexperienced handler. In an instant he had snapped off the tips of the crab's last pair of walking legs and wedged these two bits of its own body behind the hinges of its claws, effectively disabling them. The crab, disarmed, stared back at Apollo with a look of pure hatred.

We had walked only a few kilometers before we found our way blocked by a creek. The creek was narrow, but deep, and on an incoming tide the current was strong. Thus stymied, there was nothing for us to do except sit in the shade and wait for a passing canoe. Apollo assured us this wouldn't take long, and he tucked his crab into the fork of a tree and sat down. Then he told us that this was only the first of three such creeks we would have to cross.

Within a half-hour, a family from Paripi saw us and stopped. They had been clamming in the sandflats, just west of where we parted company with our boat,

ENGEL KOARE IN THE BOW, AND BEHIND HIM FREDY UNUMPARE, NEAR PARIPI.

and were now returning to the village. Their tiny canoe was full to the gunwales, and after offloading his wife, a pile of firewood, two big bags of clams, his two small children, and a packet of live coals, the boat's pilot paddled us across the inlet, two at a time. Once we were all safely on the other side, we began walking again, and he and his family reloaded their canoe and continued, with instructions from Apollo to meet us and repeat the ferrying operation at each of the next two creeks. Although it seemed like a lot of work, the family was happy to oblige, and the children, in particular, found great amusement in my wobbly entry and exit from the tiny craft.

We made better progress walking than did the canoe, which had to be poled against the tide, and at each creek we had to wait a few minutes for our ferry to catch up. By the time we crossed the final river, the Ipirawea, the sun had set, and the cooking fires of Paripi were just visible in the distance. The tide was at its lowest point. The moon was close to new, and we hiked, in almost complete darkness, across the riffled mud of the wide exposed sandbar that lay between us and the village.

We entered the village from the seaward side, and the first group of people we met were startled by our sudden appearance. Then a shout rang out, and then it was answered, and within minutes a joyous whooping arose over the entire village. By the time we were halfway to Marselus's house, we had acquired an entourage of a dozen men, and by the time we reached his big fig tree there must have been three dozen. The men were so excited that I thought they were going to physically hoist us into the air.

Huddled around Marselus's lantern, we heard the news. Every kitchen was full of sago and fish, and the men were ready to begin the *ku-kaware*. The excitement was infectious, and we felt like kids on Christmas Eve. The men were ready to begin the very next morning. When I asked what would happen first, the men just smiled.

"You will see tomorrow."

"Will the ceremony be held in the village?"

"Patience, you will see."

"What time should we be ready?"

"Don't worry, we'll get you."

WE SLEPT, AS WE HAD the week before, in Ladislaus Yaota's house. Kal, as usual, was up at the crack of dawn, and even as tired as I had been the night before, with the anticipation of the upcoming ceremony, he didn't get in more than a single cup of coffee before I was up as well. By six

194

o'clock we were all awake and sitting on the stoop with our coffee, waiting for the event to begin.

One by one, or in pairs, the men of the village, decked out in ceremonial finery, passed us on their way out of the village. We waved and cheered them on, and they smiled shyly and did their best not to be distracted by our compliments. They had painted their faces with stripes of soot, and marked their naked chests with skeletal patterns of white lime. Some added dots of ocher. Their foreheads, wrists, elbows, and torsos were tied with ribbons of palm fiber. Some wore headdresses of the long, hairy feathers of the cassowary, trimmed with cuscus or tree kangaroo pelts. Many had wrapped skirts of grass around their waists. For once the village children had something more interesting than us to stare at.

A *ku-kaware* proceeds in distinct, interrupted stages, like acts in a play. The first, called the Iriotepe, was shrouded in secrecy, a secrecy that seemed to serve ritual knowledge and drama in equal parts. By tradition, only adult men are allowed to witness the Iriotepe, and the ceremony was staged well away from the village, back in the line of trees that fringe the beach. A blind of palm fronds made sure that no casual beach stroller could see what was going on.

When the blind was pulled back and we were invited inside, we saw that the ground was littered with what could have been corpses. The men of the village were lying on the ground, dead still, their eyes closed and their bodies twisted into odd positions. Their tongues hung out, pink and swollen. A drumbeat began, very slowly at first, and for a while nothing changed. Kal stepped around the men like a war photographer documenting the scene of an atrocity. An extreme closeup here, a wide-angle shot there. Then one of the bodies twitched. Then another. Then all the bodies began to move, in time with the drumming. The men, alive now but still a little stiff, straightened up and began to dance.

The music reached a crescendo, and Frans Nawima, old and wiry, grabbed an axe and began circling a young casuarina tree. This tree had been selected earlier, and the space around it cleared for the ceremony. The tree was the reason we were here. Frans let fly with the axe and the men whooped. Then he passed it to his eldest son, Gerfasius, who also took a stroke. The men whooped again. Then his youngest son, Rikardus, and finally his son-in-law, Engel Koare. The casuarina tree fell.

The drumming stopped, and the men stripped the tree of its branches. Then they formed two rows along its length, and the drums started up again. Victor Unumpare leapt astride the tree. He shook like a man possessed. His fists were clenched, his eyes closed, and his face, a black mask of pig grease and soot, was twisted in agony, as if he were trying to spit out his own tongue. With a sudden leap, Victor advanced a meter or so along the tree, and continued his peculiar

vibrations. Then, another leap, and another. Each pause was just a little longer than expected, and every leap came as a shock.

The Iriotepe, in its ritual enactment of death and subsequent resurrection, is a way to bring back the spirits of the great men of the past, Apollo said. These spirits, awakened by the Iriotepe, will accompany the men to the forest to cut the tree from which the new canoe will be carved. The various circumstances of the deaths of these men are reflected in the various contorted positions they've assumed on the ground.

The protruding tongues at first struck me as an overly melodramatic touch, and a bit cartoonish, like "XX" for eyes. Then I realized that in the heat of the tropics a body would bloat quickly, and a swollen tongue might reasonably be the first physical sign of decomposition.

Victor's trance-like "dance" along the fallen tree awakens the spirit of the casuarina, so that it, too, can accompany the men on their trip to the forest to cut the tree. The casuarina, with its distinctive feathery leaves, is the symbol of the spirit of canoe-making, Apollo said, because like the Kamoro, it lives along the coast, and will always lead the men back home from the forest.

Frans Nawima is the *ote amoko*—literally the "owner" of the wood—and he and his sons were responsible for selecting and cutting the tree. Victor Unumpare was the owner of the spirit-awakening part of the ceremony, and by tradition he is the leader of the spirits of the casuarina and the ancestors.

The Iriotepe was an extraordinary event. Frans looks like he is close to sixty years old, and I am sure he has performed his *ote amoko* duties in the past. But Victor is young, in his thirties, and he could not have been old enough to have awakened the casuarina spirit during the last *ku-kaware* in 1970. Still his jerky, entranced progress along the tree was an astonishing performance, and most certainly what Kal would call "the real thing."

ALTHOUGH THE KU-KAWARE was being staged on our behalf, it felt at least as alive as the *karapao* we witnessed, perhaps even more so. The excitement in the village was thick enough to cut with a knife. This may actually have been enhanced by our schedule, which required that all of the various stages of the *ku-kaware* be performed in a period of just a few days. In the past these same events would have been spread out over several months.

The seasons determined the overall timing of a traditional *ku-kaware*. Preparations would take place in spring, and the tree would be cut at the end of the dry season, in April or early May. It would be left there until the heavy rains of late summer, when the men would return to the forest, hollow it out, and take advantage of the swollen rivers to float the half-completed vessel down to the coast. The finished canoe

195

ALFONS NANIPIA, PARIPI.
Wearing the *mbi-kao* during the Ametamako stage of the ceremony.

would then be ready for the season of smooth seas that begins in late September or October.

The most basic function of the *ku-kaware* is to insure that the appropriate spiritual, social, and physical preparations have been made for a group of men to safely and comfortably travel inland to the forest to cut and hollow a tree. Leaving the village for the several weeks it would take the men to select, fell, and hollow a canoe is risky. Since they would be exposing themselves to accidents and illness, and, in the old days, to attack by hostile neighbors, they would need spiritual protection. Since they would be isolated, deep in the forest, they would need faith that the rest of the village was united behind their efforts. Since the work was hard—imagine hollowing a ten-meter log in the days before steel axes—they would need a good supply of food. The various stages of the *kaware* address each of these needs.

The second stage, called Iwamapuka, was a surprisingly modest event, and took place just in front of Marselus Takati's house. A group of men stood there quietly, with Marselus presiding. Here the mask costume, the *mbi-kao,* made its first appearance as it stepped, without fanfare or warning, from the forest behind the house.

When worn by Alfons Nanipia, the *mbi-kao* looked very different from the brown bundle I had seen a week earlier. The huge chin jutted forward and the pointy head reached so high than Alfons could not himself have touched the tassel of feathers at the top. Horns poked out where there should have been ears, and another jutted from the creature's forehead. Alfons's body was shrouded in a strange vestment of palm fronds up to his armpits, as if he were climbing out of a basket. All that was visible was that horrible mask and Alfons's arms, themselves almost monstrously thick.

Alfons occupied the *mbi-kao* only in the most mundane sense; the spirit animating the costume was Mamokoro, from the casuarina tree. Mamokoro took a staff and reached with it into the crowd of men. Five or six grabbed onto it with a hand. Mamokoro led them by the staff from the crowd and, thus formed into a line, they let go of the staff and sat down. Then he went back to the crowd, and drew out another group. By the time he had finished, Mamokoro had organized the most able-bodied men of the village into a half-dozen separate groups.

Although far less dramatic than the Iriotepe, this stage is perhaps the single most important of the *kaware,* Apollo said. The groups of men selected by Mamokoro would be the working groups, and in the old days, each would produce a canoe for a single family. The family, for its part, would supply its group with tobacco, sago, and fish. In a perfect world, the Iwamapuka by itself would be sufficient to organize a canoe-making expedition. But the Kamoro, like the rest of us, do not live in a perfect world. Their world

can very easily be disrupted by the activities of malicious spirits.

The spirits of ancestors who have been properly buried and honored can be counted on to help with important and ceremonial activities, and these were the ones awakened by the Iriotepe. The spirits of people who have died under strange or accidental circumstances are another matter. These spirits, called *namuru, naoipu,* or *nokoropau*—the words all mean the same thing, Apollo said, "suddenly dead man"—are the ones who bother the living. Since they died suddenly, or under unknown circumstances, preparations were never made for their deaths, and thus they have never been properly put to rest. *Namuru* are meddlesome, and particularly dangerous to those who go to the forest to cut a canoe.

The stage of the *ku-kaware* called Namuru is designed to appease these wandering spirits, to ask them to allow the men to cut their canoe without interference. This event was simple and rather brief. On the beach in front of the village, the *mbi-kao*—this time just the mask, no elaborate costume of palm fronds—brandished the dead, yellowed leaves of the *waru* tree. The leaves of the *waru* tree contain a strong magic that calms the *namuru,* making them far less likely to disrupt the canoe-making.

The *mbi-kao* comes from the Aweyau and Miminareyau story, and there are two recognized styles of masks, one for each of the brothers. The mask representing Aweyau has a short chin or none at all; that representing Miminareyau has a long, sometimes upcurved chin. Paripi's *mbi-kao* is in the Miminareyau style, and from a Kamoro perspective it is, depending on your age, either exceptionally frightening or exceptionally ugly. The long chin is the worst part, Alo said. "It makes his face look like what the people do at night near the beach."

Except for the small, almost private Iwamapuka stage near Marselus's house, up to this point the *mbi-kao* had not entered the village. Nor were there many people around during these events, and no children at all. But the community as a whole must also support the activities of the men going out to carve the canoe, and to make this point, the spirit must enter the village. This stage was called Ametamako, literally "the way of the sago," but the connotation, Apollo said, is "the way the spirit goes." This "way" is confused and crooked, which symbolizes the difficulty of the men's upcoming task.

The Ametamako began quietly, and unannounced. The village men, dressed in their finery, simply began appearing at the far end of the village, one at a time or in small groups. As their numbers increased, they began to attract a swarm of children, bouncing and fidgeting with curiosity. At this moment the *mbi-kao* was lurking, unseen, in the bushes just outside the village.

Without warning, the *mbi-kao* charged from the forest, stumbling and reeling like an angry drunk. The

ESTUARY OF THE IPIRAWEA RIVER, NEAR PARIPI.

kids bolted in absolute terror. There was nothing faked about it, they literally feared for their lives. Their legs churned the sand like characters in a Saturday morning cartoon. I have a photograph, developed back in the United States, of the *mbi-kao* first entering the village. In the foreground is a blur, barely recognizable as a young boy. I didn't even see him go by at the time, and to create a blur like that at one-sixtieth of a second he really must have been moving.

The *mbi-kao* continued in his crooked path, charging, stopping, then charging again. A group of women danced in the front line, facing the *mbi-kao*. They wore grass skirts and had tucked the large leaves of the arrowroot plant (*Tacca leontopetaloides*) into their waistbands, and wagged their backsides in a steady rhythm. As the procession worked its way up and down the village, a few of the boys collected their nerve enough to approach the *mbi-kao*. The spirit would ignore them at first, and then, without warning, charge in their direction, which set them scampering off again. One boy of about seven, standing alone, danced about in a crude mockery of the *mbi-kao,* which would perhaps have been a brave act had he not stationed himself so far away that he was almost in Ipiri.

The Ametamako included a short play. The men grouped themselves into a single file and walked down the center of the village. Periodically, one of them would stumble and fall on the ground, as if dead. The others continued walking, and as they filed solemnly past him, each dropped a breadfruit leaf on his prostrate body.

This is an enactment of a very long story about a man named Nokoropao, Apollo said. This old man had two daughters who every day would go out into the mangrove forest to collect delicacies: shellfish, beetle larvae, and seasonal fruit. They never shared any of these with their father, however, and he grew weaker and weaker, and finally died. "See him fall?" Apollo said. "He has no strength left, that is why he can't keep up with the other dancers." The story is enacted during the *ku-kaware* as a cautionary tale, to remind the people of Paripi that they should not be like these selfish girls, or the men going out to cut the canoe will end up like Nokoropao.

The day concluded with a stage of the ceremony called Paruru, which Apollo said was "like an agreement." The men sat in a circle while Marselus and Frans Nawima, the leaders of the ceremony, gestured quietly, bringing the day's events to a satisfactory close. Then the men got up and wandered home.

As the sun was setting, with the *mbi-kao* safely gone, a group of young children acted out the perfor-

YAN WEATOA, NEAR PARIPI.
Blowing a horn during the Iriotepe.

mance. A little boy covered his face with what looked like one of his mother's blouses to play the *mbi-kao,* while the others danced, boys and girls both, their little backsides swinging in the fading light.

WITH THE MEN ORGANIZED, the spirits calmed, and the village urged to a generous spirit, it was time to cut the tree, which stood an hour's journey away in the forest. When we met the men by the river, they were already in the same state as the day before, painted and tied with ribbons of palm fiber. Even the canoes were decorated, with black flanks, white gunwales, and a chevron-like design of three or four black bars near the bow and stern. Propped near the lead boat was a staff decorated with black cassowary and white cockatoo feathers, which we dubbed the "*adat* flag," since it proclaimed allegiance to tradition, although we probably should have called it a scepter. This "flag" flew proudly, alongside the Indonesian flag, at the front of the lead canoe.

Just before setting off, one man from each of the six canoes grabbed a stout ember from a fire that had been lit on the beach and carried it to his boat. If the Kamoro stop anywhere for more than about fifteen minutes, they almost always build a fire. The embers would make it easier to start a fire when we reached the forest, and more importantly, they would provide a means to light cigarettes along the way.

Earlier that morning, the *mbi-kao* had led a posse of men down the path to the river, bringing a simple, but crucial, item—a woven mat. The mat, Apollo said, was a symbol that the men's wives have given permission for them to go cut the tree. It was a sentimental souvenir from home, a familiar, and comforting, piece of the family hearth. If this had been a full length *ku-kaware,* the mat would have been of practical use as well, giving the men something to sleep on in their shelter for the two weeks or so they would be living in the forest.

Our expedition headed off inland, the men singing and paddling in unison. With three or four men paddling, the canoes shot forward at a surprising clip, and particularly when we entered the smaller tributaries, our motor offered no significant advantage in speed.

The tree had been selected while we were off to the west, and the appropriate specimen stood at the edge of Paripi's sago grounds. We stopped our canoes deep in the mangrove forest, and walked about a kilometer along a well-used sago trail. The first part of this hike led through a tall forest of *Bruguiera,* a buttress-rooted mangrove species that populates the mud around it

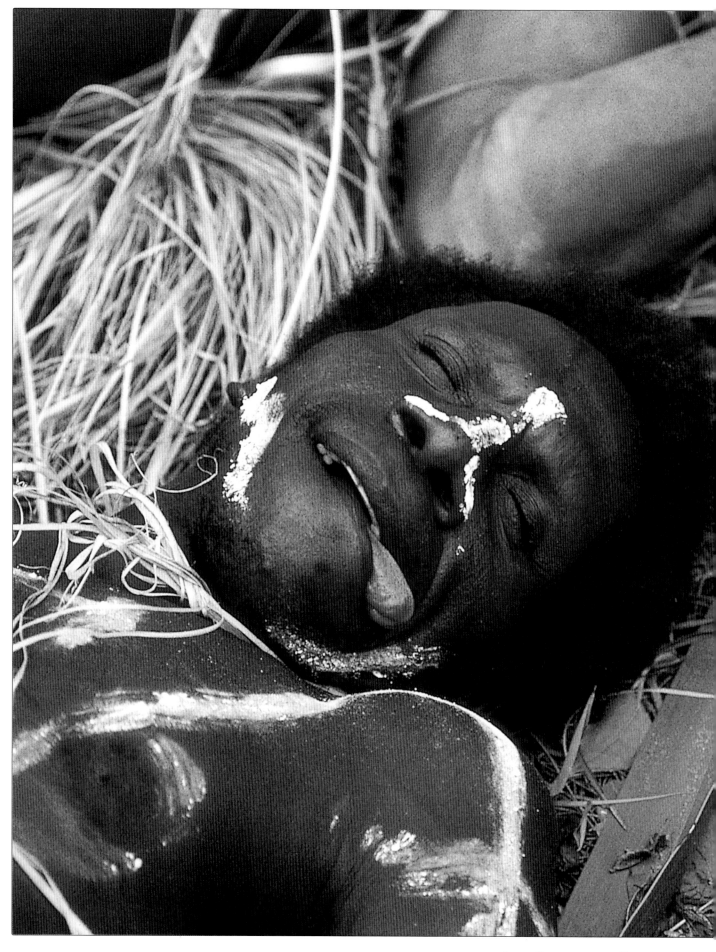

Linus Erakipia, near Paripi.
Feigning death during the Iriotepe.

with lumpy, gnome-like "knee-roots." These give the tree's root system access to atmospheric oxygen, a necessary adaptation to the constantly inundated soil. Hiking through the knees was not as difficult as it first appeared, however, and felled trees served as bridges over the the worst sections. As we neared the chosen tree, the ground became drier, and the mangrove trees gave way to sago palms, still young and scattered in this marginal area.

The *utaka* tree that had been selected for the canoe was tall, straight, and magnificent. The trunk shot up for a full thirty meters before it deigned to produce a single branch. The tree had wide buttress roots near its base, so the men built a platform about three meters high to reach the straight part of the trunk. With just three men wielding axes, the work went remarkably quickly—the tree, more than a meter across at the point where it was cut, fell in less than twenty minutes. In the meantime, the rest of the men cleared a path in which it could fall. At the last minute one man placed a branch in the cut, and the forty-five-meter tree landed exactly where it was supposed to.

The section to be used for the canoe was paced off, the trunk was cut a second time, and the resulting log was rolled ninety degrees into a position that was deemed correct for the finished canoe. The men sectioned off the top surface by placing sticks approximately where each passenger would sit, and then the chopping began.

The axe blows reverberated in the forest like firecrackers, or the sputtering of a very large engine. Since each axe rose and fell at a slightly different rate, occasional rhythms would appear from the randomness of the chopping, and then disappear again.

The Kamoro work their axes and *parang*s with a speed and precision that is sometimes difficult to believe. The platform around the base of the tree, a scaffolding of lashed poles, went up in mere minutes. A bench of stakes and split sago stems for us to sit on, and a table of the same for our cameras and gear, took just a few minutes more.

The small tree used to construct the scaffolding and other structures yields a sap that is as red and sticky as blood, and it even dries to the same brownish color. When I first saw this sap on my pants, I anxiously began looking for an injury. When the *utaka* tree fell, it opened a great hole in the canopy, and the equatorial sun reached the forest floor, exciting the insects. The men's sweaty backs proved irresistable to the biting horseflies—or pigflies, as they are called by the Kamoro, who live in a place with no horses.

Hollowing the log is very hard work. Apollo enjoyed playing the role of foreman, teasing and cajoling the men to keep their spirits up. "It's two o'clock, hurry up!" he shouted at about 11:45 a.m. One older man, working down near where Alo and I sat, looked up at the sun and said quietly to himself, "No." Nobody in the villages wears a watch, but when I had

HOLLOWING THE CANOE, NEAR THE PARIPI SAGO GROVES.

Apollo ask him what time he thought it was, his estimate disagreed with my watch by just five minutes.

After flattening the top of the log, the men began hollowing it by cross-cutting a series of slots or mortises. This was the hardest work, and it proceeded slowly. The mortises were inexorably widened until the space between them shrank to less than the length of the axe head. Then the in-between sections were split free. This seemed like the satisfying part of the job, as great chunks of wood flew out with each sideways heave on the axe. As the day progressed, the squealing of splitting wood began to be heard amidst the stacatto thumping of the axes.

The standard European trade axe, which is the only kind I have seen used in Irian Jaya, has a narrower bit and longer reach than an American axehead of the same weight, and perhaps more importantly, is easier to fit a new handle to. It lacks the poll of an American axe. Axes are used until they are worn down to the handle, and so as not to prematurely shorten their life, are sharpened as infrequently as possible. The men would occasionally steel two *parang*s against each other, or lightly dress the cutting edge of an axe with a smooth stone, but I never saw any heavy grinding or filing.

The men worked together as if each stroke had been choreographed, and yet not a single direction was given. The six axes rose and fell, centimeters from hands and feet, without a misplaced blow. The men seemed instinctively to know when one of their fellows needed a rest, and somebody would step up and relieve him without being asked. While the front lines worked the axes, the men behind them kept busy clearing brush and laying bark or palm fronds to improve the areas of bad footing around the log. Later in the afternoon, some of the men cooked up some sago. Everybody, without being told, made himself useful. A construction foreman would love this crew.

The canoe took shape from the inside out. Once the interior had been formed, the exterior was cut away to match. The vessel would be finished later, at the village, but even so the men cut a neat series of angles in the bark remaining along the gunwales so that the boat wouldn't look quite so rough on its maiden voyage.

As we watched the work progress through the late afternoon, we heard the occasional crash of trees, sometimes far away. Each time a tree fell, the men working let out a cheer. I didn't think much of this at the time, figuring somebody was just out cutting hearts of palm. It came as a shock to me when the canoe was finally pulled from its resting place and slid around the stump. A new path had been cut, and at two-meter intervals, as far as I could see down its length, logs had been laid for rolling the hollowed tree to the river. This job would be the hardest of the day, and the only way it would work was if the men kept up their speed. Putting their shoulders to their creation, they let out a great shout, and men and canoe crashed through the forest at a running pace.

We walked slowly out the same way we had come. The new corduroy road led along a different direction, as it would have been impossible to get the canoe out through the *Bruguiera* knees without actually carrying it. Just before we reached our boat, we suddenly encountered Gerardus Takati along the path. This was a surprise, because we hadn't seen him all day. His arms were full of vines, and we asked what they were for. At first, overcome with shyness, he pretended not to hear the question. Finally Apollo squeezed it out of him. "They are to make another *mbi-kao*," he said.

APOLLO AND I WERE TALKING after dinner that night when Kal ran inside from brushing his teeth. The tree behind our house, he said, was full of synchronous fireflies. Synchronous fireflies, unlike their asynchronous relatives, light up all at once, and when I went outside I saw that the tree behind Ladislaus' house looked like it had been strung with Christmas lights, although the frequency of the blinking would be too rapid for most people's tastes. Kal has an acquaintance who studies these insects, and he excitedly speculated that this might be a rare discovery. Apollo tried to let him down gently. They are common everywhere in Irian Jaya, he said, and noted, as politely as he could, that they regularly appear in the trees around his house in the middle of Timika. (In Kal's defense, although the fireflies aren't rare to Apollo, they are to entomologists, who have not yet studied Irian Jaya's synchronous species.)

That evening Apollo mentioned to me that the *ku-kaware* we were witnessing was missing a section. This stage, called the *mbi-kawane*, was the one Jan Pouwer had seen performed in 1951 as part of the funerals in Migiwia and Kaokonao. This struck me as somewhat ironic, since it was Henk H. Peeters's drawing of the *mbi-kawane* in *Antiquity and Survival* that had inspired us to come to Paripi in the first place. *Mbi-kawane* literally means "spirit-platform," and what we had missed was a performance of the *mbi-kao* that takes place on a raised platform.

"The owner of the platform was very angry that they didn't include his section," Apollo said. "He wouldn't even come along to cut the canoe."

The problem, Apollo said, was that the way the village elders interpreted the situation, a platform would have had to have been built from Marselus's house, where the Iwamapuka took place, to the edge of the mangrove river behind the village, where the canoe was to be burned and prepared. This distance is close to half a kilometer. While it isn't very far to walk, this would make an incredibly long platform.

"Apollo," I asked, "Why didn't they just build a smaller platform?"

"I don't know," he said. "Actually I don't think they thought of that."

I realized at this point that although the time schedule for our *ku-kaware* was speeded up, nobody had

even considered abbreviating or otherwise compromising any of the actual parts of the ceremony. This was probably why it felt so real. On the other hand, it also meant that we didn't get to see the *mbi-kawane,* and that the owner of this stage sat at home stewing while the others were out cutting the canoe.

Our stay in Paripi had brought back memories of Apollo's childhood in the 1940s and 1950s, a time when the village was located just west across the mouth of the Ipirawea River. Apollo's father Abraham was an important man in the village, and was a *mandar*—a kind of village foreman—under the Dutch colonial government. Despite this, he had only limited use for the innovations of the Catholic Church and the Dutch colonial government, and it was his status within the traditional leadership structure of the village that was most important. In those days, Apollo said, ceremonies like the *ku-kaware* were still routine, and traditional woodcarvings—of which we had seen so few examples on our trip—were ubiquitous.

"My father carved beautiful traditional plates, with frogs, and the hornbill, and lizards, and crabs on them," Apollo said. "I remember one in particular, it was like a platter, and had the head of the hornbill on each end. It was very long, and you had to hold it in two hands."

"At the time me and my two brothers were at boarding school—this would have been about nineteen fifty—and on visits home my father would bring us our food on this plate. Shellfish, sago, maybe fruit. Each of our portions would be placed together on the platter, and he would serve us from it."

Apollo regrets that he now has nothing that his father made. After years away from Paripi studying and teaching, the memory of that plate continued for him to be a symbol of his father, and of his own youth.

"We lost something when we went away to school," Apollo said. "Years later we asked our mother, 'Where is that old plate?' She said, 'Oh boys, it broke a long time ago.'"

"I'm sure it got broken in an argument," Apollo laughed. "Probably my father got mad and threw it at somebody."

The village of Paripi has a tight-knit quality, a kind of unity of purpose that Apollo, after many years living in the city, found as charming as I did. Both he and Alo had become very content with the village life we had been living over the last few weeks. No electricity, no noise and dust from the cars, and for Alo at least, no scrambling for work. They both constantly made comparisons to the worries and stress of life in the Timika area.

Traveling, of course, can bring its own forms of stress. One night, toward the end of our visit, Alo was uncharacteristically quiet and moody. When I asked what was wrong, he apologized for his ill temper and said he was missing his "family." Apollo and I smiled. We were quite sure what he meant.

"You're complaining after just two weeks," I said. "Think of me, I've been away from my 'family' for months."

"Ah, but the Kamoro are different," he said, the spark returning to his eyes. "We eat lots of rich food like *tambelo,* oysters, and crabs. You know what I mean."

I GREW UP less than one hundred kilometers from Baltimore, Maryland, within the culinary orbit of the Chesapeake Bay. Some people say that the finest product of this great watershed are its bluepoint oysters, but these people are wrong. Northwest Atlantic, and particularly, northeast Pacific oysters are the world's best. The Chesapeake's claim to fame is *Callinectes sapidus,* the blue crab. This animal's scientific name combines the Latin for "beautiful swimmer" and the Greek for "tasty," and carcinologist Mary J. Rathbun chose well in both cases. It is thought that more blue crabs are eaten than any other species of crab in the world, and I have certainly done my best over the years to contribute to this statistic.

The Kamoro are also fond of crabs, and the species caught here is the common Southeast Asian mangrove crab, *Scylla serrata. Scylla* does not have as elegant a name as the blue crab—it combines the Greek for "sea monster" and the Latin for "saw"—but it is the blue crab of the tropics, and probably the most common food crab in Indonesia. Like the blue crab, *Scylla* is a portunid, or swimming crab, although it doesn't particularly act like one, preferring to crawl around in the mud of the mangrove. This crab is found over a wide range, but the specimens in Irian Jaya are almost black in color, while those I have eaten in western Indonesia are lighter, a kind of dark olive green.

In the Kamoro area, crabbing is almost exclusively the work of women, who dig the little monsters from their burrows in the mud under the mangrove roots or in the banks of the tidal creeks. For some reason almost all of the crabs we were served were males, which we used to call "jimmies" around the Chesapeake. Since the Kamoro would have no reason to throw back a "sook," or female, it must be that their method of capture tends to yield males. I have read that like blue crabs, female *Scylla* retreat to the deeper channels to spawn, and perhaps this takes place in the summer. In any case, harvesting mostly males has positive consequences for maintaining the breeding population.

These crabs are delicious, either boiled or roasted right on the fire, and we ate them almost every night in Paripi. We also had fish, usually catfish, every day, and often had clams. Toward the end of the trip I

Fig. 8.1
TAMBELO.
Bactronophorus thoracites, 4/5ths of actual size. Illustration by Kevin Wiseman.

NORBERTUS MAYARAIKU, IPIRI.

YAN WEATOA, PARIPI.
When burning a canoe, sometimes things can go S-shaped.

asked Apollo if we could arrange to get some *tambelo* worms, one of the most celebrated Kamoro dishes. I wondered if they might be scarce, and I told him I'd be willing to pay a premium to whomever could find us some. He laughed. "I've been eating *tambelo* every day," he said. "I didn't think you'd want any."

The *tambelo* is a "worm" only inside quotation marks. It is a bivalve mollusk, like a clam, but the two halves of its shell, rather than serving to protect the animal, have evolved into a kind of rasp that it uses to bore into the old roots of mangrove trees. "Tambelo" is Indonesian; in Kamoro it is "pa'a."

In English the *pa'a* would be called a shipworm, or teredo, a group of animals that were the bane of sailors in the days of wooden ships. Even today, shipworms destroy wooden pilings and docks all over the world and are certainly the most destructive bivalves on the planet. Teredo is the common name for these mollusks, but there are many genera in addition to *Teredo*. I had never before heard of anybody eating one.

The Kamoro would no more cook a *tambelo* than an American or European would cook a fine oyster. A food this special must be eaten raw. When I finally tasted them I understood what all the fuss was about. The *pa'a* were superb, in taste and texture much like a sweet oyster—if anything, even richer. Apollo also

suggested marinating them in lime juice and red chili, and after twenty minutes in this mixture the worms became crisp, like ceviche. This is also pleasant, and would probably be preferred by people who are put off by the texture of oysters.

"*Tambelo* is a part of daily life, and the people eat them every day when they are out in the mangrove," Apollo said. "They taste best directly from the tree."

The shipworms live in the roots of mangrove trees of the genus *Rhizophora*, which are chopped apart with an axe to get at the worms. Another variety found in the area prefers the dead roots of a different species of tree. Apollo called this one "second-quality," and noted that it has a bitter taste. This species, like the second-rate sago grub, seems best left alone.

Shipworm taxonomy relies on the structure of the shell and, particularly, that of two odd calcified structures at the terminal end of the animal called pallets, which are used to seal its burrow. I paid little attention to these features when eating them (the pallets are removed and cleverly used to clean the animals before serving), but later Kal was able to send me a specimen in alcohol. The Teredinidae of Irian Jaya are not well studied, but the distinctive pallets of the *pa'a*—each like a tiny martini glass, with a rather large garnish— make it obvious that it is *Bactronophorus thoracites*.

206

OTAKWA.
This catch, from one of the best fishing areas on the coast, includes ariid catfish and a bull shark.

I am a great lover of oysters, but I judge the *tambelo* to be superior. Despite this, I seriously doubt that the dish would succeed in the United States. While the word "worm" might not please a scientist, it would certainly be foremost in the diner's mind. Imagine a plate of earthworms, fat ones twenty-five or thirty centimeters long, and you will understand what I mean. For most Americans no amount of lime juice and chili would help that go down.

Although clams, oysters, crabs, and *tambelo* commonly feature on the Kamoro dinner table, the definitive accompaniment to sago is fish. A biscuit of sago and a chunk of charred catfish held together in one hand satisfies the *aopao* of a meal, and nothing else is required. The Catholic missionaries, trying to get the Kamoro to eat more greens to improve their health, at first thought the problem was a lack of edible species, so they planted gardens. Their flock still didn't eat many greens. And they still don't today. During our travels, we always had to make a special request for vegetables, which were invariably *daun singkong,* the leaves of the manioc plant, or young papaya flowers. These are everywhere available, but if we hadn't asked, nobody would have thought of cooking them. The Kamoro just aren't in the habit of eating vegetables. Sago and fish are enough.

WHEN THE TIDE is at its lowest, the creek behind Paripi leading to the mangrove forest almost disappears, revealing a broad, glistening field of black mud. Metallic crabs scuttled into their burrows as we passed, and tiny mudskipper gobies, equally at home on land and in water, ricocheted up the wet banks like tossed pebbles. The mud smelled of decay, but it was a strangely pleasant odor, as of something that had been rotting for so long that it had begun to turn sweet again.

We were following a group of women from Paripi to watch them fish, a project that they found rather amusing. There was only one trail through the mud, marked by a sprinkling of buff sand against the black muck. A foot that missed the sand would sink up to the knee, so we kept our heads down. We soon came to a deeper channel, and there we climbed in a canoe and paddled off to where the women were at work.

The Kamoro use a simple but effective technique to fish in the mangrove. While the tide is low the women erect stout posts across one of the many tidal inlets. Later, when the tide is at its highest, they lash a fine, net-like barrier to the poles, taking care that it leaves no opening. This "net," called an *era,* looks like a matchstick blind about two meters across. When the tide is again low, the women return to scoop out the fish stranded by the barrier. Sometimes, at the same time they erect the posts, they chop brush and place it in their inlet to give the fish a place to hide and to encourage them to linger.

The Kamoro also fish with hooks and line, gill nets, and for larger prey such as sharks and sawfish, harpoons. If the technique will catch a fish, they use it. But the *era* is the workhorse, and feeds more Kamoro than all the other methods combined. Apollo said that the *era* is believed to be a technological import from the Kei Islands, but I was unable to confirm this. In any case, it is now so widely used that it might as well be local.

I felt more than a little unchivalrous watching two women only a little younger than my grandmother wrestling three-meter-long posts into the mud. Neither woman looked like she weighed more than forty kilograms, and working in the waist-deep water and muck, it required the full strength and body weight of both, jumping up and down, to securely plant the posts. Although the women started off dressed, I think out of politeness to us rather than modesty, they finally gave up and took off their blouses so they could better address the biting insects that plagued them during their labors. Their work was punctuated with occasional slaps, as one or the other tried to rid herself of the infuriating little insects called *agas*.

This creature is a biting gnat or midge, something like what an Alaskan would call a "no-see-um," since the insects are so tiny as to be nearly invisible. They are especially common in the mangrove swamps, and—particularly at night—on the beach. Although our visit to Paripi coincided with the middle of the rainy season, it almost never rained, and consequently we encountered very few mosquitoes, which was a welcome surprise.* The *agas*, however, were an annoyingly reliable nuisance.

My worst encounter with *agas* took place one night when, attempting to return to Timika from Timika Pantai, we became stranded at Waukutiri, a sandy spit where the Apiriyuwahu River empties into the Arafura Sea. It was late afternoon, and we were obliged to stop for the night to wait for the tide to rise. We built a fire to ward off the chill, but there was not much we could do about the *agas*. At first I thought they were beach fleas, because they are bottom feeders and attack at the ankles, or any other part of the body that is close to the sand. Because of their tiny size, socks do little to discourage their work. Unlike a mosquito, which takes its fill and leaves, the *agas* keep going, leaving itchy trails of destruction. In the morning my ankles were covered with red hieroglyphs.

I felt bad for the women working. I was wearing long pants and long sleeves and had smeared my ankles with mud, and the *agas* were still giving me trouble. And I didn't have any posts to drive into the mud.

We returned the same afternoon so Kal could photograph the *era* going up, and again the following morning, to see what had been caught. The catch was very poor, consisting mostly of a little brackish water pufferfish, each the size of a plum. This is a pretty fish, with a bright yellow bar across its eyes, but the women were looking for something to eat, and pufferfish do not generally make good eating.

Pufferfish contain a very strong neurotoxin called tetrodotoxin or TTX which is, for example, the main ingredient of a Haitian houngan's zombi potion. I had only ever heard of them being eaten for pleasure by the Japanese until Alo told me that some of the older Kamoro, who know how to prepare them, like to eat one of the larger puffers of the genus *Arothron*. Japanese chefs train for years before they are allowed to prepare *fugu*. The technique requires carefully removing the skin and organs, particularly the liver, where the toxin is concentrated. The Japanese will insist that *fugu* is delicious, but it is also an obscenely expensive—upwards of $400 a plate—and exceedingly risky meal, and I am sure it is these latter qualities that account for its popularity. For example, not all puffers are equally toxic, but the Japanese prefer the deadly tiger puffer (*Fugu rubripes*), and despite the training, an estimated fifty to one hundred people die every year eating it. I'd like to think that the Kamoro learned to eat puffer for more practical reasons.

The *era* had also trapped a couple dozen silvery herring, and these, unlike the little puffers, were kept. In season, herring appear in the area in great schools, Alo said, and at that time they are gathered by the basketful and cooked with sago in coconut leaves. We later learned that the haul was so modest because the *era* had been set too early the day before. Apollo, without telling us, had arranged this to accommodate Kal's photography, because the peak of high tide was not due until after dark.

The fishing is not equally good throughout the Kamoro area. Alo, who is himself an experienced fisherman, said it is not bad at Paripi, but at Timika Pantai, for example, one could drag a net all day long and catch just one or two fish. The very best fishing in the entire area is in the east, he said, particularly at the Otakwa River and the three or four river mouths east of it. But, like everywhere else, a fisherman's success still depends on the tides, the winds, and as often as not, plain good luck.

THROUGHOUT THE TRIP, whenever the subject of traditional ceremonies came up, whether in conversation with government officials, people from the Church, teachers, educated Kamoro like Alo and Apollo, or even just Yosef Average, there was

---

* But it only takes one, as they say. After we parted ways in Timika and I returned to the United States, Kal came down with cerebral malaria. This disease, brought on by the parasite *Plasmodium falciparum*, is far more virulent than standard *P. vivax* malaria. He was in Bali when he fell sick, and by his calculation, he must have contracted the disease while in Paripi.

Natalis Erakipia, on bow of lead canoe, estuary of Ipirawea River.
The men are heading for the sandbar to perform the Apoko Tapuma, which concludes the *ku-kaware*.

APOKO TAPUMA, SANDBAR AT THE MOUTH OF THE IPIRAWEA RIVER.

always a point where the answers to my questions would start to get a bit vague. At this point, my informants would produce euphemisms, introduce caveats, or try to skip ahead to the next subject. There was a part of the traditional ceremonies, it seemed, that people just were not comfortable talking about with a visiting writer. In my own notes, I came to refer to these as "the so-called bad parts." A typical conversation went something like this:

"So what, exactly, *are* these 'bad' parts of the *ku-kaware*?"

"Uh, well, people get distracted afterward."

"Why do they get distracted?"

"They get caught up in the festivities."

"What festivities?"

"They're tired and neglect their work."

"What festivities make them tired?"

"They stay up late."

"Doing what?"

"The *ku-kaware* symbolizes the basic elements of Kamoro life, fishing and gathering sago..."

"But what do people do when they stay up at night?"

"Of course it is not everybody."

"It's not everybody doing what?"

"The bad parts of the *ku-kaware*."

The Kamoro are not prudes, but for most of a century they have been judged by people who were. Sex is a fraught and tricky enough matter without having an unsympathetic outsider express shock and outrage at your community's sexual practices. I was unable to find a way to explain that there probably weren't too many things in the world that could be done by a man and a woman, or two men or two women, or a hundred assorted specimens of each for that matter, that would shock or outrage somebody from San Francisco.

Even Apollo seemed uncharacteristically shy about these matters. Eventually, however, I succeeded in convincing him to tell me about these "bad" parts.

For the traditional performance of the *kaware* ceremony, the men built a platform at the top of a tall pole. This platform, Apollo said, is the *kaware asli*, the "original" or "true" *kaware*. At the completion of the celebration, the adult men of the village, stark naked, climb the pole and spend the day napping on the platform at the top. They are storing up energy for later. The adult women do the same, in a special, windowless ritual structure built in the forest away from the village. After sunset, the women light fires in the building so that it fills with smoke, and the men climb down the pole and go to meet them there. In the smoke and darkness, nobody knows with whom he or she is

APOKO TAPUMA, SANDBAR AT THE MOUTH OF THE IPIRAWEA RIVER.
Galus Mauria wears the *mbi-kao.*

having sex, and as Apollo put it, "you don't have to give your name."

Once I got Apollo talking about the original *kaware,* he began to loosen up. "There are two Apollos," Alo once told me. "One is a schoolteacher; the other is just Apollo." It was just Apollo who told me about the first time he saw the *ku-kaware.*

"In nineteen forty-seven my oldest brother celebrated his nose-piercing, and the same year there was a *kaware* at old Paripi," he said, "and"—

"Wait a minute Apollo," I interrupted, "You were what, in nineteen forty-seven, maybe five years old? I thought only adult men could see the *kaware.*"

"Yes," he laughed, "but I was a naughty boy."

It turns out that on this occasion, Apollo and a couple of other young delinquents accidentally stumbled upon the building, hidden in the forest away from the village, where the ritual orgy would take place. After dark, he and his associates crept out to the building and peeked through the slats of the wall into the smoky room. The fires must have been a bit too high, because his memory of what he saw was quite clear.

"This," he joked, "is our traditional 'blue movie.'"

At one point during this movie he saw his own father, but the woman beneath him was not his mother. Unfortunately for young Apollo, his father also saw him. Abraham Takati's temper was legendary, and although he didn't stop the business at hand to attend to his wayward son, the next day Apollo received some instruction that was every bit as memorable as what he saw in the smoky room.

Every Kamoro ceremony is a time of high spirits, and these high spirits are often sexually charged. All ceremonies, including the *kaware* and the *karapao,* traditionally ended with what is called *imu,* a two- or three-day period during which license was extended by the community for every adult, married and unmarried, to experiment sexually. To provide the lovers with fuel, great quantities of *tambelo* are eaten.

Imu, in addition to being fun, seems like a good way to resolve any sexual tensions that might exist in the village. Marriages are not destroyed over these experiments because both parties understand their ritual importance and, perhaps more importantly, their temporary nature. There are many people in the United States who would like to be able to say to their spouses: "Look, don't get so worked up. After all it was just *imu.*"

Although *imu* is not the openly performed activity it once was, it has by no means disappeared. The men do not sleep naked on the post any more, but a period of *imu* still follows every ceremony, and during this period exploratory sex is condoned. In particular, Apollo said, *imu* today is an important time for young unmarried couples to experiment sexually, and they are encouraged by their parents to do so. Well, "encouraged" might not be the right word for every parent, he said, but at least they have an excuse to turn a blind eye to the matter.

Rather than meeting in the smoky building, partners today usually meet discreetly in the woods, Apollo said. To reduce the possibility of unwanted onlookers, the lovers typically work out a location for the tryst ahead of time, and invent a subtle hand signal to display when they are ready to meet. When the signal is given, he continued, the lovers slip away from the crowd quietly, one at a time, to attract as little attention as possible.

"You seem to know an awful lot about this, Apollo," I said.

He smiled. "I'm just trying to be helpful."

"You know he had quite a reputation at school in Abepura," Alo said.

"I believe that," I said.

The tradition surrounding *imu* also protects any woman who gets pregnant during the festivities. Neither her husband, if she has one, nor the community applies sanctions against her or against the child. The child is treated as belonging to her, or if she is married, to her and her husband. According to Apollo, the child is not called "bastard" or stigmatized by some other kind of negative term for "*imu* child."

This does not mean that Kamoro society is exceptionally casual about extramarital or premarital sex. Alo, when he was in his twenties, remembers a man and a woman who had had an illicit affair suffering an extremely severe punishment. They had to accept a stroke of the rattan cane from every member of the village. Their mistake was impatience. Had they waited until the *imu*, nobody would have batted an eyelid.

Alo's example, however, is probably memorable because it was so severe, and I don't think such punishment is typical today. For example, when we first stopped in Paripi, Kal visited a woodcarver in Ipiri and bought a few carvings. Neither he nor I thought they were particularly good, but it was rare to see carvings of any kind, and we wanted to be encouraging. We later found out that this man, who is in his fifties, was at the center of a village sexual scandal: he and his teenage daughter were, as the saying goes, living as man and wife.

The people of Ipiri were not at all happy about this unsavory relationship, but at the time we visited, nothing had been done about it. The man's wife died just two years before, and the relationship with his daughter was likely to be related to this psychological trauma, which may have extenuated the village's sense of the man's wrong-doing. The people of the village may also have been hoping that the parties involved would soon end it on their own. In any case, even though both villages seemed to know about the situation and to disapprove, nobody was rushing to cane this man or his daughter.

ALO AND I WERE SITTING inside Ladislaus's house, chatting and sipping our afternoon coffee, when a small child bolted across the field of vision allowed by the front door. We both laughed, and walked over to get a better look. Sure enough, Kal was photographing nearby. Adults, of course, are almost always flattered by Kal's attentions, but some of the children get scared, especially when he leans over with that big wide-angle zoom. I imagine that some kids, no matter what you tell them, can't help but think that he's a giant, bearded cyclops reaching down for a meal.

I took a sip of my coffee and, for about the four-hundredth time, got a dead fly. The first time this happened, I spit the whole mouthful out the window in disgust. Soon, it took a mouthful with three or four dead flies, or one live one, to get the same reaction. After a week or so, I learned to roll the flies—dead or alive—toward the front of my mouth with my tongue, so I could dispose of them discreetly without wasting my coffee. Somehow I couldn't quite develop the habit of just checking my cup before drinking.

The flies were only really bothersome during meals, especially when we were having fish or crabs. They became very agitated and numerous at these times, enough to affect one's appetite. In their excitement, they alight on anything moist, including your eyes. If anyone should think that eyelashes evolved for batting coquettishly and getting stuck under contact lenses, he or she needs to spend more time around flies. Eyelashes are for keeping these filthy intruders out of your eyes.

One day, when I complained that I couldn't see the catfish for its covering of *Musca domestica* or *M. paripianus* or whatever they were, Apollo disappeared to our storeroom and came back with a candle. I am afraid I was unable to disguise my skepticism, and I may have even made a crack like, "So what are you going to do with that, swat them with it?" As usual, Apollo was patient with me, and he lit the candle and set it on the table. I don't know why, but it really did drive most of the flies away. There is always something to learn.

Another troublesome insect was a species of cockroach. These creatures, a shimmery copper color, were actually quite beautiful, but they had the irritating habit of seeking out the pockets of my camera bag as hiding places. Since each was about the size of my thumb, their sudden movements could give me a start when reaching for a roll of film or a lens. But my real fear was that one would get crushed by the jostling of the bag, leaving a splat of grease to soil my equipment.

Getting rid of them was an exasperating affair. When I found one, I would empty the pocket and try to chase it out. Unfortunately, to the cockroach, the

FRANS NAWIMA, NEAR PARIPI.

EDGE OF THE MANGROVE BEHIND PARIPI.

most promising place to run to was another pocket. I once spent fifteen minutes chasing one of these insects out, and by the time I had succeeded, every lens and camera and film canister I owned sat on the table. Kal never mentioned any such trouble, but since all the zippers on his old bag froze open long ago from salt spray, I think the roaches were just free to come and go as they pleased, with no risk of ever getting trapped.

Some people would argue that the bigger the physical size of the pest, the bigger the problem, and they might be right. I mean no insult to Ladislaus's housekeeping—his house was clean and tidy—but the first night I slept there I was awakened by a rat crawling against my face. I was sleeping with my head on my bag, which was right against the wall near the corner of the room. The creature had been running down along the edge of the room when it unexpectedly found its way blocked by my bag. Scurrying around the bag, it met my face. I woke up at exactly the same time the rat realized I was not inanimate, and for a second or two neither of us quite knew what to do. The rat came up with a plan first, and shot up over my face and disappeared toward the next corner. From then on I made sure to leave a cleared perimeter around the room, and the experience was never repeated.

This animal was on the small side, so my guess is that it was the Pacific rat (*Rattus exultans*) which is common throughout the Indonesian archipelago and which I don't think is particularly verminous. The Pacific rat is one of at least six species that have been inadvertently introduced to New Guinea. The island has a few native species of *Rattus,* but zoologist Tim Flannery notes in his *Mammals of New Guinea* that these have a "distinctive odor." I'm not sure exactly what he means by this, but I don't recall my midnight visitor having any particular smell at all, and I certainly was in a position to have noticed.

Our house had its own rat-catcher as well, and it was far more disturbing than the rat. Every night a black cat would creep in and climb up on the main roof beam. Whenever it saw a rat, or a gecko, or potential prey of any other sort, it would shoot down the beam and leap after it. I don't know if this particular cat was clumsy or just overenthusiastic, but at least once a night it would slip, crashing into the coffee pot, a stack of dishes, our pressure lantern, or some other invariably noisy object. This animal was the bane of Alo's sleep. The first night, in the course of one of its pratfalls, it landed right on his face, and thereafter he could never quite relax at night. After he told me this, I always tried to sleep face down, or at least on my side.

O N THE FIRST MORNING after the canoe had been towed to the village, we walked down to the edge of the river to see how the men were coming along with the finish carving. Only a half-dozen men were working, and their strength and spirits were clearly flagging. One man, very politely, asked if we could spare a little more coffee. I was mortified. We had given the men coffee, tobacco, and sugar a week ago, but hadn't been paying attention, and they had almost run out. We had plenty left in our stores, and Apollo and I hurried back and got some. I did not want to be like the selfish girls who let Nokoropao wither away and die.

With caffeine for fuel, the work progressed at a more rapid pace, and by the following morning the canoe was ready for burning. The men had built a platform so Kal and his cameras could get a hornbill's eye view of the flames, and this time the burning went without a hitch. The new vessel expanded nicely, and was straight as a ruler. A couple of nasty splits up around the prow ornament gave the men a little trouble, but these were eventually repaired with nails and some hand-carved dowels.

The final morning of the *ku-kaware* began with a short section called Tukua Kaumare, literally "looking for fish." The *tukua* (a type of mullet) is a common fish in the area, and in this use it represents all fish. Fishing, in turn, represents all food gathering. During this enactment, the *mbi-kao* scampered across the beach, every now and then falling to the sand. "There, see, he caught one," Apollo said. The spirit continued, miming sago gathering and hunting.

"The life of the Kamoro people is closely tied to nature," Apollo said. "They can never give up this search for fish and sago. The *kaware* activities give them strength, so they can continue their food gathering. Tukua Kaumare is a symbol of this."

By late morning, the canoe was finished and decorated. It was time to take it out for its maiden voyage, and to bring the *ku-kaware* cycle to a close. A flotilla of seven canoes gathered to accompany the new vessel, which took pride of place in the center. The men, fully dressed and painted for the occasion, climbed into the canoes, and the *mbi-kao,* worn by Galus Mauria, stepped into the new canoe.

The company paddled out into the middle of the mouth of the Ipirawea River and stopped. A drum began, and the men suddenly stood up in their canoes and began singing and dancing. One man blew on a bamboo horn, which produced a low sound like a distant foghorn. The dancing and stomping grew wild, and the canoes leapt around on the water as if they were themselves living things. It seemed impossible that they didn't capsize. The singing was somber, in a minor key, and as each short verse ended, the men beat the sides of the canoes with their paddles and yelped like a pack of dogs. Then, as suddenly as they had begun, they stopped, and the dying sounds drifted across the estuary.

In silence, the canoes turned toward a deserted sandbar island far out in the mouth of the river, and the men began paddling. When the canoes slid against the sand of the island, the men noiselessly stowed their paddles and bent forward, disappearing beneath the gunwales of their vessels. The *mbi-kao* stood up, and stepped alone onto the tiny island.

The spirit seemed confused, and looked around for signs of life. There wasn't so much as a single blade of dune grass on the sand cay. As if suddenly alarmed, he leapt up in the air and began running in great circles around the island. Suddenly he stopped, and grabbing a handful of sand, he flung it high into the air. He began running and again stopped, grabbed another handful of sand, and exploded into the air. Only after he had flung sand from all four cardinal points on the island did the *mbi-kao* seem to quiet. He walked slowly to the center of the island and stopped.

The men crouching in the canoes unbent slowly, stood up, and walked ashore. Nobody made a sound. They formed a single column and headed straight for the *mbi-kao.* They didn't stop when they reached him, but continued to circle, and with the *mbi-kao* joining them, the line of men spiraled inward to the center of the island and closed into a circle. The sky was dull and hazy, and the noon sun was a gray blur. On the featureless cay, the men, circling incessantly, melted into a kind of living monument, a swirling temple of black, white, and ocher. The performance was mesmerizing. Then, abruptly, it stopped.

The men shuffled backward, creating an opening in the middle of the circle. There the *mbi-kao* squatted down and, using only his hands, dug a kind of shallow grave in the sand. In it he laid a wooden staff, the staff that had begun the ceremony in front of Marselus's house when he used it to pull the various groups of men together to work on the canoe. The *mbi-kao* brushed sand over it and stood up.

When the staff was buried, the *ku-kaware* formally ended. This final phase, Apollo said, is called Apoko Tapuma, from the Kamoro words for "stick" and "close." The men did not linger on the island afterward, and in fact they seemed to be in quite a hurry to leave. They walked briskly to the canoes and paddled back. They were probably a little afraid, Apollo said later, and did not want to hang around in case the spirit was not happy with their work. Whether or not the spirit was happy I can't say, but Kal and I were certainly happy. The *ku-kaware* was the most vibrant and fascinating event I had ever witnessed, and Kal, who has spent a lifetime photographing such ceremonies, was just as thrilled.

W E DID NOT WATCH the conclusion of the *ku-kaware* from our own boat. We borrowed a canoe from the village. Our brand-new Yamaha outboard motor was broken. "Broken" is the wrong word. In fact, the piston was seized up solid in the barrel. When he received this news Alo said nothing, and just shook his head slowly back and forth. That was all any of us could do. We didn't even have the heart to yell at Tobias. What could you say?

Tobias, we discovered, had been running the

Rofina Otokeao and Fransina Atiripuka, top, near Paripi.
Erecting a fishing weir.

LINUS ERAKIPIA AND SEBASTIANUS ATIRIPUKA, NEAR PARIPI.

engine on straight gasoline from the time we left Omba. Omba is close to two hundred kilometers from Paripi, and it is a tremendous credit to Yamaha's engineers that their engine should have lasted so long. It is not a credit to Tobias. Even overlooking the fact that our engine was carbureted to run on kerosene, not gasoline—the gasoline was aboard to aid starting, since cold engines don't like low volatility fuels like kerosene—I simply cannot fathom how anyone could think to operate a two-stroke without putting oil in the fuel. You could forget to add it, of course, but two-stroke oil contains a dye for exactly this reason. And our fuel cells were made of clear plastic. I mean, practically the only place on our boat where there *wasn't* any two-stroke oil was in the fuel cells.

I tried to imagine myself in his place. I'm back there running the engine, and it's getting worse and worse. I know something is wrong. Then I look down, and am suddenly irritated by all the foamy green bilge splashing around the bottom of the boat and soiling my feet. I know the green is from a can of two-stroke oil that tipped over and spilled, since my young assistant busted it open with a hammer and screwdriver instead of simply unscrewing the lid. At this point I'd have to believe that some kind of light bulb would go off in my head. Aha! Wait a minute. The bilge is green, but my

fuel is clear. This is backwards! And for that matter, this is a kerosene motor, so why has my fuel line been hooked up to the gasoline for the past two days?

Western travelers often speak abusively about the level and condition of technological devices in places like Irian Jaya. It is the second term in the classic complaint: "nobody speaks English and everything's broken." In Indonesia I have certainly seen some things done to machinery with a pair of pliers that made me wince, but the more I've traveled here, the more I have learned to reserve my own opinions about how to operate a piece of equipment, or how to fix one when it is broken. Technology is not culturally neutral, and there are sometimes good reasons for what looks to an American like an example of bad design, or a kind of repair technique that a English mechanic would call a "bodge." (This is not an apology for Tobias, by the way. I genuinely like the man, but until he gets some training I wouldn't let him near anything more complicated than a can opener.)

The small flashlight I'd brought with me from the United States was stolen from my room at the Sheraton Inn. This wasn't a big deal—although I do think it's significant that the only time something like this happened to me in Irian Jaya was at the only four-star hotel in the province—but it did mean that I needed to

218

VERONIKA NANIPIA, PARIPI.
Wielding torches at the *turako* performance.

buy a flashlight. The only ones available locally are the Chinese-made Tiger Head brand. These are constructed of such thin steel that, without batteries, you could crumple one like an empty beer can. They work well enough, though. The problem is the bulbs.

If my experience is any indication, a set of flashlight batteries will last longer in Irian Jaya than anywhere else in the world. Now I know why nobody complains about ABC batteries—they use them in Tiger Head flashlights. I went through the original bulb and my two spares before my batteries even worked up a sweat. The first time one burned out and I complained about it, Alo asked me to bring the bad bulb to him. I couldn't see what he planned to do about it, but decided to humor him anyway. He put the bulb back in the flashlight, with the reflector cover removed, and began flicking it with his finger. After about the fifth or sixth flick, it came back on.

I was very impressed. The technique was simple enough to understand, being a way to encourage the broken filament to weld itself back together, but I never would have thought to do it. I called Alo a genius, and he accepted my compliment, but from the way he smiled I got the impression that he wasn't the only person in the world who knew how to do this. These Lazarus bulbs didn't last very long, however,

and very soon even Alo couldn't bring them back. Then I had to rely on candles, which are fine for reading at night, but a bit unhandy when you have to take a leak at three o'clock in the morning.

Alo had told me not to expect the repaired bulbs to last very long, and warned me the others would probably go as well. The reason was that both my batteries were new. In the United States, when batteries get old you dump them both out and put in two new ones. Indonesians, Alo said, like to replace them one at a time. The bulbs are designed for this circumstance. They work well with one old and one new battery in place, but two fresh batteries quickly over-voltage them. I don't know which came first, the high-strung bulbs or the one-battery-at-a-time technique, but they work well together.

WE WERE PACKING our things to leave when two of the village leaders came to see us. You cannot leave yet, they said. We have something special planned for you this evening.

"And what is that?"

"It is a surprise."

Since the ceremony ended just after noon, we had planned to leave that day so we could visit in Kokonao for a couple hours and return to Timika. The men would not tell us what they had planned, but their mischievousness was intriguing. And we had no desire to offend the people of Paripi, who had been such splendid hosts.

Apollo and Alo seemed to have an idea what was in store, and they were strangely uneasy. They honored the village leaders' desire for secrecy, however, and would not tell me anything more than, "Don't worry, David, you'll find it interesting."

We had to wait until dark for our surprise, and although we heard activity down near the center of the village, we didn't sneak down to investigate, and spent the afternoon in the house. After dinner, someone came and told us it was time.

When we got to the middle of the village, we found that a kind of pen had been built out of coconut leaves. The walls stood about shoulder height, and the whole structure was roughly square, and maybe eight meters on a side. Inside, in one corner, stood a small group of drummers. In the middle of the pen, looking rather anxious, was a group of six young men. The entire village had gathered around the pen, sitting on the fence rails and standing two or three people deep. Some of the younger children had climbed the few short trees to get a better view over the walls of the pen.

A group of women appeared, carrying dry coconut fronds that had been tied into long bundles. Each took one of these and tested its weight and balance in her hands. Then somebody lit the end of one of the bundles. As the drums began, the rest of the woman applied the tips of their bundles to the one that was burning, and they became huge torches, each at least twice as long as the women were tall. At this point the women began to smile. They spread out around the pen, each holding her torch to the sky.

The drumming grew louder, and the men in the pen began dancing nervously. Then, in unison, the women smacked their long torches over the barrier, showering the dancers with burning embers. The men leapt and scattered like frightened insects. The song continued and the men regrouped, again dancing in an uneasy huddle in the middle of the pen. Smack!—the torches came down, and the huddle of men again exploded.

Several of the women demonstrated remarkable precision, repeatedly landing their volleys on and around the tender parts of their victim's ears and neck. Others, frustrated by their inaccuracy, resorted to stealth, sneaking their torches underneath the barrier to singe the legs of an unsuspecting victim. One older woman focused on the drummers, who were supposed to be off-limits, burning their feet just often enough to keep them anxious and on edge.

The men inside the barrier started off unprotected, but as the women's enthusiasm grew, and their blows landed with ever-increasing accuracy, friends and allies on the outside passed them baseball caps, construction hard hats, floor mats, and even banana leaves to give them some measure of protection.

The older women were having the most fun, and partway into the dance one began to disregard the rules entirely, bringing down her torch before the time dictated by the drumming or, when her torch had burned down to where it was too short to reach the men effectively, launching it like a missile into the group of dancers. By the end of the event the men were nearly panicked. They were no longer even trying to dance, but in a frantic, cowering mass, simply scurrying from side to side trying to avoid the worst of a nearly constant shower of sparks.

This performance is called *turako,* which in the most literal sense simply means "coconut frond." In the beginning, I told Apollo he should get inside and represent his village, but the very idea of this alarmed him. The men inside the pen were young and unmarried, and the "dance" is a form of showing off, an advertisement of the men's bravado and playfulness. It was not the dance itself they had been looking forward to all day, but what would follow. Though the dance was a bit rough, it was ladies' choice. And these men definitely wanted to be chosen.

The women brandishing the torches all seemed much older than the men, and almost certainly were married. This confused me at first until I noticed a group of younger women, standing together off to one side. They didn't swing the torches, but they watched the men inside very carefully. My guess is that it was these women who were making their choices for a meeting later in the woods. The fun for the married women was not in looking for a trysting partner, but simply in having carte blanche to heap some well-deserved abuse on the male of the species in general.

Later on while writing this manuscript, I came upon a reference to a "fire game" in my fragmentary copy of Pouwer. This game, my spotty English translation states, "is of a ludicrous and profane character," and the text continues to describe exactly the event we witnessed in Paripi. In the early 1950s, at least, it was performed throughout the Kamoro region. Pouwer notes that the name given to him for the dance in the village of Potowai was *tenaku,* which is the word in Kamoro for a Chinese trade ship. The anthropologist suggests that the fenced-in area represents a ship, and hypothesizes that the entertainment is a hybrid, modern form celebrating massoy gathering. This may be so, but to my eyes it was the "ludicrous and profane" part that interested the people of Paripi.

When we left the following morning the village seemed deserted. We had organized a ride back to Timika with one of Alo's cousins, who lives in Ipiri and maintains a long canoe with a fifteen-horsepower motor. After loading ourselves, our gear, and our crippled outboard, the vessel had about two inches of freeboard. As we puttered slowly along the river away from Paripi, Apollo noticed several canoes coming out of the mangroves. They were loaded down with *tambelo.* It was *imu* time in Paripi.

YOSEF IMINI, PARIPI.
As the *turako* proceeds, the torches land with ever greater frequency—and ever greater accuracy.

CHAPTER NINE

Black Sweet

New Acronyms, Old Problems

 SPENT HALF THE AFTERNOON of my last day in Timika looking for a cassette tape. One by one, Alo and I checked every market stall and shopfront that sold recorded music. Timika doesn't have a single bookstore, but there are seven places to buy music tapes. We had no luck. The problem was not the rarity of the title I was looking for, but rather its popularity. Everybody was sold out.

I was looking for a tape recorded by a band called Black Sweet. Their newest release included a song called "Dare Kokonao," which I had been repeatedly hearing around town. The song, like most popular music in Indonesia, is a saccharine ballad, this one in particular being a wistful paean to a kind of rural idyll, complete with chirping jungle birds. During the refrain, singer Ian Ulukyanan ticks off the main villages of the Kamoro coast: "Keakwa, Timika, Atuka-a-a; Omauga, Inauga, Otakwa-a-a; Ipaya, Amar, Uta, Kipia-a-a; Mapar, Potowai Buru...."

This must be the only song ever recorded that has a Kamoro setting, and although I don't know how many times I could really stand to listen to it, I wanted a copy as a souvenir. I spent a few days in Jakarta before I left Indonesia, and had the opportunity to check two stores there. In the capital I discovered that Black Sweet's popularity was a regional affair, and the clerks I spoke to assumed I must have remembered the name wrong. A friend later assured me that there was one well-stocked store in the city that would have carried the tape, but I didn't have time to check before I left.*

The members of Black Sweet are Kei Islanders from Fakfak, which until the recent division of the southwestern regency of Irian Jaya was the capital of the Kamoro area. The musicians in this band, Alo said, are former members of two bands from Irian Jaya that had been popular some years back—Black Brothers, from the provincial capital of Jayapura, and Black Papas, from Manokwari, a large town on the northeast corner of the Bird's Head.

THE BEACH AT OTAKWA.

MARSELENA APOYAU HOLDING AGUSTINA AWAKEYAU, KEAKWA.

These bands, Alo said, were too political for the government's taste, and eventually had to stop recording. Even their names represented a kind of provocation. "Black Brothers" is a direct reference to the racial pride and political solidarity of the seventies Afro-American tradition, and to Jakarta this might as well have been "Black Panthers." "Black Papas" seemed even more threatening. PAPAS is a not-so-secret acronym for Papua Pasifik Selatan, Papuan South Pacific, which did not amuse a government that considered the word "Papua" to be an implicit declaration of sympathy with the separatist goals of the OPM. Black Sweet and its predecessors also use English in their names, a decision probably dictated by fashion, given that most of the world's popular music comes from the English-speaking parts of the globe, but the government could also interpret it as unpatriotic.

The name "Black Sweet" continues this tradition. It is a direct translation of *hitam manis,* which is one of three common Indonesian metaphors for beauty. Translated idiomatically, *hitam manis* yields something like the "brown sugar" of the Rolling Stones song. If an attractive Irianese woman walked by a group of men, this phrase might accompany the raised eyebrows and appreciative whistles. "Ah, *hitam manis.*" For a lighter-skinned woman, the equivalent sobriquet is *sawo matang,* literally "ripe sapodilla," referring to a sugary fruit that has a tan-colored surface like fine moleskin. Finally, for the lightest-skinned beauties, the standard compliment is *kuning langsat,* literally "*langsat* yellow," which makes reference to the creamy smooth, lightly golden skin of the *langsat* fruit.

The band members, then, have not actually abandoned their commitment to regional and racial pride. They have simply shifted it into the register of fashion and culture, which, in addition to matching the trend set by the rest of the world, expands the market for their music and keeps the government censors at bay.

It was not a good day to be shopping in Timika. The police had set up roadblocks at the two main intersections and our taxi was stopped and searched along with all the others. The officers were looking for

---

* Alo later rounded up a copy and Kal sent it on to me.

UDILIA MANENAWA, PASIR HITAM.

"sharp objects," they said, and were perfectly polite as they asked us to stand outside the vehicle and patted us down. Nobody likes this kind of hassle, but I was a little impressed that we weren't simply waved through out of deference to the two white faces in the car.

"It's the *orang meno*," said our taxi driver, an immigrant from Java. "Yesterday the police seized a whole pile of *parang*s and bows and arrows."

Our taxi driver used the term "orang meno" to refer generally to the highland Irianese. This phrase is an example of what is sometimes called the "new language" that has developed in ethnically mixed towns in Irian Jaya, like Timika and the highland capital of Wamena. "Orang" means "person" in Indonesian, and "meno" means "friend" in the Amungme language. Translated literally, *orang meno* is nonsense, but it is understood perfectly in Timika and does not have a negative connotation. (Technically speaking, *orang meno* refers only to the Amungme, and similar constructions—such as *orang noge,* which has an equivalent derivation in the Ekagi language—have arisen for members of the other highland groups.)

Minutes after being searched, Alo and I came up empty at yet another music stall, and we turned back. We were stopped again at the very same checkpoint, and the police made us climb out of the car and submit to another search. At this point I realized that what I thought had been fair play was actually something else altogether. I can't believe that two foreigners and one Kamoro man, all of us wearing clean shirts and slacks (as usual, Alo looked the sharpest, with the only button-down shirt in the group) and carrying notebooks and camera bags, fit the profile of people who might be concealing a *parang*, though I suppose we could have dashed into the market and bought one in the five minutes since they last checked.

DURING THE TIME WE WERE AWAY in the villages of the west, Timika had come under what the Jamaicans would call "heavy manners." A conflict over funding had developed between a Moni organization and the leadership of a development foundation, which led to some tense exchanges and a small but angry demonstration. In an unrelated incident, an Ekagi man died under obscure and, some would say, suspicious circumstances. Depending on whom you talked to, he either fell from the back of a police truck on which he was hitching a ride or he was pushed from it. Normally it was not unusual for *orang meno* to walk around town with their bows and arrows, *parang*s, and other tools, but while tempers in Timika remained high, the police were taking no chances.

Timika is truly a frontier town, and unlike most parts of Indonesia, it is not what you could call friendly. You'd better lock your car here, for example, and even then don't leave anything inside that you don't mind losing. This is unsurprising to someone from the United States—in my old neighborhood, the Mission District of San Francisco, car windows are broken just for practice—but it is not something most Indonesians are used to. An expatriate friend of mine, who has lived in Indonesia for a decade, had all of her prized potted orchids stolen from her back yard in Timika while she was preparing to move. She later found out who took them: her next door neighbor, a friend of several years. People in Timika do not so much like each other as simply get along, and inter-ethnic resentment is never far beneath the surface.

This is one of the reasons Alo now lives in Pau-mako. It is not just the noise and dust of Timika that wears him down, but the anger. And the sadness.

We had heard about the events in Timika even while we were away in Ararao, through a communications network consisting of the church radio and word-of-mouth. One of the most disturbing pieces of news was that two young Kamoro men had died in an incident at the market. We could get no more details until we got back to town. By the day after we returned, Alo had discovered the identities of the men—Agus Meraweyau, originally from Atuka, and Emanuel Nokoreyau, from Timika Pantai. Both men, in their early twenties, had been living in Pulau Pisang, the little settlement where the woodcarver Paskalis Wepumi lives, and where Alo himself often stays while in the Timika area. Alo knew them both.

"They say they were drunk and fell into the well," Alo said. "But I'm not so sure."

When I heard the details of the story, I wasn't so sure, either. The men had apparently been found drowned, head down, in the well behind the main Timika market. The scattered reports Alo obtained suggested that the young men had been drinking and had traded insults with some Bugis shopkeepers. The well, which had been sealed off by the time we returned to Timika, is of the usual size. It was difficult for me to imagine even a single man, whether drunk or sober, accidentally falling down this well. For two to have done so, head first, seemed to contradict the laws of physics. I'm not a detective, but in an atmosphere where the relationship between the Kamoro and the Bugis shopkeepers is one of distrust at best—and outright enmity at worst—I would say that the rumors of insults traded between the young men and the shopkeepers are salient to this case.

MORE THAN THREE MILLION BUGIS, Sulawesi's famous seafarers and traders, are scattered throughout Southeast Asia. Their homeland is a small area on the southeast tip of Sulawesi's southern peninsula, but according to the last Indonesian census, twenty-five percent of the people who claim Bugis as a first language live outside Sulawesi. This makes them one of the most widespread ethnic groups in the country, writes French anthropologist Christian Pelras in his 1996 *The Bugis,* and makes Bugis the third most commonly spoken language in the archipelago, after Indonesian and Javanese.

Travel guides and other popular sources regularly state that the "bogeyman," the terror of every American and English child's night, is a corruption of "Bugis." This is not necessarily bad press for a people whose independence and reputation as former pirates is a source of pride (another is the legendary beauty of Bugis women). However, fortunately or unfortunately, this etymology is apocryphal. According to the *Oxford English Dictionary,* the word "bogey," in its old Scottish form "bogle," is common in literature from at least the 16th century, and in the even older form "bugge" is known from the 14th century. The similarity of the German *bögge* and *boggel-mann,* which have identical meanings, suggests an even older origin.*

In addition to their romantic tradition of piracy and beautiful women, the Bugis are also famous in the archipelago for their tempers. They are, it is said, very quick with a knife. A friend of mine who has worked in Indonesia for many years and who is given neither to exaggeration nor to mincing words put it this way: "There's no give to them. They're the hardest people you'll ever meet."

By any measure Timika is an expensive place to shop. The Indonesian department of manpower estimates that prices for food, clothing, housing, and other basic needs in Irian Jaya are thirty to forty percent higher than in western Indonesia. In an effort to keep prices down, the government subsidizes sea freight to its easternmost frontier—it calls the service Pioneer Shipping—and the amount of subsidy reaches fifty percent on a list of twenty-seven basic commodities.

The government also sets local price guidelines for nine *bahan pokok,* or staple supplies, which include things like rice, cooking oil, and sugar, and attempts through subsidies and management of supplies from government warehouses to make sure that market prices do not exceed the guidelines.† This is difficult in Irian Jaya, however. For example, at the time of my visit, the price of a kilogram of rice was supposed to be Rp 700—about 30 cents—but you would have to pay more like 75 cents a kilo at the Timika market if you actually wanted to buy any.

---

* The probable source of this confusion is the *Oxford English Dictionary* itself. The second sense of "bogy, bogey" is given as "A bogle or goblin; a person much dreaded" and includes a usage example from 1857: "Malay pirates ... those bogies of the Archipelago." A careless or overimaginative researcher, reading this line, may falsely conclude that the dictionary is suggesting an etymological relationship between the words "Bugis" and "bogies." Even such a well-received documentary as Lawrence and Lorne Blair's U.S. public television series *Ring of Fire* has made this error.

† Today only the price of rice is thus controlled.

The prices of items not part of the *bahan pokok,* like fresh meat, eggs, and canned food, are even worse. When I visited, a chicken egg in Timika cost Rp 1000, almost 40 cents. This works out to almost $5 a dozen, a price that would horrify an American shopper. Eggs from a village chicken, which like hormone-free chicken eggs in the United States are greatly preferred, cost a shocking $7.50 a dozen.

The great majority of stores in Timika, whether selling food or dry goods, are run by Bugis. There are three shops run by ethnic Chinese, and I'm sure there are a few operated by Torajans or Javanese. But if you shop in Timika, you will basically be buying from a Bugis shopkeeper. The only trouble with this, I was told by a number of Kamoro, is that the Bugis tradition of piracy seems not to be a thing of the past.

A typical way of measuring a small quantity of rice at any market in Indonesia is with a condensed milk can, and five measures yield a standard packet. Except in the Bugis shops in Timika. There it takes just four cans to make up a packet. Since a condensed milk can is no bigger in Timika than anywhere else in Indonesia, no ready explanation for this comes to mind. Perhaps the rice in Irian is twenty percent denser than usual. You wouldn't be able to test this hypothesis in a Bugis shop, however, because you won't find a scale.

"It's not about the price—it's about being cheated," Alo said, with considerable venom. "The Bugis don't weigh things."

If you buy a standard twenty-kilogram tin of rice at the Chinese shop, he said, it will weigh twenty kilos. If you buy the same tin at a Bugis shop you can be sure it will be at least two kilos light. Whenever possible the Kamoro shop at the Chinese stores. They are no cheaper than the Bugis stores, but the ethnic Chinese, Alo said, will always give you a fair deal.

Cheating, it seems, has a very long history on the south coast of western New Guinea. When Captain Webster visited the Kowiai Coast in the 1890s, he tried to buy pearls from the chief of Aiduma village, a woman he calls the "queen" or the "Rajah Prumpoean," literally "lady king."

> The queen wore a great many ear-rings, similar to those worn by the women of Aru, and also many cheap and tawdry rings, such as are to be found in a prize-packet, and which I suspect had been received for pearls and skins. I offered her a small gold chain if she would get me some more pearls, but she exclaimed, "Teda mass"—Malay for "not gold."

When Webster protested that his chain was indeed pure gold the queen had one of her assistants test it by putting it in saltwater. Since it did not turn black, like those she received from the Seramese traders, she stood by her original judgment and, to his chagrin, would not trade with him.

"Had I some cheap trinkets now, such as are to be found in the celebrated arcade in Piccadilly," he writes, "I could return laden with pearls."

IT IS UNLIKELY that the Bugis, as a people, are inherently any worse than the rest of us. The tensions that exist between the Bugis and Kamoro communities, while real, have not come about because the Bugis are recidivist pirates (and according to Pelras's research, the truth of this pirate history is itself suspect) but rather because of the clannishness of the Timika Bugis, and the bunker mentality that has developed in this settler community. Like most western Indonesians in town, the Bugis did not come to Timika because they like Irian Jaya. They came to make money. If they were suddenly given the opportunity to move their shops to South Sulawesi or Java, or just about anywhere else in Indonesia and guaranteed the same business, I don't think a single shopkeeper would choose to stay.

The Indonesian government did not formally open Irian Jaya until after the "Act of Free Choice" in 1969. Even though the territory had been under Indonesian control since 1963, except for a relatively few Javanese who came in to staff government positions, the region was closed to so-called "internal migration" from elsewhere in Indonesia until the seventies.

As the sixties drew to a close, economic conditions in Irian were worse than anywhere else in Indonesia. Most of the experienced Dutch business and government workers, and many of the relatively few Irianese in the same position, fled immediately after the transfer to Indonesia in 1963. There was another exodus in 1969. During the first years of Indonesian rule, facilities left behind by the Dutch government and Dutch-run shops were looted and destroyed. Irian Barat was a political and economic mess. In 1971, the province's $2.9 million in total exports was just over half of what it had been ten years earlier under the Dutch.

Ambitious laborers and businessmen from western Indonesia saw Irian's depressed economy as an opportunity, and began arriving in the province in ever greater numbers beginning in the early seventies. Most of these new arrivals were from South Sulawesi—Makassarese, Butonese, and particularly, Bugis. Immigrant Indonesians made up just four percent of the province's population in 1971, according to data compiled by social scientists Chris Manning and Michael Rumbiak. Today, almost half of the province's 2.1 million people are of western Indonesian heritage. Western Indonesians are concentrated in Irian's cities, and in Jayapura, for example, account for eighty percent of the population. Of these immigrants, fifty-eight percent are from South Sulawesi.

Competition for jobs is fierce in places like Makassar in South Sulawesi, and despite the high cost of living, a worker or shopkeeper can make more money in Irian Jaya. Unskilled carpenters and minibus drivers, to cite just two examples, can expect to earn in Irian several times what they would make for the same work in western Indonesia, according to Manning and Rumbiak. Bugis and Makassarese have found work in

Yohanis Maurumako, Pasir Hitam.

DRUM, SEMPAN TIMUR.

logging and lumber milling operations, and in some towns, particularly Jayapura, Merauke, Wamena, and Timika, running market stalls.

One evening when Alo was griping about the Bugis shopkeepers, he said he wished there were a Kamoro-run store in town. I think a Kamoro-run store would be a fine thing, but I had heard of a similar project in the Asmat area that ended badly, and thought I'd better tell him about it.

On my first trip to Irian Jaya in 1991, one of the Catholic brothers in Agats told me that the Asmat in Atsy, the largest village in the area, were experiencing the same kinds of problems with shopkeepers as are the Kamoro in Timika. The Church hoped to rectify the situation by helping a young Asmat man set up a small general store. The Church found him a building and stocked it with pots and pans, rice, garden tools, tobacco, and other essentials.

This man went out of business in a matter of weeks. Piece by piece, it turned out, the shopkeeper had given away all of his stock. It wasn't that he didn't understand the fundamentals of running a business. Rather, he decided bankruptcy was a better choice than ostracism by his family and friends.

If Alo opened a store in Timika, he would quickly get a large percentage of the Kamoro business. But if his experience turned out anything like that of the man in Atsy, he would also get requests from relatives and various acquaintances like: "Alo, I need a tub of laundry soap. I don't have any money right now, but you know I'm good for it." If Alo were to agree, and give his friend the soap, he would soon end up with an empty store and a stack of uncollectible I.O.U.'s. Were he to stand firm, and put up a NO CREDIT sign, people would storm out, saying, "You're as bad as the Bugis!" In fact, they would probably resent Alo even more than they do the Bugis.

Merchants throughout history have been a clannish and even surly lot, and they have never been much liked by the people who give them their money. It's a very hard thing to say "no" to one of your own. It is much easier when the customer is of a different race or speaks a different language. This is one reason why shopkeepers, particularly in the poorest parts of town, are almost always outsiders, whether they be Bugis in Timika, Chinese in western Indonesia, Indians in Africa, Koreans in New York and Los Angeles, or Lebanese in San Francisco.

THE HOMESTEAD ACT OF 1862 gave every American citizen title to a 160-acre tract of federal land—all he had to do was settle it and cultivate it for five years. This was how the vast American West came to be settled by Anglo-Saxon Americans, who were what was meant by the word "citizen" in 1862. Indonesia has its own Homestead Act, called the Transmigration Program, or *transmigrasi*.

Transmigrasi resettles families from the overcrowded provinces of western Indonesia, particularly Java, to government-selected farming sites in the more lightly populated parts of Indonesia. Those who participate in the program receive one-way sea passage, two to five hectares of land, a house and tools, and seeds for one year's planting. Relocation programs began under the Dutch in 1903, were re-imagined as part of Soekarno-era land reform in the early 1960s, and—with $560 million in World Bank support—accelerated under Suharto's New Order government in the 1970s and 1980s. From 1903 to 1999, the various programs have relocated almost four million people.

At first, Irian Jaya received very few transmigrants. By 1978 only fifteen hundred families had moved to Indonesia's easternmost province, mostly to sites near Merauke and along the north coast: Jayapura, Nabire, Manokwari, and Sorong. Following a 1977 presidential decree declaring Irian Jaya a major transmigration destination, this changed dramatically, and by 1986 more than one hundred thousand Javanese had been relocated to Irian.

Indonesia's transmigration program is extremely controversial, particularly in Irian Jaya. Although a blessing for poor whites from the east, the Homestead Act was an unalloyed curse for the American Indian, and critics of *transmigrasi* suggest the program is

TRANSMIGRATION SETTLEMENTS, TIMIKA AREA.
In the foreground is Karang Senang, former S.P.3, and behind it is Timika Jaya, former S.P. 2.

having the same result for the native Irianese. The word "swamping" is often used, and indeed the Irianese are already almost a minority in their own land. Environmentalists criticize the deforestation and other ecological disruptions that *transmigrasi* brings.

Nor have the transmigrants themselves always fared well. Sites have been chosen that are malarial, have poor soil and drainage, and are located far from potential markets, and the homes and other infrastructure accompanying them have sometimes been poorly designed or shoddily constructed by profiteering construction firms. One of the biggest problems the program has faced is that most western Indonesians are rice farmers, and few areas in eastern Indonesia are suitable for growing rice.

Recently the pace of transmigration has slowed, and the government now tries to take greater care in selecting sites and providing the kind of infrastructure needed to guarantee success. In partial answer to critics' charges that transmigration is swamping the indigenous population, since 1982 one-quarter of transmigration plots in Irian Jaya have been reserved for native Irianese.

Transmigration in the Timika area did not begin until 1984, but today there are more than eleven thousand transmigrants in the area, representing about one-sixth of the population. During the time I was researching this book, ground was broken for the tenth transmigration settlement, or "S.P.," here.

Timika is considered one of the success stories of the transmigration program. The farmers here grow mostly vegetables, rather than rice, and the mining company and the growing urban area surrounding it provides a ready market for their produce. Several of the settlements are now considered villages in their own right, and have been given names.

WHEN WE PASSED THROUGH KOKONAO on the way back to Timika, we heard that, among the several scattered violent incidents that had taken place in Timika in our absence, the office of Lembaga Musyawarah Adat Suku Kamoro or LEMASKO, the chief Kamoro development foundation, had been vandalized. This office is not far from Apollo's house, so after picking him up the next day we decided to swing by and have a look at the damage.

The office of LEMASKO—which means something like The Kamoro Traditional Council—like just about every other store, office, and business in Timika, is a dull-colored, single-story, concrete-block building set back from the main road by a gravel lot. I had visited the office several times in the past, and when we drove up my first thought was that the rumor was untrue, and the building had not been vandalized at all. Then I noticed that some of the jalousies had been broken out of the windows and, looking inside, that a few chairs and tables had been overturned.

Other than these few chairs and a table or two, the building was empty. If this had been the first time I saw the office, I would have been outraged, for it truly did look like it had been ransacked and stripped. But since I had been there before, I knew that the only things this office ever contained were a few chairs and a table, and on occasion, but not always, a couple of the LEMASKO officers. The office of this organization—which will adminster $2 million in development money this year—has never contained a single computer, fax machine, Rolodex, or filing cabinet. It never even had a telephone. The disgruntled Nawaripi Kamoro who ransacked it needn't have wasted their energy; there was never anything there to destroy.

The history of this empty office began on March 10, 1996, when disgruntled Amungme from Banti village rioted in the highland mining town of Tembagapura. By March 12, the unrest had become general in the area, and an estimated 500 to 3,000 people rioted and looted in Timika. Several people died, many were injured, dozens of houses and businesses were destroyed, and the Freeport mine was forced to shut down production for three days. Few Kamoro participated in this outpouring of anger and frustration. The Timika riots were led chiefly by Dani, Ekagi, Moni, Damal, and Nduga people, recent immigrants from the highlands who were drawn to the area by the apparent wealth and opportunity there.

Freeport-McMoRan headquarters in New Orleans was stunned by the rioting, and within a month the company had announced the creation of a new fund to increase the company's support for education, health care, and social and economic development programs for the indigenous Irianese. This would be called the Fund for Irian Jaya Development (FFIJD), and Freeport pledged to finance it with one percent of the gross revenue from its mine. To the chagrin of some in the company, only the "one percent" part seems to have stuck in the public mind. Probably only a dozen people would know what you are talking about if you mentioned FFIJD, but I doubt there is a single person in the province who doesn't know about "satu persen."

The job of managing and disbursing the money from the one percent fund fell to the Integrated Timika Development Program (Pengembangan Wilayah Timika Terpadu), better known by its Indonesian initials, PWTT, usually rendered PWT^2 and pronounced "pay-way-tay-dooah." In its first year, PWT^2 disbursed Rp 25 billion, or more than $10 million. This is a considerable amount of money, particularly in an area where many people still live outside of the cash economy, and where, in the villages at least, $1,000 would make even a large family wealthy.

ALEX MAKARE, KEAKWA.

DETAIL FROM MBITORO, ATUKA.

Some development professionals argue that this is too much money, or at least too much money too soon. The PWT² program, conceived by the provincial planning department in Jayapura to integrate government, Freeport, and community development efforts in the fast-growing Timika area, was barely out of the planning stages when the riots hit in March 1996. Government planners and the mining company had the resources and expertise to handle the sudden responsibility of $10 million, but the Irianese community, the "third leg of the stool" in the PWT² organization's own metaphor, most definitely did not.

What resulted, in June 1996, was that the planning department urged members of seven ethnic groups—the Kamoro and the Amungme from within the mining area, and the Dani, Ekagi, Nduga, Moni, and Damal from outside—to form non-profit development foundations through which these communities could participate in PWT². To finance the offices, equipment, and legal aid these organizations would require, the department authorized a one-time payment of Rp 500 million for each new foundation, or *yayasan*.

In retrospect, much can be criticized in this strategy, but at the time the PWT² organization was under pressure to do something quickly to begin distributing the vast pool of money it had been awarded. In the absence of existing Irianese institutions that could accommodate the task of evaluating, financing, and executing million-dollar projects, the planning department decided to try to buy some.

Five-hundred-million rupiah, in 1996, was $200,000. A group of people who organized themselves as a foundation according to the standards presented by PWT² were given this money in a lump sum. Yayasan Kamoro—YAKARO—formed this way, as did six others. The Rp 500 million was paid in cash. Since Indonesia then circulated no notes of higher denomination than Rp 50,000, this would be like getting $200,000 in twenty-dollar bills. And it encouraged the same behavior as would a shopping bag of worn twenties. In light of this, LEMASKO, which today represents the Kamoro in PWT², is probably lucky it has an office at all, much less one with a phone.

WHEN WE RETURNED TO TIMIKA, LEMASKO had just submitted its proposal for the following year. The amount, whittled down by PWT² staff from a Rp 20 billion request, totalled Rp 5.4 billion , or about $2 million at the time. Before this document was prepared, two members of the organization toured many of the Kamoro villages and, based on discussions with the village leaders, came up with a list of priorities for spending this year's money. Board chairman Didaktus Maoromako traveled to the Kamoro villages west of Timika to Kapiraya; executive director Cansius Amareyau visited the eastern villages to Ohotya. When I asked what their constituents had asked for, both men told me the same thing.

"The number one request," Didaktus said, "was for houses."

"In the east, too," Cansius added, "Most of the people want houses."

I was more than a little puzzled. I had just spent several weeks living in Kamoro villages, and it seemed to me that the vast majority—I'd even be tempted to say all—of the private houses I saw looked comfortable, and in reasonably good repair. Although some had galvanized roofs and some had thatch, I didn't see any with no roofs at all, or any that looked like they were about to fall down.

"Why," I asked the two men, "would people want houses?"

"Because the ones they have are no good," Didaktus said.

"What do you mean, 'no good'?"

"The old houses have a single open space inside," Cansius said.

"So?"

"The people feel this is not good," he continued. "They want new houses with separate rooms. A room for cooking, a room for the children."

"I don't follow," I said. "Plenty of Kamoro houses have walled partitions inside, and the kitchen is always separate, and out back, isn't it?"

"They want their houses to be made out of better materials," Cansius said.

"Like what?"

"In the villages they like ironwood," Cansius said, "although the people in town want concrete."

I immediately thought of my uncomfortable nights knotted up on the ironwood plank floor at Keakwa, and the sweltering afternoons in the many concrete clinics we stayed in. Then, in stark contrast, the heat-shedding, palm-mat walls and springy bark floor of Ladislaus Yaota's traditional-style house in Paripi.

"Ironwood and concrete are better materials?"

Eventually I learned that that the real reason for the new houses had nothing to do with their superiority as places to live, and everything to do with their superiority as a social statement. It was a classic case of keeping up with the Joneses, except in this case, the Joneses are Dani, Ekagi, and Moni.

"The Kamoro people ask 'Why do the highland people have new houses, and not the Kamoro people? We want the same as the others,'" Didaktus said.

One of the great frustrations of people working for the PWT² program is that it has, for the most part, turned into a house building program. In its first year, the Kamoro *yayasan* spent money on a freezer, boats, outboard motors, and nets to stake a fishing operation at Ohotya village near the mouth of the Otakwa River, but a lot of what it spent its money on was home construction: twenty-five new houses at Ohotya, fifteen at Inafita (Fanamo), and ten at Omawita (Omauga). For the second year, LEMASKO plans to open a cooperative store in Timika to sell tools, rice, and other

235

necessities at reduced prices, but what everyone continues to want, it seems, is a new house.

In the abstract, I don't see anything wrong with spending money on house-building, as shelter would seem to be an obvious prerequisite for any kind of social development program. But a house is exactly the thing that every Kamoro family already has. Tools, like outboard motors, chainsaws, and nylon fishing nets, and services, like health care and education, are the things that seemed to me to be in short supply in the Kamoro villages.

The status of new houses as the currency of disbursement of the one-percent fund can be traced back to the March 1996 riots. It was the recent Dani, Ekagi, Nduga, Moni, and Damal immigrants to the Timika area who led the riots, and their main complaint was that the jobs and opportunities they sought did not exist. Many of them, in fact, did not even have a permanent place to stay. Thus, after their *yayasan*s were chartered, the first thing they spent their money was on houses. In the first year of its operation, these five *yayasan*s together built more than two hundred new houses, all of them in Kwamki Lama, a neighborhood north of the Timika airport.* In order not to be upstaged by the others, the Kamoro and the Amungme, who already lived in the area and didn't actually need houses, ended up building them anyway.

Apollo is a boardmember of Lemasko, approximately third in command, a position he also held in the old Yakaro organization. In the original discussions on PWT², he said, the representatives decided that priorities for development spending would break down thus: 50 percent for economic development, 22 percent for education programs, 21 percent for housing, and 7 percent for administrative overhead. The reality of the spending has been very different. More than half has gone into building houses. Personally, Apollo said, he still agrees with the original priorities. But his is not the only voice in the organization.

When I was in Timika, Lemasko was facing pressure from PWT² to agree to spend no more than fifty percent of the organization's allocation on house building. Although more than double the agreed upon standard, this was still not enough for some of Lemasko's most persistent lobbyists, many of whom are not actually the organization's constituents.

Building houses in southern Irian Jaya is a very profitable business. According to PWT² records of *yayasan* spending in the first year of the one percent program, the average cost of building a home in the Timika area was $15,600. For someone from the United States or Europe, this may not seem like much for a house, but it is actually a lot of money for the simple concrete block houses that were built. Fifteen thousand dollars leaves a very healthy profit margin, and the contractors have been making a killing.†

Most construction outfits in Irian Jaya are not owned or run by Irianese, but I was told that a small community of Ayamaru people living in one of the transmigration settlements has become very active in the industry. The Ayamaru, originally from the Bird's Head, have formed a construction company, which pursues its commercial interests through a sympathetic Kamoro *yayasan* called Anamo. Since Anamo does not have the right to direct representation on PWT², it was pressuring Lemasko to make home-building a spending priority.

Relations between Anamo and Lemasko had soured over this issue, and at the time I was in Timika, *bupati* Titus Potereyauw was helping adjudicate a compromise. Apollo, who attended the meetings on behalf of Lemasko, told me that one of the problems was that the contractors had already paid out more than $11,000 in advances. The practice of a contractor paying a cash advance to a potential client is unconventional at best, and most people would simply call it a form of bribery. In any case, this system insures that the potential client, and the potential client's representatives, will work to get the PWT² money allocated to house-building, and when this is accomplished, will award the job to the contractor—if for no other reason than that they will then have the means to pay back their "loans."

SINCE THE FORMATION of the seven *yayasan*s in 1996, non-profit foundations in the Timika area have sprouted like mushrooms after a rain. Preparing the paperwork to register a *yayasan* is now a growth industry, and like an American tax attorney on April 14th, you could probably name your price for this service. The response of the PWT² organization to all these new voices clamoring for a share of the one percent fund has been to decide to recognize funding applications only from the original *yayasan*s, thus forcing the new *yayasan*s to find political representation and support for their programs in one or another of the seven recognized organizations.

What this has done is to force the Kamoro, and the members of the other ethnic groups, to find a way to sort out their differences among themselves. This process has sparked serious quarrels, such as the one that produced the broken windows and overturned furniture in the Lemasko office, but it has also led to the beginnings of a kind of group-wide political

---

* The Tipuka Kamoro consider this area to be part of their land, and outsiders building houses here have contributed to the inter-ethnic tensions in the area.

† The houses built by the Kamoro *yayasan* Yakaro were far cheaper, averaging about $5,200 each. Of all the groups represented by the orginal *yayasan*s, the Kamoro have actually spent the least money building houses. According to PWT² records, Yakaro's housing program for 1996–1997 came to Rp 645 million, less than half of what the Amungme spent, and little more than a third of what each of the other five groups spent. But the Kamoro houses were also built outside of the Timika area, and of wood, which should make them significantly cheaper. The builder's "overhead" may have been less obscene, but even $5,200 is a grossly inflated price.

LEONILA MANAMAPA AND HER SON KONSTAN, OTAKWA.
Leonila's house was built under a YAKARO program.

TITUS O. POTEREYAUW, KEAKWA.
The *bupati* addresses the crowd from the scaffolding of the *karapao* building.

process. The members of LEMASKO are now in the position of judging the suitability of various proposals from the half-dozen smaller, competing Kamoro *yayasan*s, and of combining them in a single package to propose to the PWT² board.

"LEMASKO will be conceptual," Apollo said, referring to this new political relationship, "and the small *yayasan*s, operational."

LEMASKO must also remain accountable to the Kamoro community at large. A perception of corruption at the top levels of the old YAKARO organization led to a wholesale shakeup. Several key members were essentially banished from direct participation in the PWT² process. LEMASKO has also undergone at least two serious changes of leadership, and nothing guarantees it will last, either, unless the money is handled in an open and honest way, and the members of the organization are responsive to their constituents.

One problem that LEMASKO will have to solve—and this is a problem shared by the other six *yayasan*s—is what could be called a high overhead. Of the money the organization received the first year, I think it would be optimistic to say that even one-third was actually spent on the office building and programs. This is a rate of evaporation that most people would consider unduly high.

Given this history, I asked, how does LEMASKO plan to make sure the five billion rupiah in the 1997 proposal ends up being spent on the intended programs, and not simply tucked into somebody's pocket?

Didaktus looked at me and smiled: "You can't really know another person's heart."

LEMASKO and the PWT² organization have instituted some new controls for the second year of the program. Foremost among these, Apollo said, is that the people running any given program will not get all of their money at once. They will be issued fifteen percent of their budget to start, and won't get the rest until the program has been evaluated by LEMASKO and outside representatives from the PWT² organization. If the initial money seems to have been "lost," or was not spent properly, then the program will be killed or its management replaced.

Large programs that cut across ethnic lines, such as those concerned with education and health care, have always been funded directly by the PWT² organization from the one percent fund, and their management is not handled by the individual *yayasan*s. In the first year, PWT² spent nearly two million dollars on education, upgrading a dormitory for grade school students in the Timika area, and providing scholarships for high school and university students. The scholarship program is now extensive enough that any Kamoro or Amungme student with the aptitude and interest will have the means to get a university education. The one percent fund also supports a twenty-four-hour clinic in Timika and covers the cost of treatment for any Irianese patient the clinic refers to the main hospital. PWT² also now pays for a very effective malaria control program that was started by Freeport several years ago.

When I first heard about the one percent fund and PWT², I couldn't help but be reminded of American author Terry Southern's satirical novel *The Magic Christian.* The book, published in 1959, concerns the exploits of one Guy Grand, a billionaire who amuses himself by "making it hot for them"; basically giving away money in ways designed to force the recipients into ridiculous positions, such as asking a stranger if, for $6,000, he will eat Grand's railroad ticket.

In one instance Grand, while sitting in his seat on the train, buys a hot dog from a vendor on the platform. He times the transaction so that the train is just starting to pull away when he hands over his payment for the twenty-cent hot dog. The hapless vendor begins routinely to make change for what he thinks is a $5 bill, then notices its true denomination—$500—and panics. The train is now gathering speed, and the vendor literally runs after it, knocking over his tray of hot dogs, in an ultimately vain attempt to return the bill. *The Magic Christian* is a darkly hilarious book. Southern's point is to demonstrate the tremendous power of money to turn human beings into something more like animals, and to encourage them to do things they later cannot understand.

Dropping $2 million on a community of fifteen thousand people, most of whom live in small, rural villages, is (even if unintentionally) a Guy Grand act. This is enough money to be disturbing, and like the hot dog vendor with his $500 bill, is perhaps as much of a burden as a gift. Lottery winners are famous for wasting their windfall on trivial and expensive baubles. They are equally famous for later regretting ever having won at all, and for suffering a higher than average rate of suicide.

The first year—or even the first few years—of a program as ambitious as PWT² will necessarily entail a lot of wasted money. At first the greedy people, the people whose hearts can't be known, will find a way to get some of the money into their own pockets. But is this money really wasted? When Chinese tea is made properly, the first pour is always discarded. The first pour draws out the bitterness. Once this is sacrificed, subsequent pours are smooth and fragrant.

Perhaps after the first year or two, the greediest members of the Kamoro community will be sated. And the rest of the community, and its institutions, like LEMASKO, will become experienced in the difficult and time-consuming arts of good judgment and democracy.

DEVELOPMENT PROFESSIONALS FIND the Kamoro a frustrating group of people to work with. In conversation and in texts the Kamoro have been called "difficult," "introverted," and "resistant." Very often a sharp contrast is drawn between working with the highlanders and working with the Kamoro. The highlanders, people will say, are very noisy and a lot of trouble, but at least you know what they're thinking. And when a program does get established, the highlanders will work hard at it. The Kamoro, on the other hand, are the opposite of noisy. They don't violently oppose development, but neither do they embrace it. They simply avoid any involvement at all, for reasons that remain inscrutable.

"The Kamoro?" said one friend, who has been managing various development programs in Irian Jaya for more than a decade. "Well, you can talk with the Catholic missionaries. They've been trying for a hundred bloody years and they haven't produced a lot of change, have they?"

As part of a planned expansion of mine production, Freeport hired the U.S. consulting firm Labat-Anderson to examine the company's social programs and the PWT² organization. Labat-Anderson's final report, dated July 15, 1997, states the following about the Kamoro:

> The Kamoro community faces larger and more complex socio-cultural constraints compared to the mountain people in terms of development and empowerment. Resources inherent in their traditions and culture must go through value transformation before being usefully adapted to change and development. The majority of the Kamoro are quietly resistant and show escapism towards change and development.

Although disguised somewhat by distracting contemporary constructions like "empowerment," "value transformation," and "escapism," this characterization does not fundamentally differ from Father Trenkenschuh's "dead area filled with zombies" of almost thirty years ago. The consultants do not, like Trenkenschuh, state flatly that "The future holds no hope," but the picture they paint is certainly bleak.

I read the Labat-Anderson report with interest, and I don't think it is a bad one. It is, in places, perceptive, and if not exactly trenchant—the language alone would seem to make this impossible—it is at least thorough. And there are many people who would agree with the report's assessment of the Kamoro, including many within the Kamoro community.

The strengths of the Kamoro, according to the report, include the avoidance of direct conflict with outsiders, the relative lack of animosity toward the Indonesian government and its institutions, and the prominent role of women in Kamoro society. The list of weaknesses—or "sociocultural obstacles," in the language of the report—is unfortunately twice as long. These include the "loose" structure of *taparu*, a general feeling of inferiority, a preference for "false com-

239

ARNOLDA MINAYAU, TIMIKA PANTAI.

promises," the abuse of alcohol, and the lack of a tradition of dialogue.

> The Kamoro do not have strong traditions of progress, development, and diligent effort toward difficult ends. They see no reason to, as nature has always been plentiful in supplying their needs. Development programs that need the participation of the people have not had the response hoped for, in fact it has been continuously avoided. Generally, the main motivation for joining development programs is to get free goods and money.

I suppose it is intrinsic to the nature of such a document, but when I reached this section I got a strong sense that what I was looking at was a child's report card, one that had more F's than A's, and on which the teacher had written: "Does not play well with others."

On the surface, the report's observations seem reasonable enough, but many of them come apart quickly upon reflection. Are *taparu* really "loose"? I don't doubt that the authors's understanding of *taparu* is loose (I'll readily admit the same of my own), but I do rather doubt that any Kamoro whose social obligations are defined by *taparu* would consider the institution itself "loose." And what, exactly, is a "false compromise" anyway? In particular, tying these "sociocultural obstacles" to the supposition that

"nature has always been plentiful in supplying their needs" seems specious. So it is nature herself, in her unthinking generosity, who first created the dependency relationship that has turned the Kamoro into a community of quiescent beggars?

The "plentiful nature" argument has been repeated often enough that it has now assumed the status of myth. According to its logic, the richness of the Kamoro forests and rivers, far from being a blessing, are a curse, the source of a tragic and debilitating torpor that makes it impossible for any Kamoro man or woman to rise out of bed and do some work. I remain skeptical. I have heard this argument a dozen times, and yet in my months in the Kamoro area I never once saw fish jumping into the boat, wild boar sauntering into town, or sago pounding itself. "Diligent effort toward difficult ends?" In the forest inland from Paripi, in the blazing sun of a new clearing, those axes didn't stop once in five hours.

I don't think the Kamoro are as pessimistic about their future as are the authors of this report. But then maybe the Kamoro have a different idea about which of their values they intend to transform. Money and "development programs" are not the only specie of the Kamoro realm. The most excitement I saw was in the area of Kamoro culture. With so many villages

IRMA MIYAMERO, ATUKA.

holding *karapao,* in some cases for the first time in decades, I think one could truly characterize the current period as a kind of cultural renaissance. The liveliest debates I heard, and the strongest held opinions, concerned the Seka, woodcarving, and other aspects of ceremonial life. Certainly education, health care, and economic opportunity are an essential part of the change that is coming over this part—and every part—of the world. But first you have to know who you are.

"KAMORO" REMAINS A RELATIVELY NEW identity, and it can seem to sit strangely with some people, as if they are still experimenting with how to wear it. Not everybody is even sure what it means.

When we were in Lakahia, we took a short trip up the bay to Kampung Warifi. There we met Zakarias Maramoi, the *kepala desa,* who invited us into his house for a chat. The chat quickly turned into something more like a speech, and I soon told Apollo not to bother translating anymore, because Zakarias's platitudes were giving me a headache. I was somewhat surprised to learn later that I was the only one so affected. The rest of the audience (Kal excepted) was rapt.

Zakarias reminded me more of an American politician than anybody else I met in the Kamoro area. He is

handsome, in a slightly generic way, and his speech was full of well-timed pauses and exaggerated sincerity. He liked to repeat himself for emphasis. The point he was making was one that had been recently discussed at a meeting of the *kepala desa*s of the Fakfak regency. This was whether or not the Protestant villages of the westernmost Kamoro area should properly identify themselves as Kamoro.

"In the past, with the different religions came a split," Zakarias said. "But no more. I would like to make it clear that the people of Warifi, and those of the other Kamoro villages in Fakfak regency, consider ourselves part of what should perhaps be called a greater Kamoro group. We are not a subgroup of the Kamoro, we *are* Kamoro."

In my notes I circled this statement about three times, because he repeated it about three times. At the time, it seemed to me to mean exactly nothing. Later, when Apollo and I were walking together around the village, I said something to the effect of "What a windbag, eh?," but Apollo totally disagreed. He thought it was very important that such a subject should be discussed, and felt it was significant that the Protestant villages should want to consider themselves Kamoro.

I also think Apollo was a bit impressed by

241

WILLEM YAUNIYUTA, TIMIKA PANTAI.
Willem is the chief of traditions for the village.

Zakarias's oratory skill. He gave his speech in Indonesian, and at first Apollo thought he couldn't speak Kamoro. Zakarias knew Apollo was thinking this, and after the speech, he called out to Apollo, playfully and from behind, in perfect colloquial Kamoro. "He shocked me," Apollo said, "and his accent is just like Nawaripi."

When Father Petrus Drabbe first argued in print for the general use of "Kamoro" for the people the Dutch had been calling "Mimika," he actually had two words in his collected vocabulary that he could have used: *wenata* and *kamoro*. He mentions this in his introduction to the 1947 "Folk-Tales from New Guinea," but never exactly states why he chose the latter.

Wenata is a combination of *we*, "people," and *nata*, "true, real" (also, "body"). It is a word that is still used today, and actually refers to the Kamoro people, as distinct from all other living people. If one were seeking a word that functioned in the same way "New Yorker" or "Anglo-Saxon" functions to an American, then *wenata* is the correct word, not *kamoro*. *Kamoro* refers to the same set of people as *wenata*, but it operates at a different register. It does not serve to distinguish the Kamoro from other people; rather, to distinguish them from ghosts, animals, rocks, and all other things. It is a rich, even literary word, something like "humanity," but without the word losing its ethnic and cultural distinctiveness that way it does in English. *Wenata*, by contrast, seems dull and quotidian.

The word "Kamoro" seems, to my ears, to be spoken with pleasure, and with a kind of freshness, as if the sense of shared cultural purpose that rings in this word is something newly discovered. In this it resembles the ethnic, racial, and cultural "identities"—to use the now fashionable, if vague, word—that have recently formed in the United States. But the communities celebrating identity in the United States, having rejected the enlightenment notion of essential human universality, seek to define themselves through uniqueness and "difference." The Kamoro are working the other way, trying to find a larger cultural identity within many smaller ones. They are learning what it is that the Emowai, Tukawe, and Waniawe share, not what makes them different.

The membership of Lemasko, like that of all the other new *yayasans* in Timika, is determined by ethnicity. It is a strictly Kamoro organization, and as such is beginning to play an important role in the development of a Kamoro identity, particularly a Kamoro political identity. But organizing a *yayasan* by ethnicity has also produced some problems, particularly in the area of staffing.

I once asked Apollo why, given the acknowledged shortage of Kamoro with accounting, business, and legal skills, the Lemasko organization simply didn't hire somebody who did have these skills, at least until enough Kamoro had come up through the university ranks to fill the positions themselves. If I were a member of the *yayasan*, I said, I would have voted to snap up some idealistic young Indonesian business student from the university in Jayapura, or even in Jakarta if necessary.

"The membership would only accept a Kamoro," Apollo said.

"But why, Apollo? This person would be an employee, not a voting member of the board. Isn't the organization just cheating itself by not getting the most qualified person they can?"

Apollo was patient with me: "It is, as you know, a little complicated."

We had been through this subject before. I knew that the organization did, in fact, have a member who was not Kamoro. His name is Aman Sugianto. Sugianto's position in Lemasko is controversial, and some people believe he exercises an inordinate amount of control over organization policy. His name does not appear on Lemasko's two-page list of officers and staff. But a wipe-board with Lemasko's proposed projects and funding disbursement amounts hangs on his wall, and his house has the telephone, typewriter, and other business tools that are lacking at the Lemasko office. His position seems to be something like a managing director, but it has been described to me more colloquially as, variously, "the man behind the scenes," the "mastermind," or "the brains."

Sugianto is undoubtedly a clever man. Unfortunately I never had the chance to meet him in person, because at the time that we were to join some members of Lemasko at his house for a discussion about the organization he left to attend to an unknown errand.

Sugianto's position as the "brains" of the main Kamoro *yayasan* seems odd not because he lacks the necessary skills, but because he is, as his name suggests, Javanese. On the other hand, in the eyes of some of the organization's members, he is also Kamoro. Sugianto's first wife was Kamoro, and even though he is now married to a Javanese woman, he has been able to retain a kind of residual ethnic legitimacy from that first marriage.

The kind of "dual citizenship" that Sugianto enjoys puts him in a uniquely powerful position. Despite the growing confidence in the identity "Kamoro," and despite the creation of Lemasko and the new smaller Kamoro *yayasan*s, some Kamoro still seem to harbor a residual deference toward outsiders living in the area. Perhaps this is a result of so many years under the discipline of the Catholic Church and the Kei Islander teachers, or perhaps it has some other history. But, in varying degrees, it exists. For example, the man most people considered the actual, although not the formal, leader of the Kamoro organization Yakaro was a Kei Islander. Sugianto, then, benefits from both the deference given to an outsider and the inherent trust extended to an ethnic brother.*

* Before this manuscript was completed, Aman Sugianto left the Lemasko organization.

With the arrival of urbanization, a cash economy, and all the other outside influences on the south coast of Irian Jaya, a convincing argument can be made that ethnicity is no longer the most rational way to define an interest group. The political and economic concerns of a Kamoro family living in the urban area of Timika, for example, seem closer to those of an Amungme family living in Timika than to those of a Kamoro family living in the village of Potowai-Buru. But the identity Kamoro is still too new, and interethnic institutions too weak, to yet allow for any other principle for assembling a *yayasan*.

NOT ONLY IS KAMORO ART and culture beginning to appear again, but it has even produced its own small movement of self-conscious artists and intellectuals, like the New York School of American abstract expressionists, the Group f.64 photographers of California, or the Bloomsbury Group of British writers, artists, and intellectuals.

On our long trip to the western Kamoro area, we stopped only briefly in Kokonao, because we were in a hurry to reach Paripi before dark. This caused great irritation to a man named Anakletus Maturani, who, he said, had something very important to discuss with us. We apologized that we couldn't stay, and promised to stop for longer on the way back. When we did, Anakletus hustled us to his house in the Apuri neighborhood of Kaokonao village. We had barely taken our seats when the subject of the decline of Kamoro art and woodcarving arose. Anakletus, we quickly learned, held very strong opinions on this matter.

"All of Kamoro tradition has ended because the Church objected to two small parts of the *kaware*: nose-piercing and free sex," he said, his lips quivering with anger. "What do these have to do with woodcarving, or the important parts of the *kaware?*"

By the "kaware," Anakletus means the overall cycle of Kamoro ritual life. As Apollo put it, "The *karapao* and other rituals are 'inside' the *kaware*—the *kaware* is the most basic festival." The ending of the *kaware* meant the decline of all other forms of Kamoro cultural expression: woodcarving, bark cloth making, traditional singing, and constructing and performing in *mbi-kao* masks.

"In the old times, the people who did the carvings had their children next to them, and the children learned," he said. "When the *kaware* stopped, this also ended the carving tradition."

Together with two partners, Anakletus has started an organization to promote a renaissance of Kamoro art. The men, all skilled carvers themselves, have dubbed their movement "The Caka Group." The *caka*, Anakletus explained, is a type of bird of paradise that "has not been seen in a long time." After a bit more explanation, I realized that the *caka*, pronounced "chahka," is very close to what in English would be called a phoenix.

"The culture of our ancestors is now like the *caka*," Anakletus said. "People have been waiting a long time to see who would bring this out, and that is what this group wants to do."

Anakletus, who is a former school principal, calls himself the group's chairman for "art and culture." As such, a big part of his task is historical, researching the gaps that now exist in the Kamoro cultural tradition. By his reckoning, two-thirds of this tradition has been lost, and it is his intention to help restore it. Anakletus, who has a penchant for metaphorical speech, compared the Caka Group's task to that of a carver working on a *mbitoro*.

"It is very important to realize why things are carved in the root part, and not in the rest of the tree," he said, referring to the important banner, or *tokae*, of the *mbitoro*. "We want to start with the most essential things, the root, before working on the rest of the tree."

One of the Caka Group's first and most important projects, he said, is to produce a synopsis of the various stories from the different villages in at least the western area of the Kamoro. I got the impression that Anakletus did not mean for this work to sit on a shelf. Rather than a history for academics, he imagines a work something like a musician's fake book, a well-thumbed resource for performers and artists.

"In the past, a *wou* ate all the Kamoro people," he said, referring to one version of the famous story. "Let us not let the *wou* eat us again."

ONE NIGHT IN PARIPI, after dinner, Apollo and I sat on the front stoop drinking coffee. We had been discussing LEMASKO, and the difficult and sometimes disappointing path of development and change in the Kamoro area. We were talking about the future.

To brighten up our discussion, I described the Kamoro organization ten years in the future. In my picture, the office of this healthy organization bustled with activity, with telephones ringing and people coming through the door to ask about scholarship programs for their children, new village health services, or how to order a new net for the fishing cooperative. I even made the office manager Berlinda Takati, Apollo's daughter, who would then be twenty-eight and long graduated from the computer training school in Jayapura she was currently attending. Apollo rewarded my effort with a brief smile, but his face soon clouded over again.

"Perhaps," he said, taking a sip from his cup. "I don't know."

I suppose nobody knows. Even I couldn't really generate much enthusiasm for my busy office of the future. I know it is what is supposed to happen, and I sincerely hope it does, but my heart wasn't in it. I looked out across the sand that forms the main square of Paripi. A *mbitoro*, with a strong, well-carved face,

Hiripau.

stood in front of a small *karapao* building, a leftover from the spring elections. Two men stood chatting nearby, and one suddenly burst out laughing. A hint of woodsmoke perfumed the air, and the tops of the coconut trees rustled faintly.

"It feels good to be back in Paripi, doesn't it Apollo?"

This time the smile stayed.

We didn't speak again for a long time. We just sipped our coffee and watched the red sky. Then, to myself, I imagined another scene.

O N A DRY SUMMER EVENING in the great southern tide forest, forty men urged their canoes forward with sure, soundless strokes. The sliver of moon had not yet risen, and no wind blew. It was the gloaming, not quite night, the time called *mamiki,* "the last time the eyes can see." The sky spread a great dome of steel blue over the broad river.

The canoes were charcoal black, striped and banded with bright white chalk, and floated like skeletons over the water. When they reached the meeting of two rivers, the men stowed their paddles, and the canoes drifted noiselessly to a stop. Then the drums began. A song, mournful and persistent, rose into the still air. The notes, in a strange minor key, faded oddly, dropping pitch like a siren winding down. The men's voices grew stronger and more urgent, reaching a fierce crescendo when suddenly, with a great clash of paddles on the hollow canoes, silence.

Waves of sound drifted over the murky estuary, over the tangled, dripping mangrove, over the groves of sago palm and the twisting, nipa-lined streams, over the dense, unbroken green of the inland forest, and finally disappeared, somewhere distant and unknown, in the snow-capped mountains of the interior.

The men picked up their paddles, still in silence, and moved on to the next river junction, where they repeated their song. At each junction on the way back to their village the canoes stopped, and the men wailed their strange, sad song, a song charged with pride, and strength, and ownership.

One of the canoes rode lower than the others. It was heavy and roughly hewn, the wood of its flanks still pink with sap. In the morning this canoe had stood in the forest, a magnificent *utaka* tree, towering just inland of the last of the mangrove. Now it was being introduced to its world.

Night fell before the canoes reached home, and the sky became a gauze of stars. As the men entered the final estuary, a salty tongue of the Arafura Sea, their paddle strokes turned up splashes of phosphorescence, and each canoe left a wake of blue fire.

245

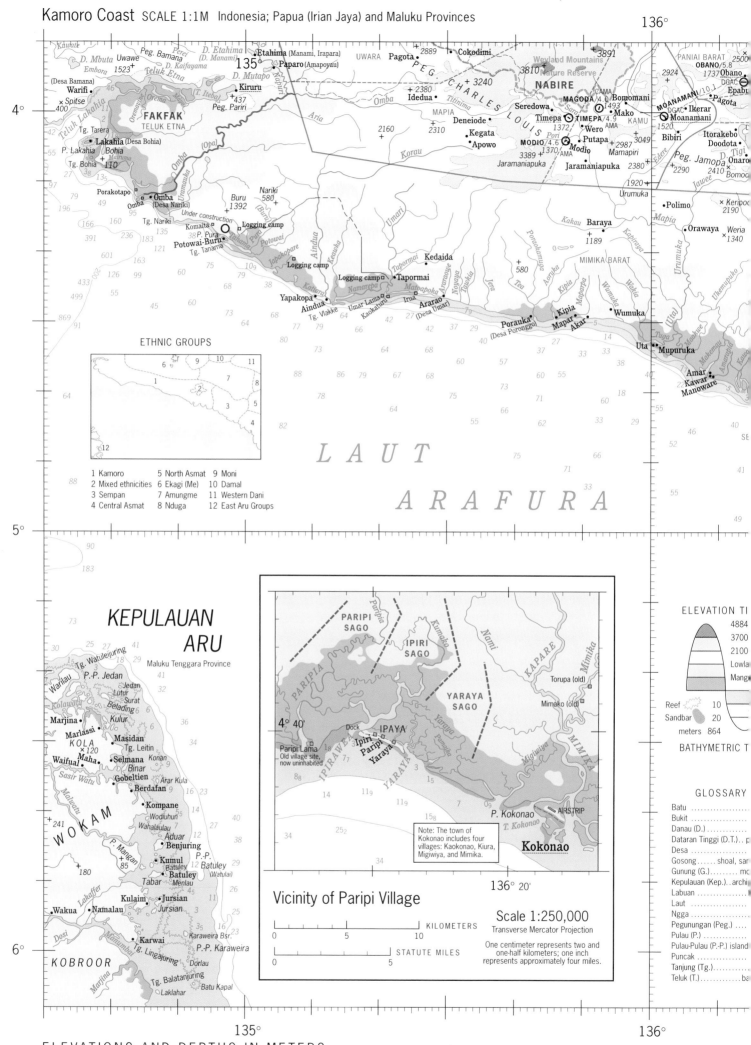

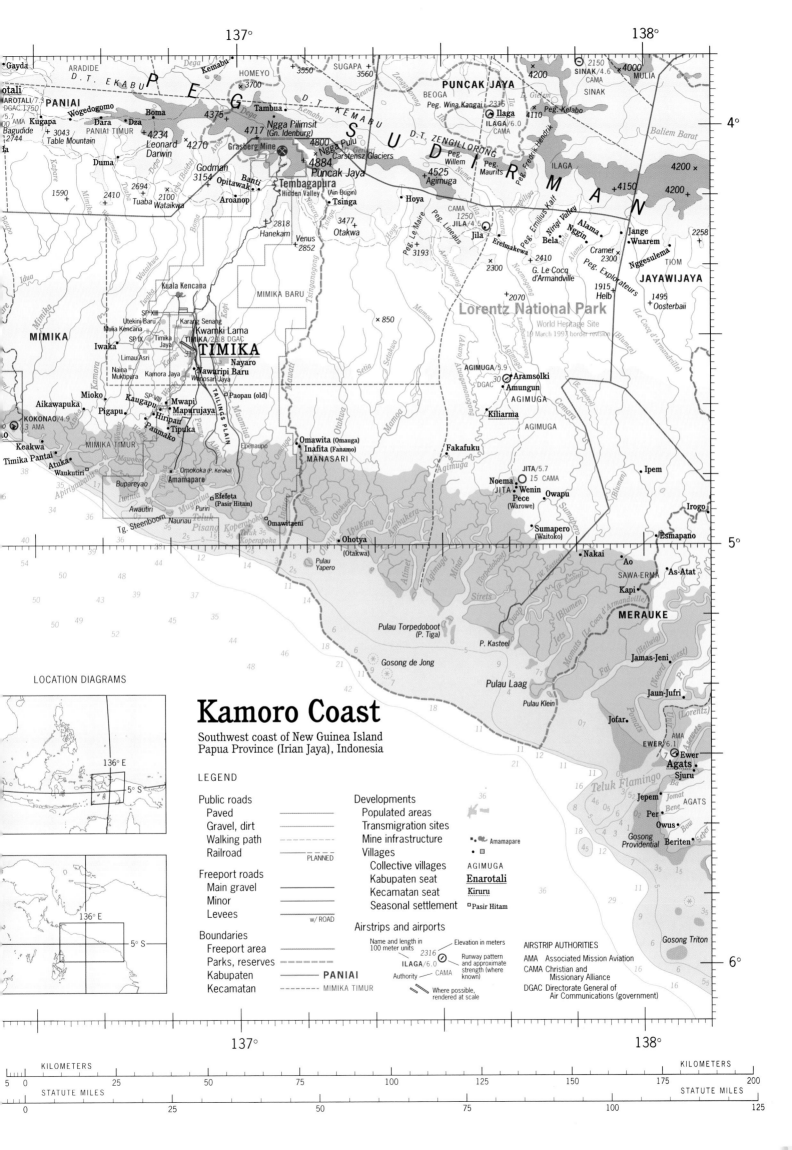

Kamoro Coast

Southwest coast of New Guinea Island
Papua Province (Irian Jaya), Indonesia

LEGEND

Public roads
Paved
Gravel, dirt
Walking path
Railroad — PLANNED

Freeport roads
Main gravel
Minor
Levees — w/ ROAD

Boundaries
Freeport area
Parks, reserves
Kabupaten — PANIAI
Kecamatan — MIMIKA TIMUR

Developments
Populated areas
Transmigration sites
Mine infrastructure
Villages
 Collective villages — AGIMUGA
 Kabupaten seat — **Enarotali**
 Kecamatan seat — Kiruru
 Seasonal settlement — □ Pasir Hitam

Amamapare

Airstrips and airports
Name and length in 100 meter units — 2316 — Elevation in meters
ILAGA/6.0 — Runway pattern and approximate strength (where known)
Authority — CAMA
Where possible, rendered at scale

AIRSTRIP AUTHORITIES
AMA — Associated Mission Aviation
CAMA — Christian and Missionary Alliance
DGAC — Directorate General of Air Communications (government)

LOCATION DIAGRAMS

136° E
5° S

136° E
5° S

KILOMETERS
5 0 25 50 75 100 125 150 175 200
STATUTE MILES
0 25 50 75 100 125

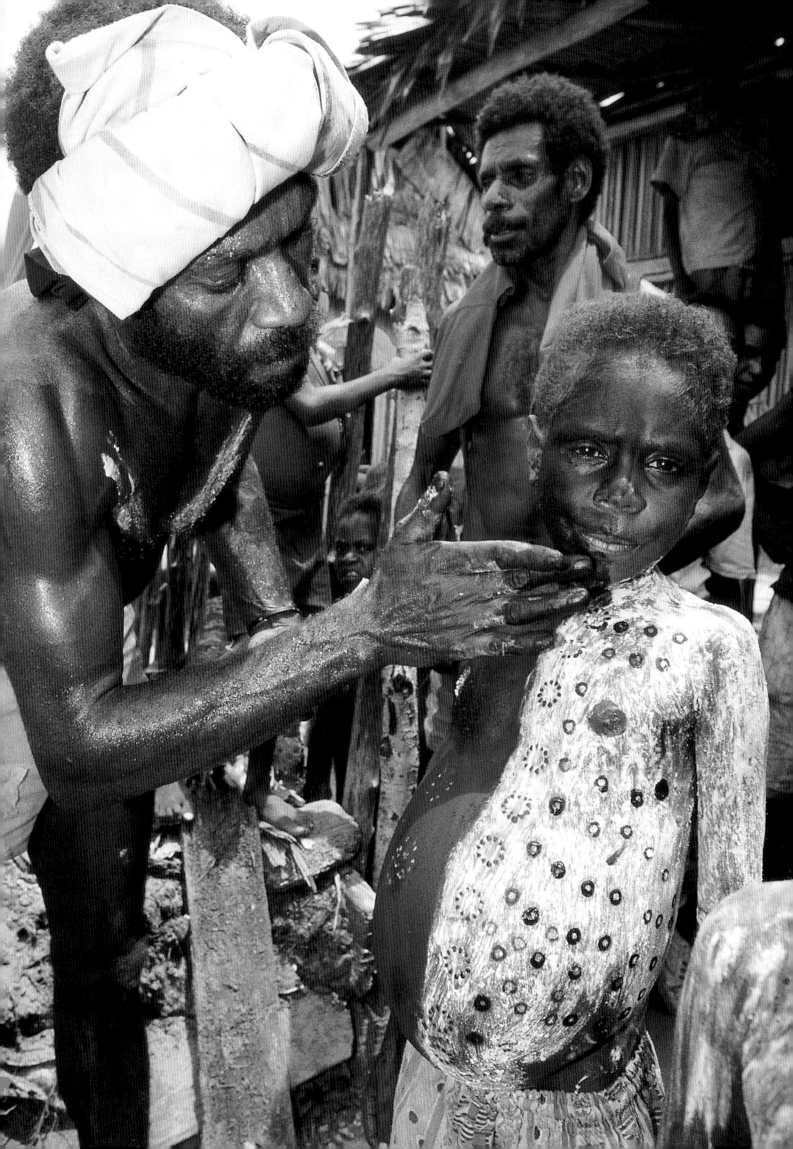

Bibliography

Abbott, R. Tucker and S. Peter Dance. 1991. *Compendium of Seashells.* 3d edition. London: Charles Letts.

Allen, Gerald R. 1991. *Field Guide to the Freshwater Fishes of New Guinea.* Publication No. 9 of the Christensen Research Institute. Madang, Papua New Guinea: Christensen Research Institute.

Andaya, Leonard Y. 1993. *The World of Maluku: Eastern Indonesia in the Early Modern Period.* Honolulu: University of Hawaii Press.

Barlow, Colin and Joan Hardjono, eds. 1996. *Indonesia Assessment 1995: Development in Eastern Indonesia.* Canberra: Research School for Pacific and Asian Studies, Australian National University and Singapore: Institute for Southeast Asian Studies.

Beaglehole, John Cawte, ed. 1955. *The Journals of Captain James Cook on his Voyages of Discovery, Vol. 1.* Cambridge: Cambridge University Press. Published for the Hakluyt Society in 5 vols.

Beehler, Bruce M., Thane K. Pratt, and Dale A. Zimmerman. 1986. *Birds of New Guinea.* Princeton, New Jersey: Princeton University Press.

Bellwood, Peter. July 1991. "The Austronesian Dispersal and the Origin of Languages." *Scientific American,* 70–75.

Bone, Robert C. 1964. "The International Status of West New Guinea until 1884" in *Papers on Early South-East Asian History,* Colin Jack-Hinton, ed. Singapore: *The Journal of Southeast Asian History.* 150–180.

Bromley, Myron. 1973. "Ethnic Groups in Irian Jaya," in *Bulletin for Irian Jaya Development* 2–3: 1–37.

De Bruijn Kops, G. F. June 1852. "Contribution to the Knowledge of the North and East Coasts of New Guinea." *The Journal of the Indian Archipelago and Eastern Asia* 6: 302–348.

Budiardjo, Carmel and Liem Soei Liong. 1988. *West Papua: The Obliteration of a People.* Surrey, England: TAPOL.

Burkill, I. H. 1935. *A Dictionary of the Economic Products of the Malay Peninsula.* With contributions by William Birtwistle, Frederick W. Foxworthy, J.B. Scrivenor and J. G. Watson. London: Crown Agents for the Colonies.

Collingridge de Tourcey, George. 1906. *The First Discovery of Australia and New Guinea... between the Years 1492–1606, with Descriptions of their Old Charts.* Sydney: William Brooks.

Crawfurd, John. 1856. *A Descriptive Dictionary of the Indian Islands & Adjacent Countries.* London: Bradbury & Evans.

Diamond, Jared M. 1997. *Guns, Germs, and Steel: The Fates of Human Societies.* New York, London: Norton.

———

KARAPAO, TIMIKA PANTAI. Albertus Kuepe decorates Natalis Onamareyuta.

———. 1992. *The Third Chimpanzee: The Evolution and Future of the Human Animal.* New York: HarperCollins.

———. April 30, 1987. "Did Komodo dragons evolve to eat pygmy elephants?" *Nature* 326: 832.

Drabbe, Petrus. 1947–1950. "Folk-tales from Netherlands New Guinea." *Oceania* 18(2): 157–175, (3): 248–270; 19(1): 75–90, (3): 224–240.

Earl, George Windsor. 1853. *The Native Races of the Indian Archipelago. Papuans.* London: Hippolyte Bailliere.

———. 1837. "Narrative of a Voyage along the S.W. Coast of New Guinea, in 1828, and communicated by G. Windsor Earl, esq." *Journal of the Royal Geographical Society of London,* 7: 383–395. London: John Murray.

"Final Social Audit Report, P.T. Freeport Indonesia." July 15, 1997. Prepared by Labat-Anderson, Inc.

Flach, M. and F. Rumawas, eds. 1996. *Plant Resources of South-East Asia* (PROSEA) *No. 9: Plants yielding non-seed carbohydrates.* Leiden: Blackhuys.

Flannery, Timothy Fridtjof. 1998. *Throwim Way Leg: Tree Kangaroos, Possums, and Penis Gourds—on the Track of Unknown Mammals in Wildest New Guinea.* New York: Atlantic Monthly Press.

———. 1995. *Mammals of New Guinea.* Chatswood, New South Wales: Reed Books and the Australian Museum.

———. 1994. *The Future Eaters: An Ecological History of the Australasian Lands and People.* New York: George Braziller.

Forrest, Thomas. 1780. *A Voyage to New Guinea, and the Moluccas, from Balambangan: Including An Account of Magindano, Sooloo, and other Islands.... During the Years 1774, 1775, and 1776.* Second Edition. London: J. Robson.

Gelpke, J. H. F Sollewijn. 1993. "On the Origin of the Name Papua." *Bijdragen tot de Taal-, Land- en Volkenkunde (Journal of the Royal Institute of Linguistics and Anthropology)* 149 (2): 319–332.

Godelier, Maurice and Marilyn Strathern, eds. 1991. *Big Men and Great Men: Personifications of Power in Melanesia.* Cambridge: Cambridge University Press.

Golson, Jack. 1997. "From Horticulture to Agriculture in the New Guinea Highlands: A Case Study of People and Their Environments." Chapter 3 in *Historical Ecology in the Pacific Islands: Prehistoric Environmental and Landscape Change,* Patrick V. Kirch and Terry L. Hunt, eds. New Haven, Connecticut, and London: Yale University Press.

Gressitt, J. L., ed. 1982. *Biogeography and Ecology of New Guinea.* Monographiae Biologicae 42 (1): 1–534, (2): 535–983. The Hague: W. Junk.

Groube, Les, John Chappell, John Muke, and David Price. December 4, 1986. "A 40,000 year–old human occupation site at Huon Peninsula, Papua New Guinea." *Nature* 324: 453–455.

Haddon, Alfred Court, and J. W. Layard. 1916. *Report made by the Wollaston Expedition on the Ethnographical Collections from the Utakwa River, Dutch New Guinea.* With a note by A. von Hügel. London: N.P.

Handbook on Netherlands New Guinea. 1958. Rotterdam: Nieuw-Guinea Instituut.

Harple, Todd S. September 1997. "Permanence and Change." Unpublished paper presented to the P.T. Freeport AMDAL Social Workshop in Abepura, Irian Jaya.

———. January 1997. "General Report on Kamoro (Mimika) History/Culture." Unpublished paper submitted to the Asian Cultural History Program, National Museum of Natural History, Smithsonian Museum, Washington, D.C.

Hilder, Brett. 1980. *The Voyage of Torres: The Discovery of the Southern Coastline of New Guinea and Torres Strait by Captain Luis Baéz de Torres in 1606.* St. Lucia, Queensland: University of Queensland Press.

Hooker, Joseph D., ed. 1896. *Journal of ... Sir Joseph Banks ... during Captain Cook's First Voyage in H.M.S. Endeavour in 1768–71....* London: Macmillan.

Irian Jaya, the Land of Challenges and Promises. 1987. Jakarta: Alpha Zenith.

Johannes, Robert E., and Michael Riepen. October 1995. "Environmental, Economic, and Social Implications of the Live Reef Fish Trade in Asia and the Western Pacific." Tasmania and Wellington, New Zealand: R.E. Johannes and Fisheries Development Associates.

Kahin, Audrey R. and George McT. Kahin, 1995. *Subversion as Foreign Policy: The Secret Eisenhower and Dulles Debacle in Indonesia.* New York: The New Press.

Kingdon, Jonathan. 1993. *Self-Made Man: Human Evolution from Eden to Extinction?* New York: John Wiley & Sons.

Knauft, Bruce M. 1993. *South Coast New Guinea Cultures: History, Comparison, Dialectic.* Cambridge: Cambridge University Press.

Kolff, Dirk Hendrik. 1840. *Voyages of the Dutch Brig of War* Dourga, *through the Southern and Little-Known Parts of the Moluccan Archipelago, and along the Previously Unknown Southern Coast of New Guinea, Performed in the Years 1825 & 1826.* Translated from the Dutch by George Windsor Earl. London: James Madden.

Konrad, Gunter, and Sukarja Somadikarta. Date unknown. "The History of the Discovery of the Birds of Paradise and Courtship of the Greater Bird of Paradise, *Paradisaea Apoda Novae Guineae.*" Publisher unknown.

Kooijman, Simon. 1984. *Art, Art Objects, and Ritual in the Mimika Culture.* Ministerie van Welzijn, Volksgesondheid en Cultuur, Mededelingen van het Rijkmuseum voor Volkenkunde, Leiden, No. 23. Leiden: E. J. Brill.

——. 1956. "Art of Southwestern New Guinea: A Preliminary Survey." *Antiquity and Survival* 1(5): 343–371.

Lagerberg, Kees. 1979. *West Irian and Jakarta Imperialism.* New York: St. Martin's Press.

Lie, Goan-Hong, 1980. "The Comparative Nutritional Roles of Sago and Cassava in Indonesia." In Stanton, W. R. and M. Flach, eds., *Sago: The Equatorial Swamp as a Natural Resource.* The Hague, Boston, London: Martinus Nijhoff.

Manning, Chris, and Michael Rumbiak. 1989. "Irian Jaya: Economic Change, Migrants, and Indigenous Welfare." Chapter 3 in Hal Hill, ed. *Unity and Diversity: Regional Economic Development in Indonesia since 1970.* Singapore: Oxford University Press. 76–106.

Mealey, George A. 1996. *Grasberg: Mining the Richest and Most Remote Deposit of Copper and Gold in the World, in the Mountains of Irian Jaya, Indonesia.* New Orleans: Freeport-McMoRan Copper & Gold.

Meek, Alexander S. 1913. *A Naturalist in Cannibal Land.* Frank Fox, ed., with an introduction by Walter Rothschild. London and Leipzig: T. Fisher Unwin.

Merrill, Elmer D. 1981. *Plant Life of the Pacific World.* Tokyo: Charles E. Tuttle. First published in 1945.

Miklouho-Maclay, Nikolai Nikolayevich [Miklukho-Maklai]. 1982. *Travels to New Guinea.* Compiled, with a forward and commentary, by Daniil Tumarkin. Moscow: Progress Publishers.

Miller, George, ed. 1996. *To the Spice Islands and Beyond: Travels in Eastern Indonesia.* Kuala Lumpur, Malaysia: Oxford University Press.

O'Brian, Flann [Brian O'Nolan]. 1973. "Slattery's Sago Saga" in *Stories and Plays.* London: Hart-Davis, MacGibbon.

Osborne, Robin. 1985. *Indonesia's Secret War: The Guerilla Struggle in Irian Jaya.* Sydney: Allen & Unwin.

Pelras, Christian. 1996. *The Bugis.* In "The Peoples of South-East Asia and The Pacific" series, Peter Bellwood and Ian Glover, eds. Oxford, U.K. and Cambridge, Mass.: Blackwell Publishers.

Petocz, Ronald G. 1989. *Conservation and Development in Irian Jaya.* Leiden: E.J. Brill.

Pouwer, Jan. 1991. "Mimika." In the *Encyclopedia of World Cultures, Volume II: Oceania,* edited by Terence E. Hays. Editor-in-chief of the ten-volume series is David Levinson. Boston: G. K. Hall. 206–208.

——. December 1970. "Mimika Land Tenure." Chapter 3 of *New Guinea Research Bulletin* 38, "Land Tenure in West Irian": 24–33. Canberra: The New Guinea Research Unit, Australian National University.

——. 1956. "A Masquerade in Mimika," *Antiquity and Survival* 1 (5): 373–386.

——. 1955. *Enkele aspecten van de Mimikacultuur, Nederlands Zuidwest Nieuw Guinea.* Staatsdrukkerij-en Uitgeversbedrijf 's-Gravenhage. "Some Aspects of the Mimika Culture, Netherlands Southwest New Guinea." Partial, privately commissioned translation into English.

Rauwerdink, Jan B. 1986. "An Essay on Metroxylon, the Sago Palm." *Principes* 30 (4): 165–180.

Rawling, Cecil G. 1913. *The Land of the New Guinea Pygmies.* London: Seeley, Service.

Rhys, Lloyd. 1947. *Jungle Pimpernel: The Story of a District Officer in Central Netherlands New Guinea.* London: Hodder and Stoughton.

Rich, T., and B. Hall. 1984. "Rebuilding a Giant Lizard: *Megalania prisca.*" In *Vertebrate Zoogeography & Evolution in Australasia (Animals in Space and Time),* Michael Archer and Georgina Clayton, eds. Carlisle, Western Australia: Hesperian Press. 393–396.

Ricklefs, Merle Calvin. 1981. *A History of Modern Indonesia, c. 1300 to the Present.* Bloomington: Indiana University Press.

Rooney, Dawn F. 1993. *Betel Chewing Traditions in South-East Asia.* Kuala Lumpur: Oxford University Press.

Rosenman, Helen. 1992. *Two Voyages to the South Seas.* A partial account of Captain Jules S.-C. Dumont d'Urville's voyages in the *Astrolabe* (1826–1829) and the *Astrolabe* and *Zélée* (1837–1840) translated and retold by Rosenman. Honolulu: University of Hawaii Press.

Ryan, John. 1971. *The Hot Land: Focus on New Guinea.* Melbourne and Sydney: Macmillan Company of Australia.

Ryan, Peter, ed. 1972. *Encyclopaedia of Papua and New Guinea,* Vols. 1 and 2. Carlton, Victoria: Melbourne University Press in association with the University of Papua and New Guinea.

Schneebaum, Tobias. 1985. *Asmat Images, From the Collection of the Asmat Museum of Culture and Progress.* Agats, Irian Jaya: Asmat Museum of Culture and Progress.

Schoorl, J.W. 1993. *Culture and Change among the Muyu.* Translated from the Dutch by G.J. van Exel. Koninklijk Instituut voor Taal-, Land- en Volkenkunde translation series 3. Leiden: KITLV Press.

Shaffer, Lynda Norene. 1996. *Maritime Southeast Asia to 1500.* In the "Sources and Studies in World History" series, Kevin Reilly, ed. Armonk, New York: M.E. Sharpe.

Silzer, Peter J., and Heljä Heikkinen Clouse. 1991. *Index of Irian Jaya Languages,* 2d edition. A Special Publication of *Irian: Bulletin of Irian Jaya.* Jayapura, Irian Jaya: Program Kerjasama Universitas Cenderawasih and the Summer Institute of Linguisitics.

Smidt, Dirk A.M., ed. 1993. *Asmat Art: Woodcarvings of Southwest New Guinea.* With contributions by Adrian A. Gerbrands, *et al.* Singapore: Periplus Editions, in association with the Rijksmuseum voor Volkenkunde, Leiden.

Souter, Gavin. 1966. *New Guinea, the Last Unknown.* New York: Taplinger Publishing Company.

Southern, Terry. 1960. *The Magic Christian.* New York: Random House.

Sowada, Alphonse A. 1984. "Kei Islanders" in *An Asmat Sketch Book 3 & 4.* Originally published in *An Asmat Sketch Book 3,* 1971. Hastings, Nebraska: The Asmat Museum of Culture and Progress and the Crosier Mission, 59–70.

Steel, Rodney. 1996. *Living Dragons: A Natural History of the World's Monitor Lizards.* London: Blandford.

Swadling, Pamela. 1996. *Plumes from Paradise: Trade Cycles in Outer Southeast Asia and their Impact on New Guinea and Nearby Islands until 1920.* With contributions by Roy Wagner and Billai Laba. Boroko, National Capital District, Papua New Guinea and Coorparoo DC, Queensland, Australia: Papua New Guinea National Museum in association with Robert Brown.

Trenkenschuh, Frank. 1982. "Border Areas of Asmat: The Mimika" in *An Asmat Sketch Book 1 & 2.* Hastings, Nebraska: The Asmat Museum of Culture and Progress and the Crosier Mission, 77–82. Originally published in *An Asmat Sketch Book 1,* 1970.

Turner, Ruth D. 1966. *A Survey and Illustrated Catalogue of the Teredinidae (Mollusca: Bivalvia).* Cambridge, Mass.: The Museum of Comparative Zoology, Harvard University.

Vaughan, J. G. and C. A. Geissler. 1997. *The New Oxford Book of Food Plants.* Oxford, New York, Tokyo: Oxford University Press.

Veevers-Carter, W. 1984. *Riches of the Rain Forest: An Introduction to the Trees and Fruits of the Indonesian and Malaysian Rain Forests.* Ill. by Mohamed Anwar. Singapore: Oxford University Press.

Van der Veur, Paul W. 1966. *Search for New Guinea's Boundaries: From Torres Strait to the Pacific.* Canberra: Australian National University Press.

Visser, Leontine E. 1989. "The Kamrau Bay Area: Between Mimika and Maluku; A Report of a Short Visit." *Irian: Bulletin of Irian Jaya* 17:65–75. Jayapura, Irian Jaya: Program Kerjasama Universitas Cenderawasih.

Wallace, Alfred Russel. 1989. *The Malay Archipelago.* Singapore: Graham Brash. First published by MacMillan & Co., London, in 1869.

Webster, Herbert Cayley-. 1898. *Through New Guinea and the Cannibal Countries.* London: T. Fisher Unwin. The title on the case is "Through New Guinea and Other Cannibal Countries."

Wilson, Forbes. 1981. *The Conquest of Copper Mountain.* New York: Atheneum.

Wollaston, Alexander F. R. 1914. "An Expedition to Dutch New Guinea." *The Geographical Journal* 45(3).

——. 1912. *Pygmies and Papuans: the Stone Age To-day in Dutch New Guinea.* New York: Sturgis and Walton.

Yule, Henry, ed. 1921. *The Book of Ser Marco Polo....* 3d Edition. Vol. 2. London: John Murray.

Zimmerman, Elwood C. 1993. *Australian Weevils.* Volume III—Nanophyidae, Rhynchophoridae, etc. East Melbourne, Australia: CSIRO.

Acknowledgments

No book belongs to its author alone, and this one is not an exception. My first and greatest debt is to Kal, who was not just the photographer of this book, but a true partner in its creation. It was Kal who first showed me Irian Jaya in 1991, and it was through his friendship and shared knowledge that I learned to love this most interesting corner of the world. Kal organized our travels and fieldwork, read drafts of the manuscript for both content and spirit, pestered our benefactor when bills needed to be paid, and worked as the most persistent kind of fact-checker one could hope for (when I grew frustrated in Berkeley trying to identify the shipworm eaten by the Kamoro, I received a courier package from Kal in Timika. In it, stuffed into a Nalgene bottle of ethyl alcohol, was a shipworm—*Bactronophorus thoracites,* I can now say with authority).

I also owe a huge debt to Aloysius Akiniyau and Apollo Takati. Their participation was not just helpful, but essential, and I simply cannot imagine this book without them in it. I'd bet that there are no two other people who could have taught me more about the Kamoro, and I'm sure there are no two other people with whom Kal and I would have had more fun in a wet boat along the Kamoro Coast. When I think of my time among the Kamoro, my most persistent memories are not of the undeniably dramatic *kukaware* or *karapao,* but these: Alo, barely able to breathe from laughter when I scared that poor kid near Kokonao; Apollo, wide-eyed and wearing his towel, hiding from the stick woman in Keakwa; or both of them, happy as five-year-old kids, walking proudly around the encampment at Kaokaturu.

Once again I must thank my editor and old friend Leigh Anne Jones. She waved away the little insecurities that gather around a freshly written text like flies, and kept me focused on the task at hand, which (and this was not always obvious to me) was to tell a story. When I could make Leigh Anne laugh I knew I was getting somewhere. Also, of course, she took out about twenty thousand commas, and made sure my digressions didn't get too windy and irrelevant.

Colleen Lye read the complete manuscript, long before it was ripe, with both pleasure and encouraging words, and tolerated the prolonged absences (and impoverishment) this research and writing required. She is a better than faithful partner.

Several other people commented on drafts of the manuscript, either in part or in whole, or provided information and assistance that is not directly acknowledged in the text. These include Stan Batey, John Cutts, Todd Harple, Leroy and Philomena Hollenbeck, Gus Kairupan, Leonard Michaels, Kalman Muller, David Reid, and Wally Siagian. Their help and encouragement was essential.

As mentioned in the preface, publisher Eric Oey of the Periplus Publishing Group was exceptionally encouraging. Eric is a student of Indonesia, and came within a whisker of pursuing an academic career in Southeast Asian Studies (I, for one, am glad for that whisker). He read the entire manuscript, and praise from him is as meaningful to me as his deciding to publish this book.

My old friend Peter Ivey provided essential help with the cover and inside page design, including finding this beautiful typeface, and designed the dust jacket for the Indonesian edition. Another old friend, Mary Chia, shepherded Kal's transparencies through color separation and proofing with her usual skill and discerning eye.

Gregorius Suharsono performed the difficult, exasperating task of seeing to the film-casting and printing of the Indonesian edition, which mostly meant spending weeks stuck in Jakarta traffic. He also took a very rough Indonesian translation of the manuscript and turned it into something much more like what its author intended. Only someone who has done this kind of work can appreciate just how demanding and frustrating this was.

As noted in the preface, Paul Murphy's role in this book was essential, and Ed Pressman and Yonaniko Salim—the other two legs of the tripod at P.T. Freeport's Jakarta community affairs office in those days—were supportive and helpful, and a joy to work with. Erry Indrasaputra, Yuli Ismartono, and Siddharta Moersjid also aided our project in various essential ways. Meike Budiyanto, faithfully from the beginning, served as liaison between us and our patron.

Lastly, but most importantly, I would like to thank the Kamoro people themselves, whose dignity, hospitality, and good humor, might, in this increasingly bitter and self-absorbed world, be even more rare than their magnificent land and culture. I consider the time I spent with them to have been a privilege.

Index